Media effects and beyond

Communication and Society
General Editor: James Curran

Fields in Vision
Television Sport and Cultural Transformation
Garry Whannel

Getting the Message
News, Truth and Power
The Glasgow University Media Group

Advertising, The Uneasy Persuasion
Its Dubious Impact on American Society
Michael Schudson

Nation, Culture, Text
Australian Cultural and Media Studies
Edited by Graeme Turner

News and Journalism in the UK
A Textbook
Brian McNair

Television Producers
Jeremy Tunstall

Talk on Television
Audience Participation and Public Debate
Sonia Livingstone and Peter Lunt

Inside Prime Time
Todd Gitlin

Media effects and beyond

Culture, socialization and lifestyles

157940745

Edited by Karl Erik Rosengren

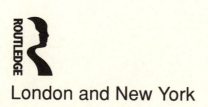

London and New York

First published 1994
by Routledge
11 New Fetter Lane, London EC4P 4EE

Simultaneously published in the USA and Canada
by Routledge
29 West 35th Street, New York, NY 10001

Typeset in Times by
Ponting–Green Publishing Services, Chesham, Bucks
Printed and bound in Great Britain by
T.J. Press (Padstow) Ltd, Padstow, Cornwall

Printed on acid free paper.

British Library Cataloguing in Publication Data

A catalogue record for this book is available from the British
Library.

Library of Congress Cataloging in Publication Data
Media effects and beyond: culture, socialization and lifestyles /
    edited by Karl Erik Rosengren.
    – (Communication and society)
    Includes bibliographical references and index.
    1. Mass media–Social aspects.   2. Mass media and
children.   3. Life style.   I. Rosengren, Karl Erik.
II. Series: Communication and society (Routledge (Firm))
HM258.M3742   1994
302.23–dc20   94–385
                                                    CIP

ISBN 0–415–09141–1

Contents

Figures

Tables

Contributors

Robert P. Hawkins is professor of journalism, University of Wisconsin–Madison, USA.

Thomas Johansson is assistant professor of sociology, University of Gothenburg, Sweden.

Ulla Johnsson-Smaragdi is senior lecturer in communication, University of Lund, Sweden.

Annelis Jönsson is associate professor of education, University of Lund, Sweden.

Fredrik Miegel is research associate in sociology, University of Lund, Sweden.

Suzanne Pingree is professor of agricultural communication, University of Wisconsin–Madison, USA.

Keith Roe is professor of communication, Catholic University of Leuven, Belgium

Karl Erik Rosengren is professor of communication, University of Lund, Sweden.

Inga Sonesson is associate professor of communication, University of Lund, Sweden.

Acknowledgements

Obviously, a book like this is the product of many people working together, with the support of a number of societal institutions. A great debt of gratitude, then, is due to various people and organizations.

Three great advisers, supporters and critics can no longer be reached by my gratitude but live on in memory: Hilde Himmelweit, Gerald Kline, Herman Wold.

Two groups of friends and colleagues have been instrumental in bringing this book about. In the first place, of course, the group of people who during two decades have been working together within the Media Panel Program, in one capacity or another, for sometimes very long, sometimes shorter, periods of time. Secondly, all those who in a number of ways acted as experts, critics, advisers, friends and supporters.

Without the generous support of a number of research councils, foundations, universities and authorities, there would have been no research programme at all.

My sincere thanks go to all these friends, colleagues and institutions. They are as follows:

People active within the Media Panel Program
Ulla Johnsson-Smaragdi, Inga Sonesson and Sven Windahl; Ulf Dalquist, Bertil Flodin, Per Hägred, Gudrun Hardardottir, Robert Hawkins, Elias Hedinsson, Ingrid Höjerback, Gunilla Jarlbro, Thomas Johansson, Annelis Jönsson, Per Källström, Inger Linderholm, Fredrik Miegel, Gunnel Norén, Gunilla Persson, Suzanne Pingree, Keith Roe, Birgitta Sandborg.

Experts, critics, friends, colleagues and supporters
David Altheide, Erik Allardt, Magnus Anshelm, Jay Blumler, Thorbjörn Broddason, Ray Brown, Gösta Carlsson, Ulla Carlsson, Stephen Chaffee, Cecilia von Feilitzen, George Gerbner, Bradley Greenberg, Torsten Hägerstraud, Karl Gustav Jöreskog, Mark Levy, Ebbe Lindell, Horst Löfgren, James Lull, Jack McLeod, Denis McQuail, Kjell Nowak, Philip Palmgreen, Rune Persson, Richard Peterson, Thorleif Pettersson, Bo Reimer, Alan Rubin,

Agneta Sternerup, Susan Strohm, Nils-Eric Svensson, Dag Sörbom, Lennart Weibull, Lawrence Wenner, Anita Werner.

Institutions, foundations, research councils
Allmänna barnhuset, The Bank of Sweden Tercentenary Foundation, The Swedish Council for Research into the Humanities and the Social Sciences, The Swedish Council for Social Research, The Swedish National Board of Education, the universities of Lund, Växjö, Gothenburg and Wisconsin–Madison.

Finally, my gratitude goes to a number of teachers, headmasters, directors of study, school directors in Malmö and Växjö – and above all to those thousands of young people and their parents who so generously gave so much of their time to the Media Panel Program.

Karl Erik Rosengren
Lund
November 1993

Part I

Introduction

Chapter 1

Culture, media and society

Agency and structure, continuity and change

Karl Erik Rosengren

This book represents an attempt to offer an overview of results gained during twenty-five years of systematic longitudinal research on mass media use by Swedish children, adolescents and young adults, and on the causes and consequences of that media use. Organized within the longitudinal Media Panel Program (MPP) at the Unit of Media and Communication Studies, University of Lund in Sweden, the research has been carried out by a team of communication scholars and sociologists of communication in close contact with European, American and Asian colleagues. The overall theoretical framework of the research venture will be presented in this chapter. Later chapters will offer specification and variation to this overall framework.

CULTURE AND SOCIETY

All human societies may be conceptualized as being composed of three closely related systems: a *cultural* system of ideas, a *social* system of actions, and a *material* system of artefacts. In empirical reality, of course, ideas, actions and artefacts are very closely intertwined, so that it may be extremely difficult to disentangle the ideational, actional and material aspects from each other. This is no argument against the analytical distinction, but it does make empirical analyses difficult, especially since there are a number of other societal subsystems, all of which, in all societies, necessarily encompass elements of those three basic systems. For theoretical purposes each of the three systems may be used to characterize any society (and from either the structural or the processual side of the system, or from both sides). It is often practical, however, to regard societies as being structured primarily by a central element in the ideational, cultural system: its value system (witness innumerable comparative studies; for a recent example, see Lipset 1993).

Actually, all societal structures may be understood in terms of two pairs of very basic value orientations:

- Cognitive/normative value orientation.
- Expressive/instrumental value orientation.

The two pairs of value orientations are defined by the four values of truth and righteousness, beauty and usefulness. These value orientations are very basic indeed. Indeed, they seem to be virtually timeless. They may be expressed in terms of four Indo-European verbs (Latin: sapere/debere, esse/facere; cf. French: savoir/devoir, être/faire) which have their functional counterparts in other families of languages. These very basic value orientations were discussed by early Greek philosophers in terms of *Logos* and *Ethos*, *Pathos* and *Praxis*. In the eighteenth century, the German poet Friedrich Schiller wrote poetry about them, as did many of his precursors and followers, and recent students of modern advertising and public relations also use them (see Pollay 1984; Nowak 1992: 182). All societal institutions have emerged out of these two pairs of value orientations, and they are still gradually developing around them. The history of basic societal structures and processes may thus be interpreted in terms of an ever-growing functional differentiation between a relatively small number of societal institutions, each based on one specific constellation of value orientations defined by the two pairs of basic value orientations (see, for instance, Parsons 1966). Within each of these institutions, the three basic systems of ideas, actions and artefacts are to be found, so that all institution-based societal subsystems may be conceptualized from an ideational, an actional and an artefactual perspective.

Figure 1.1, illustrating the 'great wheel of culture in Society', offers a typology of basic societal institutions grouped around the two pairs of basic value orientations: expressive vs. instrumental value orientation, and cognitive vs. normative value orientation (Rosengren 1984; Rosengren and Windahl 1989: 159 ff.; see, for instance, Berger and Berger 1972: 20; Giddens 1984: 17). The typology is shaped as a so-called circumplex (Guttman 1954; see Katz *et al.* 1973; Lumsden and Wilson 1981; Shepard 1978). The circumplex locates the main societal subsystems in a two-dimensional space in a way which suggests their closest 'neighbours' in society: the system of economy being located between the political and technological systems; literature, between art and scholarship, etc. The circumplex is similar, of course, to several other, more or less Weberian or Parsonian typologies of societal structures, but closest, perhaps, to that presented by Namenwirth and Bibbee (1976), which includes also the element of time, however (see Namenwirth and Weber 1987).

Figure 1.1 represents the three basic systems of ideas, action and artefacts by means of concentric circles. At the centre of the circumplex – the 'hub of the wheel' – we find culture, the ideational system of society. Culture, then, is both cognitively and normatively oriented, both expressive and instrumental. It unites and relates, one to the other, the four basic value orientations and their various subsystems. The network of broken lines relating the societal subsystems to each other tells us something about the complexity of the overall system, and of the immense communicative and co-ordinating functions fulfilled by culture: twenty-eight first order interdependencies,

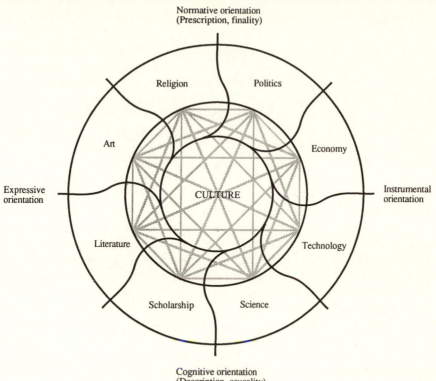

Figure 1.1 The great wheel of culture in society (Adapted from Rosengren (1984))

innumerable secondary and tertiary interdependencies and interactions. These relations connect society's institutional subsystems to each other: religion and politics; politics and science; science and technology; technology and religion, and so on, in never-ending chains of mutual interaction. All such relations may affect both ideas, actions and artefacts of the subsystems, but for pictorial convenience, the lines have been drawn going only from the system of action within one institutional subsystem to that of another.

This way of pictorial representation signals that all these relations have to be established by means of action, often by means of a very special type of action: communication. In all societies, these relations are carried out by means of interpersonal, face-to-face communication; in modern societies, they are often established also by means of mediated interpersonal communication, as well as by organizational and mass communication. As these relations continue, a never-ending process of differentiation between the various societal institutions continues. The institutions thus grow increasingly differentiated and yet remain mutually interdependent. All of them have to keep some part of general societal culture incorporated within their own substructures, continually balancing specific culture ('political culture', 'economic culture', etc.) against general societal culture. In terms of Figure 1.1., these specific cultures may be thought of as being situated within that part of the communicative network located in the action part of the great wheel of culture in society.

Culture, however, is not only a huge telephone exchange for society, connecting societal systems to each other, not only an immense exchange office converting values of one type into values of another type. It is also an important societal system in its own right, and as such it has to relate to other large societal systems, including the two basic systems of action and artefacts, as well as to virtually all institutionalized subsystems, although, paradoxically, and unlike other large societal systems, culture has no well-established institution of its own. (The institutions of art and literature, of course, deal primarily with high culture, certainly an important component of societal culture, but even more certainly not to be mistaken for societal culture.) What culture actually *does* have, however, is a set of institutions handling its relationship with the rest of society, primarily the so-called agents of socialization (see below).

The relations between culture and other societal systems form a classic problem of social science. Within a given society, four types of such relations are possible (Rosengren 1981). Figure 1.2 orders these four types in a typology. This is a typology of the relations between the ideational system of culture and the systems of actions and artefact, but it is also a typology of theories concerning these relationships.

Other societal systems influence culture

	Yes	No
Yes	Inter-dependence 1	Idealism 2
No	3 Materialism	4 Autonomy

Culture influences other societal systems

Figure 1.2 Four types of relationship between culture and other societal systems (Adapted from Rosengren (1981))

For centuries, heated philosophical debates raged along the axis of materialism/idealism, debates which were rekindled by the wave of Marxist revivalism in the 1960s and 1970s. Gradually, however, the scientific and scholarly discussions moved to the ideologically less inflammable but perhaps more realistic axis of interdepedence/autonomy – even if sometimes the old terminology has been preserved (Bell 1976; Bunge 1981; Harris 1979; Lumsden and Wilson 1981). The answer to these classic debates to a very high degree is related to the time perspective applied. Depending on the level of abstraction (Meddin 1975; cf. Johansson and Miegel 1992: 73), values may change on a time-scale ranging from millennia through centuries and decades to years and parts of a year. 'It would be strange indeed, if the relationship between culture and other societal structures would be the same under those very different circumstances' (Carlsson *et al.* 1981). More often than not, however, interdependence seems to be the best answer (see Rosengren 1981).

The horizontal relations between culture and other societal systems are important, but there is also another type of relations to be heeded, the vertical relations linking units at the macro, meso and micro levels of society to each other. (For recent discussions about these relations in ontological, epistemological, theoretical and methodological terms, see, for instance, Alexander *et al.* (1987), and especially Münch and Smelser (1987).) In these 'vertical' relations, society's culture flows from the level of society down to the individual level and back again, in modern societies often by way of the organizational level. In this ever-continuing process relating the macro to the micro level by way of the meso level, societal culture is transformed into individually internalized culture (Münch and Smelser 1987: 380 ff.; Reimer and Rosengren 1990). Since there are such factors as emergent phenomena (Münch and Smelser 1987: 367), aggregated individual culture is not the same as societal culture, of course. As a matter of fact, the relationship between these two manifestations of culture represents one of the most important problems in the sociology of culture and communication, since it may tell us something about the ontological status of culture (see Rosengren 1992a).

The vertical flow between the macro and the micro levels may also be conceived of as a flow between one societal generation and the next, as a rule conceptualized in terms of socialization (Burton 1968; Whiting 1968; Boudon and Bourricaud 1982/1989: 355–361; Gecas 1992). A number of specific societal institutions are engaged in these vertical relations; all of them may be regarded as agents of primary and secondary socialization, enculturation and acculturation (see Rosengren 1985; Rosengren and Windahl 1989: 160 ff.).

There are at least eight main types of socialization agent. Albeit, of course, in sometimes rather different shapes, three of them may be found in even the the most undifferentiated societies: the *family*, the *peer group*, and the *working group*. Three other types of socialization agent are found in somewhat more differentiated societies: *priests* (sometimes organized in churches), *teachers* (sometimes organized in schools and universities) and *law agents* (sometimes organized in courts and police forces). In our types of society we also have two other main types of socialization agent: large *social movements* and the *mass media*.

This book is primarily about the use made of mass media by young people. However, since media use is always taking place in a complex matrix of social relations, and since there is always both competition and co-operation between different types of socialization agent, we cannot deal with young people's media use without heeding also other important agents of social-ization, primarily the family, the peer group, and school. To understand socialization, we must turn, therefore, from *societal* structure to *social* structure. We must also relate the concept of structure to that of agency.

AGENCY AND STRUCTURE

In modern sociology there is perhaps no problem which has been more keenly discussed than that of agency and structure – sociology's version of general system theory's basic distinction between process and structure. (For a good overview of the agency/structure problematics, see Dietz and Burns 1992.)

Agency is understood as the capacity of acting and willing subjects within existing societal and social structures to exercise choice – 'to be able to act otherwise' (Giddens 1984: 14) – sometimes even to the extent of trans-gressing the limits established by those structures. More specifically, agency is taken to be characterized by actors' ability to undertake the following:

- Intentionally to exercise some sort of power.
- Choose between alternatives.
- Reflect on the consequences of acting (see Dietz and Burns 1992).

As Archer (1990: 82) strongly argues, any study of the interplay between agency and structure over time, any effort to 'theorize about variations in voluntarism and determinism (and their consequences)' presupposes that both terms be defined independently of each other. Structure and action, then, just as subject and object, must be kept analytically clearly separate. That is, Archer's 'dualism' is to be preferred to Giddens' 'duality' (cf. Giddens 1990).

More often than not, however, the otherwise many-faceted discussions about structure and agency have neglected the basic distinction between *societal structure* as briefly discussed in the previous section, and *social structure* as primarily defined by the four basic variables of age and gender, class and status. The distinction is important, however. Societal structures offer the general institutional framework within which, in a given society, individual and collective action may take place. Social structures define individuals' positions in a multidimensional space, the four most important dimensions of which are age, gender, status and social class. When societal and social structures have had their say, there is some space left for individual agency within which to form individual actions and patterns of actions (including, of course, more or less conscious, more or less systematically organized attempts at changing societal and social structures).

We thus have three types of patterned action (see Thunberg *et al.* 1981: 61; Johansson and Miegel 1992: 22 ff.; Reimer 1994; see also several chapters in this volume, especially Chapters 5, 10 and 12):

1 *Forms of life*: patterns of action determined primarily by societal structure.
2 *Ways of life*: patterns of action determined primarily by positions in social structure.
3 *Lifestyles*: patterns of action determined primarily by individual agency.

These are patterns analytically defined, of course. The three patterns are nested. Synthetic patterns empirically observed at the individual level ('individual lifestyles'; see Johansson and Miegel 1992), therefore, always include elements of all three types of pattern. Analytically, lifestyles may be observed as the relationship between, on the one hand, individual characteristics such as values, attitudes, interests, tastes, etc., and on the other, patterns of action, after control for relevant structural and positional variables (see Rosengren 1992b). The relationships between societal structure, individual position in the social system, individual characteristics and patterns of action are illustrated in Figure 1.3. (In statistical terms these relationships may be conceptualized as the *beta* coefficients of multivariate analyses.)

Over the decades, interest in the notion of lifestyle has fluctuated; definitions of the concept of lifestyle have been many and varied (see Chapters 10–12). There is small doubt, though, that during the last decade or so, there has been a renewed interest in the concept, at the same time as its definition has moved towards an increased accent on the role of the individual as the builder of his or her own lifestyle (see, for instance, Giddens 1991: 81). More often than not, however, the distinction between forms of life, ways of life and lifestyles is not clearly observed.

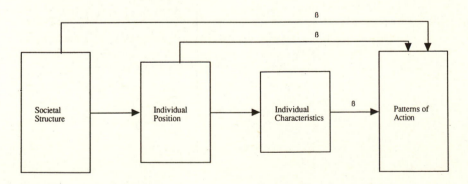

Figure 1.3 Three determinants of patterns of action

This argumentation relates quite naturally to debates which have continued for decades within socialization research. These debates have concerned characteristics of the two parties involved in all socialization processes: *society* (as represented by its agents of socialization), and the *individual being socialized* (McCron 1976; cf. Gecas 1992). In such debates, society has often been regarded as characterized primarily by either conflict or consensus. The individual socialized is often characterized either as a willing and acting subject, or as a more or less passive object of strong forces outside or within itself. When combined, the two distinctions result in a typology of socialization which is presented in Figure 1.4. The typology is highly reminiscent of a well-known typology for schools of sociology, originally presented by Burrell and Morgan (1979) and related to communication research by Rosengren (1983a, 1989a, 1993); the similarity between the two typologies offers strong validation to both of them.

Each of the two dimensions of the typology represents a number of theoretical and practical problems. A partial solution to the *theoretical* subject/object problematics (which is, of course, closely related to the agency/structure debate) is represented by the distinction between structurally, positionally and individually determined patterns of action (see above). The *practical* conflict/consensus problematics is handled in the socialization process by letting objectively existing social differences stand out as morally, politically and/or religiously motivated, so that what from a social science perspective may be regarded as a causal relation, from the individual's perspective may appear as subjectively willed, and morally proper action. By

Individual Socialized

	Subject	Object
Conflict	Radical Humanism	Radical Structuralism
Consensus	Interactionist Sociology	Mainstream Sociology

Society

Figure 1.4 A typology of approaches in socialization research

thus transforming causality into finality, socialization at the same time may transform conflict into consensus (cf. the Marxian notion of false consciousness; Boudon and Bourricaud 1982/1989: 358). However subtle it may be, this control process is never perfect. There is always some free space left, interstices in which potential dissidents may find each other and build plans for future change (in most societies, the freedom left to peer groups among young adolescents is perhaps the best example; see Rosengren 1992c). In addition, there is always more to socialization than control. All agents of socialization also provide intellectual, emotional, social and material resources which may be used by those being socialized – sometimes, in ways completely unforeseen by society and its representatives, the agents of socialization.

The control exercised and the resources put at the disposal of the agents of socialization represent two basic dimensions by means of which all socialization processes may very economically be characterized. Indeed, the two dimensions are so basic as to be applicable not only to processes of socialization but to all social groups and their internal and external interactions. The two dimensions have been independently introduced by scholars in disciplines and traditions of research such as child psychiatry (Olson *et al.* 1979; Barnes and Olson 1985) and family communication (Chaffee *et al.* 1971; Lull 1980; Jarlbro 1986; Ritchie 1991; see also Chapters 8 and 10 in this volume). Today, the best known example of this very general idea may be Anthony Giddens' notion of structure as 'rules and resources' (Giddens 1990: 301; cf. Clark 1990: 25). A systematic search would no doubt reveal that similar notions have been applied also in other types of social science. (Mary Douglas' conceptual pair of 'grid/group' (Douglas 1970; cf., for instance, Gross and Rayner 1985; Wildawsky 1989) shows some similarity, too, with the control/resources dimensions. Although the grid/group typology has been very differentially interpreted, it refers primarily to control conceptualized as within and between group structuring, leaving the notion of resources by the roadside.)

In its most general form, the typology is presented in Figure 1.5, subsuming the special cases of socialization typology just mentioned (see Rosengren 1985; cf. also Chapters 8 and 10).

The types in Figure 1.5 represent ideal types, which, of course, in their pure form are seldom or never found in reality. This should be kept in mind, but it is no argument against the typology as such. Because of its generality, the typology is relevant to both the content, the process, and the agents of socialization. In empirical research, of course, it has to be adapted and modified according to the specific circumstances at hand, and its very general dimensions probably have to be specified. The typology as it stands, though, can also be directly related to a number of problems, for instance to those three central and well-known categories of conflict and consensus originally presented and discussed by Hirschman (1970, 1981, 1985) – 'Exit', 'Voice', and 'Loyalty'.

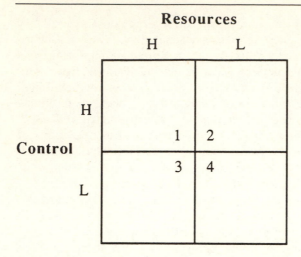

Resources

Figure 1.5 A typology of socialization conditions
H = high; L = low

In cells 1 and 3, both 'Voice' and 'Exit' seem to be most naturally applied ('Exit' being perhaps more frequent than 'Voice' in cell 1, 'Voice' than 'Exit' in cell 3, since in cell 1 (because of its high control) 'Exit' may sometimes be the only way to articulate 'Voice', while in cell 3 (because of its low control) 'Exit' may not always be very necessary). In cells 2 and 4, on the other hand, both alternatives seem to be less applicable. In cell 2, resources may not suffice for 'Voice', control may be too hard for 'Exit'. Here 'Loyalty' seems to be the natural alternative. In cell 4, neither 'Exit', nor 'Voice', nor 'Loyalty' may be very relevant at all, since cold indifference probably dampens everything. The inhabitants of this cell tend to have a weak voice, they have not much to which they might be loyal, and they may not consider exit very much – for the simple reason that they are already out.

A general conclusion to be drawn from the typology is that the independence of socializees from their agents of socialization will probably tend to be lowest in cell 2, highest in cell 3. Under the conditions of the latter cell it would probably be least difficult to arrive at that sometimes very productive outcome of a conflict: to agree to disagree.

For better and for worse, the availability of voice and exit further innovation. Processes of innovation, then, are most likely to occur in cell 3, and to some extent in cell 1. In cell 2, Roger's Innovators should be found; in cell 1, his Early Adopters (Rogers 1983), always remembering the following, of course:

1 Another word for exit is drop-out.
2 Not all exits and drop-outs are based on innovations.

In principle, the same argumentation should be valid when writ large, at the societal level. In some societies or parts of societies, for some periods of time, resources are plenty and social control, low. Renaissance Florence, and the Vienna of the early twentieth century come to mind, but less dramatic examples may certainly be found. In all countries and all times, there seem to be some regions which are more prone to innovation than others – and some which are less prone to innovation (Hägerstrand 1968). In the final analysis, this leads us back to the relationship between culture and other societal systems, this time in terms of continuity and change.

CONTINUITY AND CHANGE

Let's return for a moment to the relations between culture and other societal systems previously discussed in typological terms, and illustrated in Figures 1.1. and 1.2. Both figures actually build on the silent assumption that societies are closed systems. No societies are closed systems, however, and Figure 1.6 heeds that trivial and yet very basic truth, also turning the typological models of Figures 1.1 and 1.2 into a causally oriented model.

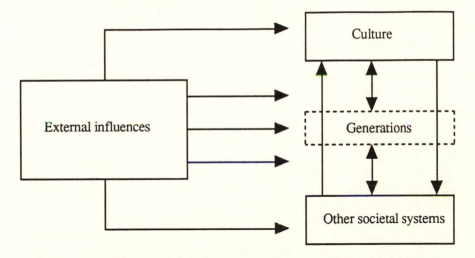

Figure 1.6 A causal model for the relations between culture and other societal systems

It will be seen that the model corresponds to cell 1 of Figure 1.2, characterized by interaction between culture and other societal systems. Two complications have been introduced: external influences from other societies, and a generational filter between culture and other societal systems.

Societies may be conceptualized as systems of ideas, actions and artefacts, but actions are carried out by human beings, also producing ideas and material artefacts. Human beings tend to live 'three score years and ten', internalizing societal culture primarily during their first twenty years or so. Their capacity for innovation as a rule being rather low after their first one or two score years, they then tend to spend large portions of their lives reproducing what has been internalized. A consequence of these basic facts of life is that there is a generational filter between culture and other societal systems, reducing the rate of innovative exchange between society's general culture and other societal systems. New ideas born within and between creative brains, new patterns of actions emerging among innovative groups of people, new types of artefacts devised and produced by *homo sapiens et faber*, therefore, are not instantaneously accepted – as innovation research has shown again and again (Hägerstrand 1968; Rogers 1983; Perry 1992). Innovations tend to be produced by relatively young generations, and the filter of relatively old generations reduces the rate of change, thus producing a certain amount of societal stability, a precarious balance between continuity and change.

The outcome of this interplay is that overall societal change tends to be relatively slow. In modern societies, all generations seem to feel they live in a period of rapid change, and perhaps they do. But changes thus perceived are often relatively superficial. The basic characteristics of societal culture as such tend to change only slowly, often passing by unnoticed until they reach some threshold value at which they suddenly become perceived and vehemently discussed: periods of clairvoyance, 'moments of madness' (see Zolberg 1972; Hirschman 1985: 90).

In order to measure such slow change, its trends, cycles, and more or less accidental variations, we need reliable instruments, indicators of societal change. In principle, there are four main types of such societal indicators: economic indicators (measuring phenomena related to wealth), objective social indicators (measuring welfare), subjective social indicators (measuring well-being) and cultural indicators (measuring the development of basic values and other central ideas). Although the terms used here to designate them may be relatively new, economic indicators have been around for centuries or even millennia; social indicators, for at least a century; and cultural indicators for at least half a century (Rosengren 1989b, 1992a; see also, for instance, Bauer 1966; Hart 1933; Sorokin 1937–41; Gerbner 1969; Klingemann *et al.* 1982; Namenwirth and Weber 1987; Rosengren 1984; Stimson 1991).

Changes in the basic value system of Sweden, its 'climate of culture' as it developed during the period 1945–1975, were studied in a research programme called CISSS (Cultural Indicators: The Swedish Symbol System, 1945–1975). Figure 1.7, featuring the development of the extent to which the basic values of freedom and equality were upheld in editorials in a representative sample of Swedish newspapers during the period 1945–1975, offers a graphic example of the way such societal change tends to proceed (see Block 1984).

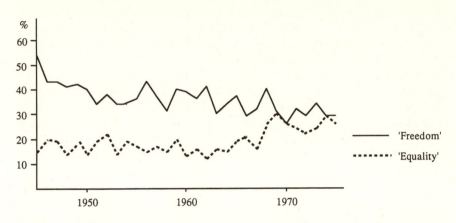

Figure 1.7 The values of 'Freedom' and 'Equality' as upheld in Swedish editorials, 1945–1975 (Source: Block (1984))

As shown by Rokeach (1973: 170), the two values of freedom and equality in combination may be regarded as defining characteristics of four basic societal ideologies:

1 *Socialism* puts a high value on both freedom and equality.
2 *Fascism* puts a low value on both freedom and equality.
3 *Communism* puts equality above freedom.
4 *Liberal capitalism* puts freedom above equality.

What Figure 1.7 tells us, then, is that during the first two decades after the Second World War, Sweden changed from being a society ideologically characterized by liberal capitalism to one ideologically characterized by socialism. This period of ideological socialism was twenty years in coming, but it lasted for only a few years. Contrary to what at the time many people believed, the notorious year of 1968 did not mark a beginning, but an end. The ideological development then took another turn. Some years later, Sweden experienced an ideologically quite different period, this time of liberal capitalism, the heyday of which – the 'moment of madness', if you will (see above) – probably was not, or will not be, much longer than that of socialism. Although these specific developments have not yet been documented by quantitative and systematic measurements and related to data from other sectors of society, this is by no means an implausible hypothesis.

Results such as these show that basic changes in societal systems tend to take quite some time to come about. They also suggest that the results of such slow processes of change, when having reached maturity, may be rather short-lived. It is as if the innumerable processes of socialization tend to be so time-consuming as not to leave much scope for the overall outcome at the macro level to be very long-lived. It may actually be true that at the micro level the times are changing always, as so many of us believe. But at the macro level change tends to be so slow that – paradoxically – periods of stability have to become rather short, something which may contribute to the widespread but false impression that times are changing at a very quick pace.

One reason for this pattern of slow change is very probably the simple fact that some powerful agents of socialization seem to be conservative almost by definition. What socialization often means is that representatives of old generations – parents and grandparents – hand over the values and opinions of their generations to representatives of the upcoming generations, their children and grandchildren. In addition, priests, teachers and law agents are not exactly known for their high level of general innovativeness (let alone their political convictions). The most innovative agent of socialization is probably the peer group, especially peer groups composed of adolescents, leading for a short period an intermediate existence between childhood and adulthood. Two types of socialization agent tend to be rather variable with respect to their innovativeness: the work group and the mass media. In both cases, their innovative capacity is probably closely related to the culture of the surrounding society: both are more innovative in a modern society than in a traditional one.

In their capacity as socializing agents, the mass media as we know them today are unique in many ways. No other type of society has had anything comparable: an agent of socialization which takes on the following tasks:

- Acts for several hours each day of the year in virtually all homes of the society.
- Establishes the agenda of political, economic, cultural discussions.
- Offers endless flows of entertainment and information.
- In addition to indirect, 'lived' socialization provides also formal, educationally oriented socialization.
- Helps to conserve existing structures of power at the same time as preparing the ground for the ever-present processes of change so vital to any modern, industrial and post-industrial society (and presumably, to all postmodern ones as well – whatever may be meant by that rather elusive term of postmodernism; see Gibbins and Reimer forthcoming).

Mass media and mass communication, then, must be important to any book which discusses the interplay between culture and other societal systems in modern societies. In this volume, they are at the very focus of interest. Let's turn to a short introductory discussion of mass media structures, uses and effects.

MASS MEDIA: STRUCTURES, USES AND EFFECTS

In terms of the previous argumentation, mass media are involved in both horizontal and vertical relations between culture and other societal systems.

Part of their task is to help strike that delicate and precarious balance between change and continuity, innovation and conservation in society and its various subsystems as discussed above. While as a rule the role of the mass media is to evaluate, interpret, and disseminate innovations produced in other societal systems, some innovations are actually created within the mass media. To some extent, at least, the mass media are innovation-producing organizations.

Mass media as innovation-producing institutions

An important characteristic of innovation-producing institutions is their reward system. The reward systems may be organized according to different principles. In each system there are different types of reward: material and symbolic rewards. Both types may be granted in different, more or less institutionalized ways. It is commonplace to distinguish between reward systems based upon market standards and critical standards (Bourdieu 1971; DiMaggio and Hirsch 1976), but there is actually a whole set of such systems: patronage of different types, market, prizes, grants, subsidies, etc. (Clark and Clark 1977; Clark 1979). Crane (1976) presented and discussed a list of four different types of reward system. Rosengren (1983b) located the four different types within a typology which orders the distinctions so that they form a Guttman scale – which, incidentally, gave rise to a fifth type of reward system (see Rosengren 1988, 1990; Rosengren *et al.* 1991). The typology is presented in Figure 1.8.

The scale generates several interesting questions. Some such questions discussed by Crane (1976) concern, for instance, the following issues:

- The degree of continuity and variety in the innovations produced under different reward systems.
- The change from one system of reward to another.
- The relationship between type of reward system and amount of resources at the disposal of the system.

The scale might also be related to other theoretical arguments, for instance, theories of professionalization and de-professionalization in the media (Windahl and Rosengren 1978; Kepplinger and Köcher 1990). It may be related, say, to the prevalence of the four types of artist listed by Becker (1982): integrated professionals, mavericks, naive artists, and folk artists. It may be related, finally, to the type of ultimate source of money available to the system: patron, market, prizes, grants, subsidies (Clark and Clark 1977; Clark 1979). The scale may have its main value as a heuristic device for theoretical work. In empirical research it probably has to be modified in various ways. The values of the scale should be seen as ideal types, seldom or never met with *in concreto*. Each of the four items of the scale has to be operationalized on its own conditions and probably also conceptualized as having more than the two values of yes and no. Overall institutions such as

Innovative product consumed mainly by fellow innovators	Material rewards allocated among innovators mainly by fellow innovators	Symbolic rewards allocated among innovators mainly by fellow innovators	Norms for innovations set mainly by fellow innovators	Ideal type of reward system	Tentative examples
Yes	Yes	Yes	Yes	Esoteric	Basic Science
No	Yes	Yes	Yes	Independent	Applied Science
No	No	Yes	Yes	Semi-independent	Technology, Elite Art and Literature
No	No	No	Yes	Subcultural	Jazz, Radical Science
No	No	No	No	Heterocultural	Mass media culture (literature, music, etc)

Figure 1.8 A Guttman scale for innovators' reward systems (Source: Rosengren (1983b))

literature or science may well be composed of sub-institutions, the innovators of which have differential degrees of control over the reward system (see the examples given in Figure 1.8).

The dynamics in and between innovation-producing institutions is considerable. There are two main types of dynamics: changes in and of the systems. Single innovations may percolate between institutions, and such movements may go both ways. *Gesunkenes Kulturgut* was for a long time a key term in European ethnography. A striking and well-known example of percolation in the other direction, as it were, is Shakespeare, who – now the dramatist *par excellence* – originally worked in a heterocultural medium, the popular theatres of sixteenth- and seventeenth-century London. At the beginning of his career he was looked down upon by the 'University Wits'. Regarding themselves as serving another system, semi-independent at the very least, and yet anxious not to be overshadowed by Shakespeare, they called him an 'upstart crowe beautified with our feathers ... that supposes he is as well able to bombast out a blank verse as the best of you' (quoted from Legouis and Cazamian 1930/1957: 411).

It would not be too difficult to find parallels to this quarrel among present-day representatives of semi-independent and heterocultural reward systems such as élite art and popular culture. Far more thorough-going than such changes *within* the systems, of course, are the changes *of* the innovation-producing systems themselves. The rise and possible fall of the public service broadcasting systems is a good example of such structural change (see Chapter 2). With respect to mass media and mass communications, a basic distinction must be made between at least two pairs of different relationships between media and innovations:

1 Innovations actually produced within the mass media system, *vs.* innovations disseminated by the media, *and*
2 Innovations discussed and criticized by the media, *vs.* innovations only reported upon by the media.

Innovations produced within esoteric reward systems (such as basic science) tend to be neglected or, at best, only reported by the media. Innovations produced within independent reward systems (such as applied science) are sometimes both reported and discussed by the media, and this may be even more true for innovations produced within semi-independent systems (such as élite art and literature). Innovations produced within sub-cultural reward systems (such as jazz, or radical science) lead a precarious existence in the media: they may be completely neglected or overwhelmed by media attention. Innovations produced within heterocultural systems, finally, are the bread and butter of media organizations and media audiences.

It may be a matter of discussion, perhaps – and certainly a matter of definition – whether the media produce any innovations at all, rather than just variations of old innovations. But to the extent that they do produce innovations, their predominant type of reward system is heterocultural, characterized by the fact that people other than fellow innovators consume the innovations, allocate material rewards, allocate symbolic rewards, and set the norms for the innovations. It should be remembered, though, that traditionally the media have kept sometimes considerable portions of available space and time open to innovations produced within independent, semi-independent and sub-cultural reward systems. This is especially true for the public service mass media. It is less true, of course, for media operating on a commercial market. Actually, this may be where the typology's utility stands out most clearly.

In terms of the typology just presented, the widespread fears of imminent changes in the quality of broadcasting programming following the transition from a public service media system to a market-oriented system could be expressed as originating in a change *from* a media system in which programming itself (and especially some types of programmes) is being produced to a considerable extent within semi-independent or sub-cultural reward systems, *to* a system in which programming itself, as well as most types of its content, is produced almost exclusively within a heterocultural reward system. The standards actually used in the different reward systems show considerable variation, of course, and this variation must of necessity affect the horizontal relations between mass media and other societal institutions, and also the vertical relations in which mass media engage in their capacity as agents of socialization. In the following section we shall discuss some such relations.

Relations between mass media and other societal institutions

Horizontally, an ever-increasing portion of the relations between large societal institutions are enacted by means of mass communication. This is so not only in the sense that mass media report and reflect such relations: in many cases the relations themselves are enacted in, by and for the mass media. Although taking place at some sports stadium or other, sports events are increasingly staged primarily for the media. The Pope offers his blessings to the thousands gathering before St. Peter's in Rome, but more important may be the millions and millions around the globe who witness the event on TV. Political discussions and decisions are often presented in the media before they are given due treatment by the formal, political authorities. In some cases, negotiations having global political consequences have actually – but only partly, to be sure – been broadcast live on the screen. Such true 'media events' may still be few and far between, but they are probably increasing in number and importance (Dayan and Katz 1992). Their importance builds on the simple fact that what is involved is *both* horizontal (national or international) relations between societal institutions, *and* vertical relations between macro, meso and micro levels.

Vertical relations between societal institutions by means of mass communication presuppose individual media use, of course. The flow from the media into individual minds may be conceptualized in terms of time perspectives ranging from hours and days to decades and centuries. A number of well-known research traditions have focussed on different parts of this broad spectrum, as follows:

- News diffusion research: hours and days (Miller 1945; Rosengren 1987; Greenberg *et al.* 1993).
- Agenda setting research: weeks and months (McCombs and Shaw 1972; Shaw and Martin 1992; Rogers *et al.* 1993).
- Spiral of silence research: months and years (Noelle-Neumann 1980/1984, 1991; Scherer 1991).
- Cultivation research: years and decades (Gerbner 1969; Signorielli and Morgan 1990; Potter 1993).
- Research on the public sphere (*Öffentlichkeit*): decades and centuries (Habermas 1962/1989, 1981/1984).

Common to these five traditions is that they deal with the communicative relationship between societal structure and individual agency – more specifically a media structure (variable over time and space), and individuals (characterized by any number of attributes) interacting with that structure and with each other. Research within traditions applying a relatively long time perspective tends to stress structural characteristics; research applying a relatively short time perspective, individual characteristics.

Individual media use and the effects of that use (both types of phenomenon being affected, of course, by macro and micro conditions) represent a broad field of research having by now been systematically cultivated for at least three-quarters of a century, at an accelerating pace (Klapper 1960; Blumler and Katz 1974; Rosengren *et al.* 1985; Bryant and Zillman 1986; Korzenny and Ting-Toomey 1992; Swanson 1992; see also Chapter 7). We know that individual use of mass media covers a large and increasing portion of most people's daily lives, that it shows considerable variation in both quantitative and qualitative terms, and that the variation is systematically related to structural, positional and individual characteristics ranging from type of society to social position in terms of age, gender and class, to individually embraced values, opinions and attitudes. The effects of individual media use may not be especially strong, but since they are many, variegated, widespread and enduring, they must be considered important. Their importance is highlighted especially in the socialization of society's young generations.

The fact that when reaching adulthood the inhabitants of many industrial and post-industrial societies have spent more hours before the TV screen than at school has become a widely spread adage which does tell us something about the comparative strength of mass media's role in the socialization process of different societies (see, for instance, Bronfenbrenner 1970). More detailed and probing scrutiny, of course, is necessary fully to assess the role of the mass media as agents of socialization. Above all, research in the field has to be theory-driven rather than goaded by some variant of those moral panics which tend to appear at the introduction of every new mass medium or variant of mass medium (see Roe 1985) .

Also, it is important not to extrapolate results gained within one society, characterized by its own variant of mass media structure, to societies with different media structures. Today, most mass communication research is located in the USA or carried out within a couple of a West European countries. Research carried out in other parts of the world – say, in Latin America and Asia, in Eastern, Northern and Southern Europe – is by no means non-existent but until fairly recently has been given less attention by the international community of scholarship and research in the field. Systematic efforts have recently been undertaken to remedy this structural deficiency, for instance by efforts to collect and systematize the incipient comparative communication research which is available (Blumler *et al.* 1992; Korzenny and Ting-Toomey 1992). Hopefully more will follow. In particular, comparisons between the role of mass media within different reward systems (see p. 18) should stand out as especially promising (not least with respect to the notion of diversity; see Rosengren *et al.* 1991; Litman 1992; Kambara 1992; Jshikawa 1994). In its way, this book tries to offer some material for future comparisons of patterns of media use in societies differentially located in geographic, socio-economical and cultural space.

ABOUT THIS BOOK

The book is divided into three parts. This introductory section has three chapters. Chapter 2 offers a bird's-eye view of Sweden and its media scene, while Chapter 3 presents the overall organization and main tenor of the research programme behind the book, the MPP.

Part II of the book offers basic results about stability and change in the media use of children, adolescents and young adults during the period 1975–1990. Chapter 4, by Karl Erik Rosengren, offers some descriptive data, an overview of media use among a number of panels and cohorts of Swedish children, adolescents and young adults. In Chapter 5, Robert P. Hawkins and Suzanne Pingree offer a temporal comparison between structural patterns of media use and other activities in 1980 and 1989 among two different cohorts of children and adolescents. Drawing on longitudinal LISREL models, Ulla Johnsson-Smaragdi in Chapter 6 examines into stability and change in levels of television viewing within and between panels of children, adolescents and young adults.

Part III of the book centres on three different types of longitudinal effect of media use in childhood and adolescence. In Chapter 7, Karl Erik Rosengren, Ulla Johnsson-Smaragdi and Inga Sonesson summarize some

long-term positive and negative effects of television viewing found in
research carried out by different members of the MPP group and mostly
published in Swedish sources not easily available to scholars outside the
Swedish research community. In Chapter 8, Ulla Johnsson-Smaragdi and
Annelis Jönsson analyse the long-term effects on self-image and schooling
of media use by children and adolescents raised in families living in different
social surroundings and characterized by a differential pattern of communication. In Chapter 9, Keith Roe takes a long look at the relationship between
media use and social mobility among children and young adults.

Part IV of the book offers three chapters on media use and lifestyle. In
Chapter 10, Fredrik Miegel presents quantitative results from his studies of
family communication patterns, lifestyle and media taste, while in Chapter
11 he summarizes a number of qualitative case studies representing individual variation within overarching patterns of lifestyles. In Chapter 12,
Thomas (Lööv-) Johansson presents a partly new theoretical framework for
understanding the lifestyle phenomenon in terms of modernity and consumer culture.

In the final part and chapter of the book, the editor looks to the future, and
discusses what new tasks for research within the Media Panel Program may
grow out of the rich and varied results offered in the previous chapters of
the book.

Chapters 4–12 of this book may be read as independent, self-contained
pieces of research about various aspects of individual media use by young
people, its causes and consequences. All of them, however, build on
empirical data collected within the Media Panel Program presented in
Chapter 3, and all of them also presuppose some knowledge about Sweden
and the Swedish media scene during the last two decades or so, which is what
Chapter 2 tries to offer.

In first chapter an attempt has been made to present an overarching
theoretical framework within which the results of the various chapters may
be interpreted and understood.

REFERENCES

Alexander, J.C. (1987) 'Action and its environments', in J.C. Alexander, B. Giesen,
R. Münch and N.J. Smelser (eds) *The Micro–Macro Link*, Berkeley, Calif.:
University of California Press.
Alexander, J.C., Giesen, B. (1987) 'From reduction to linkage: The long view of the
micro-macro debate', in J.C. Alexander, B. Giesen, R. Münch and N.J. Smelser
(eds) *The Micro–Macro Link*, Berkeley, Calif.: University of California Press.
Alexander, J.C., Giesen, B., Münch, R. and Smelser, N.J. (eds) (1987) *The Micro–
Macro Link*, Berkeley, Calif.: University of California Press.
Archer, M. (1990) 'Human agency and social structure: A critique of Giddens', in J.
Clark, C. Modgil. and S. Modgil (eds) *Anthony Giddens. Consensus and Con-
troversy*, London: The Palmer Press.

Barnes, H.L. and Olson, D.H. (1985) 'Parent–adolescent communication and the circumplex model', *Child Development* 56: 438–447.

Bauer, R.A. (ed.) (1966) *Social Indicators*, Cambridge, Mass.: MIT Press.

Becker, H.S. (1982) *Art Worlds*, Berkeley, Calif.: University of California Press.

Bell, D. (1976) *The Cultural Contradictions of Capitalism*, London: Heinemann.

Berger, P.L. and Berger, B. (1972) *Sociology: A Biographical Approach*, New York: Basic Books.

Block, E. (1984) 'Freedom, equality, et cetera: Values and valuations in the Swedish domestic political debate, 1945–1975', in G. Melischek, K.E. Rosengren and J. Stappers (eds) *Cultural Indicators: An International Symposium*, Vienna: Akademie der Wissenschaften.

Blumler, J.G. and Katz, E. (eds) (1974) *The Uses of Mass Communications: Current Perspectives on Gratifications Research*, Beverly Hills, Calif.: Sage.

Blumler, J.G. McLeod, J.M. and Rosengren, K.E. (eds) (1992) *Comparatively Speaking: Communication and Culture Across Space and Time*, Newbury Park, Calif.: Sage.

Boudon, R. and Bourricaud, F. (1982/1989) *A Critical Dictionary of Sociology*, London: Routledge.

Bourdieu, P. (1971) 'Intellectual field and creative project', in M.K.D. Young (ed.) *Knowledge and Control*, London: Macmillan.

Bronfenbrenner, U. (1970) *Two Worlds of Childhood*, New York: Russell Sage Foundation.

Bryant, J. and Zillmann, D. (eds) (1986) *Perspectives on Media Effects*, Hillsdale, NJ: Erlbaum.

Bunge, M. (1981) *Scientific Materialism*, Dordrecht: Reidel.

Burrell, G. and Morgan, G. (1979) *Sociological Paradigms and Organisational Analysis*, London: Heinemann.

Burton, R.V. (1968) 'Socialization: psychological aspects', in D.L. Sills (ed.) *International Encyclopedia of the Social Sciences*, 14: 534–545, New York: Collier-Macmillan.

Carlsson, G., Dahlberg, A. and Rosengren, K.E. (1981) 'Mass media content, political opinion and social change', in K.E. Rosengren (ed.) *Advances in Content Analysis*, Beverly Hills, Calif.: Sage.

Chaffee, S.H., McLeod, J.M. and Atkin, C.K. (1971) 'Parental influences on adolescent media use', *American Behavioural Scientist*, 14: 323–340.

Clark, J. (1990) 'Anthony Giddens, sociology and social theory', in J. Clark, C. Modgil and S. Modgil (eds) *Anthony Giddens. Consensus and Controversy*, London: The Palmer Press.

Clark, P.P. (1979) 'Literary culture in France and the United States', *The American Journal of Sociology* 84: 1057–1077.

Clark, P.P. and Clark, T.N. (1977) 'Patrons, publishers and prizes: The writers' estate in France', in J. Ben-David and T.N. Clark (eds) *Culture and Its Creators*, Chicago: Chicago University Press.

Crane, D. (1976) 'Reward systems in art, science and religion', *American Behavioural Scientist* 19: 719–734.

Crane, D. (1992) *The Production of Culture*, Newbury Park, Calif.: Sage.

Dayan, D. and Katz, E. (1992) *Media Events. The Live Broadcasting of History*, Cambridge, Mass.: Harvard University Press.

Dietz, T. and Burns, T.R. (1992) 'Human agency and the evolutional dynamics of culture', *Acta Sociologica* 35: 187–200.

DiMaggio, P. and Hirsch, P.M. (1976) 'Production organizations in the arts', *American Behavioral Scientist* 19: 735–752.

Douglas, M. (1970) *Natural Symbols*, London: Barrie & Rockliff.

Gecas, V. (1992) 'Socialization', in E.F. Borgatta (ed.) *Encyclopedia of Sociology* 4: 1863–1872, New York: Macmillan.

Gerbner, G. (1969) 'Towards "Cultural Indicators": The analysis of mass mediated message systems', *AV Communication Review* 17: 137–148.

Gibbins, J.R. and Reimer, B. (forthcoming) 'Postmodernism', in J. Van Deth (ed.) *The Impact of Values*.

Giddens, A. (1984) *The Constitution of Society. Outline of the Theory of Structuration*, Cambridge: Polity Press.

—— (1990) 'Structuration theory and sociological analysis', in J. Clark, C. Modgil and S. Modgil (eds) *Anthony Giddens. Consensus and Controversy*, London: The Palmer Press.

—— (1991) *Modernity and Self-identity*, Cambridge: Polity Press.

Greenberg, B.S., Cohen, E. and Li, H. (1993) 'How the U.S. found out about the war', in B.S. Greenberg and W. Gantz (eds) *Desert Storm and the Mass Media*, Cresskill, NJ: Hampton Press, Inc.

Gross, J.L. and Rayner, S. (1985) *Measuring Cultures*, New York: Columbia University Press.

Guttman, L. (1954) 'A new approach to factor analysis: The radex', in P.F. Lazarsfeld (ed.) *Mathematical Thinking in the Social Sciences*, New York: The Free Press.

Habermas, J. (1962/1989) *The Structural Transformation of the Public Sphere, Vol. 1*, Cambridge, Mass.: MIT Press.

—— (1981/1984) *The Theory of Communicative Action*, Boston, Mass.: Beacon.

Hägerstrand, T. (1968) 'The diffusion of innovations', in D.L. Sills (ed.) *International Encyclopedia of the Social Sciences* 4: 174–178, New York: Collier-Macmillan.

Harris, M. (1979) *Cultural Materialism*, New York: Random.

Hart, H. (1933) 'Changing social attitudes and interests', in *Recent Social Trends*, vol. I, New York: McGraw Hill.

Hirschman, A. (1970) *Exit, Voice, and Loyalty*. Cambridge, Mass.: Harvard University Press.

—— (1981) *Essays in Trespassing*, New Haven, Conn.: Yale University Press.

—— (1985) *Shifting Involvements. Private Interest and Public Action*, Oxford: Basil Blackwell Ltd.

Jarlbro, G. (1986) 'Family communication patterns revisited: Reliability and validity', *Lund Research Papers in the Sociology of Communication* 4, Lund: Department of Sociology, University of Lund.

Johansson, T. and Miegel, F. (1992) *Do the Right Thing. Lifestyle and Identity in Contemporary Youth Culture*, Stockholm: Almqvist & Wiksell International.

Jshikawa, S. (1994) 'Retrospect and prospect of the five countries joint project on quality assessment of broadcasting', *Studies of Broadcasting*, 30, 1994.

Kambara, N. (1992) 'Study of the diversity indices used for programming analysis', *Studies of Broadcasting* 28: 195–206.

Katz, E., Gurevitch, M. and Haas, H. (1973) 'On the use of mass media for important things', *American Sociological Review* 38 (2): 164–181.

Kepplinger, H.M. and Köcher, R. (1990) 'Professionalism in the media world?', *European Journal of Communication* 5: 285–312.

Klapper, J. (1960) *The Effects of Mass Communication*, New York: Free Press.

Klingemann, H.D., Mohler, P.P. and Weber, R.P. (1982) 'Das Reichtumsthema in den Thronreden des Kaisers und die ökonomische Entwicklung in Deutschland, 1871–1914', in H.D. Klingemann (ed.) *Computerunterstützte Inhaltsanalyse in der empirischen Sozialforschung*, Kronberg/Ts.: Athenäum.

Korzenny, F. and Ting-Toomey, S. (eds) (1992) *Mass Media Effects Across Cultures*. Newbury Park, Calif.: Sage.

Legouis, E. and Cazamian, L. (1930/1957) *A History of English Literature*, London: Dent & Sons.

Lipset, S.M. (1993) 'Pacific divide: American exceptionalism – Japanese uniqueness', *International Journal of Public Opinion Research* 5: 121–166.

Litman, B.R. (1992) 'Economic aspects of program quality: The case for diversity', *Studies of Broadcasting* 28: 121–156.

Lull, J. (1980) 'Family communication patterns and the social uses of television', *Communication Research* 7: 319–334.

Lumsden, C.J. and Wilson, E.O. (1981) *Genes, Mind, and Culture*, Cambridge, Mass.: Harvard University Press.

McCombs, M. and Shaw, D. (1972) 'The agenda-setting function of mass media', *Public Opinion Quarterly* 36: 176–185.

McCron, R. (1976) 'Changing perspectives in the study of mass media and socialization', in J.D. Halloran (ed.) *Mass Media and Socialization*, Leeds: Kavanagh.

Meddin, J. (1975) 'Attitudes, values and related concepts: A system of classification', *Social Science Quarterly* 55 (4): 889–900.

Miller, D.C. (1945) 'A research note on mass communication', *American Sociological Review* 10: 685–698.

Münch, R. and Smelser, N.J. (1987) 'Relating the micro and macro', in J.C. Alexander, B. Giesen, R. Münch and N.J. Smelser (eds) (1987) *The Micro–Macro Link*, Berkeley, Calif.: University of California Press.

Namenwirth, J.S. and Bibbee, R.C. (1976) 'Change within or of the system: An example from the history of American values', *Quality and Quantity* 10: 145–164.

Namenwirth, J.S. and Weber, R.P. (1987) *Dynamics of Culture*, Boston, Mass.: Allen & Unwin.

Noelle-Neumann, E. (1980/1994) *The Spiral of Silence*, Chicago: Chicago University Press.

—— (1991) 'The theory of public opinion: The concept of the spiral of silence', *Communication Yearbook* 14: 256–287.

Nowak, K. (1992) 'Magazine advertising content in Sweden and the United States: Stable patterns of change, variable levels of stability', in J.G. Blumler, J.M. McLeod and K.E. Rosengren (eds) *Comparatively Speaking: Communication and Culture Across Space and Time*, Newbury Park, Calif.: Sage.

Olson, D.H., Sprenkle, D.H. and Russell, C.S. (1979) 'The circumplex model of marital and family systems: 1. Cohesion and adaptability dimensions, family types, and clinical applications', *Family Process* 18: 3–27.

Parsons, T. (1966) *Societies: Evolutionary and Comparative Perspectives*, Englewood Cliffs, NJ: Prentice Hall.

Perry, R.W. (1992) 'Diffusion Theories', in E.F. Borgatta and M.L. Borgatta (ed.) *Encyclopedia of Sociology* 1: 487–492, New York: Macmillan.

Pollay, R.W. (1984) 'The determinants of magazine advertising informativeness throughout the twentieth century', *Written Communication* 1: 24–37.

Potter, W.J. (1993) 'Cultivation theory and research: A conceptual critique', *Human Communication Research* 19: 564–601.

Reimer, B. (1994) *The Most Common of Practices*, Stockholm: Almqvist & Wiksell International.

Reimer, B. and Rosengren, K.E. (1990) 'Cultivated viewers and readers: A lifestyle perspective', in N. Signorielli and M. Morgan (eds) *Cultivation Analysis. New Directions in Media Effects Research*, Newbury Park, Calif.: Sage.

Ritchie, L.D. (1991) 'Family communication patterns: An epistemic analysis and conceptual reinterpretation', *Communication Research* 184: 548–565.

Roe, K. (1985) 'The Swedish moral panic over video 1980–1984', *Nordicom-Information* (No. 2–3): 13–18.

Rogers, E.M. (1983) *Diffusion of Innovations*, 3rd Edn, New York: The Free Press.

Rogers, E.M., Dearing, J.W. and Bregman, D. (1993) 'The anatomy of agenda-setting research', *Journal of Communication* 43: 68–84.

Rokeach, M. (1973) *The Nature of Social Values*, New York: The Free Press.

Rosengren, K.E., (1981) 'Mass media and social change: Some current approaches', in E. Katz. and T. Szecskö. (eds) *Mass Media and Social Change*, London: Sage.

—— (1983a) 'Communication research: One paradigm, or four?', *Journal of Communication* 33 (3): 185–207.

—— (1983b) *The Climate of Literature*, Lund: Studentlitteratur.

—— (1984) 'Cultural indicators for the comparative study of culture', in G. Melischek, K.E. Rosengren, and J. Stappers (eds) *Cultural Indicators: An International Symposium*, Vienna: Akademie der Wissenschaften.

—— (1985) 'Media linkages of culture and other societal systems', *Communication Yearbook* 9:19–56.

—— (1987) 'The comparative study of news diffusion', *European Journal of Communication* 2: 227–255.

—— (1988) 'The study of media culture: Ideas, actions, and artefacts', *Lund Research Papers in the Sociology of Communication*, 10, Lund: Department of Sociology, University of Lund.

—— (1989a) 'Paradigms lost and regained', in B. Dervin, L. Grossberg, B.J. O'Keefe and E. Wartella (eds), *Rethinking Communication. Volume 1: Paradigm Issues*, Newbury Park, Calif.: Sage.

—— (1989b) 'Cultural Indicators', in E. Barnouw (ed.) *International Encyclopedia of Communications*, 1: 433–35.

—— (1990) 'Who carries the field? Communication between literary scholars and critics', in C.L. Borgman (ed.) *Bibliometrics and Scholarly Communication*, Newbury Park, Calif.: Sage.

—— (1992a) 'Cultural indicators research: A thumbnail sketch, a Swedish perspective', *Newsletter of the Sociology of Culture Section of the American Sociological Association* 6 (4): 17–20.

—— (1992b) 'Substantive theories and formal models: Their role in research on individual media use', *Lund Research Papers in Media and Communication Studies*, 4, Lund: Department of Sociology, University of Lund.

—— (1992c) 'On the conventional wisdom of soothsayers', *International Communication Bulletin* 27 (3–4): 4, 18.

—— (1993) 'From field to frog ponds', *Journal of Communication* 43 (3): 6–17.

Rosengren, K.E., Carlsson, M. and Tågerud, Y. (1991) 'Quality in programming: Views from the North', *Studies of Broadcasting* 27: 21–80.

Rosengren, K.E., Wenner, L.A., and Palmgreen, P. (1985) (eds) *Media Gratifications Research: Current Perspectives*, Beverly Hills, Calif.: Sage.

Rosengrn, K.E. and Windahl, S. (1989) *Media Matter: TV Use in Childhood and Adolescence*, Norwood, NJ: Ablex.

Scherer, H. (1991) 'Das Verhhältnis von Einstellungen und Redebereitschaft in der Theorie der Schweigespirale', in J. Wilke (ed.) *Öffentliche Meinung. Theorie, Methoden, Befunde*, Freiburg/Munich: Verlag Karl Alber.

Shaw, D.L. and Martin, S.E. (1992) 'The function of mass media agenda setting', *Journalism Quarterly* 69: 902–920.

Shepard, R.N. (1978) 'The circumplex and related topological manifolds in the study of perception', in S. Shye (ed.) *Theory Construction and Data Analysis in the Behavioural Sciences*, San Francisco, Calif.: Jossey-Bass.

Signorielli, N. and Morgan, M. (eds) (1990) *Cultivation Analysis: New Directions in Media Effects Research*, Newbury Park, Calif.: Sage.

Sorokin, P. (1937–41) *Social and Cultural Dynamics*, vols 1–4, London: Allen & Unwin.

Stimson, J.A. (1991) *Public Opinion in America: Moods, Cycles, & Swings*, Boulder, Col.: Westview Press.

Swanson, D.L. (1992) Understanding audiences: Continuing contributions of gratifications research', *Poetics* 21: 305–328.

Thunberg, A. M., Nowak, K., Rosengren, K.E. and Sigurd, B. (1981) *Communication and Equality*, Stockholm: Almqvist & Wiksell International.

Whiting, J.W.M. (1968) 'Socialization: Anthropological aspects' , in D.L. Sills (ed.) *International Encyclopedia of the Social Sciences* 14: 545–551, New York: Collier-Macmillan.

Wildawsky, A. (1989) 'Choosing preferences by constructing institutions: A cultural theory of preference formation', in A.A. Berger. (ed.) *Political Culture and Public Opinion*, New Brunswick, NJ: Transaction Publishers.

Windahl, S. and Rosengren, K.E. (1978) 'Newsmen's professionalization', *Journalism Quarterly* 55: 466–473.

Zolberg, A.R. (1972) 'Moments of Madness', *Politics and Society* 1 (Winter): 183–207.

Chapter 2

Sweden and its media scene, 1945–90

A bird's-eye view

Karl Erik Rosengren

Sweden is a relatively large country with a small population (some 450,000 square kilometres and some 9 million people; cf. United Kingdom: some 245,000 square kilometres, some 57 million people). The population is concentrated in the southern parts of the country, where the three largest cities are situated, including the capital, Stockholm. This concentration is traditional, but it increased during the first decades after the Second World War. At the same time, central authorities increased their power considerably, partly as a consequence of systematic efforts by the Social Democrat governments of those decades. In spite of strong efforts at decentralization during the 1970s and 1980s, and a process of deregulation in the early 1990s, there is no denying that compared to many other countries Sweden is still highly centralized in many respects. (For some basic information about Sweden, see, for instance, Hadenius 1990; Hadenius and Lindgren 1992.)

At the time of writing (1992/93), Sweden – just like most other European countries – finds itself in a period of dramatic economic crisis, with high unemployment figures, soaring state budget deficit, etc. From a bird's-eye view (as reflected in the *Statistical Abstracts of Sweden*), however, the development of Swedish society during the postwar period (1945–1990) has been characterized by the following trends:

- A relatively slow but steady growth of population (from seven to nine million people).
- An exodus from the countryside to townships and cities (from about 40 per cent to less than 20 per cent of the population living in the rural areas).
- A mobilization of the female labour force (from about 30 per cent to about 80 per cent in the labour force, the increase being concentrated in the public sector, especially local government employment).
- A reduction in the size of the households (one-person households increasing from some 20 per cent to some 40 per cent of all households).
- A gradual change from an industrial to a post-industrial society (in 1940 some 30 per cent, in 1990 some 70 per cent of the economically active

population were active in services, communications and administration; the 50 per cent level was reached in the mid-1960s).

- A per capita GDP which grew considerably during the first decades after the Second World War, then grew at reduced speed, and during the last few years stagnated or even diminished but still is very high, in an international perspective: US$ 26,700 in 1990, as compared to 33,100 in Switzerland; 23,800 in Japan; 23,500 in former FRG; 21,400 in the USA; 17,000 in the UK, and 6,100 in Portugal (note that such figures, of course, are subject to changes in the rates of exchange – for instance, the turmoil in the international financial markets in the early 1990s).
- A sustained growth in public sector employment (in the 1970s, some 30 per cent of the economically active population, in the 1990s, some 40 per cent), especially in local government employment , which has been able to provide a relatively high level of social welfare to the Swedish population.
- An increasing economic dependence on the world surrounding Sweden, the value of the export as part of the gross domestic product at market prices increasing from about 20 per cent in the 1960s to about 25 per cent in the 1970s, culminating at some 30 per cent in the mid-1980s, and then vascillating around 25 per cent.
- A Social-Democrat dominance of the political system for most of the period, the bourgeois parties forming governments of their own only in the periods 1976–82 and from 1991 till the time of writing (1993).

Transportation and communication are important societal processes in a large, post-industrial society with a relatively large export, and a small, widely dispersed and mobile population living in small households with relatively weakened family ties. In all modernized countries mass media structures and mass media processes form *vertical* linkages between society's macro, meso and micro levels, *horizontal* linkages between different societal institutions, and *external* linkages to other societies (see Chapter 1). In Sweden – a country characterized by very high literacy, high levels of book and newspaper reading and a strong public service broadcasting system – these functions of the mass media are more important than in some other countries.

The legal framework regulating the basic conditions of the media are included in the Swedish constitution, which has medieval roots. It comprises the following constitutional laws: the Constitution proper, the Order of Succession, the Freedom of the Press Act, and the Freedom of Expression Act. The latter Act, of 1992, provides constitutional protection for electronic media according to the same basic principles as does the Freedom of the Press Act (originally stemming from 1766). These two constitutional laws offer not only freedom of expression, prohibition of censorship and freedom of the press and other media, but also far-reaching public access to documents sent and received by authorities and protection of source anonymity. Freedom of expression crimes are handled according to a jury system not otherwise found in Swedish law. Acquittals by these juries cannot be appealed against (Vallinder 1987).

The juridical framework outlined above is backed up by a partly official, partly semi-official system of specific media laws and agreements, ombudsmen and councils, which has been shown to have strong anchorage in professional ethics and public opinion (Weibull and Börjesson 1992).

There is a Radio Council, which is a governmental agency created retrospectively to overview the programmes distributed by public service radio and TV channels (more specifically, to monitor their agreement with the radio law and the official agreements with the programme companies), and to deal with complaints against such programmes raised by individuals. Its six members, including a professional jurist, are appointed by the government and are mostly recruited from politics and the mass media. Its verdicts have to be published by the offenders.

The semi-official part of the system includes an Ombudsman of the Press, and a Press Council chaired by a professional jurist. This is a joint venture founded and carried on by the three dominating professional associations in the area: the Publicists' Club, the Swedish Union of Journalists, and the Swedish Association of Newspaper Publishers. Verdicts about editorial matters have to be published by the offenders.

With some variations, the other Nordic countries (Denmark, Finland, Iceland, Norway) show considerable similarities in their media systems. Like Sweden, they are characterized by very high literacy, high levels of book and newspaper reading and a public service broadcasting system now finding itself in competition with commercial broadcasting. During the last few years, the media systems of all Nordic countries have been characterized by a process of radical structural change – a true sea change which no doubt will have consequences for a number of the societal subsystems discussed in Chapter 1 above. This change, of course, is global, and its essence is increasing globalization. It has often been more noticeable, however, in other parts of Europe and the rest of the world than in Sweden and other Nordic countries (see, for instance, Becker and Schönbach 1989; Blumler and Nossiter 1991; Hoffmann-Riem 1992; Kleinsteuber et al. 1986; Noam 1991). Behind it lie the computer, the satellite, the parabolic aerial, the cable and the VCR – all of which helped to turn a number of monopoly public service broadcasting systems into mixed systems governed partly by the political system, partly by the market. The diffusion of a number of electronic media within the Swedish population is shown in Figure 2.1.

Various aspects of the Swedish media system and its recent changes have been presented and discussed by a number of authors, including Carlsson (1986), Gustafsson (1986), Roe and Johnsson-Smaragdi (1987), Hultén (1988), Johnsson-Smaragdi (1989), Nowak (1991), Carlsson and Anshelm (1991, 1993), Weibull (1992) and Weibull and Anshelm (1992). In the Scandinavian countries, and not least in Sweden, because of the strength of

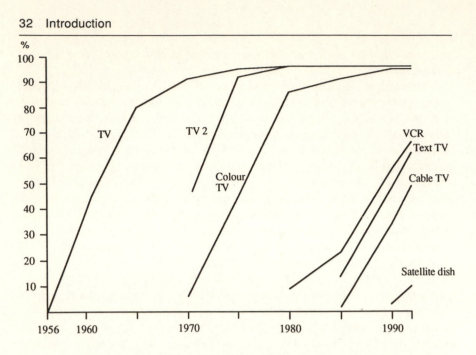

Figure 2.1 Diffusion of TV and related media in the Swedish population aged 9–79, 1956–1992 (Source: SR/PUB, Stockholm and Carlsson & Anshelm (1993))

the public service system, the change in the juridical framework necessitated by technological innovations came later than in many other countries. While these changes are far-reaching indeed, the most basic tendency characterizing the Swedish media scene during the last few decades is probably the large increase in the output of most media, as well as in the number of outlets and the size of their audiences, increases which for some media have been continuing since the end of the Second World War and which for electronic media have accelerated during the 1980s.

Here are some round figures about the growth in media output since the Second World War, borrowed from official statistics and special sources such as Carlsson and Anshelm (1991, 1993), Hadenius and Weibull (1993), Rosengren (1983) and Weibull (1992, 1993); and Weibull and Anshelm (1992):

• Books: from some 3,000 titles a year in the mid-1940s to some 12,000 in the early 1990s.
• Newspapers: from less than 3 million copies a day in 1945 to close to 5 million in the early 1990s.
• Radio (public service and private local radio): from some 60 hours broadcast a week in 1945 to some 450 hours in the early 1990s.
• Public service television: from some 10 hours a week in the mid-1950s to some 125 hours a week in the early 1990s.

Less expansive media include film and popular weekly magazines. Cinema film has experienced two serious threats: TV in the 1960s, and the VCR in the 1980s. In the former period two-thirds of all Swedish cinemas closed down; in the latter period, the number of films publicly shown in Sweden diminished from some 1,500 a year in the early 1980s to some 1,100 in the early 1990s. The total circulation of popular magazines is now somewhat below the 1945 level (some 2 million copies a week), after having oscillated around 4 million between 1955 and 1975. In relative terms, of course, this is a heavy reduction, because of the growth of the Swedish population. On the other hand there has been a considerable growth in magazines tailored to the interests of special readership groups (hobbies etc.).

Besides the basic tendency of increasing media output, some other important trends deserve mentioning (see Weibull and Anshelm 1992).

Firstly, Swedish media have experienced a process of *increasing market control*.

In terms of the 'great wheel of culture in society' (see Chapter 1), the economic and technological systems have more to say about the structure of the media system, while the normative, expressive and cognitive systems (religion and the polity, art and literature, science and scholarship) have experienced a corresponding decreasing influence. Newspapers are less closely tied to political parties and popular movements than previously. The great publishing houses have grown more market-oriented (witness, for instance, the many book clubs providing mainstream entertainment to a broad middle class) and less oriented towards a narrow cultural élite. Radio, once a great cultural, religious and political educator of national importance, to a large extent has become a medium for testing and launching hit music and/ or for local small talk and advertisements (see below). In the wings, commercial radio is waiting for its time to come.

In terms of the typology for reward systems presented in Chapter 1 (p. 18), this means that the mass media are moving well away from a semi-independent system towards a heterocultural system, a system characterized by increasing competition for audiences, leading up to demand or receiver control rather than supply or sender control. Obviously, this has consequences for the content offered by the media, for the diversity of this output, for the way that output relates to societal reality, as well as for the way it is assessed by professionals and by their audiences (see Rosengren *et al.* 1991).

Secondly and simultaneously, Swedish media have experienced a twin process of *increasing localization and transnationalization*.

Local and regional radio stations have increased in number, both inside and outside the public service system. The domestic content of one public service TV channel is produced outside the capital, Stockholm. In a similar but different vein, the position of the metropolitan press has been weakened in non-metropolitan areas, while the circulation of middle-sized local and regional newspapers has increased, as has the size of each issue.

In 1993, there were five Swedish TV channels reaching substantial portions of the Swedish audience: two licence-financed public service channels, one commercial public service channel, and two commercial channels. The former three are terrestrial, the latter two are distributed by satellite and cable. Only few and minor foreign TV channels have concentrated directly on a Swedish audience. Obviously, the foreign TV channels reaching Sweden by cable and satellite – commercial and public service channels alike – offer next to no Swedish content. Also the content of radio and television broadcasting in Sweden – be it public service or non-public service – to an increasing extent has foreign origins, mainly because music is such an increasingly dominating category of content in all radio, both broadcast and narrowcast.

In terms of the model in Figure 1.6, what this means, of course, is that the external influence on Swedish culture has grown increasingly strong during the last decade or so; very probably, it will continue to increase during years to come.

Thirdly, the trends with respect to *concentration of ownership and control* are somewhat divided.

The degree of media ownership concentration is high, but there are hardly any clear-cut tendencies. With respect to newspapers, the concentration has remained much the same during the last twenty-five years or so. The three biggest companies control some 40 per cent of the total circulation; the twelve biggest, some 75 per cent. For weeklies and magazines, the figures are somewhat higher, but declining (since the biggest group, Bonniers, has decided to gradually leave that market). It should be added that part of the daily press enjoys state subsidies. In overall terms these subsidies are small and declining (some 5 per cent of total press revenue in 1980, some 3 per cent in 1990), but they are vital to the existence of some newspapers. It is primarily Social Democrat and Centre party affiliated newspapers with powerful local competitors which enjoy subsidies, but also the leading Conservative newspaper, the *Svenska Dagbladet*, is subsidized. The subsidies are distributed according to strictly formal criteria related to readership rates in the place of publication. There is also strong legal protection against possible misuse of the state subsidies as a means of governmental control (see above). Similarly, although the most important fact about concentration in the Swedish media sector may be that the Bonnier family controls large portions not only of the newspaper market (some 20 per cent of the morning papers, some 50 per cent of the evening tabloids), but also of the markets for weeklies and comics (some 20 per cent and 50 per cent, respectively), cinema, movies (some 60 per cent) and books (some 30 per cent), it is also a fact that, by and large, the family has left the control of media content in the hands of their editors-in-chief.

When it comes to radio and television, the owner concentration was 100 per cent, of course, as long as there was a state monopoly. For radio, the monopoly was abolished, both *de facto* and *de jure*, in 1978, when voluntary organizations were granted the right to establish local, 'neighbourhood' radio stations. Fifteen years later, most radio content distributed is produced outside the public service system. In audience terms, however, the latter still dominates.

As satellite and cable techniques were introduced, the state monopoly of television was gradually abolished *de facto*, a process which started in the late 1970s, when cable systems were introduced. Today, some 40 per cent of Swedish households have access to satellite TV, as a rule by way of cable systems, most of which are owned by private or semi-private companies (the biggest being Telia, formerly a state agency, Swedish Telecom). *De jure* abolishment of the monopoly may be said to have occurred in 1989, when it was decided that a private company should be granted the licence for the third terrestrial Swedish TV channel (although the company was selected only in 1991). However, there is still a remnant of the monopoly, since the formal right to decide on terrestrial TV distribution licensing continues to rest with the government.

All in all it may be maintained, then, that the concentration of private ownership control of Swedish print media is high and stable, while the public ownership control of the electronic media distributed in Sweden is high and declining. The total output of electronic media has increased considerably during the post-war period; among the print media, books and newspapers have also increased considerably, while the output of weeklies has declined or stagnated, as has film output. These structural conditions are reflected, of course, at the micro level: the individual consumption of mass media.

In terms of daily exposure, television, radio and the morning newspaper top the media league: on an average day, between 70 and 80 per cent of the population aged between 9 and 79 expose themselves to each of these media – radio and TV having the edge before the morning newspaper. In terms of time devoted to the media, radio used to be a clear leader (a couple of hours a day, dominated by popular music and news stories), followed by TV (some two hours). The recently immensely increased TV output has put TV viewing more on a par with radio (also in the sense of having become a moving wallpaper), but it may be too early to give any precise figures here. (The situation is complicated also by the VCR, available to some 60 per cent of the population, but on an average day used only by 5–10 per cent.) Readers of morning papers spend some 30 minutes reading their daily (usually a subscribed local paper), and so do the third of the population who are readers of the often rather sensational afternoon tabloids. On an average day, one-third of the population reads a book, and they report it takes them an hour or so. Weeklies are read by some 20 per cent of the population, especially by middle-aged women.

By and large it could be said that while the recent structural changes briefly presented in this chapter may have been rather far-reaching, their effects on overall individual media use have so far been fairly modest. This is seen most strikingly in the fact that the immense increase in television output which during the last decade or so has been made available to Swedes has not (yet) resulted in any corresponding increase in actual viewing. Among small children, there was actually a decrease in viewing during the 1970s and 1980s, and so far this decrease has not been replaced by any marked increase (see Schyller 1989, 1992). Among special segments of the population, of course, the increased output may have had its effects – for instance among adolescents and young adults (see Chapter 4). Across the board, though, the impact is rather modest.

Even modest changes have consequences, however. This is illustrated in Figure 2.2 (borrowed from Cronholm *et al.* 1993). In terms of three types of activities (household chores, TV viewing, and other home-based leisure activities), the figure shows what Swedes aged 9–79 did at home on an average weekday evening in the years 1981/82 and 1991/92, respectively. It will be seen that in the early 1990s, more Swedes spent their evening time at home than during the 1980s, and that a larger portion of them them spent their time on household chores. The portion of the population who spend their time TV viewing has indeed increased somewhat, at the expense of other homebound leisure activites, which have been drastically reduced, in relative terms at least.

Even a rather modest increase in TV viewing, then, may actually have potentially important consequences. In the rest of this book we will have ample opportunities to reflect upon such relationships between media use and other activities, especially among young people. Chapter 3 will present the research programme behind the book, a programme within which we have been collecting a massive body of data on young people's media use, and its causes and consequences, during the period of dramatic structural change just outlined.

REFERENCES

Becker, L. and Schönbach, K. (eds) (1989) *Audience Responses to Media Diversification. Coping With Plenty*, Hillsdale, NJ: Lawrence Erlbaum.

Blumler, J. and Nossiter, J. (eds) (1991) *Handbook of Comparative Broadcasting*, London: Sage.

Carlsson, U. (ed.) (1986) *Media in Transition*, Göteborg: NORDICOM.

Carlsson, U. and Anshelm, M. (eds) (1991) *Medie-Sverige '91*, Göteborg: NORDICOM.

—— (1993) *Medie-Sverige 1993*, Göteborg: NORDICOM.

Cronholm, M., Nowak, L., Höijer, B., Abrahamsson, U.B., Rydin, I., and Schyller, I. (1993) 'I allmänhetens tjänst', in U. Carlsson. and M. Anshelm (eds) (1993) *Medie-Sverige 1993*, Göteborg: NORDICOM.

Gustafsson, K.E. (1986) 'Sweden', in H.J. Kleinsteuber, D. McQuail and K. Siune (eds) *Electronic Media and Politics in Western Europe*, Frankfurt am Main: Campus.

Hadenius, S. (1990) *Swedish Politics during the 20th Century*, Stockholm: Swedish Institute.

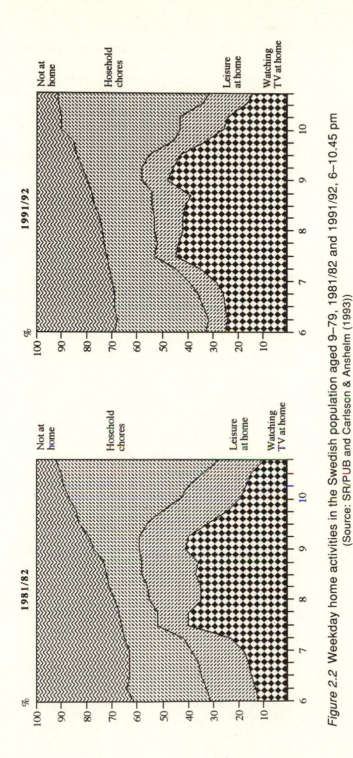

Figure 2.2 Weekday home activities in the Swedish population aged 9–79, 1981/82 and 1991/92, 6–10.45 pm
(Source: SR/PUB and Carlsson & Anshelm (1993))

Hadenius, S. and Lindgren, A. (1992) *On Sweden* (2nd edn), Stockholm: Swedish Institute.

Hadenius, S. and Weibull, L. (1993) *Massmedier. En bok om press, radio och TV*, Stockholm: Bonnier Alba.

Hoffmann-Riem (1992) 'A special issue: Media and the law. The changing landscape of Western Europe', *European Journal of Communication* 7: 147–302.

Hultén, O. (1988) 'Sweden', in M. Alvaro (ed.) *Video World Wide – An International Study*, Paris: Unesco.

Johnsson-Smaragdi, U. (1989) 'Sweden: Opening the doors – cautiously', in L. Becker and K. Schönbach (eds) *Audience Responses to Media Diversification. Coping With Plenty*, Hillsdale, NJ: Lawrence Erlbaum.

Kleinsteuber, H.J., McQuail, D. and Siune, K. (eds) (1986) *Electronic Media and Politics in Western Europe*, Frankfurt am Main: Campus.

Noam, E. (1991) *Television in Europe*, New York and Oxford: Oxford University Press.

Nowak, K. (1991) 'Television in Sweden 1991', in J. Blumler and J. Nossiter (eds) *Handbook of Comparative Broadcasting*, London: Sage.

Roe, K. and Johnsson-Smaragdi, U. (1987) 'The Swedish "mediascape" in the 1980's', *European Journal of Communication* 2: 357–370.

Rosengren, K.E. (1983) *The Climate of Literature*, Lund: Studentlitteratur.

Rosengren, K.E, Carlsson, M. and Tågerud Y. (1991) 'Quality in Programming: Views from the North', *Studies of Broadcasting* 27: 21–80.

Schyller, I. (1989) 'Barn och ungdom tittar på svensk tv', in C. Feilitzen, L. Filipson, I. Rydin and I. Schyller (eds) *Barn och unga i medieåldern*, Stockholm: Rabén & Sjögren.

—— (1992) 'TV-tittandet 1991 bland barn och ungdomar 3–24 år', *PUB*, 9.

Vallinder, T. (1987) 'The Swedish jury system in press cases: An offspring of the English trial jury?', *The Journal of Legal History* 8 (2): 190–220.

Weibull, L. (1992) 'The status of the daily newspaper. What readership research tells us about the role of newspapers in the mass media system', *Poetics* 21: 259–282.

—— (1993) 'Sweden', in J. Mitchell. and J. Blumler (eds) *Television and the Viewer Interests*, Düsseldorf: The European Institute of the Media.

Weibull, L. and Anshelm, M. (1992) 'Indications of change. Developments in Swedish media 1980–1990', *Gazette* 49: 41–73.

Weibull, L. and Börjesson, B. (1992) 'The Swedish media accountability system: A research perspective', *European Journal of Communication* 7: 121–139.

Chapter 3

The Media Panel Program (MPP) and related research

Karl Erik Rosengren

The Media Panel Program group dates its origin back to 1969, when two of its members, Professors Karl Erik Rosengren and Sven Windahl, started a series of studies focused on individual use of the media (see Rosengren and Windahl 1972, 1977). Gradually, a growing consensus emerged among the participants in the project about the necessity for a large, longitudinal study of media use among children and adolescents. There were several reasons for this, one being our interest in individuals' mass media use, its causes and consequences, another, an equally strong interest in the interplay between those very basic agents of socialization, the family, the peer group, school, and the mass media.

In 1975, after a series of preliminary studies, the Media Panel Program (MPP) was established (Rosengren and Windahl 1978). Within the MPP group about a dozen researchers, originally trained within different disciplines and all having both common and differential research interests, have since 1975 been working together for shorter or longer periods of time.

Financially, the programme has enjoyed generous support – provided to the programme as a whole, as well as to a number of specific projects within the programme – from the following organizations:

The Swedish Council for Research into the Humanities and the Social Sciences
The Bank of Sweden Tercentenary Foundation
The Swedish National Board of Education
The Swedish Social Science Council.

The Universities of Lund, Gothenburg and Växjö have provided excellent working facilities and generous leaves of absence for research, as well as a number of graduate student grants.

Today, the MPP is an umbrella organization for senior and junior scholars and social scientists working within their own projects and forming a research group with a broad range of interests, namely:

To follow successive cohorts of children and adolescents as they move through time, gradually leaving their family of origin and approaching their own families of procreation, all the time being subject to a close interplay with and between a number of basic agents of socialization (family, school, working group, peer group, and the mass media), an interplay which shapes their lives and futures, at the same time as it itself develops over time, between generations, and under different societal conditions – among which, of course, the developments of society's media structure stand out as especially important.

A basic characteristic of the research within the MPP group is that it has not been limited to a given theoretical or methodological perspective, nor has it been dedicated to research on just one substantive problem within the wide theoretical area covered by empirical MPP data. On the contrary. Within the overall theoretical framework outlined in Chapter 1, at least four main theoretical perspectives have continuously been cultivated within the MPP:

• A developmental perspective.
• A social class perspective.
• A socialization perspective.
• A lifestyle perspective.

Our research has dealt with a number of substantive aspects of individual use made of mass media by children, adolescents, young adults and their parents, as well as the behavioural, attitudinal and structural causes and consequences of that use. As a matter of course, the media use under study has continually been related to the family and peer relations, the activities, and the school and work experiences of the children, adolescents and young adults under study. A simple model which has been used to organize the thinking within the MPP is rendered in Figure 3.1. More sophisticated models have been used, of course, in the various specialized studies produced within the programme.

In methodological terms, the MPP could be described as a series of quantitative and qualitative studies from 1975 onwards carried out on children, adolescents and young adults in two towns/cities in southern Sweden. The larger one, Malmö, with some 230,000 inhabitants, lies in the centre of a metropolitan area, with Copenhagen directly across the Sound between Sweden and Denmark; the smaller one, Växjö (some 65,000 inhabitants, situated in the southern inland of Sweden) stands out as something of a Swedish Middletown.

Together, they may be taken to represent a dominant segment of the Swedish population (see Chapter 2), but obviously, the sparse countryside population of Sweden is not included – except in the data collection wave called 'Skåne 83/84' which included also the countryside population of Sweden's southernmost landscape. (For information about media use among adolescents in the countryside population, as well as its causes and consequences, see, for instance, Johnsson-Smaragdi and Roe (1986), Roe (1992).)

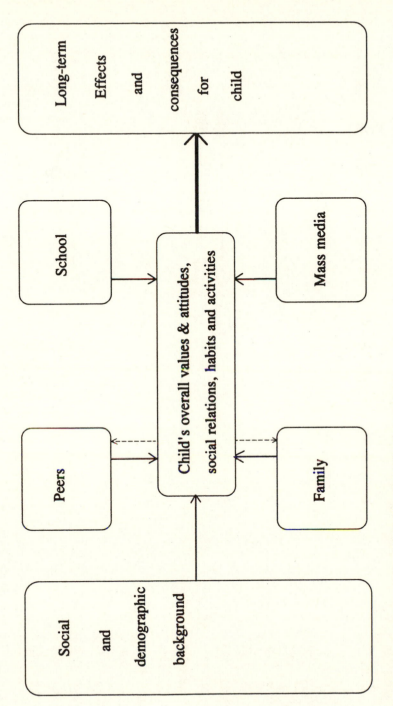

Figure 3.1 Conceptual model of the socialization process

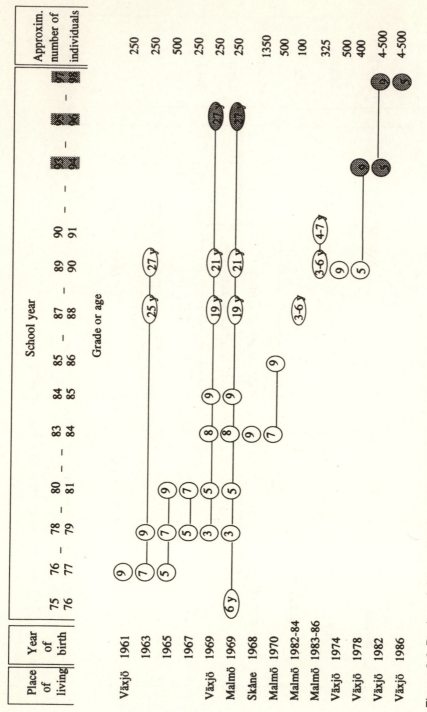

Figure 3.2 Design of data collection within the Media Panel Program

The data collection has been carried out within a combined longitudinal and cross-sectional design admitting both cross-sectional, longitudinal and diagonal analyses, thus making possible the analysis of three basic types of time-related effect: situational, maturational and cohort effects (Figure 3.2; see also Chapter 4). Since the data collection has been undertaken in two locations, we are in a position also to add spatial comparisons to the temporal ones. For logistical reasons the data collections in the two towns were as a rule undertaken during different semesters of the same school year.

The techniques used for data collection include mail and classroom questionnaires, personal interviews, essays written by school children at school, archival data, focused interviews, and long, in-depth conversations with a small number of type-representative individuals. For children and adolescents in grades 3–9 in the compulsory school system, classroom questionnaires were used, as a rule with an extremely high response rate. For older adolescents and young adults, as well as for parents, mail questionnaires were used, with response rates in the 70 and 80 per cent ranges. School grades and similar data were culled from school archives. All collection, storage and analysis of data has been undertaken with permission from, and in accordance with the rather strict regulations of the Swedish Data Inspection, an authority which quite rightly has repeatedly shown considerable interest in our work. (Further information about data collection etc. may be found in Rosengren and Windahl (1989) and in Johansson and Miegel (1992).)

During a long period of continuous research the MPP group has produced a data bank which to the best of our knowledge is unique, and in which a large mass of data related to individual media use, its causes, effects and conse-quences are stored, covering cohorts and panels of children and adolescents passing through the school system and into work or continued studies during their early adulthood. In all, the bank contains data about the following:

- Some 4,400 children, adolescents and young adults.
- Their family background, activities and relations.
- Their relations to peers and their school experiences (including school grades etc.).
- Their media use, lifestyles, present occupation and activities, *as well as*
- Their plans for the future.

Relevant information and data from their parents have also been collected on several occasions. If – as we hope – it will prove possible to maintain and update it properly, this data bank will for many years to come remain a rich resource for the study of a number of different relations between, on the one hand, children, adolescents and young adults, and on the other, their families (of origin and of procreation), school, peer group, mass media use, working position, etc. In future studies, it will become possible to study the kind of family life which these former youngsters are and will be leading as they gradually enter the phase of adult life and their own family of procreation.

Sonesson, I. (1979) *Förskolebarn och TV*, Malmö: Esselte studium (*Pre-school children and television*; with a summary in English).

Hedinsson, E. (1981) *TV, Family and Society: The Social Origins and Effects of Adolescents' TV Use*, Stockholm: Almqvist & Wiksell International.

Roe, K. (1983) *Mass Media Use and Adolescent Schooling: Conflict or Co-existence?*, Stockholm: Almqvist & Wiksell International.

Johnsson-Smaragdi, U. (1983) *TV Use and Social Interaction in Adolescence. A Longitudinal Study*, Stockholm: Almqvist & Wiksell International.

Roe, K. (1985) 'Swedish youth and music. Listening patterns and motivations', *Communication Research* 12: 353–362.

Jönsson, A. (1985) *TV – ett hot eller en resurs för barn?*, Lund: CWK Gleerup (*TV – a threat or a resource for children*; with a summary in English).

Jönsson, A. (1986) 'TV – A threat or a complement to school?', *Journal of Educational Television* 12 (1): 29–38.

Flodin, B. (1986) *TV och yrkesförväntan: En longitudinell studie av ungdomars yrkessocialisation*, Lund: Studentlitteratur (*TV and adolescent's occupational socialization. A longitudinal study*; with a summary in English).

Johnsson-Smaragdi, U. and Roe, K. (1986) 'Teenagers in the new media world. Video recorders, video games and home computers', *Lund Research Papers in the Sociology of Communication* 2, Lund: Department of Sociology, University of Lund.

Jarlbro, G. (1986) 'Family communication patterns revisited: Reliability and validity', *Lund Research Papers in the Sociology of Communication* 4, Lund: Department of Sociology, University of Lund.

Jarlbro, G. (1988) *Familj, massmedier och politik*, Stockholm: Almqvist & Wiksell International (*Family, mass media and politics*; with a summary in English).

Johnsson-Smaragdi, U. (1988) 'Audience response to the new media situation in Sweden', *Lund Research Papers in the Sociology of Communication* 11, Lund: Department of Sociology, University of Lund.

Johnsson-Smaragdi U. and Roe, K. (1986) 'Teenagers in the new media world', *Lund Research Papers in the Sociology of Communication* 13, Lund: Department of Sociology, University of Lund.

Sonesson, I (1989) *Vem fostrar våra barn – videon eller vi?*, Stockholm: Esselte Studium (*Who brings up our children – the VCR or we?*).

Rosengren, K.E. and Windahl, S. (1989) *Media Matter: TV Use in Childhood and Adolescence*, Norwood, NJ: Ablex.

Johansson, T. and Miegel, F. (1992) *Do the Right Thing. Lifestyle and Identity in Contemporary Youth Culture*, Stockholm: Almqvist & Wiksell International.

Roe, K. (1992) 'Different destinies – different melodies: School achievement, anticipated status, and adolescents' tastes in music', *European Journal of Communication* 7: 335–357.

Rosengren, K.E. (1992) 'Substantive theories and formal models: Their role in research on individual media use', *Lund Research Papers in Media and Communication Studies* 4, Lund: Department of Sociology, University of Lund.

Rosengren, K.E. (1992) 'The structural invariance of change: Comparative studies of media use. (Some results from a Swedish research program)', in J.G. Blumler, J.M. McLeod and K.E. Rosengren (eds) *Comparatively Speaking: Communication and Culture Across Space and Time*, Newbury Park, Calif.: Sage.

Figure 3.3 Chronological list of some main publications within the Media Panel Program

The research undertaken has been reported in a great number of publications, local, national and international. Space does not permit even short summaries of these results. Results from the first three data collection waves within the MPP were presented in Rosengren and Windahl (1989). Results from later waves were presented in Johansson and Miegel (1992) and in a number of other publications. Figure 3.3 presents a list of the main publications produced by members of the MPP group during the last few years. Chapters 4 to 12 in this book offer numerous results from both early and later data collection waves undertaken within the MPP.

REFERENCES

Johansson, T. and Miegel, F. (1992) *Do the Right Thing. Lifestyle and Identity in Contemporary Youth Culture*, Stockholm: Almqvist & Wiksell International.

Johnsson-Smaragdi U. and Roe, K. (1986) 'Teenagers in the new media world', *Lund Research Papers in the Sociology of Communication* 2, Lund: Department of Sociology, University of Lund.

Roe, K. (1992) 'Different destinies – different melodies: School achievement, anticipated status, and adolescents' tastes in music', *European Journal of Communication* 7: 335–357.

Rosengren, K.E. and Windahl, S. (1972) 'Mass media consumption as a functional alternative', in D. McQuail (ed.) *Sociology of Mass Communications*, Harmondsworth: Penguin.

Rosengren, K.E. and Windahl, S. (1977) 'Mass media use: Causes and effects', *Communications* 3: 336–352.

Rosengren, K.E. and Windahl, S. (1978) 'The Media Panel Program: A Presentation', *Media Panel Reports* 4.

Rosengren, K.E. and Windahl, S. (1989) *Media Matter: TV Use in Childhood and Adolescence*, Norwood, NJ: Ablex.

Part II

Media use: differentiation, change and stability

Chapter 4

Media use under structural change

Karl Erik Rosengren

INTRODUCTION

Aspects and determinants of mass media use

In all industrial and post-industrial societies mass media form very important linkages:

1 Between the great societal subsystems (horizontal linkages between, say, economy and polity, religion and science) *and*
2 Between the macro, meso and micro levels of society (vertical linkages).

The latter linkages may be conceptualized in terms of primary and secondary socialization. When it comes to mass media and the use of mass media, the very general phenomena of primary and secondary socialization have their more specific counterparts in a range of phenomena conceptualized in terms such as diffusion of news, agenda setting, spirals of silence, cultivation, effects research, etc. (see Chapter 1).

Whatever the perspective applied, however, all these traditions of research presuppose (or assume) knowledge about a more basic phenomenon: the individual use made of the mass media and their contents. This chapter deals with some basic aspects of mass media use by Swedish children, adolescents and young adults from about 1975 to about 1990.

Within the MPP, data have been collected about the individual use made of a wide range of mass media: dailies, weeklies, radio, television (broadcast, satellite and cable), VCR, film and music recorded and distributed in various ways. There is no doubt, however, that two partly overlapping types of media use are overwhelmingly dominant among young people: television viewing (by way of broadcasting, cable (CTV), satellite (DBS) or video(VCR)) and listening to music (by way of radio, television or some recording device or other). In this chapter, therefore, attention will be focused on television viewing and listening to music among children, adolescents and young adults. Between them, these two types of media use represent a great, heterogeneous and highly variable slice of the lives of young people. (Data about the use of other media by young people have been published in a number of previous MPP reports. For an overview of early MPP data about media use, see Rosengren and Windahl 1989; for more recent data, see Sonesson and Höjerback 1989; Höjerback 1990; see also Chapters 5 and 6.)

Regardless of the medium chosen, any student of individual media use must distinguish between at least four aspects of that use (see Rosengren and Windahl 1989: 18 ff.):

1 Amount of use (in terms of units of time spent or units of media content used).
2 Type or genre of media content used and preferred (news, editorials, soap operas, etc.).
3 Type of relation established with the content used (identification, para-social interaction, etc.).
4 Type of context of media use (alone or with somebody else, media use being primary or secondary activity, etc.).

In this chapter – indeed, in most parts of this book – the most basic of these four aspects will be in focus: amount of media use.

There is a lot of variation in television viewing and listening to music among young people. As was noted in Chapter 1, all variation in human action – including all four aspects of individual media use – is determined by long- and short-term variation in the following factors:

1 Societal structure (including media structure).
2 Individuals' position in social structure: age and gender, class and status.
3 Personal characteristics: values, attitudes, opinions, etc.

Between them, these three types of determinant produce an immense variation in individual media use, especially if time is included in the analysis.

This chapter deals with similarities and differences, homogeneity and heterogeneity, stability and change in young people's mass media use, primarily with respect to amount of television viewing and listening to music as determined by a given societal structure and individuals' position in that structure. Towards the end of the chapter, we will give special attention to the difficult question about the relationship between changes in societal structure and individual media use as partly determined by the individual's position in social structure.

The study of media use: research design, methodology and techniques

The reason the MPP was initiated was a conviction that social phenomena are best understood as they develop and change. Starting out from this conviction it was only natural to turn to a study of media use as it develops among children and adolescents. In its turn, this choice called for a longitudinal design able to disentangle the three different causes of temporal variation: age,

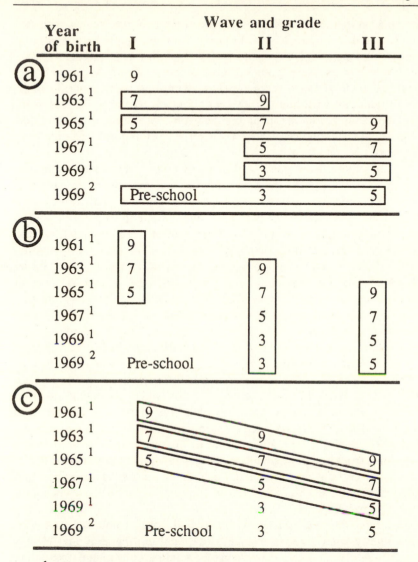

Year of birth	Wave and grade		
	I	II	III

ⓐ
1961 [1]	9		
1963 [1]	7	9	
1965 [1]	5	7	9
1967 [1]		5	7
1969 [1]		3	5
1969 [2]	Pre-school	3	5

ⓑ
1961 [1]	9		
1963 [1]	7	9	
1965 [1]	5	7	9
1967 [1]		5	7
1969 [1]		3	5
1969 [2]	Pre-school	3	5

ⓒ
1961 [1]	9		
1963 [1]	7	9	
1965 [1]	5	7	9
1967 [1]		5	7
1969 [1]		3	5
1969 [2]	Pre-school	3	5

[1] Data gathering for the Växjö study.
[2] Data gathering for the Malmö study.

Figure 4.1 Three modes of analysing data collected within a combined cross-sectional/longitudinal design (first three waves within the MPP)

generation (cohort), and situation. Only the combined panel/cross-sectional design presented in Figure 4.1 (cf. Figure 3.2 above) can achieve that, and even this design can achieve it only imperfectly (Riley 1992; Ryder 1992).

The design admits three types of comparison: vertical, horizontal, and diagonal. In each of these three types of comparison, one of the three sources of temporal variation is kept under control. By means of combined vertical, horizontal and diagonal comparisons, provisional information about the separate influence of the three sources of temporal variation may be arrived at.

In *vertical* comparisons (say, within the 1976/77 MPP data collection wave), the *situation* is kept constant; age and generational effects remain. This type of comparison is undertaken in most cross-sectional studies, as a rule with a view to explore the effects of age – sometimes without paying much attention to potential effects of generation, not to speak of the interaction between age and generation. Vertically computed means (that is, within the different MPP data collection waves) may provide some information about qualities common to a given situation. Under favourable conditions, therefore, comparisons between vertically calculated means may provide some information about the unique effects of situation as such (see however, Ryder 1992: 228).

In *horizontal* comparisons (say, within the MPP panel born 1965), *generation* is kept constant; situational and age effects remain. This is the type of comparison undertaken in most panel studies, often with a view to include the study of age effects, and sometimes without paying too much attention to potential situational effects, not to speak of the interaction between age and situational effects. Horizontally computed means (that is, within the different MPP panels) may provide some information about qualities common to individuals from a given generation. Under favourable conditions, therefore, comparisons between horizontally calculated means may provide some information about the unique effects of generation (cohort) as such (see however, Ryder 1992: 228).

In *diagonal* comparisons (say, within the diagonal composed of ninth-graders), finally, *age* is kept constant; situational and generational effects remain. Diagonally computed means (that is, within groups of equal age) may provide some information about qualities common to individuals of a given age. Under favourable conditions, therefore, comparisons between diagonally calculated means may provide some information about the unique effects of age as such (see however, Ryder 1992: 228).

Comparisons of the types here discussed are regularly undertaken in cohort studies, often using the rectangular design facilitating distinctions between the three temporal sources of variation (see Riley 1992). Based as they tend to be, however, on secondary analysis of available cross-sectional statistics, not on panel data, cohort studies are handicapped when it comes to argumentation about effects of individual characteristics on the same or different characteristics at a later point of time. The combined panel/cross-sectional design used in the MPP, on the other hand, admits such argumentation; at the same time it is the design which most efficiently (although by no means perfectly) admits that the three different effects of age, generation and situation be distinguished from each other.

Later in this chapter, some MPP data about amount of television viewing and listening to music among Swedish young people will be presented, in principle organized in an overall research design such as the one just described. In other chapters, this design will be more intensely exploited, in attempts to disentangle the differential effects of age, situation and generation not only on separate characteristics of media use, but also on clusters and temporal patterns of media use.

Amount of media use may be conceptualized in two quite different ways:

1 In terms of habits of consumption, usually measured by means of interview or questionnaire, and
2 In terms of actual consumption during a given time period, usually measured by means of interviews or questionnaires (diaries etc.), by means of people-metres (BBC 1987–93; Hasebrink and Krotz 1992; Webster and Lichty 1991), or by more direct observations, for instance, televised observation (Gunter and Svennevig 1987) or the so-called ESM technique, in which the individual reports his or her activities at random intervals (Csikszentmihalyi and Kubey 1981; Kubey and Csikszentmihalyi 1990; Lööv and Rosengren 1988; Lööv and Miegel 1989; Rosengren 1991a).

The two ways of conceptualization concern two quite different phenomena which unfortunately are sometimes confused. Habits are dispositional phenomena, in principle similar to other dispositional phenomena, for instance, attitudes, while actual consumption is just that: a type of actual behaviour. It is well known that attitudes and actual behaviour are less than perfectly correlated, and the same holds true for media habits and actual media behaviour during a given period of time (see Rosengren and Windahl 1989: 29 ff.). The reason this is so is that habits depend on relatively stable factors such as societal structure (including media structure), social position (age, gender, social class, etc.), and basic values, etc. which characterize the individual, while actual behaviour is much more situationally determined (in the case of media use, say, by daily variations in media output; see, for instance, Weibull 1985). To use one of the two types of measurement as a criterion variable for the other, in an attempt at validity measurement, therefore, seems to be less well-advised (see van der Voort and Vooijs 1990).

Distinctions such as these are valid, of course, not only for television but also for other types of media use, say, newspaper reading, or listening to music. They should be kept in mind when comparing descriptive data from different times and countries.

The MPP data about amount of television viewing and listening to music to be presented and analysed in the following section were collected mainly by means of classroom and mail questionnaires about a number of activities, attitudes and background data (see Rosengren and Windahl 1989: 29–38). As a rule, the type of media use measured was habitual media use, but in some data waves actual media use was also measured. The data collection was organized within the combined panel/cross-sectional design described in Chapter 3 and further discussed in this section.

TELEVISION VIEWING AND LISTENING TO MUSIC UNDER STRUCTURAL CHANGE

Young people's acceptance of new media appliances

Young people like to watch television, and to listen to music. Small wonder, then, that the new communication channels and equipment entering the Swedish media scene during the 1980s and 1990s – satellite and cable TV, the VCR and the CD – tended to reach young people quickly. According to semi-official statistics about 'actual viewing' (see above), on an average day in 1992, 36 per cent of the total Swedish population watched cable and/or satellite television; among those aged 9–14 and 15–24, the corresponding figures were 53 per cent and 49 per cent, respectively (Cronholm 1993: 317). In 1985, 23 per cent of the total population had a VCR in their home; in 1991, 58 per cent. Among those aged 9–14, the corresponding figures were 35 per cent and 85 per cent, respectively (Anshelm 1993: 340). On an average day in 1979, 1 per cent of the total population watched video, but the figure was 3 per cent among those aged 9–14. In 1992, the corresponding figures were 6 per cent and 12 per cent, respectively (Anshelm 1993: 342). And in 1991, 31 per cent of the total population had a CD-player; among those aged 15–19, the corresponding figure was 58 per cent (Burnett 1993: 388).

   How did these new media appliances affect young people's media use? More specifically, during this period of thorough-going structural change, what happened to television viewing and music listening among young people in Sweden? Our MPP data offer detailed and precise answers to those questions, the combined panel/cross-sectional design sometimes letting otherwise unnoticed tendencies stand out relatively clearly.

Amount of television viewing and listening to music, 1975–1990

Figures 4.2 and 4.3 show the amount of television viewing and listening to music among the Malmö and Växjö panels of children, adolescents and young adults during the period 1975–1990.[1] (The panels are denoted by V and M for Växjö and Malmö, respectively, followed by the panel's year of birth.) Both TV viewing and listening to music are measured as habits, by means of classroom and mail questionnaires. Television viewing includes broadcast,

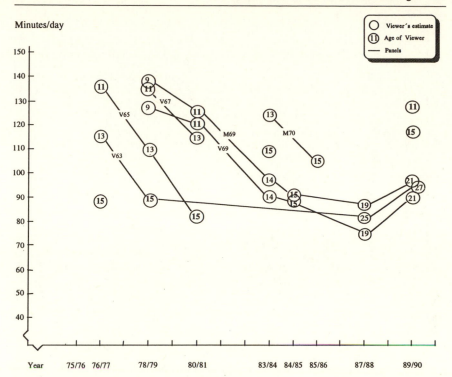

Figure 4.2 Stability and change in amount of TV consumption, 1975–1990
(means)

cable and satellite television, but not VCR (see below). Note that the units
of measurement in the two figures are very different: for television, minutes
per day; for music, days per wcck. Based on a relatively large chunk of time
(a whole day) and one single question as it is, the latter measure is much
cruder than the former, which is based on minutes per day and six or eight
questions (for further technical details, see also below).

What do the two figures tell us? The first impression is the high amount of
variation. Take the age span 9–15, for instance (roughly corresponding to
grades 3–9 of the figures). We see that during these years the habit of TV
viewing is reduced from more than two hours a day to less than an hour and a
half a day (panels V63, V65, V69 and M69), a reduction which for the three
long panels (V63, M69, V69) continues at least till age 19. The change in
listening to music is even larger, although it goes in the different direction. The
amount of listening to popular music is roughly doubled from grade 5 to grade
9 (panels M69 and V69), and the increase goes on at least to the age of 21.

This large variation showing up within age spans which in current media
statistics are often indiscriminately lumped together, does provide some food
for thought. (Swedish semi-offical statistics, for instance, as a rule use age
intervals such as, say, 9–14, 15–24 or some such variant.) In the following

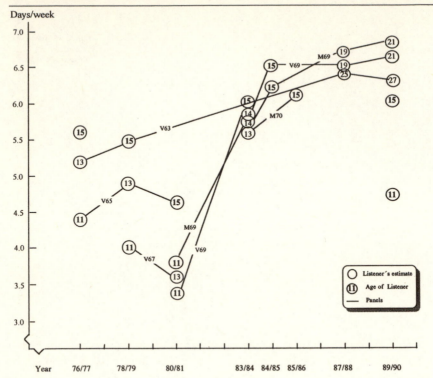

Figure 4.3 Stability and change in amount of music consumption, 1976–1990
means

sections we shall discuss some sources of this variation, starting with a
methodological artefact.

Dependency of descriptive results on the operationalization used

As data collection within the MPP proceeded, a change in Swedish leisure
habits was definitely established, a change which had really begun in the
1960s and 1970s. Due to the change from a six-day week to a five-day week
in the labour market, Friday night gradually became the equivalent of the
Saturday night of previous times. With some lag, the school system followed
suit in that schools started to be closed on Saturdays, too, just like offices and
factories. This change proceeded at rather different pace in different school
districts. For children and adolescents, the real breakthrough in this respect
must have come some time around 1973, when, after a fairly long transition
period, an official decree closed all Swedish schools on Saturdays.

At the time, most members of the MPP group had children at school. As
late as in 1975, however, when the MPP started, we still must have felt that
Friday was more similar to Thursday than it was to Saturday, for in the six-

question battery on which we built our media consumption index, we preferred to group the days of the week that way (asking for time of viewing on weekdays (i .e. Mondays–Fridays), Saturdays and Sundays, respectively): 'In a normal week, how many weekdays do you ususally watch TV (1, 2, 3, 4, 5) – If you watch on a weekday, for how long do you usually watch (Less than an hour, about an hour, an hour and a half, etc.).' As always in panel studies, we then had to stick as long as possible to the original operationalizations, in order to maintain direct comparability. For the M70 panel, however, which at its start was conceived of as a rather independent panel, we felt free to heed the change in leisure habits which had meanwhile definitively taken place. (So we did in the one-off 'Skåne' study, a cross-sectional study of 15-year-old youngsters in the southernmost landscape of Sweden.) Consequently, Friday, Saturday and Sunday were treated as individual days, while the remaining four 'real' weekdays were lumped together. The six-item battery was thus changed into an eight-item battery: 'How many Fridays (Saturdays etc.) a month do you usually watch TV? (1, 2, 3, 4) – If you watch on a Friday, for how long do you usually watch? (Less than an hour, about an hour, about an hour and a half, etc.).' As a result of this, the level of TV consumption stood out as considerably higher for the V70 panel (and for the one-off 'Skåne' study) than for the previous ones (see Figure 4. 2). In the last two waves of the earlier panels we felt that we had better change to the more adequate eight-item battery.

The long and the short of all this is a caveat with respect to figures about actual level of media consumption based on survey questions (see Comstock and Paik 1987: 13). To a considerable extent, such figures are dependent on the formulation of the question and/or the build-up of the index. In studies comparing media habits between countries, the risk of meeting with such artefactual differences should be even higher. For instance, US children are reported to have a viewing time double that of Norwegian children, with Swedes coming somewhere in between (se Rosengren and Windahl 1989: 21). But only very careful comparisons could reveal how much of those differences are methodological artefacts, and how much are due to differences in media structure and general societal structure (for instance, the difference between the commercial US radio and television system on the one hand, and on the other the Scandinavian monopoly public-service type of system prevailing in the 1970s and most of the 1980s). In later sections of this chapter we will give more attention to that problem.

The fact that the absolute level of media consumption is tricky to measure does not mean that relative levels cannot be measured, of course. In Figures 4.2 and 4.3 the important fact to observe is not the absolute levels, but the strong dynamics observable in relative terms: the enormous increase in the importance of music during adolescence, and the corresponding reduction in the importance of television viewing. With respect to these two media, then, adolescence is really – as with respect to so many other phenomena – a period of dramatic upheavals. It deserves pointing out, though, that in the midst of upheaval, there is considerable stability. Stability in consumption, though, is perhaps an even more tricky phenomenon to conceptualize and operationalize than is consumption itself (see Chapter 6). But before turning to stability, we shall have to discuss temporal change and variation and the three main sources thereof.

Age, generation and situation

Methodologically and theoretically, the variation displayed in Figures 4.2 and 4.3 may be understood as caused by age (maturation), generation and situation. In this case, age effects should be theoretically interpreted primarily in terms of development theory, which is able to provide a quite convincing interpretation of the fact that in early adolescence children move away from family-oriented to peer-oriented activities (for example, away from watching public service television together with their parents in the living room, instead turning to listening to music together with their friends, preferably somewhere out of reach of parental control). This type of temporal effect seems to be quite strong in our case.

Generational effects should not be expected to be very strong within the relatively short time period under study, some fifteen years. Closer analysis does reveal, however, that already during the short time-span covered by the first three waves (3–4 years), some traces of generational effects are discernible (see Rosengren and Windahl 1989: 26). According to the same analysis those situation effects were not as strong as age effects.

A situational effect is clearly visible in Figure 4.3: listening to music is much lower in 1980/81 than in earlier and later waves (as compared with the two previous waves, some 20–30 per cent lower). This affects the development within all four panels measured in that wave, so that they differ from the overall pattern of continually increasing listening during adolescence, a pattern most clearly discernible in comparative analysis of cross-sectional patterns. As a consequence of this deviation, panel V65 gets an A-shaped profile (see Johnsson-Smaragdi 1983: 115 ff.; Rosengren and Windahl 1989: 106). Without our combined panel/cross-sectional design, this situation effect might have been erroneously interpreted as a maturational phenomenon. Similarly, the increase from age 11 to age 14, which is much more dramatic for panels V69 and M69 than is otherwise the case, might have been taken as showing a general developmental phenomenon, rather than being the joint product of situational and developmental effects which it actually is.

The strong situational effect on listening to music in 1980/81 was observed also at the national level (Berg 1982). Speculating on its causes, one may think of changes in either media structure or music fashion. (For the interplay between structural change and fashion cycles, see Peterson and Berger 1975.) Actually, analysing trade statistics, Burnett (1990, 1992) was able to show that in the early 1980s there was a down period in popular music in Sweden, thus confirming the downfall in the popularity of punk music which in Sweden was generally felt to take place around 1980.

Be that as it may. The overall methodological lesson to be drawn from Figures 4.2 and 4.3 is that when analysing descriptive data about media use, it is an advantage to have access to both narrow age categories and a combined cross-sectional/longitudinal design, preferably based on panel data. Broad categories and cross-sectional or panel data alone may result in quite misleading results. In addition, it is well to remember that empirical data about the absolute level of consumption are heavily dependent on both the conceptualization and the operationalization of media use (habit vs. actual consumption, type of measurement, etc.).

Keeping these lessons in mind, we shall now return to the problem of situational effects, this time writ large.

SITUATIONAL EFFECTS WRIT LARGE: MEDIA STRUCTURE CHANGING

A special case of situational effects: structural change

In the previous section we were able to observe a very probable situational effect for the year of 1980, the plausible explanation of which was a change in popular musical fashion. In this section we will be discussing a situational effect of much larger size – indeed, a change of a size which makes the use of the term 'situational effect' somewhat dubious. We shall turn to effects of a change not *in* the system, but *of* the system.

Let's return for a moment to Figure 4.2, featuring television viewing. Actually, there are some signs of the beginning of another situational effect to be perceived in that figure: the increased viewing among the 15-year-old ninth-graders of the new MPP cohort, V74, first measured in school-year 1989/90. In the latest data collection wave the ninth-graders of this cohort watched 117 minutes a day, while their comrades of the same age in panels V61, V63 and V65 watched 88, 89 and 82 minutes, respectively. In technical terms, this difference might be classified as a situational effect. But what we see is something else, something more important.

We noted in Chapter 2 that in the late 1970s the monopoly of the Swedish public service television system was *de facto* abolished when cable television was introduced (while the *de jure* abolishment occurred a decade later). The actual growth of access to commercial television by way of CTV and/or DBS among the population came much later than the *de facto* abolishment, of course. In early 1986, some 5 per cent of the population had such access, in early 1989 some 17 per cent, and in mid-1991, some 40 per cent (Cronholm 1993: 309). We have already seen, however, that among youth the penetration of various new communication gadgets was faster and more widespread than among adults, and much the same tendency can be seen for CTV: in 1989 30

per cent of our MPP youngsters in grade 9 had access to satellite television
by way of cable. Those who had access watched 145 minutes a day (broadcast
plus cable TV); those who did not, 105 minutes (Höjerback 1990: 5, 11) – a
difference of some 40 per cent, a figure which is in rough accordance with
national figures collected for somewhat broader age categories. This is what
lies behind at least part of the comparatively high viewing among ninth-
graders of cohort V74 to be observed in Figure 4.2 (another factor being the
difference in measurement technique discussed above).

It would seem, then, that the incipient structural change of the Swedish
television system had already exercised some influence on the viewing habits
of the perhaps most susceptible part of the population, the adolescents.
Another structural change had even stronger effects. Let's turn to the VCR.

In 1989, 74 per cent of the ninth-graders of cohort V74 had a VCR in their
home. Those who had a VCR, watched 5.9 hours video a week; those who
had not, 1.9 hours a week, either by means of renting a 'video box', or in the
homes of friends having access to the family VCR (Höjerback 1990: 5, 15).
In terms of the statistic used in our TV viewing measurements, these figures
correspond to 51 and 16 minutes a day, respectively.

The measurements of viewing previously discussed in this chapter do not
include VCR viewing, which was always separately measured. In order to
arrive at the total time spent before the screen, therefore, the VCR figures
have to be added to the TV figures used in Figure 4.2. Figure 4.4 shows – for
cohorts V69, V74 and V78 – the total time spent before the screen, watching
not only broadcast and cable television, but also video.

We see how, because of the introduction of the VCR, the general decline
in TV viewing during adolescence and early adulthood, repeated again and
again in Figure 4.2, is reduced and turned into a rise after age 14 (grade 8),
a tendency which remains and is being strengthened during later years of
early adulthood. Note that the VCR figures refer to the whole cohort, thus
including those without home access to VCR. The corresponding rise for
VCR owners only, of course, would have been even steeper.

Figure 4.4 includes also the corresponding figures for cohorts V74 and
V78. Two observations can be made. The figures for both TV alone and 'TV
plus video' are much higher for the later cohorts. The decline from age 11 to
age 15 is less steep among those cohorts. How are these striking differences
to be explained?

Part of this difference no doubt is a methodological artefact (TV viewing
measured by an eight-question battery, instead of a six-question battery; see
above). The first substantive observation, however, is that the data for the
two new cohorts, V74 and V78, reflect the situation in 1989, while the
corresponding data from the old cohort, V69, reflect the situations in 1980
and 1984, respectively. (Had the x-axis of the figure referred to chronological
time rather than to age intervals, the dots and lines for the two later cohorts
would have been located to the very right of the figure.) In 1989, cable

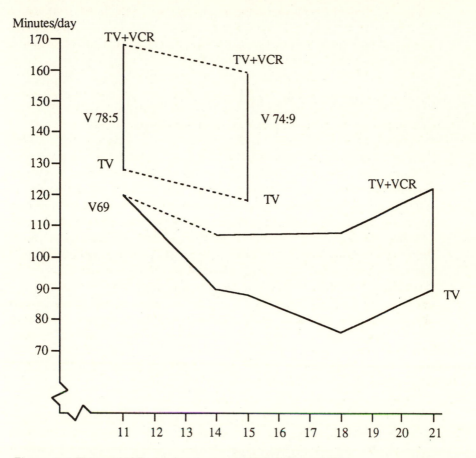

Figure 4.4 TV and VCR viewing in panels V69, V74 and V78

viewing was widespread, while in 1980 and 1984, it was still unusual. The differences in 'pure TV viewing' observed between the early and late cohorts, therefore, partly express an increase in viewing caused by cable and satellite.

Similarly, the difference between early and late cohorts observed in video viewing at age 16 (grade 9) is also to be explained primarily in terms of structural change. In 1989, of course, the VCR was much more widespread than in 1984 (see above). Consequently, much more time was spent video viewing by the ninth-graders of the V74 cohort than by those of the V69 cohort (see Chapter 6).

Finally, we note that the slope of the lines connecting pure TV viewing at ages 11 and 14 is much steeper for the previous cohort than for the two later ones. What remains to be seen is what will happen to the slopes of the later cohorts from age 11 and onwards. Only continued research can provide an answer to that question, but it seems to be a fair guess that what has happened

during the last decade is a true sea change, not only in the levels, but also –
and more interestingly – in the whole dynamics of TV viewing among
adolescents and young adults. Let's turn to a closer study of that dynamics,
in terms of a somewhat broader framework.

Individual maturation under structural change

In Rosengren (1991a) an attempt was made directly to compare the relations
between changes in music listening and television viewing during adolescence, by means of averaging and standardizing procedures applied to the
MPP data collected up to 1987. (Unweighted, age-wise means were first
calculated for Malmö and Växjö data separately, then for the two towns
together. Finally the means were standardized to 100, while the dispersion
was kept unstandardized.) The end result was Figure 4.5, showing two curves
with some similarity to traditional S-curves of growth and diffusion (Brown
1989; Perry 1992). The curves were interpreted, in terms of development
theory, as reflecting biological, cognitive and social development.

According to a basic observation by Brown *et al.* (1974), the individual's
need structure during late childhhood and early adolescence changes, in that
a set of intermittently felt needs ('spasmodic' needs in the expressive

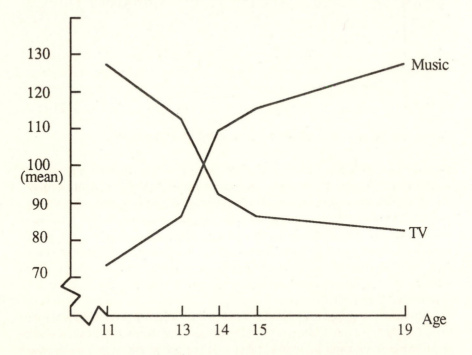

Figure 4.5 Development of TV viewing and listening to music during adolescence, all Malmö and Växjö panels, 1976–1987

terminology used by Brown and his co-authors) are added to a set of more or less constant needs. These new, spasmodic needs naturally call for increased control of the adolescents' environment. In terms of the typology of social-ization patterns discussed in Chapter 1 (Figure 1.4), the socializees are no longer satisfied being objects. They want to be subjects.

In terms of media use, all this means that mere access to a given medium is no longer enough. Adolescents feel they need to control media use themselves. Consequently, they increasingly try to escape the relatively tight control of the family, turning instead to the peer group, which provides better opportunities for satisfaction of this new set of needs. At the same time, they turn from the family medium of television to the peer medium of music, which comes to them by way of media more controllable by them (primarily radio, record-player, tape recorder, CD-player, and VCR). What actually takes place is a thorough-going functional reorganization of adolescent media use called forward by basic biological, cognitive and social development. This functional reorganization is neatly illustrated by the two curves of Figure 4.5, based on MPP data about television viewing and listening to music collected during the period 1975–1987. In terms of the three basic types of temporal effect – age, situation, and generation – the figure illustrates a strong age effect on individual use of the basic mass media.

Now, Figure 4.4 suggests that Figure 4.5 may no longer offer a valid picture of development and media use during childhood, adolescence and early adulthood. Biological and cognitive development is still the same among young humans, of course, but the media structure of modern society is changing. Consequently, young people develop their social and cultural identities by means of different media than previously. Figures 4.6 and 4.7 nicely illustrate this basic change.

In principle, both figures are built in the same way as Figure 4.5. Figure 4.6 synthesizes data collected during the first three waves (1976–81). Figure 4.7, besides covering a longer period of time, is built on data from cohort V69 (the 11 year olds that have also provided two data points among the scores of points on which Figure 4.6 is built). Just like Figure 4.5, Figure 4.6 does not include video viewing and cable/satellite viewing (since both phenomena were almost unknown in Swedish homes of that time period), while Figure 4.7 includes not only broadcast television viewing, but also time spent before the screen enjoying cable and video viewing – that is, from the time period when these media were made available to our youngsters (in Figure 4.7, from the age of 14). Now, what do these figures tell us?

Let's first compare Figures 4.5 and 4.6. The latter, of course, covers the same time period and the same period of life as the left-hand part of the former, with the important exception that there is no data for age 14 (those data in Figure 4.5 stemming from later cohorts). The somewhat longer time intervals of Figure 4.6 is why the typical S-character of the curves of Figure 4.5 has disappeared. Otherwise, the main tendency is intact: a drastic

Standardized amount of
viewing and listening

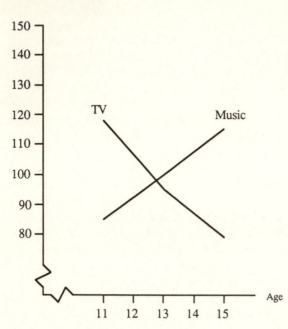

Figure 4.6 Development of TV viewing and listening to music during the first
three waves of data collection, 1976–1981

reduction of TV viewing, and equally drastic increase of listening to music.

In the left-hand side of Figure 4.7, we find much the same tendencies. In the right-hand side of the figure, however, things are different. After the age of 14, the regular decline in TV viewing is suddenly replaced by an increase, in the end bringing the combined TV and VCR viewing up to the level of music listening (in the relative terms of the figure, of course). That is, at the age of 21, TV viewing is back at the very high level found at age 11, while at the same time listening to music at age 21 has roughly doubled since age 11.

What we see is not a situational effect of the type exemplified by the temporal drop in music listening in the1980/81 season. It is not just a short spell of rain or sunshine. It is more like a change of climate, a change of structure. That change has at least four important components.

Firstly, of course, it is due to the breakthrough of CTV and VCR in Sweden. Secondly, is the fact that an ever-increasing portion of teenagers started getting a TV set of their own. Thirdly, CTV and VCR offer a type of content which had not been prevalent in the Swedish monopoly public service television: programmes aimed directly at people around 20 years old, preferably video music distributed by VCR or cable. Fourthly, in the face of the vigorous competition from CTV and VCR, the Swedish public service

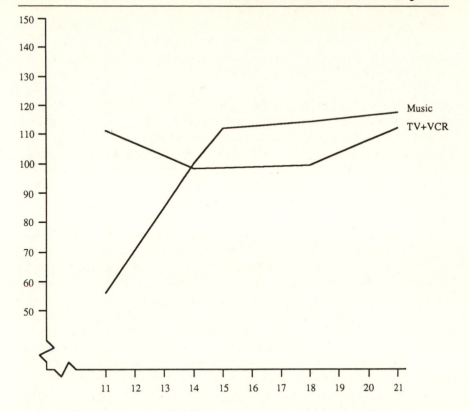

Figure 4.7 Development of TV and VCR viewing and listening to music from age 12 to age 21 in panel V69

television slowly adapted its output, so that it was also more suited to the taste of a previously neglected segment of the public: those aged 15–25. In more abstract terms, there was a structural change from a system characterized mainly by supply/output control to one characterized to some extent by demand/receiver control. (In the terms of Figure 1.8, the change was a transition from a semi-independent reward system to a heterocultural one.)

Together, the four types of structural change taking place during the 1980s moved the TV medium within the control of young people, now offering content well suited to their tastes. As a result the age-related media habits of young people were subject to a radical change, illustrated in the contrast beween the media habits of the cohorts in Figures 4.4, 4.6 and 4.7.

The question immediately following is whether – and if so, how – this change in age-related effects will prove constant, so that it will materialize in a more or less permanent difference between the media habits of generations growing up before and after the still ongoing structural change in the Swedish media scene. Will there be a generational effect on media habits, visible not only for a time between young people of different generations, but also in the long run between middle-aged and elderly people from different generations? Will the 'generational filter' discussed in Chapter 1 and shown in Figure 1.6 become operative?

We cannot tell, of course, but it would hardly seem to be an unreasonable assumption that the changing pattern of age effects observed will be gradually cemented in a generational effect, remaining until future structural change will bring about new long-term changes in media habits. After all, the previous pattern to a large extent was caused by young people's wish to enjoy full control of the medium so important to them: music. Regardless of whether or not, as they grow older, they want to continue with their high consumption of music, there is no reason to leave at an adult age the medium they will have been preferring since they were toddlers.

The enormous amount and breadth of future TV output distributed by way of public service and commercial broadcast, cable and satellite TV and by way of the VCR – easily available news and commentary, fiction and music alike – will have no counterpart in any other medium. Very probably, therefore, the TV viewing pattern being established will to an increasing extent become similar to the radio listening pattern already prevailing: a choice among channels rather than programmes, occasional switching between channels for information and commentary instead of music and entertainment – and very probably a heavy dose of popular music in whatever medium viewed and listened to.

It is also likely, finally, that the ongoing change in the media structure has already contributed, and will continue to contribute, to a tendency which during the last few decades has grown increasingly stronger: the tendency to define and express one's lifestyle in terms of musical taste.

In Sweden (as in many other countries), relatively early, striking examples of this tendency are represented by the 'jazz' and 'swing' crazes occurring around 1920 and 1940, respectively, and bringing many good citizens into what has later been called a moral panic (Roe 1985). In the early 1920s, of course, radio broadcasting was only in its infancy, and there were only few and primitive gramophones. Even in the early 1940s – with television still waiting in the wings, and neither the VCR nor the CD yet invented – the medium for popular music was the gramophone rather than the staid Swedish public service radio of the time (which offered one hour of gramophone music, starting with a military march, an accordion piece somewhere in the middle and rounding off with a classical piece or two).

In their most outspoken forms, therefore, the jazz and swing crazes as sources of an individual lifestyle probably concerned only very small minorities, just as is today the case with a number of narrowly defined specialties in modern popular music. What has changed during the last fifty years or so is that recorded and mass distributed music is widely used to define and express one's lifestyle (see, for instance, Innis 1992: 283 ff). This is so not only among advanced connoisseurs of a particular special taste. Even those travelling in the middle of the road use some variant or other of mainstream music several hours a day to define, express and maintain their more or less consciously chosen lifestyle (see Chapters 10–12).

The thorough-going structural change of the Swedish mass media scene which started in the 1980s and has not yet finished will no doubt help to re-inforce this secular tendency. For large parts of the population – probably a majority – music will form an integrating element of their lifestyle. The choice whether to receive that music by way of radio, cable or broadcast television, VCR or CD or tape recorder will depend on the time of the day, the other activities simultaneously exercised, and – as always – a host of contingencies.

Class, gender and media use under structural change

So far we have been discussing the interplay between, on the one hand, structural change and time-related effects (such as those of age and generation), and on the other, television viewing and listening to music. We shall now turn to the interplay between influences from structural change and influences stemming from the two positional variables of gender and social class.

In most societies, working-class people watch more television than middle-class people, and men more than women. This is also what we have found in our MPP studies. Working-class boys are the most avid watchers; middle-class girls, the least avid, with middle-class boys and working-class girls coming in between (Rosengren and Windahl 1989: 25; Roe 1992). With listening to music, it's somewhat more complicated. In previous MPP studies we have found that working-class girls tend to listen the most; middle-class girls, the least. The differences are much less outspoken, though, and they tend to vary over time (Rosengren and Windahl 1989: 107).

Whether, and to what extent, such patterns are affected by changes in the media structure is a quite different question, of course, and it is also a much more difficult question to answer. As is so often the case, once the question is posed and analysed, it dissolves into a number of different questions, each with an answer of its own. How are the relationships to be conceptualized, for instance? – As differences between levels? – If so, in absolute or relative terms? – Or, perhaps, in terms of some coefficient or other? – And if so, with or without controls for one or more relevant variables?

Results from a thorough-going analysis of data from later MPP waves suggest that with respect to TV viewing, the general pattern of relationships between class, gender and media use is much the same before and during the ongoing structural change, while the pattern may be changing when it comes to the relationship between social class, gender and music (Höjerback, 1990; see also below).

Actually, it is probably too early to issue any definitive statement about the effect of the changing media structure on the relationship between basic

positional variables such as gender and social class, and central socio-cultural
activities such as TV viewing and listening to music. It could be expected,
however, that during periods of structural change such relationships should
be more stable than, say, the overall amount of consumption of this or that
medium in the population at large.

After careful consideration of a quite considerable amount of various
analyses, it was decided that the best way to approach the problem would be
to present a few simple tables based on partial correlations between social
class, gender, TV viewing and listening to music. Tables 4.1–4.4, provide

Table 4.1 Relationship between gender and TV viewing, 1976–1990[1]

	1976/77	1984/85	1989/90
Grade 5	–.21***	–	–.14*** (–.16***)
Grade 9	–.27***	–.34*** (–.36***)	–.22*** (–.20***)

[1] Partial product-moment correlations, controlling for social class. Coefficients within parentheses refer to viewing including VCR.

Table 4.2 Relationship between social class and TV viewing, 1976–1990[1]

	1976/77	1984/85	1989/90
Grade 5	–.25***	–	–.15*** (–.16***)
Grade 9	–.28***	–.29*** (–.26***)	–.25*** (–.27***)

[1] Partial product-moment correlations, controlling for gender. Coefficients within parentheses refer to viewing including VCR.

Table 4.3 Relationship between gender and listening to music, 1976–1990[1]

	1976/77	1984/85	1989/90
Grade 5	–.09	–	.11*
Grade 9	.05	.14	.25***

[1] Partial product-moment correlations, controlling for social class. Coefficients within parentheses refer to viewing including VCR.

Table 4.4 Relationship between social class and listening to music, 1976–1990[1]

	1976/77	1984/85	1989/90
Grade 5	–.05	–	.01
Grade 9	.13	.09	–.01

[1] Partial product-moment correlations, controlling for gender.

information about the relationships between gender and social class, and TV viewing and listening to music among fifth- and ninth-graders, respectively. In each table, one of the two positional variables is conceptualized as the independent one, while the other is being controlled for. There are three points of measurement, but in the middle measurement, no data were available for the fifth-graders (see Figure 3.2). In the right-hand part of the TV tables, the coefficients have been calculated both with and without the inclusion of VCR viewing.

Let's start with gender and TV viewing. The coefficients of Table 4.1 tell us that by and large there has been no drastic change in the relationship between gender and TV viewing before and after the period of structural change. As before, girls watch less TV than do boys. The relationship may have become somewhat weakened, however, especially among children aged 11–12. This is the case whether VCR viewing is included or not. Turning to the relationship between social class and TV viewing (Table 4.2), we find, as expected, that working-class children watch more than middle-class children. Here, too, the importance of the positional variable seems to have been reduced for the fifth-graders, but not for the ninth-graders (again regardless of whether VCR is included or not).

With music, however, it is another matter. Here the volatility is much more striking. The coefficients for gender and listening among fifth-graders change sign between 1976 and 1989: first boys listen somewhat more than girls, then it is the other way round. Among the ninth-graders, girls listen more to music than boys all the time; the strength of the relationship increases linearly over time, however, and in 1989 it has become significant at the .001 level.

Table 4.5 Listening to music in cohort V74, grade 9, 1989 (hrs/week)

Social Class	Gender	
	Boys	Girls
Working class	14.9	18.7
	(57)	(80)
Middle class	13.7	20.4
	(144)	(122)
Upper class	11.2	24.0
	(52)	(44)

Source: Höjerback (1990: 18)

When it comes to music and social class, the pattern is even more complicated. According to Table 4.4, there is next to no relationship found anywhere, but that result is actually an artefact, stemming from complex interactions between the variables of gender and social class in their influence on listening to music. On the one hand, girls listen more than boys regardless of within which social class we compare them; on the other, working-class *boys* listen *more* to music than do middle-class boys, while working-class *girls* listen *less* than middle-class girls. This interaction is spelled out in Table 4.5 corresponding to coefficients .25*** and -.01 in Tables 4.3 and 4.4, respectively. (The four three-dimensional tables corresponding to the remaining four pairs of coefficients in Tables 4.3 and 4.4, in their turn, show somewhat different, but in principle the same patterns of interaction.) We may conclude, then, that while the influence of gender on listening to music has become stronger and more consistent, so that girls now listen more to music than do boys, the influence of class on listening to music remains more ambiguous.

Trying to summarize these complicated patterns we find that, as a result of the ongoing changes in the media structure, the influence of both gender and social class on TV viewing may have been somewhat reduced for fifth-graders but not for ninth-graders, while the influence of gender on music has become stronger, so that, regardless of class, girls now listen more than boys. The influence of social class on music is ambiguous, and no clear change has been found. Especially among old adolescents, then, TV viewing is still very much determined by the two positional variables of social class and gender, while for music, gender seems to emerge as the most consistently important determinant.

Table 4.6 Total amount of media use in cohort V74, grade 9, 1989 (hrs/week)

	+CTV +VCR	+CTV -VCR	-CTV +VCR	-CTV -VCR	Diff.
Boys					
Working class	57.1	50.5	48.3	41.7	15.4
Lower middle class	47.3	43.1	41.6	37.4	9.9
Upper middle class	37.3	33.9	33.5	29.8	7.8
Diff.	19.8	16.6	14.8	11.9	**27.3**
Girls					
Working class	49.5	46.2	47.1	43.8	5.7
Lower middle class	46.4	42.9	44.7	41.2	5.2
Upper middle class	48.6	46.3	44.7	42.4	6.2
Diff.	3.1	3.4	2.4	2.6	**7.1**

Source: Höjerback (1990: 27)

In an attempt to characterize the dynamics of the overall situation, Höjerback (1990: 27) analysed the relationship between, on the one hand, gender and social class, and, on the other, young people's total media use in families with and without access to CTV and VCR (total media use including broadcast TV, CTV, VCR, radio, music, and dailies). Her results are summarized in Table 4.6. Since there was no possibility of distinguishing between primary and secondary media use, and since obviously there is a considerable overlap between the categories (music coming to us by way of all electronic media), the absolute level of consumption *per se* is not a very interesting figure. Very interesting, however, are the considerable differences in *patterns* of media use existing between, on the one hand, boys and girls of different social origin, and on the other, adolescents with and without access to CTV and VCR.

The introduction of the new media of CTV and VCR seems to have struck differently among boys and girls. Working-class boys, much more than upper-middle-class boys in particular, took the new media (and especially CTV) to their hearts, which sent their overall media consumption soaring. Among the girls, the impact was less, and for them, the VCR seems to have been at least as important as the CTV. By and large it could be said that the overall variation in media use is much larger for boys than for girls. Actually, there is only little variation to be found among the girls, and what variation there is, is stronger between girls with and without access to CTV and VCR than between girls of different social origin (controlling for class and access, respectively). With boys, both sources of variation are quite strong, and their total influence is striking indeed. Working-class boys with access to CTV and VCR spend twice as much time with media than do upper-middle-class boys without such access (some 57 hours vs. some 30 hours). The corresponding difference for girls is only about seven hours.

The end result of these complex processes of interaction between social class, gender and a changing media structure, then, is that in quantitative terms, at least, the girls stand out as much more homogeneous in their mass media use than the boys. (The overall difference between their highest and lowest category is only 7.1 hours a week, vs. 27.3 hours for the boys.) The quite impressive difference in total mass media use between working-class boys with access to the new media and upper-middle-class boys without such access, no doubt must add considerably to already existing differences in the whole way of living of these social groups.

Changes in media structure, then, seem to have added to already existing differences between young people from different walks of life. Whether these and other results will remain stable as individual media use gradually adapts to old and new changes in media structure is hard to tell, especially as the period of change has not yet finished. Perhaps during years to come there will not be a period of stability in media structure corresponding to that which prevailed in many West European countries during the 1960s, 1970s and early 1980s. Under such premises, the importance of continued longitudinal studies of young people's media use stands out as ever more important.

SUMMING UP

The study of individual media use under structural change is no simple matter. A number of theoretical, conceptual, methodological and technical problems must be solved; several key decisions must be taken before presenting any results.

Theoretically, the distinctions made in Chapter 1 must be heeded. Change in media structure is change in one sector of the overall *societal* structure. The *social* structure as represented by the four basic dimensions of age and gender, class and status and their influence on individual action may or may not be affected by that change.

Conceptually, the difference between different aspects of media use (amount of use, type of content used, type of relation established to content used, type of context of media use) must be heeded, as well as the distinction between media use conceptualized as habit and as actual behaviour.

Methodologically, the research design used should offer some possibility of differentiating between the three basic aspects of temporality: age, generation and situation.

Technically, considerable attention should be given to the simple fact that different operationalizations will affect the absolute level of media use reported. Some thought should also be given to the fact that differences in operationalizations may very well also affect the relationships reported between media use and a number of dependent and independent variables.

In this chapter, media use has been studied in terms of its most basic aspect: amount of use. Use, in its turn, has been regarded in terms of habits. Since habits are more stable than actual behaviour, the more accidental and ephemeral aspects of media use have been left outside our equations. This choice of conceptualization should make our results more reliable and stable over time.

Methodologically, we have been able to draw on the most powerful design available to survey research: the combined cross-sectional/longitudinal design described in Chapter 3. The influence of differential operationalizations have at least to some extent been neutralized by means of standardization procedures; some remaining differences were revealed by the combined cross-sectional/longitudinal design. By means of the design we were also able to detect a situational effect on listening to music among Swedish adolescents which otherwise might well have been interpreted as an effect of age or generation.

The most basic problems discussed in the chapter, however, have concerned the relationship between changes in media structure as part of the overall societal structure and individual media use as determined by positions in the social structure (age, gender and social class).

We first noted that effects of changes in the media structure seem to reach young people more rapidly than old people – at least in the sense that young people gain access to new media appliances more quickly than do old people. We then proceeded to a renewed analysis of a fact often mentioned in previous research, namely, that the maturation processes playing such an important role in the lives of young people also exert strong influence on their media habits. During adolescence – characterized as it is by 'spasmodic' needs for mood control – the need for expressive media contents such as music, as well as for individual control of media use, suddenly grows much stronger.

Concretely, this means that adolescents feel they need not only *access* to music media; they also need tight *control* of their contents. Since in the 1960s and 1970s Swedish television did not offer much music, and since adolescents were seldom in control of the living-room TV set, they left television, instead turning to listening to music which reached them by way of other media, primarily radio and the tape recorder. All this changed, however, in the early and mid-1980s when CTV and VCR entered the scene, when there was an old and/or small TV set available in their own room, and when even Swedish public service TV started to offer popular music for young people. Expressive media content was as important as before to adolescents; now they could have it also by way of television. The pattern of influence on individual media use exerted by the positional variable of age, then, was drastically changed, so that the heavy reduction in TV viewing primarily observed during the teens is no longer to be found.

An intriguing question is whether this age-related change in patterns of media use will gradually turn into a generation effect. Only continued research will be able to provide an answer to that question. Much the same goes for potential changes in the influence exerted by those two important positional variables, gender and social class. As far as we can tell today, both gender and social class seem to keep their influence on the use of television (gender possibly having become somewhat less important). Contrariwise, gender may have become *more* important as a determinant of listening to music, in that adolescent girls and young women now seem to listen more to music than do adolescent boys and young men. Although there has hardly been any change *per se* in the social structure as defined by the positional variables of age and gender, social class and status, a change in the media sector of the societal structure may thus have influenced the strength and character of the influence exerted by a positional variable in the social system of action.

In the following chapters, the perspective will be broadened; the analyses will be sharpened and deepened in various ways. Not only causes but also effects of mass media use will be scrutinized. A close look will be taken at stability and change in media use. Not only societal structure and social position but also individual characteristics will be regarded as determinants of media use. And individual media use will be regarded as one component of those complex patterns of actions called lifestyles – in their turn determined by individual characteristics such as individually held basic values and more or less specific phenomena at the attitudinal level (such as interests, tastes, principles, convictions).

NOTE

The figures were drawn by Dr Ulla Johnsson-Smaragdi, who in Chapter 6 will use some of them for basically different purposes.

REFERENCES

Anshelm, M. (1993) 'Video', in U. Carlsson and M. Anshelm (eds) *Medie-Sverige 1993*, Gothenburg: NORDICOM.

BBC (1987–93) *Annual Review of Audience Research Findings*, London: John Libbey.

Berg, U. (1982) 'Mediebarometern 1982', *Pub informerar* December.

Brown, J.R., Cramond, J.K. and Wilde, R.J. (1974) 'Displacement effects of television and the child's functional orientation to media', in J.G. Blumler and E. Katz (eds) *The Uses of Mass Communications*, Beverly Hills, Calif.: Sage.

Brown, M.A. (1989) 'Diffusion', in E. Barnouw (ed.) *International Encyclopedia of Communications* 2: 31–36, New York: Oxford University Press.

Burnett, R. (1990) *Concentration and Diversity in the International Phonogram Industry*, Gothenburg: Department of Media and Communication.

—— (1992) 'The implications of ownership changes on concentration and diversity in the phonogram industry', *Communication Research* 19: 749–769.

—— (1993) 'Fonogram', in U. Carlsson and M. Anshelm (eds) *Medie Sverige 1993*, Gothenburg: NORDICOM.

Comstock, G. and Paik, H.J. (1987) *Television and Children: A Review of Recent Research*, Syracuse, NY: ERIC.

Cronholm, M. (1993) 'Satellit- och kabel-TV', in U. Carlsson and M. Anshelm (eds) *Medie Sverige 1993*, Gothenburg: NORDICOM.

Csikszentmihalyi, M. and Kubey, R. (1981) 'Television and the rest of life', *Public Opinion Quarterly* 45: 317–328.

Gunter, B. and Svennevig, M. (1987) *Behind and in Front of the Screen*, London: John Libbey.

Hasebrink, U. and Krotz, F. (1992) 'Muster individueller Fernsehnutzung', *Rundfunk und Fernsehen* 40: 398–411.

Höjerback , I. (1990) 'Nya medier – nya klyftor', *Lund Research Papers in the Sociology of Communication* 27, Lund: Department of Sociology, University of Lund.

Innis, P.H. (1992) *The Emergence of Rocknroll in American Popular Music*, Hanover, NH and London: Wesleyan University Press.

Johnsson-Smaragdi, U. (1983) *TV Use and Social Interaction in Adolescence. A Longitudinal Study*, Stockholm: Almqvist & Wiksell International.

Kubey, R. and Csikszentmihalyi, M. (1990) *Television and the Quality of Life*, Hillsdale, NJ: Lawrence Erlbaum.

Lööv, T. and Miegel, F. (1989) 'Vardagsliv, livsstilar och massmedieanvändning. En studie av 12 malmöungdomar', *Lund Research Papers in the Sociology of Communication* 16, Department of Sociology, University of Lund.

Lööv, T. and Rosengren, K.E. (1988) 'The experience sampling method (ESM)', *Lund Research Papers in the Sociology of Communication* 9, Department of Sociology, University of Lund.

Perry, R.W. (1992) 'Diffusion theories', in E.F. Borgatta and M.L. Borgatta (eds) *Encyclopedia of Sociology 1*, New York: Macmillan.

Peterson, R.A. and Berger, D.G. (1975) 'Cycles in symbol production: The case of popular music', *American Sociological Review* 40: 158–173.

Riley, M.W. (1992) 'Cohort perspectives', in E.F. Borgatta and M.L. Borgatta (eds) *Encyclopedia of Sociology*, New York: Macmillan.

Roe, K. (1985) 'The Swedish moral panic over video 1980–1984', *Nordicom Review* 1: 20–25.

—— (1992) 'Different destinies – different melodies: School achievement, anticipated status, and adolescents' tastes in music', *European Journal of Communication* 7: 335–357.

Rosengren, K.E. (1991a) 'Media use in childhood and adolescence: Invariant change?', *Communication Yearbook* 14: 48–90, Newbury Park, Calif.: Sage.

—— (1991b) 'How do you feel?' (Review of Kubey, R. and Csikszentmihalyi, M. (1990) *Television and the Quality of Life*), *Journal of Communication* 41 (1): 143–145.

Rosengren, K.E. and Windahl, S. (1989) *Media Matter: TV Use in Childhood and Adolescence*, Norwood, NJ: Ablex.

Ryder, N.B. (1992) 'Cohort analysis', in E.F. Borgatta and M.L. Borgatta (eds) *Encyclopedia of Sociology*, New York: Macmillan.

Sonesson, I. and Höjerback, I. (1989) 'Skolungdomars medievanor före och efter videon'. *Lund Research Papers in the Sociology of Communication* 12, Department of Sociology, University of Lund.

van der Voort, T.H.A. and Vooijs, M.W. (1990) 'Validity of children's direct estimates of time spent television viewing', *Journal of Broadcasting & Electronic Media* 34 (1): 93–99.

Webster, J.G. and Lichty, L.W. (1991) *Ratings Analysis. Theory and Practice*, Hillsdale, NJ: Lawrence Erlbaum.

Weibull, L. (1985) 'Structural factors in gratifications research', in K.E. Rosengren, L.A. Wenner and P. Palmgreen (eds) *Media Gratifications Research. Current Perspectives*, Beverly Hills, Calif.: Sage.

Chapter 5

Looking for patterns in lifestyle behaviours

Suzanne Pingree and Robert P. Hawkins

INTRODUCTION

The lifestyle concept has had a recurring fascination for social scientists. The hope, whether stated explicitly or not, has been to grasp at something closer to the essence of social life than the study of either individual behaviours or social categories will permit. However, realizing this hope requires some means of dealing with multiple aspects of individuals and social groups more or less simultaneously. How are multiple behaviours in different spheres integrated into coherent and meaningful organizations, and why do these integrations occur? In addition, implicit within the lifestyle concept is the notion of difference or variation – that individuals differ from each other in systematic and meaningful ways.

Attempts to apply these ideas to media-related behaviours have developed rapidly in recent years. Rosengren and Windahl (1989), in research that provided the direct impetus for that reported here, described nearly thirty adolescent activities with parents, friends and organizations according to a circumplex organized around the two dimensions of parent vs. peer and organized/planned vs. unplanned/spontaneous activities (see Figure 5.1). Mass media use was related to the circumplex by correlating use of individual media to each activity separately for subgroups defined by the social positional variables of gender, age, and social class. That is, different adolescent activities are related to use of television than to use of books or pop music; furthermore, these patterns also differed between subgroups. While the authors did not phrase their results in lifestyle terms, they did speak of variations in how media use is 'embedded in patterns of social interaction' (p. 203).

Rosengren and Windahl (1989) suggested that these differences indicated both developmental and lifestyle variation in the meaning of mass media to adolescents. However, while their analyses stimulate and suggest a lifestyle interpretation, they are necessarily limited – as are snapshots that suggest but cannot show motion. Working with one media use variable at a time makes it difficult to assess the degree of independence of the conclusions: we can

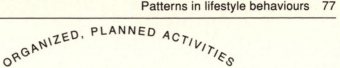

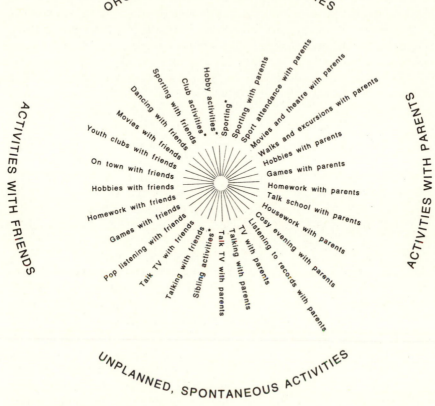

Note: * Not necessarily with parents or friends

Figure 5.1 A quasi-circumplex of adolescent activities

see multiple aspects of parent and peer activities simultaneously, but only for one slice of media lifestyle at a time. Similarly, it is not possible to assess the degree of independence of the activity variables to which media use is related, or even the validity of the circumplex itself.

In addition, basing the subgroups on social positional variables implicitly assumes both that social position is the key determinant and that gender, age and class adequately represent social position in distinguishing media life-style. Treating these three as dichotomies would already produce eight subgroups, but additional variables might also be relevant, and the number of subgroups grows by multiplication to numbers that are clearly unmanage-able and uninterpretable (over a thousand for ten variables).

A further development is contained in Johansson and Miegel's (1992) analysis of lifestyle and identity in youth culture. In attempting to construct an integrated theory of lifestyle, they focused on personal values, attitudes and actions (including a range of media activities and details on the content of media used and preferred), and they attended to simultaneous determination by social structure, social position and the individual. Operationally, they locate the 'lifestyles' within each element as the factor dimensions of each of these elements (i.e. a factor analysis for values, one for music taste, one for activities, etc.), and then correlate taste and activity factors with values and social position variables.

Importantly, because Johansson and Miegel (1992) wanted to allow for lifestyle stemming from several levels of determination, they both defined and measured lifestyle entirely in terms of lifestyle variables themselves (rather than social position), which matches the approach we describe here. However, because their quantitative analyses correlated factor scores from different elements for the whole sample, they provide a better sense of how these lifestyle elements relate to each other overall than of differences in lifestyles.

Our approach in this chapter agrees in part with Johansson and Miegel (1992). We also look first for tools for simplification and understanding within the phenomena themselves. But beyond this, what we are suggesting is the utility of characterizing groups of these lifestyle media behaviours as 'patterns' of behaviour. In Rosengren's terms (see Chapter 1), we look first for patterns relating media use and social activities as 'lifestyles' (patterns of action determined by the individual), although subsequent analyses may attribute some of the variation to 'ways of life' (patterns determined by position in social structure) or to 'forms of life' (patterns determined by social structure itself). In other words, we want to see whether we can make some progress toward reducing the complexity in lifestyle media behaviours by looking for distinctly different patterns in the behaviours themselves, instead of for a common solution. This approach assumes that individual behaviours are sufficiently complex that we need to measure them as they co-occur, in clouds of interrelated variables, but that they are not so idiosyncratic that each individual has her/his own cloud.

As an analogy, we are reminded of Brenda Dervin's argument about attempting to customize messages of information campaigns to make them more useful for the general public. Doing so based on demographic or other enduring characteristics of individuals quickly bogs one down in far too many subgroups, as suggested above. But distinguishing instead between communication-related perceptions of individual situations requires only about a half-dozen categories, with another half-dozen categories of resulting questions greatly tightening the understanding of the situation (Dervin et al. 1982).

Thus, we see lifestyle media behaviour as potentially composed of many variables, and the differences between individuals as occurring in multiple dimensions at once. Treating each behaviour as a separate dependent variable would be unworkable, while linear combinations (such as in canonical correlation) search for best-fitting summaries at the expense of differences. In other words, there is considerable opportunity and promise for analytic approaches utilizing *patterns* in which individuals are grouped in multi-dimensional spaces according to communication lifestyle behaviours. Such patterns of interpretation or exposure would be composites of behaviours (which have perhaps been more successful than defining patterns as specific behaviours; cf. Greenberg *et al.* 1988; Pingree *et al.* 1991).

To pursue these ideas about communication lifestyle behaviours, we re-examined the circumplex of adolescent activities, looking for a method of approach that would satisfy several criteria. First, we wanted to test the assumed two-dimensional structure of parent/peer activities, and also to determine the extent to which individual activities were independent of each other. Second, we wanted to incorporate use of various media more directly and simultaneously into the circumplex, in hope that this would give a more direct sense of how mass media fit with and relate to other adolescent activities. Third, we wanted to be able to locate subgroups that differed in their jointly-considered patterns of media and circumplex activities, defining the subgroups by the patterns themselves rather than by external variables, although subsequent examination of any such subgroups should consider such variables. Finally, because the environment adolescents face is changing rapidly, perhaps especially in the range and nature of mass media available, we wanted to compare two different time periods.

RESULTS

Our analyses were of data collected by the Media Panel Group (Rosengren and Windahl 1989) from fifth- and ninth-year school students (about one year older than US students in those school grades) in the same Swedish city in 1980 and 1989. While this community of course shared in the global changes in media and society, it is worth noting that the nature of and access to television changed even more, from two commercial-free channels in 1980 to multiple imported channels and wide availability of videotapes by 1989 (see Chapter 2).

In each year of the survey, the number of respondents in one of these grades was considerably larger than the other, which could have produced age biases in both factor and cluster analyses. Also, a few variables had larger amounts of missing data than others. Thus, we first discarded cases with missing data on these variables and then randomly sampled from the remainder to end up with samples of approximately equal sizes for each age group (179 fifth grade and 182 ninth grade in 1980, 372 of each age in 1989).

Dimensions of adolescent activities

As a first step in locating commonalities and patterns of behaviours, we factor analysed the 29 circumplex items in each of the 1980 and 1989 Media Panel surveys, using the whole sample each time instead of conducting separate factor analyses for age, gender or social class subgroups. While different subgroups might have had different factor structures, sample sizes would have been marginal even for two separate subgroups (let alone eight!). Further, separate analyses would have necessarily prefocused the analysis on social positional factors, instead of leaving the source of variation open and grouping entirely in terms of the variables themselves.

(The response scales differed slightly between 1980 and 1989, with the earlier providing finer resolution for very frequent performance and the later survey providing more discrimination for rare events. However, since the stems were generally identical and the response scales in each case provide a five-point ordinal scale, an analysis focusing on correlations rather than absolute values should be unaffected by this difference.)

Although the original conceptualization organized these behaviours along two dimensions (with parents vs. with peers and organized/planned vs. unorganized/unplanned activities), our factor analyses both confirmed some of the central ideas and elaborated on them. To begin with, as shown in Tables 5.1 and 5.2, there were many more than two dimensions underlying adolescents' responses to these questions.

For 1980, we characterize the factor solution as follows:

Factor 1 *Parent Non-routine* activities. Frequency of occurrence of a variety of leisure-time activities with parents. These were not, of course, unusual activities; the point is that they are not routine and often require some organization and planning.

Factor 2 *Parent Routine* activities. Frequency of routine, unplanned interactions, such as discussing schoolwork, getting help with lessons or doing chores.

Note that these two factors corresponded reasonably well to two of the quadrants of the initial conception. However, they did not correspond to the two underlying theoretical dimensions, since they did not contain negative loadings from the "other side" of the circumplex.

Factor 3 *Friend Teen* activities. Frequency of going out with friends, talking with them, or listening to music (either with friends or with parents), all of which suggest a youth-culture orientation. This factor was less consistent with the circumplex idea, since the activities that make it up were dispersed around the original circumplex. And it is worth noting that there is some overlap between this factor and non-routine activities with parents.

Factor 4 *Friend Home* activities. Frequency of engaging in schoolwork, hobbies or games with friends, or simply belonging to clubs. Except for the latter, these activities were all on one side of the original circumplex: with friends, but neutral on planned vs. unplanned.

Table 5.1 Factor analyses of 1980 circumplex activities

Factor	1	2	3	4	5	6	7
1. Parent Non-routine							
1. parent cinema	.79						
2. parent spectate	.71						
3. parent cosy	.69						
4. parent walk	.68						
5. friend cinema	.67						
6. parent games	.60			.34			
7. parent sport	.58						
8. parent hobby	.51			.35			
9. friend dance	.43		.37				
10. parent lesson	.41	.40					
2. Parent Routine							
11. parent talk		.78					
12. parent housework		.71					
13. parent talk school		.65			.35		
3. Friend Teen							
14. friend music			.74		.35		
15. friend talk			.66				
16. friend town	.37		.59				
17. parent music	.38		.41				
4. Friend Home							
18. friend lessons				.74			
19. friend hobby				.50			
20. friend games				.47		.32	
21. clubs				.40			
5. TV Talk							
22. parent talk TV					.69		
23. parent TV					.65		
24. friend talk TV					.63		
25. hobby					-.37		.35
6. Friends/Sports/Clubs							
26. friend sport						.74	
27. friend clubs	.31					.45	
7. Sibling Sports							
* sibling activity							.63
28. sports						.42	.46
% variance	22%	7%	6%	5%	5%	4%	4%

Note: * This variable was not included in the 1989 survey. All loadings above .30 are shown.

Table 5.2 Factor analyses of 1989 circumplex activities

Factor	1	2	3	4	5	6	7
1. Parent Non-routine							
10. parent lessons	.69						
6. parent games	.61						
7. parent sport	.61		.49				
8. parent hobby	.60					.39	
17. parent music	.54						
4. parent walk	.51			.46			
3. parent cosy	.46			.41			
1. parent cinema	.43						
2. Friend Home							
14. friend music		.74					
15. friend talk		.70					
24. friend talk tv		.60					
* friend tv		.57					
20. friend games		.52					
18. friend lessons	.46	.49					
3. Sports/Clubs							
28. sports			.83				
26. friend sport			.75				
21. clubs			.67				.40
2. parent spectate	.45		.57				
4. Parent Routine							
11. parent talk				.72			
13. parent talk school				.70			
12. parent housework	.31			.59			
5. Friend Out							
5. friend cinema					.72		
9. friend dance		.32			.67		
16. friend town		.49			.60		
6. Parents and TV							
23. parent TV						.69	
22. parent talk TV						.59	
27. friend/club						.32	
7. Hobbies							
25. hobby							.82
19. friend hobby							.63
% variance	20%	11%	8%	6%	4%	4%	4%

Note: Row numbers indicate an item's position in Table 5.1, to simplify comparison.
* This variable was not included in the 1980 survey. All loadings above .30 are shown.

Factor 5 *TV Talk*. Frequency of watching and talking about television with either friends or parents. This factor represents the juncture of family and friends for one very focused context of activity.

The final two factors may be relatively minor.

Factor 6 *Friend Sports and Clubs*, both fairly organized activities.

Factor 7 *Siblings and Sports*. Activities with siblings and participating in sports, originally conceived as on opposite sides of the circumplex.

Table 5.2 presents the comparable factor solution for 1989, using almost identical questions (the tables note two exceptions) with students of the same ages as in 1980. To facilitate comparison, items are identified by their number from the 1980 factor structure, and, where possible, the factors are named similarly.

Factor 1 *Parent Non-routine* activities.

Factor 2 *Friend Home* activities.

Factor 3 *Sports and Clubs*.

Factor 4 *Parent Routine* activities.

Factor 5 *Friends Out*.

Factor 6 *Parents and TV*.

Factor 7 *Hobbies*.

The two factor structures can be compared more directly in Table 5.3, which maintains the order of items and places a factor from each year with the most similar factor from the other year. Overall, there were substantial similarities between the factor structures, especially in that the two parent factors (*Routine* and *Non-routine* activities with parents) were very similar across time. Two activities with friends (cinema and dance) that were included in *Parent Non-routine* in 1980 moved out in 1989, and more overlap was visible with the otherwise unchanged *Parent Routine* factor, but these were minor. Basically, the division of parental activities into two groupings (independent of activities with friends or alone) remained.

The relationships between the 1980 and 1989 friend factors were more complex. In 1980 the two factors were nearly equal in eigenvalue; in 1989 one was nearly three times the size of the other. The dominant friend factor in 1989 (*Friend Home*) drew its variables equally from the two different 1980 friend factors and from the *TV Talk* factor. As such, it became a much more general factor, more compatible with the circumplex idea than its pre-decessors, covering a wide range of unplanned activities with peers.

Other items that were part of the two 1980 friend factors migrated away. Listening to music with parents, associated with teenage activities in 1980, joined the *Parent Non-routine* factor in 1989, while hobby and club items joined topic-specific factors. The remaining item in the 1980 friend factors, going to town with friends, in 1989 formed its own more focused factor of going out with friends, joining with cinema and dance that in 1980 aligned with *Parent Non-routine*.

Table 5.3 Comparing 1980 and 1989 circumplex factors

	Factor order numbers													
	1	1	2	4	3	5	4	2	5	6	6	3	7	7
	'80	'89	'80	'89	'80	'89	'80	'89	'80	'89	'80	'89	'80	'89
Parent Non-routine														
1. parent cinema	x	x												
2. parent spectate	x	(x)										x		
3. parent cosy	x	x		(x)										
4. parent walk	x	x		(x)										
5. friend cinema	x					x								
6. parent games	x	x					(x)							
7. parent sport	x	x										(x)		
8. parent hobby	x	x					(x)							
9. friend dance	x				(x)	x		(x)						
10. parent lesson	x	x	(x)											
Parent Routine														
11. parent talk			x	x										
12. parent housework		(x)	x	x										
13. parent talk school			x	x					(x)					
Friend teen														
14. friend music					x			x						
15. friend talk					x			x						
16. friend town	(x)				x	x		(x)						
17. parent music	(x)	x			x									
Friend Home														
18. friend lessons				(x)			x	x						
19. friend hobby							x						x	
23. friend games							x	x			(x)			
21. clubs							x					x	(x)	(x)
** friend TV								x						
TV Talk														
22. parent talk TV									x	x				
Z3. parent TV									x	x				
24. friend talk TV								x	x					
25. hobby									x				(x)	x
Friend/Sports/Clubs														
26. friend sport											x	x		
27. friend clubs	(x)									x	x			
Sibling Sports														
* sibling activity													x	
28. sports											(x)	x	x	

Note: X denotes a final factor solution primary loading greater than .40.
   (x) denotes a secondary loading greater than .30.
   * This variable was not included in the 1989 survey.
   ** This variable was not included in the 1980 survey.

The 1980 factor 5, watching TV with parents and talking about it with parents or friends, was still recognizable in 1989, but was limited to parents. Talking about TV with friends, along with the newly added 'watching TV with friends', moved to factor 2 (*Friend Home* activities) in 1989.

The two minor (and not terribly clear) factors in 1980 were much more distinct in 1989. A strong *Sports/Clubs* factor incorporating both friends and parents emerged in 1989, and the final factor dealt exclusively with *Hobbies*.

Overall, distinctions were clearer in 1989 than in 1980. There was sharper definition and division between parents and peers, but also sharper definition of contexts and locations of activities as well. The only exception to this trend was the pulling-apart of a singular television factor in 1980, but even this more clearly separated the spheres of parents and friends. However, while these changes are interesting and may be suggestive of important trends, it is still clear that there was substantial continuity from 1980 to 1989 in the ways adolescents organized their life with parents and peers.

Clusters of activity and media use

Given this, the next question is how adolescents relate media use with these dimensions. However, while the above analyses sought to *reduce* the large number of specific measures of adolescent activities to a small set of dimensions, locating use of various media within the dimensions of the circumplex requires a different approach. Correlating use of each medium with each of the dimensions would be somewhat informative, but even though the factor scores are at least in principle uncorrelated, use of various mass media is certainly not, so that correlations would have to be evaluated for redundancy.

But even trying to avoid this problem through multiple regression or canonical correlation would actually miss our main point. Any of these correlational techniques seeks a best *overall* solution – the average or aggregate or most common set of relationships between mass media use and activities with parents and friends. We suspect that there are instead different ways of combining media use and the circumplex activities (different lifestyles, one might say), and therefore we need to use a different technique.

Our attempt to locate styles uses cluster analysis to identify groups of adolescents who are similar to each other on a set of activity and media use variables, while different from other groups or clusters who share a different constellation of behaviours. Since these are subgroup analyses, we can look for patterns within the parent and friend activity variables even though these variables are uncorrelated across the sample as a whole. And finally, this approach attempts to locate the styles based on patterns in the behaviours themselves, rather than by first defining subgroups by social position variables.

For the 1980 cluster analysis, the seven circumplex factor scores were entered along with amount of use of eight mass media (television, radio, newspapers (combining the news-oriented morning papers and the afternoon tabloids), books, weekly magazines (typically aimed at a subgroup – teens, women, men), comics (books, weeklies, series), music, and cinema). Use distributions were highly skewed for a few variables, so square root transformation was used in the cluster analysis. However, Tables 5.4 and 5.5 present the means using the original metrics as shown. Note that the scales differed for some variables in the two surveys, which limits comparisons of absolute magnitudes but should have little effect on the clustering procedures.

Since cluster analysis typically generates the number of clusters requested (there is no common decision statistic or default comparable to the eigenvalue of factor analysis), solutions were produced for four through seven clusters. Picking one solution to interpret involved first examining the balance of cluster sizes for each solution. The four- and five-cluster solutions each placed 78 per cent of the 1980 sample in only two clusters. The six- and seven-cluster solutions each placed 62 per cent in their first two clusters (and 20–21 per cent in the third). However, the seven-cluster solution had one very large cluster and many smaller ones, making the six-cluster solution both the most balanced and the most interpretable.

The first cluster (see Table 5.4), a fairly small group, combined high levels of *Parent Non-routine* activity, *Friend Teen*, *TV Talk* and *Friend Sports/ Clubs*, while being merely moderate on the *Parent Routine* and *Friend Home* dimensions. They were also very heavy users of all eight media. This active and outgoing group was largely younger boys.

The second cluster, also quite small, was similarly high on *Parent Non-routine* and *TV Talk*, but also *Friend Home*, while being lower than other groups on *Parent Routine* activities and *Sibling/Sports*. They were heavier than average users of television, radio, books and comics, while lighter users of newspapers, music and films. They were also mostly boys and they were *all* fifth graders.

Note that while the first two clusters were similar in social position and share some behaviours (*TV Talk*, *Non-routine* activities with parents, and heavy use of four media), they differed on *Friend Home* and *Parent Routine* activities, and three other media use variables.

The third cluster, again a small group, was higher on *Friend Teen* and *Sibling/Sports*, but lower on *Parent Non-routine*, *Friend Home*, *TV Talk* and *Friend Sports/Club*. They were heavy users of newspapers, music and films, while being light users of books, weeklies, comics, radio and especially television. They were mostly older and girls.

The fourth, largest group, was low on *Parent Non-routine* and *TV Talk* activities, and moderate on the other five circumplex variables. They were moderate to light users of most mass media. They were older, equally divided between boys and girls, and were the only group higher in social class than the others.

The fifth group, also large, was simply moderate on all circumplex

Table 5.4 1980 clusters

	Outgoing, Heavy Media 1	Friends and TV, TV/Books 2	Teens, No TV 3	Unconnected, Media Moderate 4	Moderates, Magazines 5	TV Talk, Moderates 6
Activity Factors						
parent non-routine	.67 b	.34 ab	-.36 cd	-.31 c	-.04 ad	.15 a
parent routine	.02 a	-.40 a	.08 a	.09 a	.11 d	-.18 a
friend teen	.49 b	-.09 a	.75 b	-.07 a	-.07 a	-.08 a
friend home	.02 ab	.44 bc	-.17 ac	-.07 ab	-.11 a	.11 ab
TV talk	.53 a	.73 a	-.57 b	-.34 b	.07	.37 a
friend sports/club	.28 a	-.19 a	-.24 a	.02 a	-.07 a	.13 a
sibling/sports	-.16 a	-.27 a	.29 a	.09 a	-.13 a	.08 a
Media Use						
TV use (hours per week)	21.33	27.10	1.99	5.72	10.80	15.72
radio use (hours per week)	8.45 b	6.57 ab	3.15 a	3.94 a	3.73 a	5.15 a
newspaper (number read)	1.54 b	1.07 ac	1.47 bc	1.38 ab	1.45 b	1.42 ab
books (how many in three weeks)	2.00 ab	2.80 b	1.41 a	1.58 a	1.83 a	1.68 a
weeklies (never to often, 0–3)	1.46 b	1.20 ab	.88 a	1.24 b	1.35 b	1.17 ab
comics (never to often, 0–3)	2.54 b	2.47 b	1.47 a	1.69 a	1.91 ac	2.19 bc
music (never to daily, 0–7)	4.46 ac	3.13 bcd	5.12 a	4.37 a	3.44 bcd	3.92 ab
cinema (never to weekly, 0–8)	2.96 b	1.87 a	2.53 ab	2.15 a	1.95 a	2.05 a
Demographics						
gender (1 = boy, 2 = girl)	1.32 ace	1.33 acde	1.65 bc	1.56 bd	1.52 be	1.34 a
grade (1 = 5th, 2 = 9th)	1.29 ab	1.00 b	1.76 c	1.70 c	1.45 a	1.39 a
socioeconomic status (range 1–5)	1.20 a	1.11 ab	1.18 a	2.01 b	1.41 a	1.45 a
N =	28	15	17	115	110	77

Note: The labels for each cluster first describe their relative circumplex activities and then their media behaviour. Means with like superscripts do not differ at $p < .05$.

Table 5.5 1989 clusters

	Connected, Newspapers 1	Unconnected, Video/Comics 2	Friends, Heavy Media 3	Low Parents, Books 4	Moderates, Light Media 5	Connected, Heavy Media 6
Activity Factors						
parent non-routine	.17 b	.08 ab	-.64	-.14 ac	.02 ab	.24 bc
friend home	.19 bc	-.29 a	.44 b	-.06 ac	-.03 ac	.59 b
sports/clubs	.29 a	.17 a	-.53 c	.01 ab	-.12 b	.04 abc
parent routine	.41 a	-.35 b	.27 a	-.23 b	.15 a	.43 a
friend out	.36 b	-.25 c	.77 a	.04 b	-.12 bc	.34 ab
parent TV	.26 bcd	.22 bcd	-.15 ad	-.10 a	-.04 ac	.70 b
hobby	-.01 a	-.12 a	.28 a	-.08 a	.12 a	.23 a
Media Use						
TV use (hours per week)	14.27 a	18.57 b	19.31 b	13.18 a	12.38 a	25.28
video (hours per week)	4.85	5.89 a	6.20 a	3.57 b	3.47 b	14.1 a
radio use (hours per week)	6.47 bc	5.43 ac	9.22 b	4.20 a	3.78 a	7.59 bc
newspaper (hours per week)	1.85	.57 ab	1.06 c	.58 a	.76 b	.71 abc
tabloid (hours per week)	2.43 b	.54 a	.95	.52 a	.50 a	2.08 b
books (hours per week)	1.33 a	.62 ab	4.13 b	3.87 a	.77 c	3.17 c
weeklies (hours per week)	1.23	.34 ab	3.23 c	.28 a	.38 b	2.98 c
comics (hours per week)	1.65	3.90	.75 ab	.65 a	1.13 b	5.30
music (hours per week)	15.80 a	10.20 a	25.30 b	9.88 a	11.80 a	25.70 b
cinema (never to monthly, 0–4)	1.74 b	1.22 a	2.22 c	1.35 a	1.40 a	1.62 abc
Demographics						
gender (1 = boy, 2 = girl)	1.60 a	1.18 a	1.89 b	1.38	1.64 a	1.75 ab
grade (1 = 5th, 2 = 9th)	1.58 ad	1.28 b	1.88	1.61 cd	1.50 a	1.38 abc
socioeconomic status (range 2–10)	5.62 a	6.34 a	5.70 a	6.15 a	6.27 a	5.62 a
N =	53	68	27	179	187	16

Note: The labels for each cluster first describe their relative circumplex activities and then their media behaviour. Means with like superscripts do not differ at $p<.05$.

measures. They were also generally moderate in media use, although they used weekly magazines more than did others, and were less likely to use music, radio or films. They were of mixed age and gender.

The sixth group, still fairly large, was not sharply distinctive, being only moderately higher on *TV Talk* and moderately lower on *Parent Routine*, and generally moderate for the media use variables. Like the first group, they tended to be younger and boys.

A similar cluster analysis was conducted on the 1989 sample, using the slightly different circumplex dimensions, and with some alteration of the media use variables. First, newspaper use was measured separately for the morning papers and the tabloids, and amount of video viewing was added. In addition, almost all media variables were measured in minutes or hours per week (rather than by 'how often' scales), producing skewed distributions in most cases; the cluster analyses used transformed variables, but the original scales were used for the means in Table 5.5. Once again, six clusters proved to be the best solution. Four-, five- and seven-cluster solutions all grouped many more individuals into the largest cluster. (However, the order of the clusters in Table 5.5 is not the original, essentially arbitrary order produced by the computer program; we have altered the order to facilitate comparisons to 1980 to be presented in Table 5.6.)

The first 1989 cluster seemed very connected to almost all aspects of the circumplex, higher than average on all but one, and especially high on *Parent Routine* and *Sports/Clubs*. It was moderate in its use of most media, but higher than average on use of newspapers and tabloids. The cluster was fairly mixed in age and gender but with a few more girls and ninth-graders. None of the clusters was significantly different from the others in social class as indexed by parental occupations.

The second cluster was not very connected to the family and friend circumplex: slightly above average on *Sports/Clubs*, *Parent Non-routine* and *Parent TV* activities, but the lowest of the groups on the other four factors. They were heavy video and comic users, but low on all print media, as well as on music and cinema (which one might consider adolescent media). They were mostly young and almost all boys.

The third group was quite high on the friend factors and quite low on *Parent Non-routine* and *Sports/Clubs*. They were heavy users of all mass media except comics and tabloids, especially radio, books, weeklies, music and films. They were almost all older and girls.

The fourth group, almost as large as the fifth, was moderate to below average across the circumplex factors, particularly the two parent factors. They were very heavy book readers, but among the lightest users of all other media. They tended to be older and boys.

The fifth cluster, a large group, was generally moderate on all circumplex factors (slightly above average on *Parent Routine* and *Hobby*, slightly below on *Friend Out* and *Sports/Club*). They were light to very light users of almost all media, tended to be girls, and were evenly divided between fifth- and ninth-graders.

The sixth cluster, a very small group, was also very connected to most aspects of the circumplex (although not *Sports/Clubs*), in five cases the strongest of all six groups. They were substantial consumers of almost all media (except that they were moderate in newspaper use) and highest of the groups on television, video, comics, and music. A majority were fifth-graders and three-quarters were girls.

Table 5.6 presents an attempt to relate the 1980 and 1989 clusters. In comparing clusters, we looked first for similar loadings on the seven circumplex factor dimensions, and then examined similarities in media use. Overall, we found two close matches (the second and fifth clusters) and two matches that were close on the circumplex variables but weak on media use (the first and fourth clusters). In addition, there were two cases where the match on the circumplex variables was only moderately good (the third and sixth clusters). In one of these, the match on media use was fairly good; in the other it was weak.

More specifically, the Friends and TV, TV/Books cluster from 1980 (a small group, all fifth grade and mostly boys high on *Parent Non-routine* and

Table 5.6 Comparing 1980 and 1989 lifestyle clusters

						Cluster Number						
	80 1	89 1	80 2	89 2	80 3	89 3	80 4	89 4	80 5	89 5	80 6	89 6
Activity Factors												
parent non-routine	+	+	+	(+)	−	−	−	(−)				+
parent routine		+	−	−		(+)		−	(+)	(+)	(−)	+
friend home		(+)	+	−	−	+					(+)	+
friend teen/out	+	(+)	(−)	−	+	+	(−)		(−)	(−)	(−)	+
TV talk/parent TV	+	(+)	+	(+)	−	−	−	(−)			+	+
sports/clubs	+	+	−	(+)	−	+				(−)	(+)	
siblings/hobby	−		−	−	+	+				(+)		+
Media Use												
TV	+	(−)	+	(+)	−	+	−	−		−	(+)	+
video	na	(−)	na	(+)	na	(+)	na	−	na	−	na	+
radio	+		+		−	+		−	(−)	−	(+)	
newspapers	+	+	−	−	−							
tabloids	na	+	na	−	na		na	−	na	−	na	+
books			+	−	−	+	−	+		−	(−)	(+)
weeklies	+			−	−	+		−	(+)	−	(−)	+
comics	+		+	−	−	−	(−)	−	(−)			+
music	(+)		−	−	+	+	(+)	−	−	−		+
films	+		−	−	(+)	+		−	−	−		

Note: + or − indicates a mean substantially above or below the grand-mean (usually the highest or lowest group). (+) or (−) indicates a mean moderately above or below the grand mean.

TV Talk while low on *Parent Routine* and *Friend Teen)* corresponded on five of the seven dimensions with the Unconnected, Video/Comics 1989 cluster (a larger group, but also mostly fifth grade and boys), although the 1989 group reversed the 1980 group on *Sports/Clubs* and *Friend Home* (where, we should note, the factor structure realigned somewhat). The two clusters were also quite similar in their media use: high on television and comics, low on newspapers, music and films, and differing only in books. Thus, this at-home, entertainment-oriented lifestyle of some younger boys appeared to continue in fairly stable fashion through the 1980s.

The Moderates, Magazines 1980 cluster (a large group of mixed age and gender, generally moderate on the circumplex but above average on *Parent Routine* and below average on *Friend Teen* and *Friend Home*) matched very well to the Moderates, Light Media 1989 cluster (also a large group, of mixed age and with more girls than boys). Besides the similarity in their circumplex activities, the two groups were also very similar in being light users of almost all media, so that this pattern also seemed to persist.

The 1980 Outgoing, Heavy Media cluster generally matched the circumplex variables of the 1989 Connected, Newspapers cluster: high *Parent Non-routine*, *Friend Teen/Out*, *TV Talk/Parent TV*, and *Sports/Clubs*, although in 1989 this cluster is also more involved in home-based activities with parents and peers than in 1980. However, despite the circumplex match, the two groups differ more in their media use than they are similar. They were both heavy newspaper users and moderate on books and music, but were opposite on television use. And while the 1980 group used a number of other media quite heavily, the 1989 cluster was only moderate. In addition, the 1980 group was mostly young boys, while the most comparable 1989 group was more than half ninth-graders and girls. All of the above suggests a shift between 1980 and 1989 in the meaning of this particular circumplex mix: despite considerable stability in the pattern of activities, in some sense it has migrated to be associated with a different mix of media use by people from different social positional categories.

Similarly, the 1980 cluster named Unconnected, Moderate Media was very similar in circumplex activities to the 1989 cluster named Low Parents, Books. Both were generally moderate on the circumplex factors, but below average on *Parent Non-routine* and *TV Talk/Parent TV*. However, the two clusters matched well on only two media use variables (low use of TV and comics), while they were opposite on two others (books and music). More to the point, the 1989 group were light users of all media except books, while the 1980 cluster was simply moderate. Both groups were older, but the 1980 group had slightly more girls and the 1989 group had a majority of boys. Thus, the pattern of being unconnected to parents and peers also seems to have shifted in its association with mass media.

The match between the TV Talk, Moderates group in 1980 (a moderate-sized group with a majority of young boys) and the Connected, Heavy Media group of 1989 (a small group composed mostly of younger girls) was fair in the circumplex variables. They were both moderately high in *Friend Home*, *TV Talk/Parent TV*, and *Sports/Club*, and both were moderate in *Siblings/Hobby*, but the groups were opposite on *Parent Routine* and *Friend Teen/Out*. The match between the two was also only fair on media use variables: high on TV use and moderate on radio, newspaper and films, but opposite on books and weeklies. Given the opposite directions on two circumplex factors and the different genders, we are inclined to see these two as different lifestyle combinations that merely happen to overlap on several measures, and not necessarily a continuing pattern.

Finally, the 1980 cluster named Teens, No TV (a small group with a majority of girls and mostly older) has some circumplex similarities to the 1989 cluster named Friends, Heavy Media (a small group mostly of older girls): both are low on *Parent Non-routine* and *TV Talk/Parent TV*, high on *Friend Teen/Out*, and moderate on *Parent Routine*, although they are opposite on *Friend Home* and *Sports/Clubs*. However, they were opposite on media use variables as often as they were similar: high on music and films, low on comics, and moderate on newspapers, but opposite on television, radio, books and weeklies. This suggests that the lifestyle of low involvement with parents for older girls was shifting to incorporate more television, radio, books and weeklies, to go along with its original emphasis on music and movies.

DISCUSSION

In pursuing both differences in adolescent lifestyle and a methodology conducive to their expression, our first goal was to achieve a better overall understanding of the circumplex of adolescent behaviours, and test the two-dimensional theoretical structure underlying it. Initially, our seven-factored analyses appeared to undercut the original conception. Besides being numerous, none of the factor dimensions crossed through the centre of the circumplex with corresponding negative loadings on the opposite side (in fact, the entire factor structure was conspicuous for the nearly-complete absence of negative loadings altogether). However, we think it would be manifestly unfair to conclude from these results that the original concept of the circumplex is not viable. Instead, our analyses provide an important elaboration.

Figures 5.2 and 5.3 summarize the 1980 and 1989 factor structures visually in a way that allows direct comparison to the original circumplex conceptions. Each concentric circle represents one of the seven factors, with the darkened portion of the arcs being items loading .40 or greater on that factor. Since the factors generally still occupy wedges of the original circle, it is more accurate to say that the factor structure relates well to the original two-dimensional theoretical conception, but that the factors are vectors of varying width rather than dimensions. In other words, the parent–friend and planned–unplanned dimensions are important organizing principles, but adolescents' behavioural activities are oriented toward sectors of the circumplex rather than toward the dimensions themselves. Furthermore, it seems reasonable to regard these orientations toward different sectors as relatively independent of each other, so that individuals may hold varying combinations of these orientations.

In particular, the two figures illustrate the centrality of the parent vs. friend distinction in adolescents' orientations, a distinction that became much clearer between 1980 and 1989. In 1980 there was overlap of parents and peers at both the top (organized, planned) and bottom (unplanned, spontaneous) of the circumplex, and several factors sprawled across quadrants and

Factors
1. Parent Non-Routine
2. Parent Routine
3. Friend Teen
4. Friend Home
5. TV Talk
6. Friends/Sports/Clubs
7. Sibling Sports

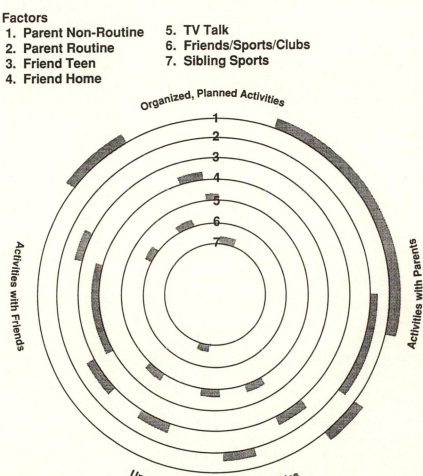

Figure 5.2 1980 factor structure of adolescent activities mapped onto the circumplex model

Factors
1. **Parent Non-Routine** 5. **Friend Out**
2. **Friend Home**   6. **Parent & TV**
3. **Sports/Clubs**   7. **Hobbies**
4. **Parent Routine**

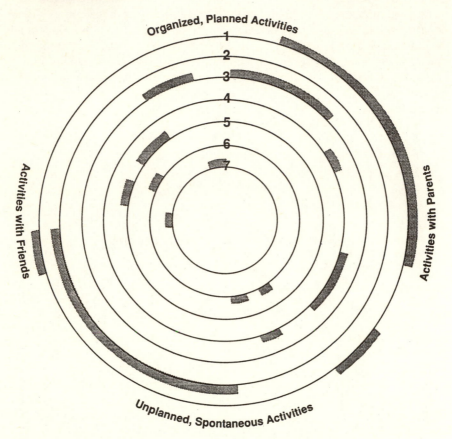

Figure 5.3 1989 factor structure of adolescent activities mapped onto the circumplex model

each other, leaving irregular gaps. By 1989 the overlap remained only in the realm of sports, clubs and spectatorship, and factors which generally combine contiguous items from the original circumplex.

Further focusing on the 1989 structure's better match to the circumplex, one can see that within the two domains of friends and parents, the original conception fares quite differently. For friends, the distinction between the few remaining planned activities (*Friend Out*) and the larger mass of less-organized, often home-bound activities (*Friend Home*) clearly is the vector analogue of the original dimensions. For parents, however, the organization of activities is much less clear. While the largest vector (*Parent Non-routine*) contains most of the activities planned or organized with parents, it also spreads well into the unplanned activities (doing lessons, cosy evening together), thus providing a very diffuse, unfocused orientation to parents. In addition, this dimension overlapped in one-third of its range with routine activities with parents, which in turn overlapped with the *Parent TV* dimension.

It is important to note that these overlaps do not result from individual activities loading simultaneously on two dimensions, but instead from a dimension skipping over some activities and including others farther around the circumplex. In other words, planned vs. spontaneous does not adequately capture the distinctions adolescents now make in their activities with their parents. We suspect, instead, that the 'non-routine' activities were generally pleasant and/or involving, while the 'routine' activities were also emotionally neutral and uninvolving.

These changes from 1980 to 1989 are also intriguing in suggesting cultural shifts that further distinguished home and peer environments. While this is purely speculation, it may be that in 1980 Swedish adolescents saw much more overlap between the worlds of home and friends than they did by 1989. This is not to say that they are spending more or less time with one than the other, simply that time spent with each has become distinct from and uncorrelated with time spent with the other. The one exception to this trend is the emergence of the Sports/Clubs vector of organized, planned activities spanning parents and friends.

The next step in our analyses was to attempt to locate patterns or styles in the way in which adolescents assemble these vectors of activities with their use of various mass media. Each of these resultant clusters suggests a different way to organize one's interaction with parents and friends, and each uses a certain mix of mass media. A wide variety of combinations were observed. Some patterns were characterized by heavy involvement with most aspects of peer and parent activities, while others were unconnected with any and yet others were moderate throughout. The activity factors were also independent in these clusters, in that about half the groups were more involved with some subpart than others (parents vs. peers, routine vs. non-routine, or content specific). Similarly, groups evidenced various combinations of media use and combinations of media use with the activity factors.

While variation in social structure was of course not available, several of these clusters seemed related to the social positional variables of gender and grade level, but other clusters were thoroughly mixed, and the clusters generally mixed social class (as measured by parental education), implying key contributions of the individuals themselves. Some of these clusters were quite stable from 1980 to 1989, but others changed considerably in how the circumplex activities mixed with use of mass media or shifted in their relation to social position characteristics. Explanations for this stability and change are necessarily speculation, but will need to take account of the changing media environment, Swedish and European cultural trends, generational changes in social relationships, and so on.

The limitations of this secondary analysis suggest some avenues for further research. As we see it, the main weakness is that we have based these factors and clusters purely on behaviour – frequency of activities with parents, peers and various mass media – without regard to the content and affective loading of those interactions. A key further step will be to add content to the purely behavioural measures used here. For one thing, as Johansson and Miegel (1992) suggest, these lifestyle clusterings should also be groupings of individuals who share values. The same should be true for media use gratifications. Furthermore, we constantly found ourselves tempted to explain media use patterns by referring to presumed patterns of content that may or may not have been present in the messages used. The nature of the content (genres, themes, expressed values) should be at least as important to lifestyle and should be more distinct in the styles than were the channels. Taking account of such variables should greatly sharpen the claim of this approach to tap lifestyles.

Beyond this, the next stage might well be to determine how much difference these lifestyles make. What are their consequences? Do they lend themselves to different media effects or different susceptibility to effects? Do they contain cognitive style differences as well, or different chances for social success? All these questions are equally legitimate and equally beckoning. But for the moment, the main lesson is that the conception of lifestyles as different approaches to the world can be matched with a methodology of differences as well, one that locates the differences in the phenomena themselves instead of in the social context alone.

REFERENCES

Dervin, B., Nilan, M. and Jacobson, T. (1982) 'Measuring aspects of information seeking: A test of a quantitative/qualitative methodology,' in M. Burgoon (ed.), *Communication Yearbook 6*, Newbury Park, Calif.: Sage.

Greenberg, B.S., Heeter, C. and Sipes, S. (1988) 'Viewing context and style with electronic assessment of viewing behaviour', in C. Heeter and B.S. Greenberg (eds), *Cableviewing*. Norwood, NJ: Ablex.

Johansson, T. and Miegel, F. (1992) *Do the Right Thing: Lifestyle and Identity in Contemporary Youth Culture*, Stockholm: Almqvist & Wiksell International.

Pingree, S., Hawkins, R.P., Rosengren, K.E., Johnsson-Smaragdi, U. and Reynolds, N. (1991) 'Television structures and adolescent viewing patterns: A Swedish–American comparison', *European Journal of Communication* 6: 417–440.

Rosengren, K.E. and Windahl, S. (1989) *Media Matter: TV Use in Childhood and Adolescence*, Norwood, NJ: Ablex.

Chapter 6

Models of change and stability in adolescents' media use

Ulla Johnsson-Smaragdi

STABILITY AND CHANGE

No doubt Sweden has changed during the last decade – fast, thoroughly and seemingly irrevocably. To varying degrees these changes affect many different sectors of society. One sector radically altered is the Swedish media scene. During the last decade a series of both powerful and attractive mass media have became available to the public at large. The VCR was introduced in the beginning of the 1980s; in the middle of the decade, satellite and cable television became increasingly diffused; the access to personal computers in the home has increased, as has also the number of games played on these computers or on TV and video – all of them quickly adopted, not least by families with children and adolescents. At the same time access to CD-players, personal stereos (Walkmans) and tape recorders has increased, especially among adolescents (see Chapter 2).

As a result of these processes, the entire range of mass media and mass media fare has been radically enlarged. There are now more options as to what and when to watch or listen, where to see/listen to it, together with whom and through which medium. Such changes in the media structure inevitably affect individual use of mass media. More than before individuals are now able to decide about their amount of use and to compose their own 'media menu' with their own preferences and likings. Individual media use has to be comprehended against the background of the media structure existing at a given point in time.

Regardless of what changes may be going on in this or that media structure, the period from childhood through adolescence into adulthood is generally turbulent. So much change occurs so fast in these years. Young people develop at a different pace along biological, cognitive, social and emotional dimensions. As a consequence, their use of, and their relations to, the media are also subject to continuous change.

Given the combination of a turbulent period of life at the micro level and a period of structural change at the macro level, will there be any persistent patterns of media use? In order to be stable over time and space, patterns of media use probably have to be firmly anchored in basic biological, psychological and social conditions. Variations in such patterns may depend on variation in structural conditions, for example, on the ever changing balance between family, peers, school and the mass media.

An important problem to be discussed in relation to stability and change is when something may be considered stable or changing. Stability and change are not to be regarded as fixed properties, but rather as a continuum with two opposite poles. If anything, stability and change are a matter of degrees – we are always more or less stable, more or less changing.

There are also different types of stability. Stability may be referred to in absolute or relative terms, at the individual or aggregate level, with reference to rank or structure. Usually we distinguish between four types of stability, namely, 'relative', 'level' and 'ipsative' stability, and 'structural invariance' (Mortimer *et al.* 1982: 266–270; cf. Johnsson-Smaragdi 1983: 84, 1992; Rosengren 1991: 54).

Relative stability is stability in individuals' ranks or differences with respect to a given phenomenon. It indicates that, in relation to other members of the group, individuals retain much the same position over time (e.g., with respect to amount of television viewing over time). *Level stability* is stability in the quantity of a phenomenon over time (e.g., quantity of television watched). *Ipsative stability* is stability in the ordering of attributes of an individual over time, examining the relative importance of, for example, various interests at different points in time. *Structural invariance*, finally, refers to the degree of continuity in the structure of the phenomenon under study. Structural invariance exists, for example, when there is a persistent pattern of relations, independently of time period and cohort.

Structural invariance may be expressed in *qualitative* terms (the overall structural pattern is the same) or in *quantitative* terms (the coefficients are of the same magnitude) (Rosengren 1991: 85). Both aspects are important when considering the stability of a structure, even if the former stands out as the most crucial criterion.

When analysing the stability or change of a certain phenomenon, access to data that permit both analyses over time and the opportunity to undertake replications is mandatory. Both cohort and panel data are required. A combination of cross-sectional and panel studies carried out in different locations admits phenomena to be compared over time and space – within, as well as between, panels and cohorts. Since panels admit coupling of data at the individual level, they admit strong causal modelling of causes and effects, including long-term effects. By comparing panels based on different cohorts, it is possible to study the structural stability and temporal invariance of longitudinal models. By comparing panels from different locations, it is possible to study invariance over space.

In all empirical research, the way concepts and variables are measured is, of course, of utmost importance. In longitudinal research this becomes even more crucial. A given concept must cover the same phenomena over time – even if the manifest indicators of a latent concept or variable sometimes have to be changed, for empirical, theoretical or methodological reasons.

MEDIA USE IN CHILDHOOD AND ADOLESCENCE

Young people are not born with an innate tendency to use media in certain ways. They are successively *socialized* to use the media as they do. The home environment – shaped by social class, parents' education, interaction and communication patterns in the family, attitudes towards, and use of, different media and by a host of other phenomena – influences media habits and media relations. Other, increasingly important socialization agents include peers, the school and the neighbourhood. Media habits are formed early in life, continue to develop and change throughout childhood and adolescence, but do not become established until later in life.

Within a given society, the amount of time spent by individual children and adolescents on television and other media differs widely, depending on a variety of background variables, as well as on social and individual characteristics and interests. Swedish children generally start watching television early in life. Already at the age of two, children show an interest in television. At the age of three they pay closer attention to the programmes, and many of these very young children have even become regular viewers. The hours spent in front of television gradually increase with age until late childhood. From this age on, the time devoted to television is again reduced, reaching a minimum during the middle and later teenage years. Instead, listening to music becomes ever more important (Rosengren and Windahl 1989: 23; Sonesson 1989: 50; Rosengren 1991: 55).

In the late 1980s, however, this general pattern seems to have become less pronounced, in that during late childhood and adolescence television viewing no longer decreases as flagrantly as before. Thanks to cable television, foreign satellite programmes are now accessible most of the day, featuring a content which is often very attractive to children and adolescents (Filipson and Rydin 1989; Höjerback 1990; see also Chapter 4 above). Children and adolescents turn to satellite television more than do other groups. This is so in Sweden, and probably in other countries as well (see, for example, Becker and Schoenbach 1989).

Simplified, it may still be said, however, that during the adolescent years there generally occurs a dramatic shift in media use. Adolescents tend to reorient their media use by reducing their use of mainly home-oriented media, like TV and books, while at the same time they tend to increase their use of more peer-oriented ones, like VCR and music.

While the specific ages at which the peak in viewing and the following decline is located may vary, a similar television viewing pattern may be found in many countries. This invariance in the viewing pattern of children and adolescents from various countries is found despite the fact that the overall level of television consumption varies a great deal, reflecting the amount of television output, the composition of the total media scene and – perhaps most importantly – subcultural values as well as the overall culture permeating society.

STABILITY IN MEDIA

In order fully to appreciate the ongoing change in individual media use among children and adolescents caused by changes in the overall media structure, it is necessary to have access to baseline data against which new tendencies may stand out as clearly as possible. It is also necessary to realize that individual change is not even and uniform, but rather characterized by a great deal of turbulence. There are 'sprinters' and 'laggards' among the adolescents, changing their media use faster or slower than the rest of the young audience.

If a group of adolescents continues to view about the same average amount of TV over a certain time period, its viewing is characterized by a high level of stability. Nothing is said about the relative stability, though. There may still be a lot of turbulence and change in viewing time by some individuals within the group – among these the laggards and sprinters are to be found. Whether the TV viewing is stable or changing in one or both of these aspects, the structural relations between viewing TV and using other media – or between TV viewing and other aspects of behaviour – may still be invariant, or they may be changing in qualitative as well as in quantitative terms. Level stability or level change, relative stability or relative change, structural invariance or structural change – the possible combinations are manifold.

Thus, behaviour may be stable or it may be changing with time. If changing, the process may be due to *age*, to *generation* or to *situation* (see Chapter 4). As discussed above, media use changes as small children become older and then grow into adolescents – an effect of age. This effect is best studied by means of longitudinal data covering individuals over an extended period of time. Likewise, the time period in which you are born, for example, if you are born in the early 1960s or in late 1970s, may affect the media behaviour. This generation or cohort effect is best studied by comparing the same age-groups belonging to cohorts born at disparate time periods. Finally, the historical context and media structure at a given time period may, of course, also influence how media is used – a situational effect. This effect is often hard to distinguish from the generation effect. It takes a combination of cross-sectional and panel studies to separate these two effects (see Chapter 4).

In the sections below we will successively analyse the different aspects of stability with reference to, above all, TV viewing, but also to some degree to music listening and VCR use among children, adolescents and young adults studied in the Media Panel Program (see Chapter 3).

Level stability

Figures 6.1–6.3 illustrate the stability and change in amount of TV viewing (not including VCR), music listening and VCR viewing for different cohorts and panels. The two former figures span a time period of some fifteen years, from the mid-1970s to the early 1990s, while the third figure covers the last eight years of this time period. The opportunity to follow the stability and change in media use at the aggregate level – including several panels based on different cohorts – during such an extended period of time is met with only seldom.

In Figures 6.1 and 6.2 we may study level stability in at least two respects, namely, by comparing stability for different age-groups *within the same panels (cohorts)* and by comparing stability for the same age-groups *belonging to different panels (cohorts)*. By comparing within panels we may study how the use of a medium increases or decreases with age, here from childhood through adolescence to adulthood. By comparing specific age-groups we may instead study how the use of a medium changes with the time period. Thus, we may compare 15-year-old adolescents in 1976 with those of the same age in 1984 or 1989. Furthermore, it is possible to compare

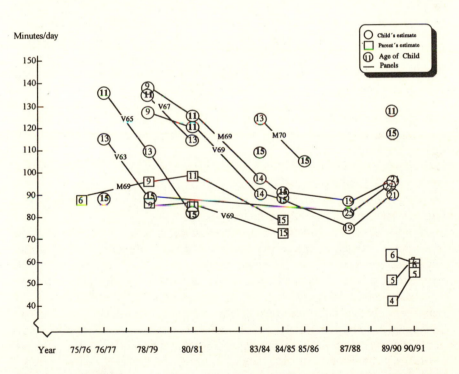

Figure 6.1 Stability and change in amount of TV consumption, 1975–1991 (means)

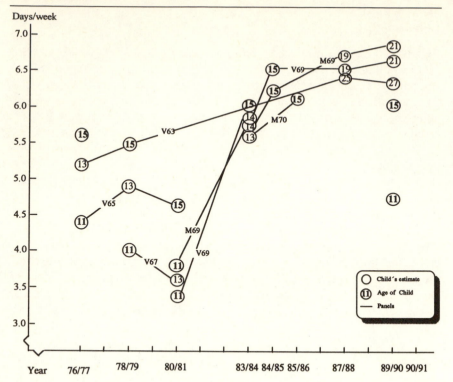

Figure 6.2 Stability and change in amount of music consumption, 1976–1990 (means)

also the slope of the curves formed by the different panels. Does media consumption in the different panels develop similarly, making the curves take on the same general form?

The overall impression conveyed by a first review of Figures 6.1 and 6.2 is that level stability seems to be low, in the quantity of both television watched and music listened to. But is the level stability equally low both within panels and between specific age-groups?

Comparing *within* panels, we find considerable level *instability* both in television viewing and music listening: television viewing decreases, while music listening increases. When approaching adulthood this general trend seems to be broken. Around the age of 20, television viewing slowly begins to increase again, while music listening more or less tends to stabilize. This may be referred to as an age effect. (We may note here that music consumption is rather crudely measured, as the habit of listening to music in number of days per week – the only comparable measure available over the period of some fifteen years.)

There are results suggesting that from the middle of the 1980s the reduction in television viewing was less pronounced than in the beginning of the decade

(Höjerback 1990; see Chapter 4). If this is the case it ought to be evident from the slope of the curves formed by the panels. By comparing the two earlier panels (V63 and V65) with the two latter (V69 and M69), indications of this might be found. The slopes (that is, the decrease) have indeed become less pronounced in later years. There is thus a trend towards a somewhat higher overall level stability in viewing by age, which may be due either to a situational or a generational effect. This is the combined result of a lower viewing level among the 11 year olds in 1980 than in 1976, and a higher viewing level among the 15 year olds in 1985 than in 1980.

As for music listening there seems to be indications of the reversed tendency, that is, the increase in listening with age has become more pronounced in later years. However, there are several problems in comparing music listening over time as evident from Figure 6.2. For instance, music listening in 1980/81 stands out as something fairly apart. It is an effect of the situation at this concrete time period (Burnett 1990: 135), an effect impossible to detect without access to a combined cross-sectional and longitudinal design. Still, it is possible to compare the increase in amount of listening between 13 and 15 years of age in the panel of V63, with the same ages in the panel of M70 and also with the increase between 14 and 15 years in the panels of V69 and M69. It indicates that the increase in music listening during adolescence was more pronounced in the middle of the 1980s than it was in the late 1970s.

From comparing within and between panels we now shift instead to comparisons *between cohorts*, or specific age-groups. We have access to several cohorts made up of 11- and 15-year-old adolescents, which we may compare with respect to their viewing and listening levels over the time period of some fifteen years covered by our data.

The 11 year olds are the most keen television viewers, and, according to their own estimates, this age-group is marked with considerable *level stability*. They view about as much television in 1989 as they did 1980 and 1976. There is only a slight decrease visible in their viewing level over this approximately fifteen-year time period. However, the expansion of television output has obviously been followed by an increase in consumption among the 15-year-old adolescents. Cable television is now available to the greater part of the population, providing expanded channel and programme options. Among adolescents, music video programmes are especially popular. This increase in viewing began in the middle of the 1980s, but is obvious until the end of the decade. It results in a *lower* level stability for television viewing in this age group. Also music listening has increased during the time period of study among both 11 and 15 year olds. The increase in listening is less marked than for television viewing, but clearly noticeable.

Figure 6.3 shows amount of VCR viewing. In Sweden the medium began its diffusion in the early 1980s, and it was rapidly diffused to a fairly large segment of the population, especially to families with children and adolescents. By 1984, 36 per cent of these households had access to a VCR. Large

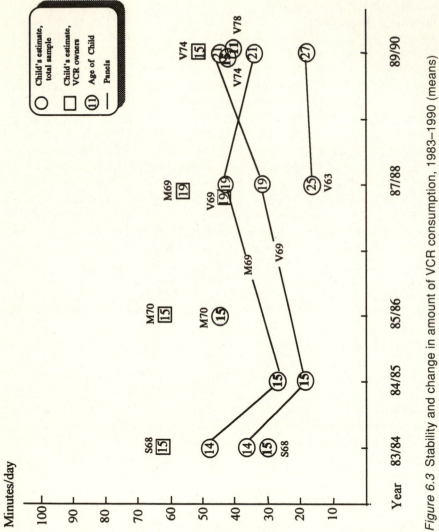

Minutes/day

Child's estimate,
total sample ○

Child's estimate,
VCR owners □

Age of Child ⑪

Panels —

Year 83/84 84/85 85/86 87/88 89/90

Figure 6.3 Stability and change in amount of VCR consumption, 1983–1990 (means)

geographical variations in access existed, however, especially between large cities and small towns or rural areas. In Malmö, for example, 45 per cent of households with children owned a VCR at this point in time, compared to 30 per cent in more rural areas. In 1989, VCR ownership in Malmö had risen to about 75 per cent of households with adolescents.

Stability in VCR use during this period is very difficult to discern, as the medium was rapidly diffusing among the population. This is true especially for comparisons within panels. We had better stay content to compare VCR use in specific age-groups within different cohorts. Best suited for such a comparison are the 15 year olds, since for this age-group we have measurements from both the middle and the end of the 1980s. Among the total sample, containing both VCR owners and non-owners, VCR use has increased slightly during the period, from about half an hour a day to about three-quarters of an hour. But this increase among the total sample also mirrors the increase in ownership. Let us compare this with VCR use among VCR owners only. We then notice that the use in the ownership group has actually declined. This indicates that the early owners were also the more interested ones and consequently used the medium to a larger extent. In 1989, when about 75 per cent of the households with children had a VCR in their home, there are also less interested viewers among this group, and more irregular viewers.

Relative stability

Relative stability shows the individual's stability in his/her position within a given group. If the whole group is changing uniformly, with little fluctuation in the relative positions of group members, relative stability is said to be high. (Nothing is said about the amount of level change, however.)

Which degree of relative stability could we expect? It is to be remembered that in general, adolescence is a period of great changes, in physical, biological, social, emotional and cognitive terms. All these changes in interests, preferences and activities occur with differential pace within individuals as well as between individuals (Stattin and Magnusson 1990: 7 ff.; Rosengren 1991: 61). Low relative stability in television viewing indicates that individuals are not always found where they were left, that is, on either a high or low viewing level relative to the age-group.

Relative stability in TV use

The amount of television viewing changes with age. Starting from nothing, it increases from infancy to late childhood, when it tends to stabilize for a longer or shorter period of time. In adolescence a decrease in viewing tends to occur – a decrease that only some years ago was fairly drastic, but now is considerably less pronounced – only to be followed by another increase somewhat later in young adulthood. It thus seems more relevant to refer to change rather than to stability in viewing levels during this period of life.

However, there are substantial individual differences in amount of viewing. Some are regular viewers; others are more sporadic in their viewing. Some view quite a lot; others, considerably less. Such differences may be established by analysing subgroups of children and adolescents.

A quite different but related question is whether individuals tend to retain their relative positions as high, low or average viewers during their life course, or do they, in relative terms, sometimes tend to be low and perhaps irregular viewers, while at other times in life they tend to be regular high-consumers? To what extent is there individual 'mobility' in relative amount of TV viewing? (Note that lack of relative stability is not necessarily due to either a general reduction or to an increase in viewing time.) In order to analyse stability at the individual level, access to longitudinal data is necessary.

Which degree of relative stability could we expect? In late childhood and early adolescence great changes occur in many different areas, both physical, biological, social, emotional and cognitive. Changes in interests, preferences and activities occur with differential pace within individuals as well as between individuals. Consequently, the relative stability in television viewing could be expected to be fairly low, and especially low in the early teens, when biological development is very fast.

The existence, or non-existence, of individual stability in media use is important in relation to possible effects and consequences of that use. If the stability is low, the effects are likely to be reduced. An important question, then, is this: what is the amount of relative stability? There are many ways to answer that question. Three such ways will be presented here, each method looking at the individual stability from different points of view and with shifting degrees of abstraction:

1 Plot diagrams, showing an individual's position related to two points in time and relative to the positions of all other individuals.
2 Split the cohort and then study the transition frequencies between high and low TV consumption.
3 Longitudinal LISREL models.

Let's start with the most obvious method.

In order to analyse relative stability at the individual level, viewing at age 11 has been related to that at age 15, and viewing at age 15 to viewing at age 21. In figures 6.4 and 6.5 the relationship between TV viewing time at different ages is illustrated. Changes occurring in an individual's relative position are revealed by this analysis. The medians are marked by thicker lines in order to facilitate the interpretation. Likewise, the regression lines have been included in the plots.

By and large the diagrams in the two cohorts give the same general picture – one of great variation and dispersion. This is more true in the first diagrams

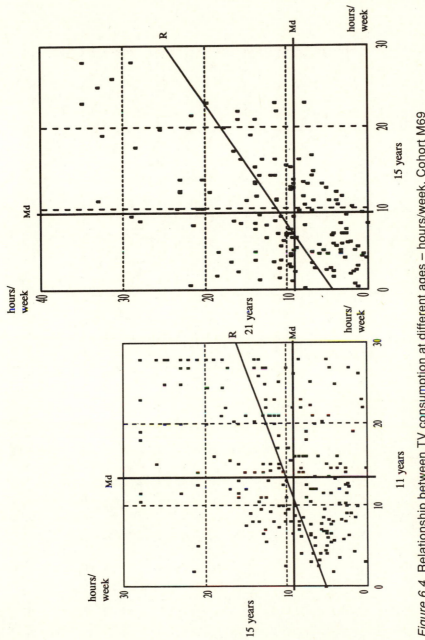

Figure 6.4 Relationship between TV consumption at different ages – hours/week. Cohort M69
(Md = median, R = line of regression)

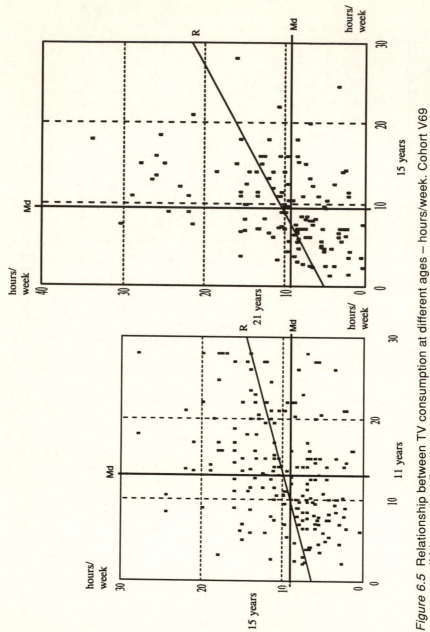

Figure 6.5 Relationship between TV consumption at different ages – hours/week. Cohort V69
(Md = median, R = line of regression)

and less so in the latter. Individuals are less dispersed in the M69 cohort (Figure 6.4) than in the cohort of V69 (Figure 6.5), and less when they are older than when they are younger. In both cohorts the main part of the adolescents in the second diagram are concentrated towards the bottom left. This is shown by the median, which divides the scale within one-third or one-fourth of the total range at ages 15 and 21, respectively.

There is a slight tendency towards a band running from the bottom left to the top right, though, a pattern showing that as one variable increases, so tends the other one to do so. The correlations between TV viewing at different ages in the two cohorts are shown in Table 6.1.

Table 6.1 Correlations between TV viewing at different ages in two cohorts (zero-order correlations)

Age	Cohort M69		Cohort V69	
	11 years	*15 years*	*11 years*	*15 years*
15 years	.42		.34	
21 years	.28	.54	.40	.40

It is obvious that there is a substantial number of individuals who have changed their viewing considerably from ages 11 to 15 and from ages 15 to 21. Some have increased their viewing above average, others have decreased it. Children *increasing* their viewing as they enter adolescence certainly go against the stream. They are not just 'laggards', i.e. late or slow changers; they are more 'obstinates'. They are to be found above the diagonal, that is in the upper left part of the diagrams. Maybe these are the adolescents who have turned to satellite and cable TV, there finding programmes more suited to them. Children and adolescents *decreasing* their viewing more than the average may be the 'sprinters', but the term could then represent at least two different categories within this group.

In the first place, it could stand for those children who have decreased their viewing above average; for those who in some sense exaggerate the decreasing trend and, thus, travel farther in changing their relative position. They would be found well below the diagonal, in the bottom right. This group is the first that comes to mind when talking about 'sprinters'. There may well be another kind of 'sprinters', however, those who begin to change their viewing before the rest of the group, at an earlier age. In this sense of the word, the 'sprinters' would be the forerunners, the leaders, of all change or trends – be it increasing or decreasing trends.

There are also stable viewers. If stable in relative terms they go with the stream – decreasing their viewing at an average rate, thus preserving their relative position within the group as expressed by the line of regression. They are 'mainstreamers'. Others may be stable in absolute terms, not changing the amount of time devoted to TV viewing. These children would centre around the diagonal in Figures 6.4 and 6.5, unmoved by maturational trends or by changes in the media structure. Those children are really stable.

As we have seen in Figures 6.4 and 6.5 most youngsters are not high or low television viewers all the time. On the contrary, there is a good deal of individual change and mobility. This individual mobility in TV viewing time is summarized by the data in Figures 6.6 and 6.7. The individual stability has now been expressed in terms of transition frequencies between high and low TV consumption – 'high' and 'low' being defined in relative terms, as below or above the median, so that the age-related, overall ups and downs of average consumption has been controlled for. These figures demonstrate where those who at 11 years of age were classified as 'heavy' and 'light' viewers, were to be found four and nine years later. Figures on the arrows denote transition proportions; figures in the boxes, proportions of the total number originally classified as heavy or light viewers remaining in the same category or moving between categories from 11 to 15 to 21 years of age. The proportions are calculated on those remaining in the sample at each age.

The close resemblance of the transition figures is striking. At the age of 16, about two-thirds of the adolescents in both cohorts still remain in the

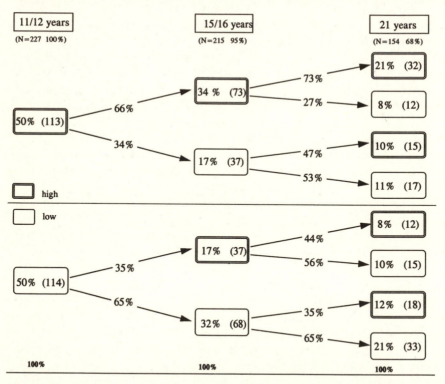

Figure 6.6 Stability and change in TV viewing over time – transition frequencies. Cohort M69 (median split of age groups)

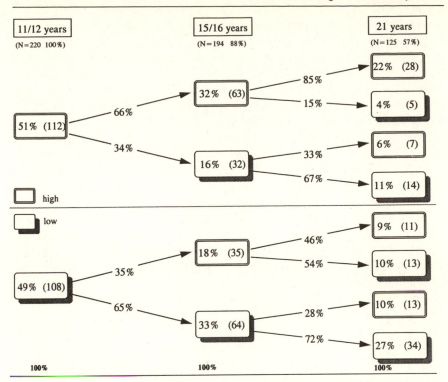

11/12 years
(N=220 100%)

15/16 years
(N=194 88%)

21 years
(N=125 57%)

51% (112)

66%
34%

32% (63)
16% (32)

85%
15%
33%
67%

22% (28)
4% (5)
6% (7)
11% (14)

☐ high
☐ low

49% (108)

35%
65%

18% (35)
33% (64)

46%
54%
28%
72%

9% (11)
10% (13)
10% (13)
27% (34)

100%   100%   100%

Figure 6.7 Stability and change in TV viewing over time – transition
frequencies. Cohort V69 (median split of age groups)

category into which they were classified four years earlier – regardless
of whether they were once classified as high or low viewers. Of these, about
two-thirds continue to be in their original category even at 21 years of age.
About one-third of the adolescents change category, some between 11 and
16 years, others between 16 and 21 years of age. Some change for good,
others change back and forth between the two categories.

Now, looking at the percentage of adolescents remaining in their original
category, we find that from 50 per cent of high and low viewers, respectively,
after four years this share has decreased to about 33 per cent, and after five
more years the share is 20–25 per cent. The decrease, as well as the share of
adolescents remaining constant, is remarkably similar in the two cohorts,
both for high and low viewers. However, there is a somewhat different picture
if we look at the adolescents that at 21 years of age remain in the same
category as that into which they were originally classified at the age of 11
(V69: 22+6+10+27=65 per cent and M69: 21+10+10+21=62 per cent). These
adolescents are to be considered as the 'stable' viewers – stable in the sense
that they remain in, or return to, the same viewer category over the years.

Some adolescents, changing between the high/low categories as shown in the 'transition figures', were found to be very close to the median splitting the cohorts (see Figures 6.4 and 6.5). Some of these have in relative terms been classified as low at one point in time and as high at another, and vice versa. Thus, there may seem to be more change than there really is. This problem may be handled by further summarizing the amount of change and stability in adolescents' TV viewing by expressing relative stability by means of coefficients in longitudinal structural models.

In a longitudinal model it is possible to establish the longitudinal causal influence of a variable on itself. The level of relative stability in media use may thus be studied in the structural part of a LISREL model. The level of relative stability is expressed in quantitative terms, summarized by the magnitude of the coefficients attached to the arrows linking television viewing at different points in time. In Figures 6.8 and 6.9, the relative stability in TV viewing over twelve years, from the age of 9 to 21, is analysed with longitudinal data from two equally aged cohorts in two different towns in southern Sweden.

Amount of television consumption between the ages of 9 and 15 years was measured by means of six questions tapping the weekly amount of broadcast and cable television (but not VCR) viewing (number of days and hours per day on weekdays (Mon.-Fri.), Saturdays and Sundays). At 19 and 21 years of age, television consumption was measured by means of eight questions, as Friday evenings had been separated from the weekday measure and separate questions had been asked. On the basis of these six or eight questions two indices have been built, one for weekdays and one for weekends, which make up the manifest indicators (WD;WE) of the latent variable, that is, weekly TV viewing. (For a detailed discussion of these manifest indicators, see Johnsson-Smaragdi 1992.)

Gender and social background are background variables in the model (the latter being measured by an index (low–high) combining father's and mother's occupational status). The relative stability in TV consumption is thus controlled by these variables, thereby eliminating their effect on the coefficients of stability. However, we may still study the influence of these background variables on amount of TV viewing. The LISREL models show that both gender and social background directly influence the amount of TV viewing. Boys are generally viewing more television than girls, as are also children from homes characterized by a relatively low social background.

In the LISREL models in Figures 6.8 and 6.9 the stability coefficients fluctuate between .29 and .79. The degree of relative stability is, of course, dependent on the time elapsed between the measurements. The shorter the period, the higher the stability as indicated by the LISREL coefficients. By examining the total effects of TV viewing on itself over time – stripped of influences from background variables – it is possible to establish the more long-term stability in viewing. Overall the total effects (Table 6.2) indicate

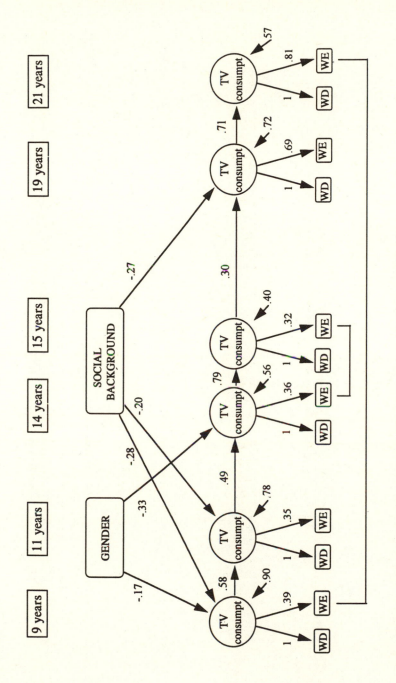

9 years | 11 years | 14 years | 15 years | 19 years | 21 years

N=142-252 DF=66 X2=76 Prob.=.20 GFI=.95 AGFI=.91 RMR=5.0 Coeff. of determ.=.34

Figure 6.8 LISREL model of stability and change in TV consumption between ages 9 and 21. Cohort M69 (only statistically significant paths are presented)

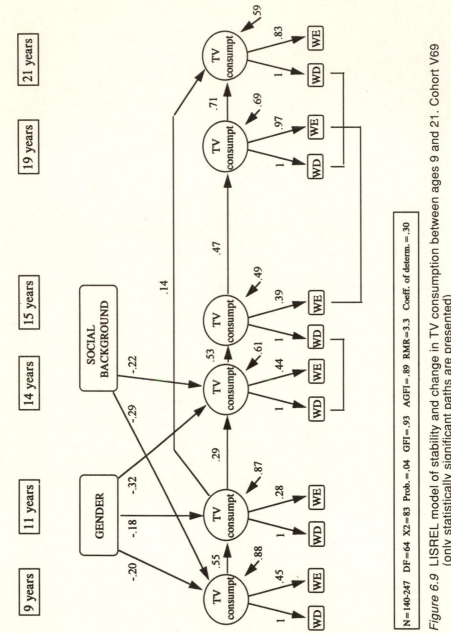

N=140-247 DF=64 X2=83 Prob.=.04 GFI=.93 AGFI=.89 RMR=3.3 Coeff. of determ. =.30

Figure 6.9 LISREL model of stability and change in TV consumption between ages 9 and 21. Cohort V69 (only statistically significant paths are presented)

that, relatively speaking, there is more change than stability in TV viewing. Over time the stability coefficients turn out to be fairly weak. Comparing cohorts M69 and V69 we may note that stability in viewing is somewhat higher in the former cohort than in the latter, especially in childhood and early adolescence. The long-term influence from early viewing on later viewing in early adulthood is, however, stronger in cohort V69.

Table 6.2 Total effects from earlier TV viewing on later viewing in two cohorts (LISREL coefficients)

Age	Cohort M69					Cohort V69				
	9	11	14	15	19	9	11	14	15	19
11 years	.58					.55				
14 years	.28	.49				.16	.29			
15 years	.22	.39	.79			.09	.15	.53		
19 years	.07	.12	.24	.30		.04	.07	.25	.47	
21 years	.05	.08	.17	.21	.71	.11	.19	.18	.33	.71

The relative stability in TV viewing may be compared with the relative stability in, for example, school grades. In cohort V69 the stability in TV viewing between ages 14 and 15 years (as measured by zero-order correlations) was .60 and in school grades .94, while in cohort M69 it was .68 as compared to .92 in school grades. Behind the less than perfect stability coefficients of the structural LISREL models lies the fact that not all youngsters remain in the same category of consumption – they are not high or low TV viewers all the time.

Despite this, individual TV viewing tends to be somewhat more stable in the beginning and in the end of the period studied – that is, in childhood and in young adulthood, respectively – than it is during adolescence. Comparing the two periods with equal intervals between measurements, the relative viewing level turns out to be most stable at the end of the age period, that is, between 19 and 21 years of age. This is only to be expected, both considering the fact that many habits are not really established before adulthood, and the fact that the most turbulent teenage period has now passed. The proportion of unexplained variance in TV viewing at the age of 21 is .59 and .57, respectively, indicating that between them, the three variables of earlier TV viewing, gender and social background are able to explain no less than about half the variation in TV viewing at this age.

Hitherto the analyses have mainly been preoccupied with different aspects of stability in one medium at a time. We have seen that the use made of a medium fluctuates both with increasing age and over historical time. Both stability and change were present in different aspects to different degrees under different circumstances. But nothing has yet been said as to how the use made of various media is structured. It is now time to turn to analyses including several media at a time in order to examine the structural stability of media relations.

Structural stability

During the last decade the Swedish media scene has experienced a period of thoroughgoing structural change, a change that has concerned the type of media available to the public as well as the media fare and options offered to that public (see Chapters 2 and 4). Inevitably, structural changes will affect individual media use – in the short as well as in the long run – and it will affect children and adolescents more than adults. In this perspective it is necessary to ask to what degree invariance in structural relations over time and space will exist in an ever-changing society.

Each pair of media may be functionally different or functionally equivalent (Adoni 1985; Johnsson-Smaragdi 1986). In the former case one medium cannot easily be replaced with another; in the latter, the media may be interchanged and substituted for each other. In this case one of the media may even tend to become more or less superfluous, in society as a whole or for specific groups within that society. Among the functions for individuals commonly ascribed to the media are cognitive, emotional, escapist and social functions. Any medium, of course, may fulfil more than one function.

Media use may be viewed as a form of adaptive behaviour. In adolescence, with its turbulence and rapid development, a reorganization process takes place in media use. This process may be explained by adolescents' biological, cognitive, social and emotional development calling forward new needs and requirements. These requirements, ranging from occasional to ever-present, the adolescents try to satisfy in different ways, including media use. In this context it becomes important to have control both over the medium and over the selection of its content, as well as access to suitable content (Brown *et al.* 1974; Brown 1976; see also Chapter 4).

The changes in the media scene have made possible an increased individual control over media and their use, not least through the new media and distribution forms on the market, offering a new kind of content more suitable to the adolescent public. As a consequence, adolescent use of various media has been subject to change and reorganization.

Structure of media consumption

A reorganization of media use in adolescence may thus be due to two different forces at work: a developmental process in adolescence at the individual level, and a societal process altering the media structure at the macro level and, thus, the relations between different media and the options available to the public. A reorganized media use depending on such structural changes could best be traced by comparing same-aged cohorts located at different points in time, for instance before the change process, in the beginning of it and when it is well under way. The alteration, or invariance, of the structural relationships between various media are graphically presented in Figure 6.10. Structural relations between six to seven media in four separate cohorts from the same place at different points in time dispersed over a fifteen-year period are analysed by means of zero-order and partial correlations. Two of the observation points are situated before the change in the media structure began in the early 1980s and two after the change process was initiated.

In the first two cohorts (V61 and V65), measured in 1976 and 1980, respectively, the structural relations between six media – TV, cinema, radio, music, comics and books – are studied. The VCR was not yet introduced. In the V69 cohort another medium, comics, is missing due to the absence of any questions about their use. The VCR had its market take-off during the years 1981–83. In 1984 more than a third of the adolescents had a VCR in their home, and many more had the opportunity to use a VCR together with their peers. In 1989 the proportion of adolescents with home access to a VCR had risen to about three-quarters. In the meantime, the TV medium itself had also changed. By the advent of cable and satellite TV the media fare and programme options had been radically enlarged, and adolescents often had started turning to these new programme options, at the expense of the old national channels. These, in their turn, also had to accommodate to the new media situation by altering their programme policy.

A first grasp of the relations between the various media may be found from studying the correlations in the four cohorts. Are there any invariant relations between the media or are they changing and reorganized during the course of the decade? The *first* observation is that of the number of correlations possible (between 15 and 21 in each cohort) about one-third turn out to be significant at least at the .01 level. The *second* observation is that although the correlations shown between the media are significant, most of them are relatively weak. A *third* fact worth noticing is that the majority of the correlations between the media are positive, that is, use of one medium is accompanied by use of others as well. The only negative relations found are between reading books and watching TV in two of the cohorts and between books and cinema-going in 1976 (V61).

Relations may be invariant in quantitative terms (the coefficients are of the same magnitude) and/or in qualitative terms (the patterns of structural relations are the same). Both aspects are important when considering stability, even if the latter stands out as most crucial (Rosengren 1991: 85).

Are there any signs of invariance or are the relations between the various media during the fifteen-year period studied rather characterized by change? First, in qualitative terms the relations seem to be marked more by change than by stability. Only one relation is found to be invariant over time, namely, that between music listening and going to the cinema. This relation is stronger

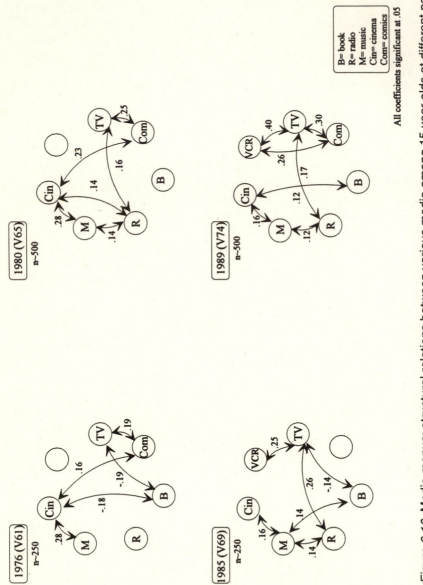

Figure 6.10 Media menus: structural relations between various media among 15 year olds at different points in time between 1976 and 1989 (zero order correlations)

at the first two points in time (.28) than in the later two (.16). This structural relation does not disappear or change in magnitude even after controlling for the influence of gender and social background by means of partial correlation.

Three other relations are found invariant in three out of four cohorts, namely, those between music and radio listening (.14, .14, .12), between radio and TV (.16, .26, .17) and between TV and reading comics (.19, .25, .30). Quantitatively, these structural relations thus seem to be fairly stable. It may be noted, though, that the relation between TV and reading comics grows stronger over time. The first two of these relations withstand the control of influences from the background variables both qualitatively and quantitatively. However, the relationship between TV viewing and reading comics is partially due to the influence of the background variables. When this influence is controlled for by means of partial correlations, the relationship disappears in the first cohort and diminishes in magnitude in the two others, from .25 and .30 down to .19 and .22, respectively.

VCR and TV viewing are also strongly related and this grows stronger with time (.25 and .40 in 1985 and 1989, respectively). This change may be due to the rapidly growing access to VCRs among the adolescents or to a real change in their use and significance, the two media being increasingly intertwined, or to both of these factors. The corresponding partial correlations are, in this case, .15 and .36.

Most of the media analysed seem to contribute to the structuring of media use, and they also seem to be used in an inclusive way, that is, the more of one, the more of other media. Sometimes book reading makes an exception to this. In 1976, reading of books is negatively related to both TV viewing and cinema going. Also in 1985, the relation between TV and books is negative, while in 1980 and 1989 there is no relation between these two media. However, the negative relation between books and cinema in 1976 has changed to a positive relation in 1989. These relations are, however, strongly dependent on gender and social class. Looking at the partial correlations, the relationships between books and other media disappear, with one exception – the relation between TV and books in 1985 that does not change at all.

There has been a structural change or reorganization, in that the VCR has found its place among the other media. In 1989 there are fairly strong relations between the use of TV, VCR and comics. These media all rely on the image of pictures. In comparison with the situation in the 1970s and the beginning of the 1980s, the role of TV also seems to have become more important with time. Cable and satellite TV, as well as changes within the old TV medium, have had an impact on the adolescent use. While the VCR may have found its place within the structure of young people's media use, cinema may well be on its way out. Whether adolescents attend cinemas or not has more or less become unrelated to their use of other kinds of mass media. The last pertains also to books – reading has relatively little to do with use of other media. This fact becomes even more obvious when analysing the partial correlations that control for the influence of gender and social background.

A fact worth noting is that rather few structural relations are found to remain invariant over time. This is probably due not only to structural changes in the media world; the pattern of relationships is not changing consistently enough. Rather, it points to the importance of not putting too much emphasis on a single analysis or study, but instead to make frequent comparisons and replications, between studies as well as over time.

If individual development during adolescence results in a reorganized media use this could best be traced by longitudinal analyses following the same adolescent cohorts during an extended period of time. Such an analysis is graphically presented in Figure 6.11, showing the structural relations between various media (cross-sectionally and longitudinally) in a cohort of adolescents, following them from age 11 in 1980 until 21 years of age in 1990. In this longitudinal analysis the two cohorts V69 and M69 have been joined together to ensure a sample sufficiently large for this type of analysis.

Looking first at the structural relations cross-sectionally the dominant impression is change. Not one single structural relation between the various media endures over the full time period covered. The pattern of relations changes completely from childhood to young adulthood. The relations existing in adolescence, however, remain the same in young adulthood, qualitatively and mainly also quantitatively. At 11 years of age there are many simultaneous structural relations and an inclusive media use seems to exist. At the age of 21 there are about as many relations, but the pattern is hardly an inclusive one. At 15 years of age, in the middle of adolescence, there are considerably fewer relations between the different media; of those existing, two are negative.

At 11 years of age all media included – with the exception of books – have positive relations to each of the other media. Book reading, on the other hand, is mostly unrelated – children at this age read equally much or equally little independently of their use of other media. The only exception to this is a negative relation between the reading of books and of comics. Books continue to be either unrelated or negatively related to other media at an older age, but now the negative relations are those between reading books and watching TV or VCR. All these negative relationships in childhood and adolescence are partly due to differences between gender and in social background, causing a differential media use (see Rosengren 1991). When analysing the partial correlations, controlling for these background factors, the negative relationships between books and the other media disappear at these early ages, but remain unaffected, though somewhat lowered, at 21 years of age. The habit of use, developed during childhood and adolescence, seems to have become established.

Another pattern is found in the case of comics and music. The role of these

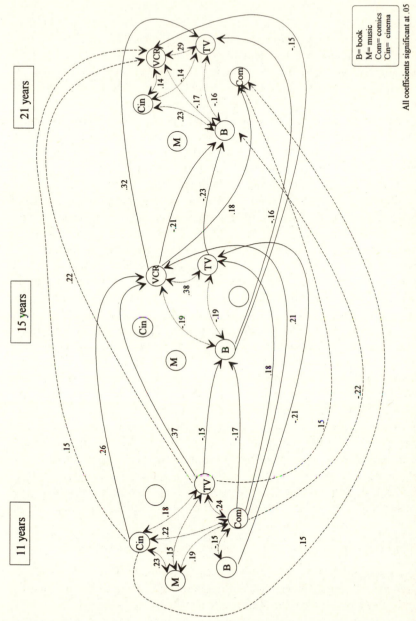

11 years | 15 years | 21 years

B= book
M= music
Com= comics
Cin= cinema

All coefficients significant at .05

Figure 6.11 Relationships between use of various mass media – simultaneously and over time. Cohort VM69
(Zero order correlations)

two media in the lives of adolescents has also changed. At the age of 11, children who read comics and listen to music also use other media more than do other children. Ten years later there is no relation whatsoever between reading comics or listening to music and use of other media. This fact strengthens the reorganization hypothesis. Reading comics seems to have become independent of the extent to which other media are used. As for music, there is no longer any variation in the variable and, hence, no correlation possible. Everybody listens to music just about equally much (in this case, partly an effect of our crude instrument of measurement).

As mentioned above, in childhood and adolescence book reading was either unrelated or negatively related to the amount of consumption of most other media. But reading books and cinema-going correlate positively in young adulthood – as they also did among the 15 year olds in 1989 (cohort V74; see Figure 6.10). We can only speculate about the kinds of books read and the kinds of cinemas attended – whether intellectual or more escapist functions (or both) are satisfied. The role of the cinema seems also to have changed over the years. This change may depend on individual development, or on the restructuring of the media society, or on a combination of these factors.

There are several longitudinal relations between the media, especially from the age of 11 and onwards. In general, those longitudinal relations are low but positive – except when books are involved. Relations between books and any other media are all negative over time – independently of whether use of books comes before or after use of other media. Thus, reading books at age 11 means less television viewing at age 15 and less television viewing at age 15 means more book reading at age 21. Conversely, those adolescents viewing a lot of television – and using the VCR more – at the age of 15 also read fewer books when they are 21 years. Books, then, may well represent a strong fortress against the tidal wave of popular media culture!

TV viewing and cinema going at the age of 11 promote the use of VCR later in life. Those who read comics in childhood also view more television and VCR in adolescence, and they read fewer books when grown up. Both the simultaneous and the longitudinal relationships indicate a reorganization of the media use. Some of the reorganization seems to be due to the changing media structure, some to individual development from childhood to adulthood.

Learning media habits: structure of parent–child interaction

Children do not learn to use media in a social vacuum. Those closest to the children set the terms for their media use, influencing the child in a number of subtle ways, making media use more or less tempting. The child, in its turn, decides – deliberately or not – how to use the media and to sort out which medium to use – when, how, and for what purpose. As time goes by and the interaction goes on, this process is constantly being shaped and reshaped, actions and reactions being successively modified. The socialization process is thus complex and subtle, and it affects every aspect of life. It is actually not one process, but many. In addition, the different processes are mutually interdependent in a complex pattern of interaction.

Several social learning mechanisms may transmit parental values and patterns of behaviour to children. Throughout childhood and early adolescence, the family is expected to play a decisive role in shaping the attitudes and habits of the children. Learning processes of special relevance to media use are modelling, reinforcement and social interaction. All families draw more or less consciously on these processes in bringing up their children. To a varying degree, each of these processes is supposed to play its decisive role in shaping media habits.

Within the family the ever-ongoing processes of interaction and communication between parents and children are assumed to be of great importance for children's television habits. Parents' positive and negative emotions towards diverse phenomena are noticed by the child. In this way parental attitudes may be powerful in shaping children's attitudes. The processes are, of course, complex, subtle, and difficult to define precisely.

The term 'reinforcement' refers to parents' use of rewards and punishments, of approval and disapproval, in order to shape their child's attitudes on many issues, and to make it behave in a certain way. In relation to television viewing, for example, parents may stimulate their children's viewing of certain programmes, while disapproving or restraining their viewing of other programmes. Children become conscious of their parents' opinion of television and its content, an opinion that may be transferred to, and eventually more or less taken over by, the child.

The concept of modelling refers to learning by observation. Modelling means that the child consciously or unconsciously imitates, and perhaps identifies with, another person's behaviour and actions. Bandura (see, for example, Bandura and Walters 1963; Bandura 1969) was among the first to state that children *learn* their personality through experience and through interacting with family and peers within the framework of a given culture or sub-culture. Modelling has a unique role to play in social development during childhood. The most effective way to teach new ways of acting and their consequences to a child is to show the behaviour requested to the child. Modelling means that the child tends to behave as the parents behave. Even when parents do not try to influence their children's behaviour, they may be setting examples which the child will later on imitate. For instance, if parents view a lot of television, the child also tends to view quite a lot. Modelling may be short term – as when the child explicitly imitates a specific act – or more long term – when, for example, the child learns adult behaviour through identification with a person or with a role at a more general level (see Brown 1965: 395).

In previous empirical research parents' and children's television viewing has been found to correlate (McLeod and Brown 1976; Johnsson-Smaragdi

1983: 162; Johnsson-Smaragdi and Höjerback 1989). By multivariate analysis of longitudinal data it has been demonstrated that parents' amount of television viewing influences their children's amount of viewing, both simultaneously and over time. An overt behaviour is thus learned and imitated (Johnsson-Smaragdi 1983). The influence does not seem to be entirely due to modelling, however, since both reinforcement and social interaction also have been shown to have a strong, indirect influence on the process (Johnsson-Smaragdi 1992). The above discussion, as well as the analyses presented below, draws heavily on the latter work.

Figure 6.12 presents a so called meta-model of parents' influence on their children's television viewing (for meta-studies, see Hunter and Schmidt 1990; Sonesson 1990). The meta-model summarizes invariant parts resulting from replicated analyses of a longitudinal structural model performed on three different cohorts (Johnsson-Smaragdi 1992). The magnitude of the total influence of a given variable on another is summarized in a meta-table (Table 6.3), drawing on three original tables.

The family communication climate (Chaffee *et al.* 1971; Jarlbro 1986, 1988: 45; Ritchie 1991) is essential for the general attitudes and outlooks of its members; it structures the interaction and communication going on in the

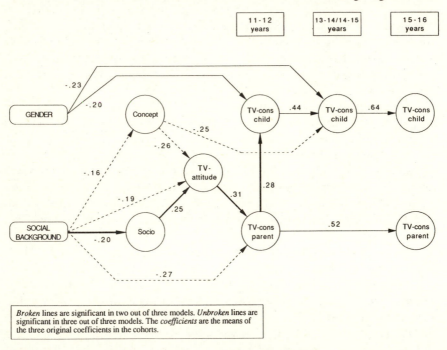

Broken lines are significant in two out of three models. *Unbroken* lines are significant in three out of three models. The *coefficients* are the means of the three original coefficients in the cohorts.

Figure 6.12 Cohorts V65, V69 & M69: meta-model of structural invariance for the 'Family interactions models'
Source: Johnsson-Smaragdi 1992.

Table 6.3 Cohorts V65, V69 and M69: Meta-table: means of total effects in three 'Family Interaction Models'

| | BACKGROUND | | FAMILY COMMUNICATION 'Interaction' | | ATTITUDE 'Reinforcement' | TV BEHAVIOUR | | | | |
| | | | | | | 'Modelling' TV parent | | 'Reversed modelling' TV child years of age | | |
	Gender	Social class	Concept	Socio	TV Attitude	Time I (Child 11)	Time III (Child 15)	11–12	13–14	15–16
Parent										
Concept	—	.11	—	—	—	—	—	—	—	—
Socio	—	-.20	—	—	—	—	—	—	—	—
TV attitude	—	-.18	-.17	—	—	—	—	—	—	—
TV parent										
Time I (Child 11 years old)	—	-.24	-.05	—	.31	—	—	—	—	—
Time III (Child 15 years old)	-.04	-.20	-.12	—	.17	.55	—	.06	.14	—
TV child										
11–12 years old	-.20	-.15	-.02	.11	.16	.28	—	—	—	—
13–14 years old	-.31	-.15	-.17	.06	.09	.18	—	.44	—	—
15–16 years old	-.22	-.10	-.15	.04	.00	.15	—	.37	.64	—

Source: Johnsson-Smaragdi 1992
Note: * Figures in italics show the means from two out of the three tables.

family. Thus it plays an important role in the socialization process of the children. There are two main types of communication pattern: socio- and concept-orientation. Socio-orientation is characterized by stressing social harmony and trying to avoid controversy and to repress anger, while concept-orientation emphasizes intellectual values, trying to stimulate flexibility, even to challenge other people's views (Hedinsson 1981: 33; Jarlbro 1988: 26; see also Chapter 1).

Socio-orientation and concept-orientation are two radically different ways of relating to the social world. It is the structure of parent–child communication that the child learns to generalize, though, not the specific communication content (Chaffee *et al.* 1971; Hedinsson 1981: 33; Jarlbro 1986, 1988: 45).

The pattern of communication is highly relevant for the media use of family members. For instance, socio-oriented parents have been found to have a more positive attitude to television viewing than concept-oriented parents. Parents with a positive attitude towards television also watch more television (Sonesson 1979; Jönsson 1986; Sonesson and Linderholm 1992). This attitude is consciously or unconsciously conveyed to their children, and, in its turn, affects the children's viewing level. These are, above all, processes of social interaction, possibly with instances of subtle reinforcement.

The parental attitude towards television is also supposed to influence the children's viewing level by way of the process of reinforcement. Parents' attitudes towards television have been measured by a scale originally developed by Brown *et al.* (1974) and adapted to Swedish conditions (see Sonesson 1979: 105; Jönsson 1985: 68; Rosengren and Windahl 1989: 196). Two dimensions from this scale are included in the present analyses, namely, a generally positive attitude towards television, and a more specific attitude regarding television as by and large stimulating for the children.

Amount of weekly consumption of television, both broadcast and cable but not VCR, is identically measured for children and parents over time – by means of six questions tapping the weekly amount of viewing (see Johnsson-Smaragdi 1992).

Turning now to the meta-model in Figure 6.12, it may be noted that it shows an invariant chain of influence: a chain flowing from parents' social background, to socio-orientation, to parental television attitude, to parents' television consumption and, finally, to children's television.

Of the three learning processes discussed above, modelling seems to be the most influential – on the assumption that the influence from parents' viewing on that of their children is primarily regarded as an instance of modelling. The total influence from parents' viewing is fairly strong, both simultaneously and also, on the whole, over time (Table 6.3). This is the closest to an invariant influence to which we have come so far. Thus, the amount of parental television viewing exerts a relatively strong influence on children's amount of viewing – independently of the particular process, or maybe blend of processes, at work (and independently of background variables such as social class, and intervening variables such as family communication climate and television attitudes).

The substantive interpretation of these invariant relations is that parents' television viewing is *directly* influencing children's viewing level simultaneously. Indirectly there is also considerable influence over time. Both types of influence are to be interpreted mainly in terms of modelling. As parents view television, so do children.

Furthermore, neither parental attitudes to television, nor their pattern of communication seem to have any *direct, invariant* influence on children's viewing, but Table 6.3 tells us that there are fairly strong indirect influences, mainly conveyed through parents' own television viewing. These influences should be interpreted as expressing instances of social interaction and subtle reinforcement affecting children's amount of viewing. Those processes thus seem to constitute a differentiated background against which the viewing patterns of parents and children are formed. The differential occurrence and strength of these influences indicate that social interaction is a subtle process, subject to influences from variable conditions in the immediate environment as well as in the overall social structure.

An important conclusion can be drawn from these replications of the longitudinal LISREL models: *Structural invariance seems to be a matter of degrees rather than an absolute property.* The invariance turned out to be far from complete – at least, that is what our models tell us.

The basic processes forming children's media habits must be assumed to be fairly general and stable. We have found some invariant structural relations over time, summarized in the Meta-model just discussed. The invariance is far from complete, however, at least in part due to the restructuring of the media landscape. It is to be remembered that the models analysed are relatively simple. What about the invariance of more complex models? This question concerns the degree to which invariance in structural relations over time and space actually do exist in an ever-changing society, and, if so, in which areas. Only continued theoretical, methodological and empirical work will provide an answer to that question. Theory and methodology have to be jointly applied in carefully designed studies in relevant areas, preferably longitudinal studies, admitting systematic replications. Otherwise, casual, haphazard research will dominate at the expense of long-term, theoretically anchored work, and there will be no possibility at all of knowing whether our findings are indeed based on invariant structural relations.

CONSEQUENCES OF STABILITY OR CHANGE

The Swedish media scene has been radically altered during the last ten to fifteen years. There are now more options to choose among – more media, more channels, several methods of distribution, a greater output of, and, maybe, more diversified media fare. Such thorough changes in the media structure inevitably affect individual use of mass media, including how the 'media menu' is composed and altered over time.

The differences in amount of media use between individuals or specific groups of individuals will probably become more marked in an expanding media system. It is also probable that there will be more individual change and turbulence over time, due both to individual development and historical change. Thus, in the long run, what will happen to the stability in media use? Will there be more stability in one respect than in another, for example in level stability but not in relative or structural stability? Can we expect an increasing number of 'sprinters', 'obstinates' and 'laggards' (adolescents that in some respect deviate from the average trend) and/or higher stability within specific subgroups of viewers, i.e. more 'mainstreamers'? We do not know, of course, but a fair guess may be that the average 'normal' adolescent will become rare and that future media use will be more marked by change than by stability.

Media use is in many respects habitual; founded early in life, developing and changing during childhood and adolescence due to both internal and external forces in children's lives. The habit of viewing may be strong, but not so strong that it cannot be changed. Media use may be viewed as a form of adaptive behaviour. There are many forces influencing a child's viewing level and habits, trying to change and reorganize it in one direction or another. Probably these forces will become even stronger in the future.

In a quickly changing media environment, parents in the future may be less able than now to exert any influence. Children and adolescents are usually among the first to pick up new influences and to act and react in accordance with these (Johnsson-Smaragdi and Roe 1986; Johnsson-Smaragdi 1989: 121). Besides the parental influence on children's television viewing, there may be other, increasingly more important, sources of influence in the multi-media and multi-channel society – for example, the peer group. Besides, adherence to certain lifestyles within specific subgroups may become even more important. In order to find stable structural relationships it may be increasingly necessary in the future to break down the population under study into narrowly defined subgroups. It will also become increasingly important to include all relevant variables in the analyses – to build more complex models and perform more stringent analyses. It is also essential not to put too great weight on single analyses and studies, not even longitudinal ones. Carefully designed studies admitting systematic replications and comparisons over time and space are to be preferred. Otherwise there will be no possibility at all of knowing whether our findings are indeed based on invariant structural relations, or in which respects the relations are changing.

REFERENCES

Adoni, H. (1985) 'Media interchangeability and co-existence: trends and changes in production, distribution and consumption patterns of the print media in the television era', *Libri* 35 (3): 202–217.

Bandura, A. (1969) 'Social learning theory of identificatory processes', in D.A. Goslin (ed.) *Handbook of Socialization Theory and Research*, Chicago: Rand McNally.

Bandura, A. and Walters, R.H. (1963) *Social Learning and Personality Development*, New York: Holt, Rinehart & Winston.

Becker, L.B. and Schoenbach, K. (1989) (eds) *Audience Responses to Media Diversification. Coping With Plenty*, Hillsdale, NJ: Lawrence Erlbaum.

Brown, J.R. (1976) 'Children's uses of television', in J.R. Brown (ed.) *Children and Television*, London: Collier Macmillan.

Brown, J.R., Cramond, J.K. and Wilde, R.J. (1974) 'Displacement effects of television and the child's functional orientation to media', in J.G. Blumler and E. Katz (eds) *The Uses of Mass Communications: Current Perspectives on Gratifications Research*, Beverly Hills, Calif.: Sage.

Brown, R. (1965) *Social Psychology*, New York: The Free Press.

Burnett, R. (1990) *Concentration and Diversity in the International Phonogram Industry*, Gothenburg: Department of Media and Communication.

Chaffee, S.H., McLeod, J.M. and Atkin, C.K. (1971) 'Parental influences on adolescent media use', *American Behavioral Scientist* 14: 323–340.

Filipson, L. and Rydin, I. (1989) *Children's and Adolescents' Television Viewing*, Stockholm: SR/PUB.

Hedinsson, E. (1981) *TV, Family and Society. The Social Origins and Effects of Adolescents' TV Use*, Stockholm: Almqvist & Wiksell International.

Höjerback, I. (1990) 'Nya medier – nya klyftor? Ungdomars medieanvändning i ett tioårs-perspektiv', *Lund Research Papers in the Sociology of Communication* 27, Lund: Department of Sociology, University of Lund.

Hunter, J.E. and Schmidt, F.L. (1990) *Methods of Meta-analysis: Correcting Error and Bias in Research Findings*, Newbury Park, Calif.: Sage.

Jarlbro, G. (1986) 'Family communication patterns revisited: reliability and validity', *Lund Research Papers in the Sociology of Communication* 4, Lund: Department of Sociology, University of Lund.

—— (1988) *Familj, massmedier och politik*, Stockholm: Almqvist & Wiksell International.

Johnsson-Smaragdi, U. (1983) *TV Use and Social Interaction in Adolescence. A Longitudinal Study*, Stockholm: Almqvist & Wiksell International.

—— (1986) 'Tryckta kontra audiovisuella medier – konkurrens eller samexistens?', *Wahlgrenska stiftelsens rapportserie* 3.

—— (1989) 'Sweden: opening the doors – cautiously', in L. Becker and K. Schoenbach (eds) *Audience Responses to Media Diversification. Coping With Plenty*, Hillsdale, NJ: Lawrence Erlbaum.

—— (1992) 'Learning to watch television: longitudinal LISREL models replicated', *Lund Research Papers in Media and Communication Studies* 5, Lund: Department of Sociology, University of Lund.

Johnsson-Smaragdi, U. and Höjerback, I. (1989) 'Replikation av en LISREL-modell på nytt urval. Likheter i barns och föräldrars TV-konsumtion', *Lund Research Papers in the Sociology of Communication* 13, Lund: Department of Sociology, University of Lund.

Johnsson-Smaragdi, U. and Roe, K. (1986) 'Teenagers in the new media world. Video recorders, video games and home computers', *Lund Research Papers in the Sociology of Communication* 2, Lund: Department of Sociology, University of Lund.

Jönsson, A. (1985) *TV – ett hot eller en resurs. En longitudinell studie av relationen mellan skola och TV*, Lund: Gleerups.

—— (1986) 'TV: A threat or a complement to school?', *Journal of Educational Television* 12(1): 29–38.

McLeod, J. and Brown, J.D. (1976) 'The family environment and adolescent television use', in R. Brown (ed.) *Children and Television*, London: Collier Macmillan.

Mortimer, J.T., Finch, M.D. and Kumka, D. (1982) 'Persistence and change in development: The multidimensional self-concept', in P.B. Baltes and O.G. Brim (eds) *Life-Span Development and Behavior* 4, New York: Holt, Rinehart & Winston.

Ritchie, L.D. (1991) 'Family communication patterns', *Communication Research* 18 (4): 548–565.

Rosengren, K.E. (1991) 'Media use in childhood and adolescence: invariant change? Some results from a Swedish research program', in J.A. Anderson (ed.) *Communication Yearbook* 14: 48–90, Newbury Park, Calif.: Sage.

Rosengren, K.E. and Windahl, S. (1989) *Media Matter. TV Use in Childhood and Adolescence*, Norwood, NJ: Ablex.

Sonesson, I. (1979) *Förskolebarn och TV*, Stockholm: Esselte Studium.

—— (1989) *Vem fostrar våra barn – videon eller vi?*, Stockholm: Esselte Studium.

—— (1990) *Ängslan – ett personlighetsbegrepp i svensk skolforskning*, Stockholm: Skolöverstyrelsen.

Sonesson, I. and Linderholm, I. (1992) 'Förskolebarns mediebeteende och den sociala miljön', *Lund Research Papers in Media and Communication Studies* 3, Lund: Department of Sociology, University of Lund.

Stattin, H. and Magnusson, D. (1990) *Pubertal Maturation in Female Development*, Hillsdale, NJ: Lawrence Erlbaum.

Part III

Young people and media use: individual, class and socialization

Chapter 7

For better and for worse: effects studies and beyond

Karl Erik Rosengren, Ulla Johnsson-Smaragdi and Inga Sonesson

INTRODUCTION

Modern media and communication studies may be said to have started as a consequence of a moral panic (Cohen 1972/80; Roe 1985) about the effects of the new mass medium of film. At the initiative of the US Motion Picture Research Council, the so-called Payne Fund Studies were carried out in the late 1920s by a number of leading sociologists and psychologists including, for instance, Herbert Blumer, Philip Hauser and L.L. Thurstone (see Lowery and De Fleur 1983: 31 ff.). A couple of decades later, for similar but different reasons, comic magazines for children and adolescents triggered another moral panic. Again research into the effects of individual use made of mass media was carried out, this time by a psychiatrist who, incidentally, found an enthusiastic sympathizer in a Swedish professor of social medicine (Wertham 1954; Bejerot 1954; cf. Lowery and De Fleur 1983: 233 ff.).

Meanwhile, although somewhat less inclined to be seized by moral panics, leading members of the pioneering generation of communication scholars – for instance, Carl Hovland, Paul F. Lazarsfeld, and Wilbur Schramm – had also become much preoccupied by effects studies. About a decade after the introduction of television, the stage was set, then, for a couple of path-breaking, rather comprehensive effects studies in Europe and America (Himmelweit *et al.* 1958; Schramm *et al.* 1961), soon to be followed up by a number of studies more or less specifically focused on the media and violence problematics (for instance, Baker and Ball 1969; Comstock *et al.* 1978; Pearl *et al.* 1982; Surgeon General 1972). This tradition, of course, is still very much alive (see below).

Besides these broad developments, a number of other types of media effects – both positive and negative – were dealt with within the effects research tradition at large, the innumerable studies of which have been summarized and anthologized in several volumes such as Bradac (1989), Bryant and Zillmann (1986), Klapper (1960) and Schulz (1992). Hearold (1986) made a meta analysis of more than 1,000 positive and negative effects studies of television on social behaviour, finding that the average size for prosocial television contents on prosocial behaviour was far higher than that for antisocial television content on antisocial behaviour.

Parallel with the mainly effects-oriented studies, that other broad tradition of research on individual use of the media – uses and gratifications research, originally inaugurated by the group around Lazarsfeld and Merton at Columbia – continued to grow (see, for instance, Blumler and Katz 1974; Rosengren, Wenner and Palmgreen 1985; Swanson 1992). Increasingly often, the originally rather marked divide between effects and uses and gratifications tended to disappear in studies of individual media use.

The Media Panel Program tries to combine the two perspectives of effects and uses and gratifications research in a 'Uses and Effects' approach (Rosengren and Windahl 1989: 8 ff.; Windahl 1981). We also make a distinction between effects and consequences; the former being related to the type of content consumed, the latter, to the media use as such (Windahl 1981; cf. Cramond 1976). We try to relate our approach to the four aspects of media use listed in Chapter 4:

1 Amount of media use.
2 Type or genre of media content used and preferred.
3 Type of relation established with the content used.
4 Type of context of media use.

Within the MPP group, we are in a position to heed both short-term and long-term effects and consequences, since our combined cross-sectional/longitudinal approach offers opportunities for studies ranging from the observation of immediate, cross-sectionally observed effects and consequences to that of effects and consequences which remain – or appear – only after several years.

While most effects studies have been concerned with what has been regarded as harmful effects (say, an increased tendency to violent behaviour), we are equally interested in positive and negative effects. Indeed, our uses and effects approach makes us realize that the good is sometimes the mother of the bad: long-term effects which from most reasonable perspectives must be considered harmful often have their origin in short-term positive effects more or less consciously sought for by the individual user of mass media (see below). For this reason also, then, the predominantly causal perspective of effects research must be combined with the predominantly finalistic perspective of the uses and gratifications research (see Rosengren and Windahl 1989: 211 ff.).

This chapter starts with a type of consequence not often mentioned in traditional effects studies: consequences of media use for future media use by the individuals themselves or by other family members (see the notion of stability analysed in Chapter 6). Viewing breeds viewing. We note that the idea of consequences of media use for future media use may be applied not only to amount of use, but also to the other three aspects of media use: type of content used and preferred, type of relation established with the content used, and type of context of media use.

Starting from a typology of television consequences developed within the MPP, we then turn to consequences and effects of media use on other phenomena: characteristics and qualities of individuals as well as more or less stable patterns of actions and activities stemming from media use as such and from media use of special types of content. In so doing, we concentrate, of course, on new MPP results not otherwise presented in this volume. A number of other effects and consequences will be dealt with in the following two chapters in this section of the book. In the next section of the book, yet a different perspective on the relationship between media use and other activities will dominate.

CONSEQUENCES OF MEDIA USE FOR MEDIA USE

In Chapters 5 and 6, by Pingree and Hawkins, and Johnsson-Smaragdi, respectively, we saw that the use of some media tends to correlate, often positively, sometimes negatively. Although patterns of such correlations may change during and after periods of structural change, they seem to be stable enough to merit further study. There are at least two different ways of interpreting such relationships.

Especially in cross-sectional studies, perhaps, co-variation between amount of use of different media may be taken to indicate a pattern of living supposedly characteristic for this or that type of society, this or that type of segment within the population, this or that group of individuals sharing some basic values or attitudes. By and large, that is the perspective applied in Chapter 5 (see also the notions of forms of life, ways of life, and lifestyle as discussed in Chapter 1 and Chapters 10–12). When the correlations are longitudinal, however, it seems to be more natural to regard them as measures of stability, as in the previous chapter by Ulla Johnsson-Smaragdi. And stripped of the influence of basic positional variables such as gender and social class, these longitudinal relationships actually bring to mind the notion of causality. Amount of media use at one point in time may be regarded as partly *caused* by amount of media use at a previous point of time (see Chapter 6, p. 112). Obviously, the same type of argument may be applied also to aspects of media use other than amount of use, for instance, relations established with the media content used.

There are a number of different types of media relation which have been discussed in the literature. The two relations which have been the most preferred by media scholars are probably identification and para-social relation (PSI). The latter type of media relation, originally inaugurated by Horton and Wohl (1956), explicated by Rosengren and Windahl (1972) and recently reviewed by Hippel (1992), has also been a focus of interest in the Media Panel Program. Briefly, it could be characterized as a quasi-interaction between viewer and some *persona* on the screen. Identification has also been given much attention within the MPP. Identification may be short term or long term, and we have been most interested in long-term identification: a relation in which the viewer – often for relatively long periods of time after the viewing – tends to identify, more or less superficially or deeply, with a *persona* on the screen, say, the hero or heroine of this or that series or serial. A combined index of PSI, short-term and long-term identification called 'TV Relation' was used in most MPP waves of data collection (see Rosengren *et al.* 1976; Rosengren and Windahl 1989: 38 ff.).

Figure 7.1 presents a LISREL model of the causal relations between amount of TV consumption and TV relations during childhood, adolescence and early adulthood. Before turning to these causal relations, however, we note what we have had opportunity to note several times before, namely, that gender and social background are powerful determinants of media use.

Girls watch less TV than boys, but they are more inclined to establish TV relations. Upper-class youngsters watch less TV than do working-class youngsters. But in early adulthood, at the same time as they are less inclined to enter into TV relations, they seem to watch somewhat more (perhaps because as students they lack the money necessary for frequent disco visits and such like). In general, TV relations are less influenced by background variables than is TV consumption, possibly because they may be related to some personality variable or other (see Rosengren and Windahl 1977).

The intricacies of such causal relationships between aspects of media use and background variables are interesting as such, but in this connection we are more interested in discussing the causal relationships within aspects of media use itself. It is striking to note how – even after control for the two powerful background variables of gender and social class – the so-called stability coefficients for TV consumption are quite strong. What is really striking, however, is that this applies not only to amount of viewing but also to that much more subtle and presumably fleeting variable of TV relations – indeed, the coefficients for the relations are even stronger than those pertaining to the amount of viewing. (The total effect of viewing upon viewing may be calculated as the sum of direct and indirects of early viewing on later viewing. For such total effects, see corresponding figures in Chapter 6.) In causal terms this means that not only does viewing breed viewing; relationships also breed relationships.

What we see is the strong power of media habits. Once a TV fan, chances are you will remain one – even after having passed that period of turmoil called adolescence. Expressed in stronger terms, what we see is not only the development and conservation of a habit, but also a process of habituation, sometimes resulting in mild forms of media dependency, 'addiction'. This type of dependency is described, for instance, by McQuail and Windahl (1981); see also Rubin and Windahl (1986). (Similar phenomena may be observed for most media, as well as between different media. For examples

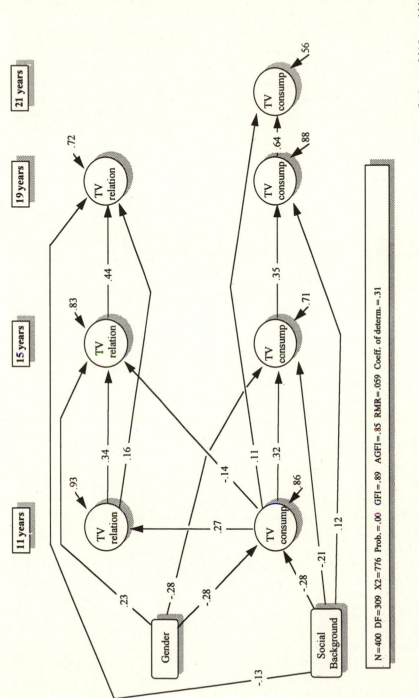

| 11 years | 15 years | 19 years | 21 years |

N=400 DF=309 X2=776 Prob.=.00 GFI=.89 AGFI=.85 RMR=.059 Coeff. of determ.=.31

Figure 7.1 LISREL model of TV consumption and TV relations between ages 11 and 21 – structural part. Cohorts M69 and V69 (only statistically significant paths are presented)

of positive and negative relationships between, say, early and late book reading and use of other media, see Chapter 6.)

The consequences of heavy TV viewing among youngsters are often the concern of parents, teachers and other citizens, sometimes for good reasons. One good reason for such concern, we have just seen, may well be the fact that viewing often turns into a habit, so that it could be said that viewing itself causes and ensures continued viewing. On the assumptions that viewing may reduce other activities, and/or that effects and consequences of viewing are sometimes harmful, this is a result of childhood viewing which should be, and often is, a matter of some concern.

Actually, the influence of amount of viewing on amount of viewing is not limited to one's own viewing. In Chapter 6, Ulla Johnsson-Smaragdi showed that parental viewing is a strong causal factor behind children's viewing – even after control for background variables (see also Johnsson-Smaragdi 1992). Interestingly, she also showed that children's viewing may exert an influence on parental viewing, especially in mid-adolescence when (during a public-service regime, at least) many youngsters leave mainstream television for music which reaches them through other media (see Chapter 4). In cases where the youngsters remain seated before the screen, however, so do their parents, it seems (cf. Johnsson-Smaragdi 1992). For both parties involved in the process, the 'context' aspect of viewing is at play (see above): joint viewing by parents and children alike.

This observation is strengthened by the fact noted by Rosengren and Windahl (1989: 83 ff.) that parents' TV viewing diminishes with the age of their children. This is the result of a form of dependency other than the mild form of addiction described above: structurally rather than individually generated dependency – a type to be understood in terms of dependency theory as developed by Ball-Rokeach and her associates (Ball-Rokeach and De Fleur 1976; Ball-Rokeach 1985, cf. Ball-Rokeach 1988). Small children make parents stay at home, make them dependent on home-bound pleasures – television, for instance. As the child grows older, this dependency is gradually reduced, and consequently children and parents alike leave television for the real world. It remains to be seen, however, whether these tendencies will survive the changes in media structure which have already taken place but which may not yet have reached their end.

It should be added, finally, that the influence of viewing on viewing is not limited to the three aspects discussed so far: amount of viewing, relations established with TV content, and context of viewing. Also type of content preferred and consumed at one time influences type of content consumed at a later point in time. In an attempt at untangling the longitudinal relationships between television content preferences in childhood and early adulthood, Dalquist (1992) followed amount of television viewing and content preferences among cohorts V69 and M69 from the age of 11 (grade 5) to age 21, including data from five data collection waves and both panels in a

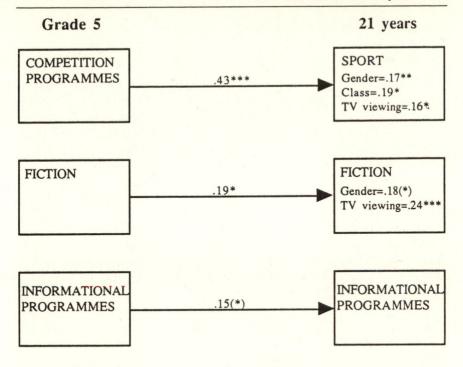

Figure 7.2 Long-term stability in media preferences (beta coefficients)
(Source: Dalquist 1992)

number of sequential MCA analyses. As it turned out, a relatively clear-cut pattern of preferences was established fairly early: sports, contests and competitions stood out as a special interest already at age 12, an interest which persisted into early adulthood and had next to no relations with other preferences and interests.

Three other groups of preferences articulated already at the age of 12 and remaining until the age of 16 were directed towards fiction, youth programmes and informational programmes, respectively. At the age of 19, the young adults reshuffled these three groups into two groups of preferences: one consisting of entertainment programmes, action fiction and comedy fiction; another, of informational programmes and high culture programmes. After control for gender, social class, town of living and amount of viewing, the stability (beta) coefficients for the various preferences as measured in two contingent waves of data collection varied between some .20 and some .60, depending on the temporal distance between the waves and the type of preference (sport showing the highest coefficients).

In a final attempt to assess also long-term stability in type of TV content preferred, Dalquist (1992) took a look at the long-term stability of preferences for the following programmes:

a) Sports, contests and competitions.
b) Fiction.
c) Informational.

The preferences were measured in grade 5 (age 12) and at age 21, again within the collapsed cohorts M69 and V69. The results obtained are shown in Figure 7.2. As it turned out, the beta coefficients – again after control for gender, social class, town and TV viewing – were significant and quite substantial: .15 and .19 for preferences for informational programmes and fiction, respectively, and .43 for sports programmes. Given the many variables controlled for, as well as the nine years' interval betweeen the two waves of data collection, the coefficients are quite impressive, especially that for sports. What they show is that the basic foundations for television content preferences are laid at an early age, and that they are quite stable.

In summary, then, after control for a number of basic background variables, and in a long-term perspective, media use, having once been initiated, breeds media use. As far as TV is concerned, this seems so for all four aspects of media use: amount, content preferences, relations established with content used, and context of media use. This fact should not be forgotten when in the next section we turn to a discussion, not about consequences of media use for media use, but about effects and consequences of media use on other, and perhaps more important, activities.

ACTIVITIES AND CHARACTERISTICS FOLLOWING TV USE

In an attempt to clarify the relationships between TV use and other activities, Rosengren and Windahl (1989:179 ff.) created a three-dimensional typology providing seven different types of such relationships (since two of the eight theoretically possible types coincide):

1 *Supplement*: other activities stimulate TV use.
2 *Prevention*: other activities reduce TV use.
3 *Substitute*: lack of other activities calls for TV use.
4 *Passivity*: both TV use and other activities low.
5 *Activation*: high TV use stimulates other activities.
6 *Leeway*: low TV use leaves room for other activities.
7 *Displacement*: high TV use reduces other activities.

In terms of this typology, we then made an overview of results gained in a number of previous MPP studies – primarily by Sonesson (1979, 1986, 1989) and Johnsson-Smaragdi (1983, 1986) – of the relationship between television viewing and other activities, including both parental viewing and children's viewing, as well as parental and children's activities. Contrary to some previous results we were able to conclude that

For parents and children alike, from preschool to grade 9, over various aspects of TV use and social interaction, we have found that TV does not reduce interaction. If anything, it does the opposite. Children high on TV are socially better integrated and more active. In preschool they are more apt to have a close friend. In grade 5, they interact more with parents and peers, and in grade 9 those who interact more with their parents also watch more TV. Only when it comes to organized leisure activities (sports, hobbies, etc.) did we find negative relationships. But here the influence ran from activities to TV viewing. A high amount of organized leisure activities reduced TV (prevention), a low amount of organized activities may have admitted – even called for – much TV (substitute). TV as substitute was found also for the parents. But TV did not reduce or admit the organized activities of the children (no displacement or leeway effects). (Rosengren and Windahl 1989: 188 f.)

We then proceeded to conclude that while these results were in disagreement with early American results, they agreed with some relatively recent results obtained in Europe and other regions outside the USA, arguing that the early US results referred to a period when TV was something relatively new and extraordinary, while our results referred to a period in which TV was a phenomenon well integrated in everybody's daily life. The 1989 results have received further support in later MPP studies, for instance, by Sonesson (1990). The analyses undertaken by Ulla Johnsson-Smaragdi and Annelis Jönsson in Chapter 8 show that, for girls, at least, a high amount of TV viewing in grade 5 resulted in increased interaction in grade 9. In retrospect one realizes, though, that present-day changes of the media structure may well change all this. (Whether that is so still remains to be seen, of course.)

What was clear already in the late 1970s and early 1980s, was that while TV viewing had hardly any passivating consequences at the time, it certainly was activating in more than one sense. Not only did it increase interaction with friends and parents; there are also clear signs that it increased other, less positive activities and characteristics.

The subject area most persistently pursued by mass communications studies with an effects/consequences perspective no doubt is the relationship between viewing, aggressiveness and violent behaviour (see the introductory section of this chapter). This specific subject has been given considerable attention within the MPP since its start in the mid-1970s (see Rosengren and Windahl 1989: 215 ff.). A series of studies undertaken on the M69 cohort actually focused specifically on this problem (Sonesson 1979, 1986, 1989, 1990), producing a wealth of detailed results which for space reasons cannot be rendered in any detail in this chapter. The main outcome of the studies is clear enough, however.

In her studies in the area Sonesson (1979, 1986, 1989) consistently applied a combined uses and effects perspective. Individual media use not only has its effects and consequences, but also its reasons and causes. In combination,

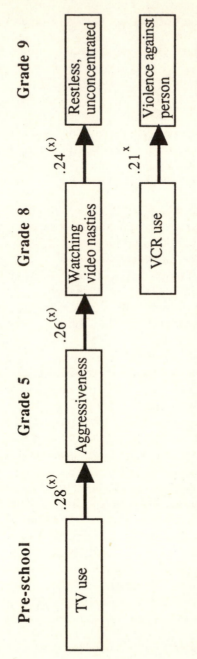

Pre-school   **Grade 5**   **Grade 8**   **Grade 9**

TV use $\xrightarrow{.28^{(x)}}$ Aggressiveness $\xrightarrow{.26^{(x)}}$ Watching video nasties $\xrightarrow{.24^{(x)}}$ Restless, unconcentrated

VCR use $\xrightarrow{.21^{x}}$ Violence against person

Figure 7.3 Chains of effects and consequences of TV and VCR use among boys in panel M69 (beta coeffinients)

the two processes proceeding and following media use may result in long chains of finality/causality and effects/consequences: spirals of interaction between individuals and their media environment stretching over decades. In Sonesson (1989) a number of such chains are presented, covering the period from pre-school (age 6) to grade 9 (the last year of the compulsory school system, age 15). They are summarized in an impressive series of consecutive MCA analyses of the relationship between mass media use and tendencies towards aggressiveness, restlessness and/or anxiety. Here is a condensed summary of these results, differentiated for boys and girls.

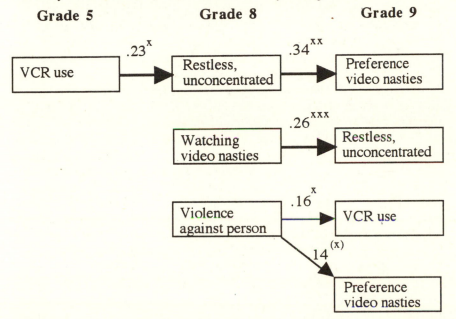

Figure 7.4 Chains of effects and consequences of TV and VCR use among girls in panel M69 (beta coefficients)

The amount of boys' TV viewing in pre-school affected tendencies to (relatively mild) aggressiveness in grade 5 (beta .28). In its turn, this aggressiveness led to high viewing of video violence and horror content in grade 8 (beta .26), which in its turn led to restlessness and lack of concentration (beta .24) in grade 9; VCR viewing in grade 8 (including, of course, the video nasties) led to (relatively harsh) aggressiveness against people in grade 9 (beta .21) – all coefficients after control for social background and previous aggressiveness, restlessness, lack of concentration, etc. (gender being controlled for by homogenization). For girls a similar chain of uses and effects was found, although with other types of effect. Here the amount of VCR viewing in grade 5 led to restlessness, lack of concentration and attention in grade 8 (beta .23), which in its turn led to high preferences for violence and horror video content in grade 9 (beta.34) – again after extensive controls for relevant variables (social background, previous lack of concentration, previous media use and media preferences, etc.).

Disregarding for the moment the specifics and the details of these studies, what these and similar MPP results convincingly show is that media use has effects and consequences for children which may stretch over years, probably decades. We also see how such effects and consequences come about in spiralling uses-and-effects chains of interaction between individual characteristics (aggressiveness, restlessness, etc.) and media use (media preferences, amount of viewing, type of content viewed), in a way which is in agreement with a number of other studies in the area, and especially, perhaps, with the so-called reciprocal cognitive models summarized, for instance, in Linz and Donnerstein (1989) and implemented, for instance, in a large, relatively recent international comparative study (see Eron and Huesmann 1987; Huesmann and Eron 1986). They are not in agreement, however, with results arrived at within the same comparative study as interpreted by Wiegman *et al.* (1992). Nor are they in agreement with a recent meta analysis of gender differences in the effects of television violence (Paik 1992), which surprisingly found no or only small gender differences. There will always be deviant results, of course. Sometimes such results will result in new and unexpected insights, sometimes they may be explained in terms of specific circumstances (as cleverly done, for instance, by Turner *et al.* (1986) with respect to the otherwise deviant results presented by Milawsky *et al.* (1982)).

The debate goes on. It may well be that future combinations of uses-and-effects models and reciprocal cognitive models will be able to solve some of the differences found in the literature. The fact that aggressive commercials have been shown to enhance and facilitate aggression (see, for instance, Caprara *et al.* 1987) makes it mandatory to continue and replicate longitudinal studies, especially in countries which have recently experienced a restructuring of the media scene making such commercials a standard part of many young people's media fare. Also, while most results suggest rather weak effects in terms of proportion of explained variance, those effects are virtually globally endemic, and even a small portion of all violence in all countries must represent immense, almost staggering amounts of violence. In addition, Rosenthal (1986) convincingly showed that even seemingly modest amounts of explained variance may represent considerable amounts of actual reduction or increase of this or that type of behaviour.

Regarded in this perspective, it will be an important and fascinating task of future research within the MPP to follow up the spiralling chains presented above from grade 9 and onwards, a task which is quite feasible and which, as a matter of fact, has already been approached (Johnsson-Smaragdi and Jönsson, forthcoming). Preferably, such studies should be combined with similar studies of related subject areas, such as, for instance, school achievements and occupational plans and choices, an area which has also already been given considerable attention within the research programme.

Using the PLS approach (see Jöreskog and Wold 1982; for a short comparison of the PLS and LISREL approaches, see also Rosengren and Windahl 1989: 263 ff.), Jönsson (1985, 1986) showed that under positive and negative circumstances heavy viewing may have positive and negative effects on children's school marks – circumstances being defined as family background, context of viewing, type of content viewed and preferred. Under favourable circumstances – having parents with a critical view towards TV, viewing together with parents, viewing programmes created for children and adolescents etc. – TV viewing in pre-school and early school years showed up in better school marks in grade 6 (age 12), while opposite conditions had opposite effects and consequences (see also Rosengren and Windahl 1989: 221 ff.). In LISREL analyses carried out separately for boys and girls of the V65 cohort, on the other hand, Flodin (1986) found only a weak influence of amount of TV viewing in grade 5 on school marks in grade 6, and no influence on occupational expectations in grade 9 of viewing in grades 5, 7 and 9 (Flodin 1986; cf. Rosengren and Windahl 1989: 236 ff.); related results will also be presented in Chapter 8. We thus have results which point to *no* effects of TV viewing on school results and occupational plans, and results which suggest such effects.

Jönsson (1985, 1986) used a different statistical approach in her analyses than did Flodin (1986) and Johnsson-Smaragdi and Jönsson in Chapter 8, but common to the two statistical packages, PLS and LISREL, is that they very efficiently control for all relevant variables included in the analysis, so that the unique influence of one variable upon another stands out clearly. The main reason for the difference between the results presented by them, therefore, probably is a different one: the fact that Jönsson not only heeded amount of viewing but included also contextual background factors to viewing, and – at least equally important – that she was able to include also *type of content viewed*. Hers was a mixed consequence/effects model, then, presumably stronger than the pure consequence model used by Flodin. Also, Jönsson's main result – that, depending upon the circumstances, effects of TV viewing on scholastic achievements may be positive or negative – agrees with, provides comparative corroboration of, and adds new knowledge to the main message of an overview of the area published at about the same time (Ball *et al.* 1986). It also agrees with a rather different perspective quickly touched upon in the second section of this chapter: a lifestyle perspective, which actually brings us beyond the effects perspective in the strict sense of the word.

BEYOND THE EFFECTS PERSPECTIVE

We noted above that correlations between the use of different media may be interpreted either in causal terms (so that the use of one medium supposedly leads to the use of another) or as expressing a pattern of living (so that use of different media is taken to express the way the individual has come to lead his/her life). The choice between the two perspectives is often related to the time perspective applied, so that cross-sectional studies invite the pattern perspective; longitudinal ones, the causal perspective. But just as in cross-sectional studies a causal perspective may be applied, it is quite possible, of course – although not very common, perhaps – to apply a pattern perspective to longitudinal data. In so doing, we would be able to see how the emergence of patterns of media use interacts over time with the emergence of other patterns of actions and characteristics, be they structurally, positionally or individually determined. In such a perspective a narrowly defined effects perspective breaks down.

An attempt at such a longitudinal, pattern-oriented design was made by Jarlbro and Dalquist (1991), who comparing social background at age 11 and educational status at age 21 for members of cohorts M69 and V69 classified the young adults as either 'Climbers', 'Droppers', 'Stable Working Class' or 'Stable Middle Class'. The media use among members of the four categories was then studied by means of a number of MCA analyses, controlling for gender, place of living and, when applicable, other relevant variables. Here are some results obtained, complementing in an interesting way more traditional analyses showing that working-class children watch more TV etc:

- Working-class children with low TV viewing at the age of 12 tended to be climbers at the age of 21 (beta: .32).
- Middle-class children with high TV viewing at the age of 12 tended to be droppers at the age of 21 (beta: .41).
- Droppers tended to have high TV viewing at the age of 21 (beta .31), to often visit restaurants (beta .22) and to be heavy VCR users (.36).
- Climbers and Stable Middle-Class young adults tended often to visit libraries (beta .28 and .36, respectively).

These results should only be regarded as tentative, of course, but they are suggestive indeed, and what they suggest is a quite subtle pattern of anticipatory socialization (Merton 1963: 265 ff.) rather than the strictly causal processes relevant to an effects perspective (see also Chapter 9 by Keith Roe, where a similar perspective is theoretically elaborated and empirically illustrated). It is hardly high or low TV viewing *per se* which sends youngsters up or down the social ladder. What we see, rather, is youngsters starting to choose their future, more or less consciously and intentionally, more or less compelled by strong but often hidden forces within themselves and outside of them, in their surroundings. Starting to form their lives, they sometimes make a virtue out of necessity (choosing and liking whatever under the circumstances seems to be the thing to do, given their ambition or lack of ambition), sometimes they seem very consciously, very deliberately to choose patterns of living corresponding to their inner cravings and inherent capacities (see Chapters 1 and 13). What we see, then, is specific patterns of values, attitudes and actions emerging out of a common *form of life*, patterns which are partly determined by social position (*ways of life*), partly by individual choice (*lifestyles*).

Analyses of this and similar types transcend both effects studies and uses and gratification studies, but they are quite consistent and compatible with a uses and effects approach as applied within a lifestyle perspective, and they cast an intriguing light on the discussions about socialization, agency and structure referred to in Chapter 1. With or without the intentions of the individual actors, different ways of using mass media – whether consciously chosen by the actors or not – contribute to the shaping of young people's present and future life. Young people often use mass media to express their basic values, their beliefs and opinions, their tastes and whims, and in so doing they help society to fulfil the more or less subtle sorting procedures which its agents of socialization – in this case, primarily, family, school, mass media – have been applying for as long as the young people have been alive. It almost looks as if the young people themselves choose a pattern of media use which later on affects them in a way which to the outsider may sometimes seem tragic and sometimes cynical, sometimes very conventional and sometimes quite unexpected.

In the next two chapters of this part of the book, and in the three chapters in Part IV, the perspective just outlined will be further detailed, extended and developed.

REFERENCES

Baker, R. and Ball, S.J. (eds) (1969) *Violence and the Media*, Washington, DC: US Government Printing Office.

Ball, S., Palmer, P. and Milward, E. (1986) 'Television and its educational impact: A reconsideration', in J. Bryant and D. Zillman (eds) *Perspectives on Media Effects*, Hillsdale, NJ: Erlbaum.

Ball-Rokeach, S. J. (1985) 'The origins of individual media systems dependency: A sociological framework', *Communication Research* 12: 485–510.

—— (1988) 'Media systems and mass communication', in E.F. Borgatta and K.S. Cook (eds) *The Future of Sociology*, Newbury Park, Calif.: Sage.

Ball-Rokeach, S. and De Fleur, M.L. (1976) 'A dependency model of mass media effects', *Communication Research* 3: 3–21.

Bejerot, N. (1954) *Barn, serier, samhälle*, Stockholm: Folket i Bild.

Blumler, J.G. and Katz, E. (eds) (1974) *The Uses of Mass Communications: Current Perspectives on Gratifications Research*, Beverly Hills, Calif.: Sage.

Bradac, J.J. (ed.) (1989) *Message Effects in Communication Science*, Newbury Park, Calif.: Sage:

Bryant, J. and Zillmann, D. (eds) (1986) *Perspectives on Media Effects*, Hillsdale, NJ: Erlbaum.

Caprara, G.V., D'Imperio, G., Gentilomo, A., Mammucari, A., Renzi, P. and Travaglia, G. (1987) 'The intrusive commercial: Influence of aggressive TV commercials on aggression', *European Journal of Social Psychology* 17: 23–31.

Cohen, S. (1972/80) *Folk Devils and Moral Panics* (2nd edn), Oxford: Martin Robertson.

Comstock, G., Chaffee, S., Katzman, N., McCombs, M. and Roberts, D. (1978) *Television and Human Behavior*, New York: Columbia University Press.

Cramond, J. (1976) 'The introduction of television and its effects upon children's daily lives', in R. Brown (ed.) *Children and Television*, London: Collier-Macmillan.

Dalquist, U. (1992) 'Om ungdomars val av TV-program. En longitudinell studie', *Lund Research Papers in Media and Communication Studies* 2, Lund: Department of Sociology, University of Lund.

Eron, L.D. and Huesmann, L.R. (1987) 'Television as a source of maltreatment of children', *School Psychology Review* 16 (2): 195–202.

Flodin, B. (1986) *TV och yrkesförväntan. En longitudinell studie av ungdomars yrkessocialisation* (with a summary in English), Lund: Studentlitteratur.

Hearold, S. (1986) 'A synthesis of 1043 effects of televison on social behavior', in G. Comstock (ed.) *Public Communication and Behavior*, vol. 1, Orlando, Fla.: Academic Press.

Himmelweit. H., Oppenheim, A.P. and Vince, P. (1958) *Television and the Child*, London: Oxford University Press.

Hippel, K. (1992) 'Parasoziale Interaktion. Bericht und Bibliographie', *Montage/AV* 1(1): 135–150.

Horton, D. and Wohl, R.R. (1956) 'Mass communication and para-social interaction', *Psychiatry* 19: 215–229.

Huesmann, L.R. and Eron, L.D. (eds) (1986) *Television and the Aggressive Child: A Cross-national Comparison*, Hillsdale, NJ: Erlbaum.

Jarlbro. G. and Dalquist, U. (1991) 'Mot alla odds. En longitudinell studie av ungdomars sociala mobilitet', *Lund Research Papers in the Sociology of Communication* 30, Lund: Department of Sociology, University of Lund.

Jensen, K.B. and Rosengren, K.E. (1990) 'Five traditions in search of the audience', *European Journal of Communication* 5: 207–238.

Johnsson-Smaragdi, U. (1983) *TV Use and Social Interaction in Adolescence. A Longitudinal Study*, Stockholm: Almqvist & Wiksell International.

—— (1986) 'Familjen, kamraterna och TV-tittandet', in K.E. Rosengren (ed.) *På gott och ont: Barn och ungdom, TV och video*, Stockholm: Allmänna barnhuset.

—— (1992) 'Learning to watch television: Longitudinal LISREL models replicated', *Lund Research Papers in Media and Communication Studies* 5, Lund: Department of sociology, University of Lund.

Johnsson-Smaragdi, U. and Jönsson, A. (forthcoming) 'TV viewing and the social character – a long term perspective', *Lund Research Papers in Media and Communication Studies*, Lund: Department of Sociology, University of Lund.

Jönsson, A. (1985) *TV – ett hot eller en resurs. En longitudinell studie av relationen mellan skola och TV* (with a summary in English), Lund: Gleerups.

—— (1986) 'TV: a threat or a complement to school?', *Journal of Educational Television* 12(1): 29–38.

Jöreskog, K.G. and Sörbom, D. (1988) *LISREL 7. A Guide to the Program and Applications* (2nd edn), Chicago: SPSS Publications.

Jöreskog, K.G. and Wold, H. (eds) (1982) *Systems under Indirect Observation: Causality, Structure, Prediction*, Amsterdam: North Holland.

Klapper, J. (1960) *The Effects of Mass Communication*, New York: Free Press.

Korzenny, F. and Ting-Toomey, S. (eds) 1992 *Mass Media Effects Across Cultures*, Newbury Park, Calif.: Sage.

Linz, D.G. and Donnerstein, E. (1989) 'The effects of violent messages in the mass media', in J.J. Bradac (ed.) *Message Effects in Communication Science*, Newbury Park, Calif.: Sage.

Lowery, S. and De Fleur, M.L. (1983) *Milestones in Mass Communication Research*, New York: Longman.

McQuail, D. and Windahl, S. (1981) *Communication Models for the Study of Mass Communications*, London: Longman.

Merton, R.K. (1963) *Social Theory and Social Structure*, rev. and enlarged edn, Glencoe, Ill.: Free Press.

Milawsky, J.R., Kessler, R.C., Stipp, H.H. and Rubens, W.S. (1982) *Television and Aggression: A Panel Study*, New York: Academic Press.

Paik, H. (1992) 'Gender and the effects of television violence: A meta analysis' (Paper presented to the AEJMC convention, Montreal, August 1992).

Pearl, D., Bouthilet, L. and Lazar, J. (eds) (1982) *Television and Behavior. Ten Years of Scientific Progress and Implications for the Eighties*, Washington, DC: Government Printing Office.

Roe, K. (1985) 'The Swedish moral panic over video 1980–1984', *Nordicom Review* 1: 20–25.

Rosengren, K.E. (ed.) (1992) 'Special issue on audience research', *Poetics* 21 (4).

Rosengren, K.E., Wenner, L.A. and Palmgreen, P. (eds) (1985) *Media Gratifications Research: Current Perspectives*. Beverly Hills, Calif.: Sage.

Rosengren, K.E. and Windahl, S. (1972) 'Mass media consumption as a functional alternative', in D. McQuail (ed.) *Sociology of Mass Communications*, Harmondsworth: Penguin.

Rosengren, K.E. and Windahl, S. (1977) 'Mass media use: causes and effects', *Communications* 3: 337–351.

Rosengren, K.E, and Windahl. S. (1989) *Media Matter. TV Use in Childhood and Adolescence*, Norwood, NJ: Ablex.

Rosengren, K.E., Windahl, S., Håkansson, P.A. and Johnsson-Smaragdi, U. (1976) 'Adolescents' TV relations: Three scales', *Communication Research* 3: 347–366.

Rosenthal, R. (1986) Media violence, antisocial behavior, and the social consequences of small effects', *Journal of Social Issues* 42 (3): 141–154.

Rubin, A.M. and Windahl, S. (1986) 'The uses and dependency model of mass communication', *Critical Studies in Mass Communication* 3: 184–199.

Schramm, V., Lyle, J. and Parker, E.B. (1961) *Television in the Lives of our Children*, Stanford: Stanford University Press.

Schulz, W. (ed.) (1992) *Medienwirkungen. Einflüsse von Presse, Radio und Fernsehen auf Individuum und Gesellschaft*, Weinheim, Germany: VCH Verlagsgesellschaft.

Sonesson, I. (1979) *Förskolebarn och TV*. Malmö: Esselte Studium.

—— (1986) 'TV, aggressivitet och ängslan', in K.E. Rosengren (ed.) *På gott och ont: Barn och ungdom, TV och video*, Stockholm: Allmänna barnhuset.

—— (1989) *Vem fostrar våra barn – videon eller vi?*, Stockholm: Esselte Studium.

—— (1990) 'Barn i satellitåldern', in U. Carlsson (ed.) *Medier Människor Samhälle*, Göteborg: NORDICOM.

Surgeon General (1972) *Television and Growing Up. The Impact of Televised Violence*, Washington, DC: Government Printing Office.

Swanson, D.L. (1992) 'Understanding audiences: Continuing contributions of gratifications research', *Poetics* 21: 305–328.

Turner, C.W., Hesse, B.W., and Peterson-Lewis, S. (1986) 'Naturalistic studies of the long-term effects of television violence', *Journal of Social Issues* 42 (3): 51–73.

Wertham, F. (1954) *Seduction of the Innocent*, New York: Rinehart.

Wiegman, O., Kuttschreuter, M. and Baarda, B. (1992) 'A longitudinal study of the effects of television viewing on aggressive and prosocial behaviours', *British Journal of Social Psychology* 31: 147–164.

Windahl, S. (1981) 'Uses and gratifications at the crossroads', in G. C. Wilhoit and H. de Bock (eds) *Mass Communication Review Yearbook* 2.

Chapter 8

Self-evaluation in an ecological perspective: neighbourhood, family and peers, schooling and media use

Ulla Johnsson-Smaragdi and Annelis Jönsson

SELF-ESTEEM AND THE ECOLOGICAL DEVELOPMENTAL MODEL

Our perception of ourselves is of essential significance to what we feel we are able to accomplish, as well as to the goals for which we strive. Further, the way we perceive ourselves is important not only for our behaviour, but also for our mental well-being.

Self-evaluation or self-esteem may be studied from different angles. It is possible, for example, to study self-evaluation as a conceivable *cause* of certain kinds of behaviour or conditions. Or self-evaluation may be regarded as an *effect*, i.e. as a result of other factors influencing self-evaluation. Another possibility is to study self-esteem simultaneously as a cause and as an effect.

Studies of self-evaluation have usually started from either psycho-dynamically inspired theories, emphasizing the intra-individual development in the spirit of Freud and Erikson, or from socio-psychological theories. In the latter case the individual's development in terms of socialization is emphasized.

In this analysis we have chosen to study self-evaluation mainly from a socio-psychological perspective and, thus, to perceive self-evaluation as a result of continual interaction between the individual and his/her environment, including family, school, peers, mass media and the neighbourhood (see Figure 8.1).

The analysis starts from Bronfenbrenner's ecological model of human development. This model is based on an interactional view, where the interplay between the individual and his/her environment is emphasized (see Bronfenbrenner 1979; Andersson 1986). The model is used because it is in accordance with our understanding of the process of socialization and of the individual's development.

Bronfenbrenner views the child as an active individual, who develops in constant interaction with its environment. In the theory of human ecological development, the environment is described as a series of coherent structures

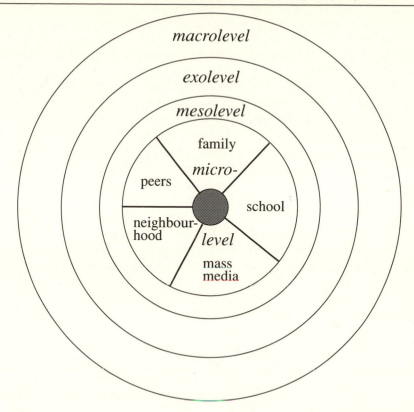

Figure 8.1 Bronfenbrenner's model of the ecology of human development
(Source: Andersson 1986; supplemented with mass media)

and systems (Figure 8.1). The family, pre-school/school, peers and the
housing area are the most important settings for the growing child. To the
small child, the parents and the family are naturally most essential. A
network of relations is developed within the family; a network which
influences the child, and which the child itself influences. In Bronfenbrenner's terminology such a network is called a microsystem. As the child
grows older, it will be part of an increasing number of such microsystems.
A more prominent place will be given to school with its network of relations,
to peers and to the neighbourhood. Bronfenbrenner does not mention mass
media in this context. In this chapter, however, mass media – in this case,
TV and video – have been added to the ecological model. Earlier studies have
shown that TV and the video appear early in the lives of children. Families
gather in front of the TV, and peers gather in front of the VCR (Johnsson-
Smaragdi 1983; Jönsson 1985; Sonesson 1989). Many children are better
acquainted with persons whom they see on TV and video than with real people
around them. Studies have also shown that children and adolescents interact

with media in different ways (Rosengren and Windahl 1989; Comstock and Paik 1991) and that, in their turn, media interact with school, peers, the family and the neighbourhood (Johnsson-Smaragdi 1983, 1986; Jönsson 1985, 1986, 1989, 1991).

The microsystems are not independent, but interact with each other. Taken as a whole, the relations between the microsystems form an overall system – the mesosystem. Thus, the children's self-image is affected by each of the microsystems not only directly, but also indirectly by the interactions between the microsystems. School, for example, is involved in such an interplay. School's significance for children's self-image depends not only on how the child is treated by its schoolmates and teachers, and on how the child handles the demands raised by school. Indirectly, the child's self-image is affected also by the way the school interacts with other microsystems. Their parents' attitude towards school, and the socio-cultural climate in which the children grow up, are very important, of course, to the school's potential to influence the children. The atmosphere of the neighbourhood, the attitudes and ways of relating to each other which dominate among its inhabitants, have not only a direct, but also an indirect influence on the development of the children. The attitudes and ways of relating which develop within a neighbourhood affect the other microsystems, and, thus, also indirectly the children. In addition, the same conditions also have a bearing on the other microsystems: the media and the peer group.

The mesosystem, in its turn, is affected by the next level – the exolevel. The community's supply of services, the working conditions of the parents and so forth, also make up a network, which in Bronfenbrenner's model is called the exosystem. The children do not have immediate contact with these systems and, therefore, are only indirectly affected by them. The next level of the model is the macrolevel, where the more comprehensive, ideological, economical, historical and political evaluations and conditions make up different macrosystems.

Mead has made essential contributions to our understanding of the ways in which our self-esteem or self-perception develop. According to Mead (1934, 1969), we are born without a 'self'. As a result of our social experiences, our 'self-consciousness' gradually develops. Mead starts out from interactional theory, thus emphasizing the role and importance of interaction. According to his mirror theory our self-perception is created by our taking over the reactions, as well as the attitudes to our own actions, of people around us. This view has been summarized in a sentence which we find illustrative: *I am not the one I think I am, and I am not the one you think I am; I am the one I think that you think I am.*

Trust in people, and in our own ability, is founded early in life. Erikson (1963) regards the care received in early childhood as essential for the development of fundamental security and trust, which, in its turn, is basic to the development of the identity to come. The basis for the most fundamental self-esteem consists of being loved and appreciated for who you are. At a later stage in childhood we develop the external self-esteem, which is mainly related to performing and managing. By realizing that we are good at something, when, compared to others, we seem to be competent, and when we feel that we live up to the expectations of people around us, the external self-esteem is reinforced.

During the pre-school years, children's self-esteem is comparatively diffuse, and their ideas about themselves are rather exaggerated. Between the age of 6 and 11/12, children find themselves in the 'phase of latency' (psychoanalytical terminology) or in the 'period of rest' (a psychosexual perspective). In a psychosocial perspective, however, the period is important. During this period two important aspects are forcefully introduced, namely, work and the peer group. Work, as well as contact with peers, takes place mainly in school. During this age, children grow increasingly able to discriminate between different areas of competence when they evaluate themselves. They are now more interested in their cognitive and social competence as compared to others. Positive self-esteem builds, above all, on success in school and popularity among peers. To learn that you are good enough, are able to handle things, and that you are accepted, is now especially important. In other words, school is very much responsible for the development of the child's self-image.

In a series of studies it has been established that individuals having a positive self-image – that is to say, who believe in themselves – act and behave differently from those who do not have this kind of self-confidence. Children with a high degree of self-reliance are often described as more active and curious, more inclined to take responsibility and to act on their own initiative. They are usually better liked and more accepted among their peers. Good relations with peers and acceptance in the group strengthen self-esteem, as does success in school (Johanneson 1966; Skaalvik 1982; Beane and Lipka 1984). Jarlbro (1988) also points to the connection between young people's self-image and their relations with peers. She indicates that it is often a matter of reciprocal, 'circle' effects; a positive self-image results in good relations with peers, which further strengthens the positive self-image. Correspondingly, a negative self-image will contribute to worse relations with peers, which fortifies the negative self-image.

One of school's most important tasks is to strengthen each pupil's desire and trust in his or her ability to learn. However, the ability of schools to live up to these aims varies. Some students learn to believe in their own capability, and to explain possible failures by external factors such as bad luck, the nature of the assignment, etc. Other students leave school with ruined self-confidence or a further strengthened negative self-image. They have learnt to explain possible failures by saying 'I am not good enough' (Donelson 1986).

PURPOSE AND METHOD

In this study we try to show – from the perspective of the ecology of human development – how a group of children (born 1969; cohort M69; see Figure 3.2 p. 42) estimate their self-image at 11, 15 and 21 years of age and how their estimates depend on a number of factors, including gender and social background, neighbourhood, school grades, mass media and peers. The study is based on longitudinal data collected within the Media Panel Program by means of classroom and postal questionnaires, schemes of teacher's estimates, and register data. Rosengren and Windahl (1989) offers a review of the research results from the first three waves of data collection within the Media Panel Program.

Among many other subjects, the children and adolescents in the panel were questioned about their media habits, their activities with peers, and their self-esteem. Their parents were also questioned, for example about their media habits, attitudes and their standards of upbringing. The original sample included about 250 children: 133 girls and 119 boys. After fifteen years, 72 per cent (165) of the original group remained.

Our main object is to illustrate to what extent different experiences within the microsystems – the neighbourhood, the family, the peer group, media and school – are reflected in the way girls and boys evaluate themselves at different ages. We also want to elucidate the way the microsystems interact. Thanks to the longitudinal design it is possible to estimate what importance early socialization experiences have for adolescents' self-evaluation later in life.

Our self-image is created as we gradually take over the reactions of people around us to our behaviour. In a historical perspective, society's expectations and reactions to the behaviour of boys and girls have certainly changed to some extent, but despite this there are some traditional elements in the way we treat boys and girls. From birth, boys and girls meet different expectations and, thus, also differential treatment from people around them. In his survey of previous research, Block (1983) notices that there are considerable differences in parents' attitudes towards sons and daughters. In the upbringing of boys, performance, competition, independence and emotional control are often emphasized, while obedience, responsibility and care are emphasized in the upbringing of girls. In a study carried out among Swedish school children at the junior level, Einarsson and Hultman (1984) show that girls are more subjected to over-protection and control than are boys. Early in life girls learn to forego their striving for independence. Instead they seek appreciation for their very lack of self-assertion. The differential treatment is also likely to be reflected in how boys and girls estimate their self-image. Consequently, we will study the self-perception of boys and girls, as well as its development during childhood and adolescence, separately.

DESCRIPTION OF VARIABLES

Self-image was measured by Rosenberg's test of self-evaluation (1965). In this test self-esteem is estimated by a number of statements such as '*I often feel worthless*' and '*I have plenty of good qualities*'. The first measurement was based on a 4-degree scale; the following two on a 5-degree scale. The scales ranged from 'Do not correspond with' (value 0) to 'Correspond completely' (values 3 and 4, respectively). This test of self-evaluation taps general self-esteem; it is not specifically focused on cognitive or social competence. Reliability was measured by Cronbach's alpha, which on the first occasion was (.70) and on the following two (.86) and (.87).

The group of variables called 'Activities with peers' concerns how often you meet peers and do things together with them, and also how many different activities you are engaged in with peers. Questions concerning these peer activities cover a wide range of activities, from 'just being with peers' to more organized sports and hobby activities. It is a rather rough measure, which does not include any other qualitative aspects than those related to the content of the activities.

TV consumption is measured by means of six questions (at the age of 21, with 8 questions; see Chapter 4) tapping the amount of broadcast and cable television viewing on weekdays (number of days and hours per day), and at weekends (number of Saturdays and Sundays (later also Fridays) per month and number of hours on each of these days). VCR consumption is measured by means of four questions about amount of viewing on weekdays (number of weekdays and hours per day) and at weekends (number of times during the weekend and number of hours each time). On the basis of these questions two indices have been built, measuring the number of hours devoted to TV and VCR during an average week.

The data from the school sector include cognitive measures – results from tests of school readiness, marks and choice of course level at the senior level in compulsory school. The tests of school readiness, given at the school start, include three-part tests intended to measure the children's knowledge of letters, their spatial ability and their numeric perception. Cronbach's alpha for each of the three tests was (.80). When leaving grade 6, the average of the marks includes Swedish, Maths, General Subjects and English. When leaving grade 9, the average includes Swedish, Maths, English, Science Subjects and Civics. The marks vary between 1 and 5, where 5 is the best. (In grade 6, the average was 3.2; in grade 9, 3.3.) We have also taken into account whether the children have followed a general or an advanced course in English and Maths, i.e. taken a limited (general) or a more extensive course in these subjects. In the group under study, 30 per cent of the pupils attended the general course, and almost 45 per cent attended the advanced course in both subjects. Some 25 per cent of the children had chosen the general course in one of the subjects and the advanced in the other.

The social background of the family is measured by using information on the parents' occupations. Information on the mother's level of education and the family communication climate when the children were 11 years old, is also included.

Family communication climate is measured by a scale developed by Chaffee *et al.* (1971, 1973). The scale has been adjusted to Swedish conditions. The scale includes two factors, namely, *socio-oriented* communication (based on statements such as *'It's better to give in than argue in a discussion'* and *'Discussions should be held in a nice and pleasant tone'*), and *concept-oriented* communication (including statements such as *'It's important to speak one's mind even if other people disagree'* and *'Children have the right to criticize and discuss the ideas of grown-ups'*). The scale was administered to the parents of the adolescents in grades 5 and 9 (age 11 and 15). On both measurement occasions, the reliability was measured by Cronbach's alpha; in grade 5 it was (.87) for socio and (.65) for concept, and in grade 9, (.82) and (.55), respectively.

In the scales, a value of zero means total absence of socio- or concept-orientation. The higher the point on the scale, the more the socio- or concept-oriented communication in the family. Analysis of the scales showed that all the families in the study were to be found on the upper part of the scales. Above all, this concerns the concept-oriented scale, where the variance is very restricted. This means that most families score high both on socio- and on concept-oriented communication.

The two family communication scales have been dichotomized and then combined, whereby four family types can be discerned (see Figure 8.2). The figure implies that the measurement instrument does not cover the whole range of the two concepts. In the figure it is also stressed that you may be more or less concept- and/or socio-oriented. Thus, it is more a question of degrees than absolute differences. The family types are described in more detail in Chaffee *et al.* (1971, 1973). Results from Swedish studies on family communication types are presented in Jarlbro (1988), Rosengren and Windahl (1989) and in Chapter 10 of this volume.

Information about the socio-economic structure of the neighbourhood is mainly based on the income tax returns among its inhabitants. The neighbourhoods have been divided into four groups, classified from 1 to 4, where 1 means *high* socio-economic status and 4 means *low*.

STABILITY OVER TIME

Stability over time is of great interest in longitudinal studies. In Johnsson-Smaragdi (1983, 1992; see also Chapter 6) different concepts of stability are discussed in some detail. Relative stability is defined as *'stability in individuals' ranks or differences with respect to a given phenomenon'*. It indicates *'that in relation to other members of the group, individuals retain*

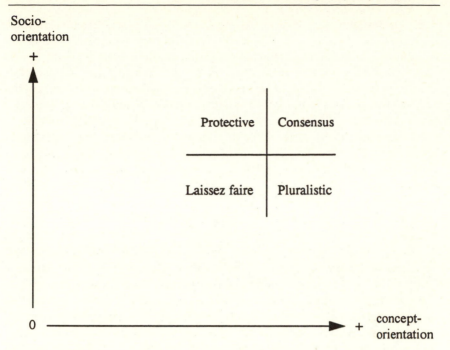

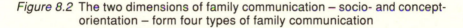

Figure 8.2 The two dimensions of family communication – socio- and concept-
orientation – form four types of family communication

much the same position over time'. Relative stability is measured by means
of correlations between the same variables on different occasions; it describes
the individual's stability in relation to the group.

Table 8.1 presents the coefficients of stability for the self-image between
ages 11 and 15, and between ages 15 and 21, respectively.

Table 8.1 Stability in the estimation of self-image (Pearson correlation coefficients)

	11 years	⇔	15 years	⇔	21 years
Totals:		.38		.47	
Girls:		.38		.37	
Boys:		.29		.27	

In previous studies (Samuels 1977; Rosenberg 1979) it is emphasized that
the self-image grows more stable with age and more resistant to external
influences. According to Rosenberg (1979) the self-perception is usually not
stabilized before the age of 18. Ahlgren (1991) shows correlations between .46
and .69 for tests of self-evaluation carried out with an interval of one year. The
lowest degree of stability was found for the age-groups between 13 and 14.

In the present study the time intervals between the measurements are 4 and 6 years, respectively. The stability differs with regard to gender; girls show a higher degree of stability than boys. Whether the coefficients of stability in Table 8.1 can be considered as strong or weak is a matter of judgement. A much more stable variable is achievement at school as measured by grades and test results. Here, the coefficients of stability are .60 between 7 and 11 years of age and .70 between 11 and 15 years of age, for both girls and boys. On the other hand, the coefficients of stability for activities with peers show about the same stability over time (between .34 and .37) as does self-image, which is natural considering that the types of activity change with age. Corresponding results are also shown in Johnsson-Smaragdi (1983).

SELF-IMAGE AMONG GIRLS AND BOYS

Much research has been devoted to studying what factors in our surroundings are important to the way we perceive ourselves. Gender is a factor which in a series of studies has proved to be of importance in the context (Zahran 1966; Roe 1989; Alsaker *et al.* 1990). Corresponding results were also arrived at in this study. In Table 8.2 a standardized average value is presented (m/r, i.e. the average value is divided by the range of the scale to facilitate comparisons between the occasions of measurement). Thus measured, self-image may vary between 0 and 1.

Table 8.2 Standardized average self-image (m/r) at ages 11, 15 and 21; controlling for gender and social background

	11 years m/r	15 years m/r	21 years m/r
Gender:			
Boys	.66	.72	.77
Girls	.61	.57	.64
p	<.01	<.001	<.001
Social background:			
Lower	.62	.63	.69
Middle	.63	.64	.70
High	.66	.64	.71
p	ns	ns	ns

Irrespective of age, boys have a more positive self-image than girls of the same age. Generally they seem to have a less critical view of themselves than girls. They are more pleased with themselves and their looks, and they have more trust in their ability than the girls. Gender differences increase with age. Corresponding age differences between how boys and girls estimate their self-image are presented in other studies (for instance, Ahlgren 1991). One explanation for the increase in the gender differences in self-estimation in the teens is that through the socialization process girls become more aware of the fact that men have more power and prestige in society than women have. Girls also meet appreciation for the very same lack of independence and lack of self-assertion. A consequence of this gender-specific socialization is that girls tend to be more self-critical. Low self-estimation is a means for girls to be obedient to the cultural expectations directed towards them.

Self-image has also been analysed with regard to social background. The differences in how people in different social groups estimate their self-image are only marginal. When combining gender with social background in order to study the self-image, differences occur between the subgroups, however (Table 8.3).

Table 8.3 Standardized average value for self-image at ages 11, 15 and 21; combined control for gender and social background

Social background:	11 years m/r			15 years m/r			21 years m/r		
	low	middle	high	low	middle	high	low	middle	high
Gender:									
Boys	.66	.66	.66	.71	.74	.72	.77	.79	.77
Girls	.60	.61	.66	.58	.57	.54	.66	.60	.64
p	ns	ns	ns	<.001	<.001	<.01	<.01	<.001	<.01

At the age of 11, the differences between the self-image of boys and girls from different social groups are only marginal. When they get older, however, the situation changes. Irrespective of social background, boys have a more positive self-image than girls, both at 15 and 21 years of age. The gender differences at each social level are statistically significant. However, when analysing self-image within each gender group with regard to social background the differences are not found to be significant.

SELF-IMAGE SEEN FROM THE PERSPECTIVE OF THE ECOLOGY OF HUMAN DEVELOPMENT

On several occasions it has been confirmed that the climate of communication within the family is of importance to children's and young people's self-perception and trust in themselves and the world around them. Rosenberg (1965) was one of the first to demonstrate parents' importance for the child's self-esteem. Among other factors he found that the child's self-esteem was influenced more by the extent to which parents showed an interest in their children, encouraged and supported them, than by social background. Children who were not encouraged and did not feel appreciated by their parents showed a lower degree of self-estimation than others. The children seem to have internalized what they perceived as their parents' view. Corresponding results are presented by a series of other scholars (Greenstein 1969; Thomas 1974; Baron and Byrne 1987; Pölkki 1990).

Two theoretical models of the development and preservation of self-perception, namely, symbolic interaction and social learning, are presented in Openshaw *et al.* (1983). According to the theory of symbolic interaction, self-perception is seen as a joint result of parents' attitude towards the child and the interaction between child and parents. The theory of social learning, on the other hand, emphasizes parents' role as models; parents' self-evaluation is assumed to influence that of the child. In previous research it has also been shown that social learning and symbolic interaction affect the self-perception in different ways at different stages in people's lives (Gecas *et al.* 1974).

In the model of the ecology of human development, the environment is regarded as consisting of a series of coherent structures and systems. For children and adolescents, the most important local settings are the family, the neighbourhood, peers and school. The importance of these local settings for the development of the self-image is analysed in Table 8.4. The statistical analyses are based on MCA (SPSS). Each independent factor has been analysed separately, controlling only for social background. It was not possible to analyse the factors contemporaneously, which means that the influence from the other independent factors could not be controlled for. The main reason is that the groups become relatively small when boys and girls are analysed separately.

An important reason for choosing MCA for the analyses was that this method provides opportunities to study whether or not the relations established are linear. Another reason was that we wanted to use MCA exploratory, thus being able to catch tendencies in the material. As the groups analysed are relatively small, more importance has been put on the strength of the relationships (beta) than on tests of significance. Table 8.4 is a compilation of five separate MCA analyses. Only beta coefficients over (.15) are presented.

The results support the importance of the family for our self-image. The family communication type is related to self-evaluation both at the age of 11 and at the age of 15. At the same time there are some interesting gender differences. Generally, the family type seems to be more important for girls' self-image than for that of boys. (How the different types of family affect the self-image of boys and girls at different ages is more closely accounted for in the next section.) A strong linear relationship also exists between the education level of their mothers and the girls' self-image, while the corresponding relation is missing for boys (their fathers' educational level was not available). In the group of girls with extremely high self-perception, more than 20 per cent had mothers with college or university education. Among the girls with extremely low self-image, only 3 per cent had highly educated

Table 8.4 Self-image of boys and girls at ages 11 and 15 in different microsystems with control for social background (cross-sections)

| | Self-image of boys | | Self-image of girls | |
	11 years beta	15 years beta	11 years beta	15 years beta
Family: mother's educational level	–	–	.34	.26
family communication type	.18	.17	.33	.27
Neighbourhood: socio-economic status	.19	–	.19	–
Mass media: TV-consumption	.17	.18	–	–
VCR-consumption	#	.19	#	–
School: grades	.33	.28	.18	.25
stream	#	.26	#	.20
Peers: activities with peers	.18	.17	–	–

Note: # = information missing
      (–) = beta coefficients <.15

mothers. One explanation of the large gender differences is that the girls
identify themselves with their mothers, while the boys do not. In other words,
independent and well-educated mothers seem to strengthen their daughters'
self-images. During the teens the connection between the mother's level of
education and the girl's self-images decreases slightly.

From Table 8.4 it can also be concluded that school is important for young
people's self-esteem. To perform well and prove that you can cope with
school's cognitive demands, by, for instance, having good marks and being
able to make a more demanding choice of courses, is important for self-
evaluation. The relation is strongest for boys, especially at the age of 11. At
this age the children are in the phase of latency. They then experience a
crisis of maturation, primarily concerning the struggle between feelings of
competence and inferiority (Erikson 1963). The importance of school results
to the self-image of girls increases gradually, and in the teens it is
comparable with that of boys. An interesting difference may be found
between boys and girls with regard to the importance of family and school
for their self-image. In these age-groups, it seems that school means more
to the self-esteem of boys than the family does, while the opposite tendency
is prevalent among girls.

The connection between self-perception and success in school has been established in many, mainly American, investigations. This is true for school-related as well as a more general self-perception (Coopersmith 1967; Nash 1974; Prendergast and Binder 1975; Simon and Simon 1975). Hansford and Hattie (1982) show that success in school is more strongly related to self-esteem than is intelligence. The connection between self-perception and school achievement is also shown in surveys based on Swedish school children; those successful in school had a more positive self-perception (Taube 1987; Roe 1989). At the same time Roe states that in the research on self-evaluation the stress has usually been on the parents' attitudes towards the child, while the importance of school experiences in the context has often been disregarded. The relation between self-perception and success in school, however, does not tell anything about the direction of the relationship, that is, what is the cause and what is the effect. Roe points out that low self-evaluation can be both a cause and an effect of bad results at school.

On the other hand, both media and peers seem to play a less important part in the way boys and girls evaluate their self-images in the age-groups in question. Nevertheless, media and peers are more important to boys' self-perception than to that of girls. The relations accounted for are weak, but linear.

The socio-economic structure of the neighbourhood has some importance for the self-image of 11-year-old children. The connection is not linear, though. Highest self-esteem is found in areas of either high or low status, while the self-esteem is slightly lower in the areas in between. One possible explanation could be that a sense of community develops more easily in homogeneous and segregated environments; in its turn, this may contribute to increased security and self-evaluation. However, the neighbourhood's importance for the self-image decreases with age, which probably is due to the fact that the 15-year-old adolescent is less dependent on the physical, local environment than the 11-year-old child. Since teenagers are less dependent on the local environment, this is of less importance to them.

In a study of self-evaluation among school children from different minority groups, Rosenberg (1965) found that the close community affects the school children's self-evaluation most. He also found that black children in segregated schools had higher self-esteem than those who went to integrated schools. To live in a segregated minority group is more positive for self-perception than to live as a minority group in a majority group. In a study of retarded pupils Lagerroth and Nilsson (1992) presented corresponding results.

FAMILY TYPE AND SELF-IMAGE

Parents' attitudes towards their children – that is, to what extent their attitudes are characterized by support and encouragement or control and prohibition – have in many situations been identified as central factors in the socialization process. Researchers with a symbolic interactionist perspective have often claimed that supportive behaviour from the parents gives the child a feeling of being an accepted and competent person. Therefore, supportive parent behaviour is presumed to be positively related to the child's self-perception (Rosenberg 1965, 1979). Rollins and Thomas (1979) describe two different kinds of controlling parent behaviour, namely, induction, which means that the parents point out the consequences in which a certain kind of behaviour will result, and coercion, which means that the parents exercise power to attain the desired behaviour. Unlike coercion, induction is considered to strengthen self-esteem positively.

Socio-oriented family communication, as described by Chaffee *et al.* (1971, 1973), can be compared to what Rollins and Thomas (1979) describe as induction, while concept-oriented communication can be compared to supportive parent behaviour. Socio-oriented and concept-oriented family communication have been combined into four family types, namely, '*Laissez-faire*', 'Pluralistic', 'Protective' and 'Consensus' (Figure 8.2 above). Average values for the different family types, with simultaneous control for age and gender, are presented in Table 8.5, based on a number of MCA analyses. The average values are standardized by dividing the average with the range of the scale, in order to make the averages more comparable. The differences between family types are not significant, but show interesting tendencies.

The relationships between self-image and family type were .18 for boys and .27 for girls, both at the ages of 11 and 15 (beta).

Table 8.5 Self-image for boys and girls at ages of 11 and 15 in different family types (standardized means)

Family communication	Self-image of boys		Self-image of girls	
	11 years m/r	15 years m/r	11 years m/r	15 years m/r
Laissez-faire	.60	.70	.56	.50
Protective	.65	.71	.65	.61
Pluralistic	.67	.74	.59	.56
Consensus	.69	.77	.65	.60

Boys, as well as girls, who grow up in '*Laissez-faire*' families, have a more negative self-image than other children. Above all, this applies to girls. Researchers such as Rosenberg (1965), Coopersmith (1967) and Greenstein (1969) have previously presented similar results; children growing up in this type of communication climate show a lower degree of self-esteem. A communication climate characterized by '*Laissez-faire*' is easily interpreted as an inadequate commitment and indifference from the parents towards the child. Not being confirmed gives the child a feeling that the parents do not care, and because of this, the child may feel worthless.

On the other hand, 'Consensus' families with high socio-oriented as well as concept-oriented family communication seem to strengthen the self-image of boys and girls alike. The results correspond with what Rollins and Thomas (1979) and Rosenberg (1965, 1979) describe as induction and supportive parent behaviour, respectively.

However, the 'Pluralistic' family type with high concept-orientation and low socio-orientation, and the 'Protective' family type with low concept-orientation and high socio-orientation, seem to affect girls' and boys' self-images in different ways. In the 'Protective' family type girls have a tendency to a somewhat higher self-image than in the 'Pluralistic' family type. In this type, on the other hand, the boys tend to have a better self-image than in the 'Protective' family type. The differences are marginal, however.

For girls, family types which include socio-orientation – 'Consensus' and 'Protective' types – seem to strengthen the self-image positively, while family types which lack this kind of orientation tend to create a more negative self-image. The age of the girls is of no importance in this context. Tendencies to please, to listen to other people, not to argue and so on are often characterized as female qualities. To adapt oneself to existing norms and ideas leads to positive reinforcement from other people, thus strengthening the girls' self-image. Society's expectations of boys are more in accordance with the characteristics of concept- orientation, that is, being firm, not giving in, not being afraid of discussions, and to demand respect for one's opinions.

INTERACTION BETWEEN MICROSYSTEMS

In the model of the ecology of human development, the interaction between the different microsystems is strongly emphasized. Family, school, peers, media and the socio-economic structure of the neighbourhood each have direct influence on the development, and also an indirect influence, by way of the interaction between different microsystems interacting. This interaction takes place within what Bronfenbrenner calls the mesosystem. We have tried to show the interaction between the microsystems by means of zero-order correlations, which are presented in Figures 8.3a and b and 8.4a and b. (Family type is not included in the interaction models, since it is measured on the level of a nominal scale.)

There is interaction between nearly all the different microsystems. Families with a certain kind of social background make for certain types of housing area, are influenced by, and also influence the character of the area. The character of the neighbourhood influences the atmosphere and activities of the school, but also what peers you meet and what kind of activities are available. The use of media also interacts with the culture and the atmosphere in the neighbourhood, as well as in school and among peers.

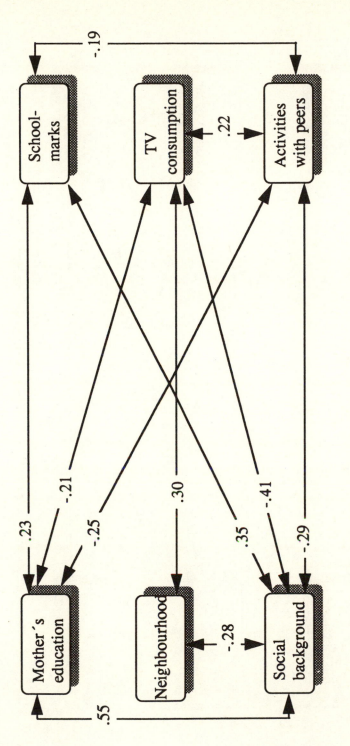

Figure 8.3a Interaction between microsystems. Girls, age 11 (bivariate correlations)

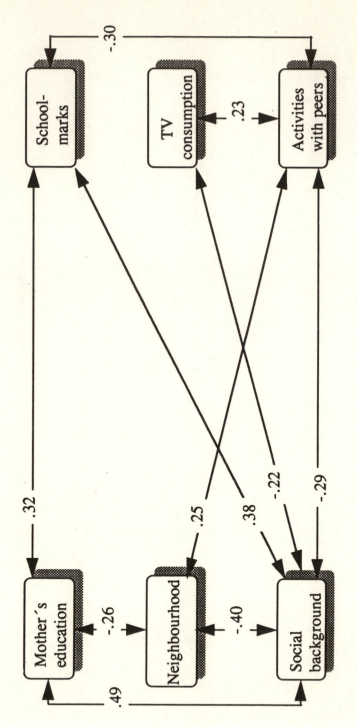

Figure 8.3b Interaction between microsystems. Boys, age 11 (bivariate correlations)

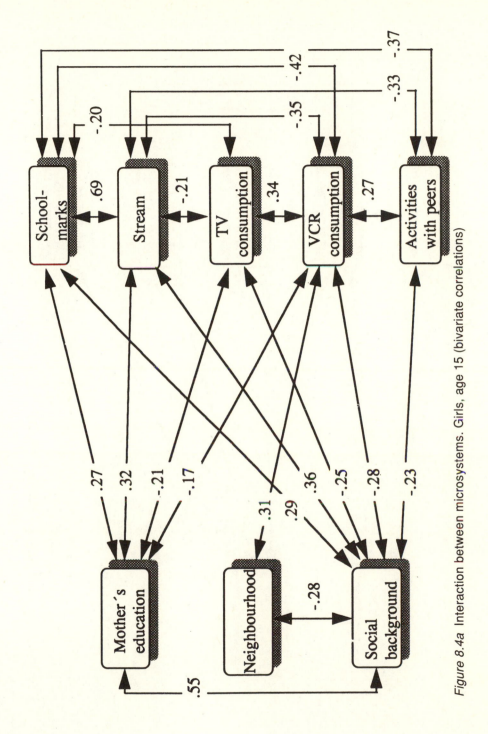

Figure 8.4a Interaction between microsystems. Girls, age 15 (bivariate correlations)

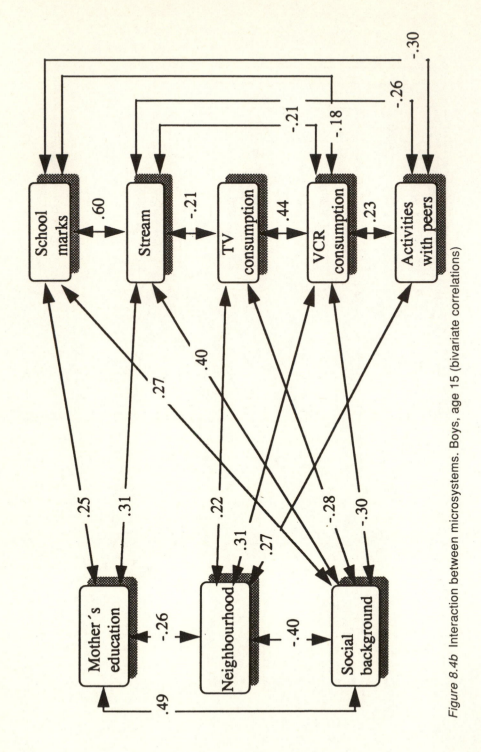

Figure 8.4b Interaction between microsystems. Boys, age 15 (bivariate correlations)

SELF-IMAGE FROM A LONGITUDINAL PERSPECTIVE

The individual's self-image develops and forms in interaction with the surroundings. During childhood and adolescence the self-image is rather unstable. It does not stabilize and become more resistant to external influence until adulthood (Rosenberg 1979).

By using the ecological perspective of human development, we try to show how the self-image has developed and been formed over time through interaction with the microsystems in which the child has been growing up. We try to show to what extent earlier experiences within the microsystems – the neighbourhood, the family, peers, the media and school – affect how girls and boys evaluate themselves in adulthood. Our main question is if, and to what extent, the different microsystems have any long-term effects on the self-image.

Thanks to the longitudinal design of this study, we are able to describe the importance of earlier experiences to the way young people estimate their self-images later in life. In order to show the complete influence on the self-image, we have analysed the interplay over time with LISREL – a programme of analysis by means of which multivariate causal relations between latent variables may be estimated showing both direct and indirect influences (Jöreskog and Sörbom 1988; Johnsson-Smaragdi 1983, 1992).

Just as before, boys and girls have been analysed separately. All microsystems included in the previous cross-sectional analyses – family circumstances, the socio-economic structure of the neighbourhood, school results, activities with peers, mass media habits and self-image at the ages of 11 and 15 – were also included in the first LISREL analyses. In a second step, the LISREL model was reduced to include only those microsystems which turned out to affect the self-image at the age of 21. In all the analyses, the self-image at the age of 21 made up the effect variable.

The first LISREL analyses (Figures 8.5 and 8.6) show that there is interaction between the different microsystems, for both boys and girls. In this case, the interaction is stronger between the microsystems over time, and less strong between the contemporary microsystems, which is quite remarkable, since it is usually more difficult to demonstrate influence over time.

The previous cross-sectional analyses showed a relationship between, on one hand, self-image and on the other hand the different microsystems (see Table 8.4). However, in the LISREL analyses, showing the complete structure and its relations, interaction could not be established to the same extent as in the MCA analyses. Since the LISREL model allows the unique influence between variables to stand out, at the same time controlling for other variables, the importance of interaction between separate variables is reduced.

However, interesting circle effects may be distinguished in the LISREL model. At the age of 11, activities with peers affect the ambitions in school, resulting in either a positive or a negative circle, from the standpoint of school and society. In a *negative circle*, children having many peer activities at the age of 11, later choose less advanced courses in the senior level of comprehensive school, which in its turn leads to lower school marks when leaving school at the age of 15/16. At this age, adolescents with low school marks spend more time with peers than do their associates with higher marks. In the *positive circle* we find children who spend less time with peers at the age of 11. Those children later tend to choose advanced courses in the senior level of comprehensive school, and they also have higher marks when leaving school. This also means that they may have less time for, and maybe also less interest in, peer activities.

These circle effects, which are valid for boys as well as for girls, may be interpreted to show that young people who do not succeed at school compensate for their failure by turning to the peer group. This may be an alternative way to strengthen their self-image. It is worth noting that these relations remain even after the influence from all other variables is eliminated – including the environment when growing up (i.e. family and neighbourhood) and individual factors (i.e. school-readiness and earlier self-esteem).

The restricted LISREL models (Figures 8.7 and 8.8) show that the previous childhood environment and individual factors such as school-readiness have both a direct and an indirect influence on how young people estimate their self-images at the age of 21. However, there are essential differences between boys and girls in this regard, as is evident from a comparison between Figures 8.7 and 8.8. Table 8.6 shows the total effects on self-esteem at the age of 21, that is, a summary of direct as well as indirect effects in the reduced LISREL models.

The social background does not seem to affect boys' self-evaluation. For girls, on the other hand, there is an indirect influence from the social background via choice of course to the senior level of the elementary school – the higher the social background, the lower their self-esteem at the age of 21 (see Table 8.6). Girls with a higher social background to a larger extent choose advanced courses at senior level. However, it is primarily the school marks that determine the choice of stream. Girls choosing advanced courses – with their higher degree of difficulty and tougher competition among the pupils – to a larger extent had lower self-esteem six years later than had those who completed less demanding courses.

One explanation of the fact that girls who, by their choice of advanced courses, demonstrated high goals and levels of ambition show a more self-critical attitude at the age of 21, is probably an increased awareness and experience of the many hindrances which exist for girls trying to make a career. Although showing competence, expectations and high demands on themselves, girls often experience difficulties in asserting themselves on the male scene. More than men, women interpret their 'failures' as 'it is me that is not good enough', while men are more inclined to put the blame outside themselves, in this way protecting their self-image (Donelson 1986).

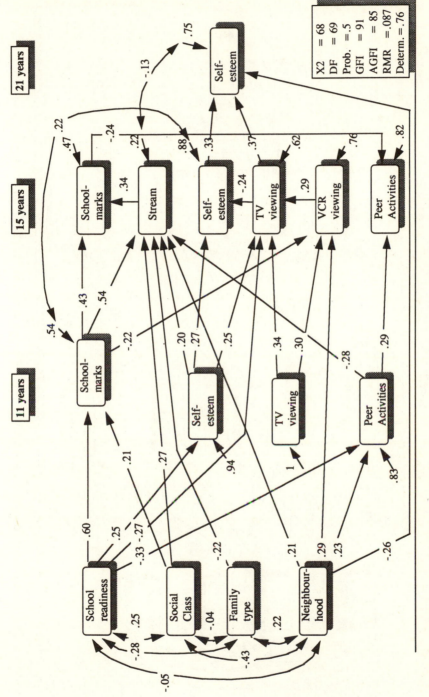

Figure 8.5 Self-esteem in an ecological development perspective: a longitudinal LISREL model. Boys. Cohort M69

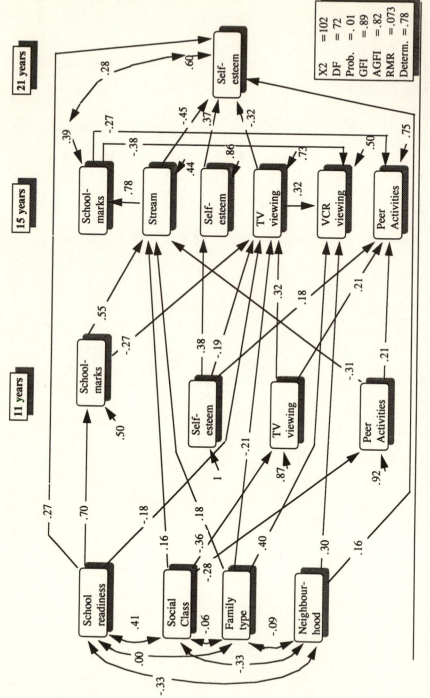

Figure 8.6 Self-esteem in an ecological development perspective: a longitudinal LISREL model. Girls. Cohort M69

Girls with lower ambitions do not to the same extent confront the often tough, male-dominated world of professions. The goals of those girls are usually more easily obtained.

Lööv and Jarlbro (1989) show in their study that boys to a greater extent than girls expect an occupation with a high status. They conclude that girls do not expect to be able to fulfil their occupational dreams to the same extent as do boys.

The gender-specific socialization, stimulating lack of both independence and self-assertion among girls, probably also explains some of the difficulties which girls have in asserting themselves. This gender specific socialization is a handicap in the competition with men.

For girls, there is a direct positive influence from school-readiness at the age of 7 to self-esteem at the age of 21 (.29). The corresponding influence is completely missing for boys. However, the total effect over time from school-readiness to self-esteem is essentially lower (.16; see Table 8.6), which depends on the strong negative effect (-.55) from stream on self-esteem at the age of 21. The tests of school-readiness may be seen as a form of intelligence test. The differences between boys and girls could thus be interpreted to show that girls have a more realistic view about their ability than have boys. Another interpretation is that boys' self-evaluation reflects society's traditional way of appraising boys and girls rather than their actual ability.

Brock-Utne (1983) maintains that it is inherent in schools' reproductive function to teach girls to accept the prevailing structure of power, according to which women have both lower income and lower status than men. Girls are systematically brought up to adjustment, at home as well as at school. In different ways school mirrors the male dominance in society. In several studies it has been established that boys dominate the classroom interaction. Wernersson (1977) found that teachers directed most questions and tasks to boys. Boys received more help and encouragement than girls, and they also had more opportunities to talk and express themselves than had girls. Similar results have also been presented by Becker (1981), Einarsson and Hultman (1984), Crossman (1987), and others. In several studies (Spender 1982; Brock-Utne 1983; and others) it has been shown that textbooks and teaching aids often offer a picture in which boys and men are the actors, something which, of course, further reinforces the male dominance in the teaching situation.

In the long run the socio-economic character of the neighbourhood during the years of growing up influences boys more than girls. Boys from areas with lower socio-economic status have a more negative self-esteem than boys who have grown up in high status areas. For girls this relation does not exist.

During the years of growing up, when the children had a more immediate contact with the neighbourhood, it was above all the homogeneity of the area

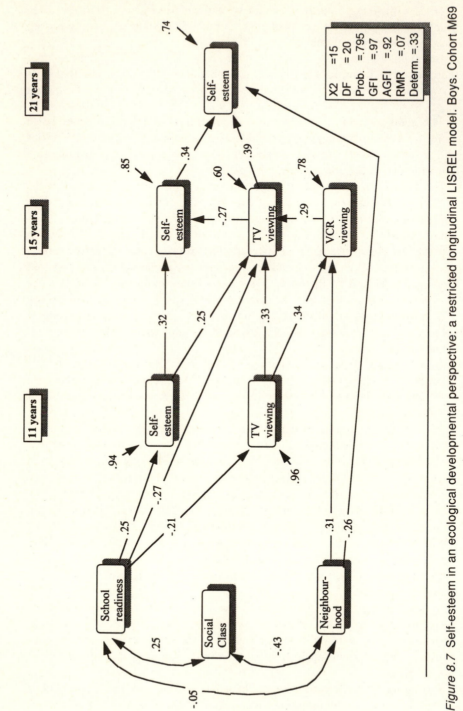

Figure 8.7 Self-esteem in an ecological developmental perspective: a restricted longitudinal LISREL model. Boys. Cohort M69

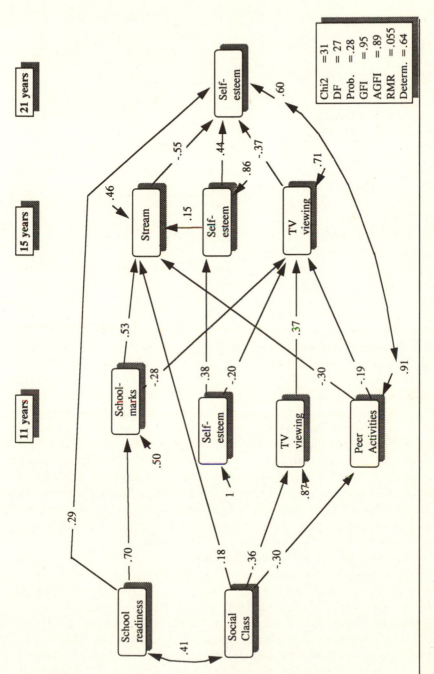

Chi2	=31
DF	= 27
Prob.	=.28
GFI	=.95
AGFI	=.89
RMR	=.055
Determ.	=.64

Figure 8.8 Self-esteem in an ecological developmental perspective: a restricted longitudinal LISREL model. Girls. Cohort M69

Table 8.6 Total effects on self-esteem at the age of 21 (from Figure 8.7; LISREL coefficients)

| | Self-esteem at 21 years | |
	Boys	Girls
Social background	–	–.12
Neighbourhood	–.23	–
School-readiness, 7 years	–.06	.16
Self-esteem, 11 years	.18	.21
TV consumption, 11 years	.13	–.14
Peer activities, 11 years	–	.24
School marks, 12 years	–	–.19
Stream, 15 years	–	–.57
Self-esteem, 15 years	.34	.37
TV consumption, 15 years	.29	–.37
VCR consumption, 15 years	.09	–

in socio-economic terms that influenced the self-image. Children and adolescents growing up in genuinely low or high status areas, had a more positive self-image than those growing up in areas with a more heterogeneous population. The level of status, in other words, did not seem to be essential for the self-esteem at the ages of 11 and 15.

The neighbourhood's level of status during the years of growing up appeared, however, to be essential for self-esteem at the age of 21. At this age many adolescents have moved from their home and are some distance from their childhood environment. This result is, however, valid only for boys. The total effect is –.23, which means that boys growing up in high status areas have a more positive self-image than boys from areas with low status. The boys' social belongingness is not reflected in their self-evaluation until young adulthood, however. The socio-economic status of the environment during childhood is important for girls' as well as for boys' self-esteem, but there is an interesting difference. For girls, it is primarily the status of the family which is important, while for boys it is above all the status of the neighbourhood which affects their self-esteem at the age of 21. An explanation may be that girls spend more time at home and usually have a closer relation with their parents, while boys usually spend more time outside home in the vicinity and, thus, are more affected by the character of the area than girls.

The relation between TV viewing and boys' and girls' self-esteem shows some interesting differences. For boys, high TV consumption during childhood leads to more positive self-esteem at the age of 21. For girls the relation is the opposite: high TV consumption leads to low self-esteem.

A possible explanation of the gender differences is that boys and girls prefer different programmes. Besides sports, boys prefer different kinds of action programmes with male role models who outdo most people when it comes to courage, initiative and independence. Girls, on the other hand, prefer serials, where the main theme is relations and intrigues, usually with traditional feminine ideals. The female role models are usually presented as more dependent and passive, sometimes lacking self-reliance (Feshbach *et al*. 1979).

Media also give us a picture of what kind of people are important in society. Abrahamsson (1985) has studied the age and gender distribution in the most popular fiction programmes shown on Swedish TV. Her analyses show an overwhelming over-representation of men. It is men who act and have the power, while women usually have a subordinate role. When women appear in fiction programmes they are normally young and attractive. Men, on the other hand, are present in all age groups. In Houston *et al*. (1992) it is shown that women – together with minority groups, children and retired people – are under-represented in American TV programmes. When present in the programmes they are very stereotypically pictured and often also in a negative way. Ageing among women is more negatively portrayed than ageing among men (Davies and Davies 1986).

Ziehe (1989) claims that we live in a culture which teaches us to wish the most out of life. The gap between what the individual wishes to achieve and what is possible in reality has increased in modern and post-modern society. It is most likely that mass media have a considerable power when it comes to creating dreams. Not being able to fulfil one's high expectations about beauty, power and admiration can easily lead to a sense of failure and to the development of a negative self-image. Studies of the importance of mass media to our self-evaluation are relatively few, though.

According to our results, Ziehe's discussion seems to apply for girls only. The picture of men and their role in society which mass media present, instead seems to strengthen boys' self-image. Men have the leading role in media as well as in society. The subordinate role is usually occupied by women – in media as well as in society. In other words, TV seems to have diametrically opposite consequences for girls and boys. It strengthens boys' self-esteem and weakens that of girls. Zuckerman *et al*. (1980) found that girls who spend much time in front of the TV had a more negative attitude towards their own gender. Gerbner *et al*. (1986) also point to the importance of TV in cultivating attitudes among viewers. According to Kohlberg (1966), girls as well as boys tend to assign more power and prestige to the male role, something which according to Kohlberg depends on their awareness of the fact that men have greater power in society. Their own insight that there are differences in prestige between the genders probably contributes to girls' self-critical attitude.

CONCLUDING DISCUSSION

In order to study adolescents' self-image we started from Bronfenbrenner's model of the ecology of human development. Our main object was to ascertain to what extent different experiences within the microsystems of the neighbourhood, the family, the group of peers, media and the school are reflected in the way girls and boys evaluate themselves at different ages, and also how the microsystems interact between themselves. We regard mass media, above all TV, as an important microsystem in children's lives.

Self-evaluation develops and is formed over time in interaction between the individual and his or her surroundings. This interaction is manifested in somewhat different ways for boys and for girls. Interaction with more immediate microsystems, such as the family, seems to mean more to girls' self-evaluation, while external factors, such as the character of the neighbourhood, means more to boys' self-evaluation. Our results show, then, that there are great differences between the way girls and boys evaluate themselves. They also show that different factors influence their self-evaluation. Bjerrum Nielsen and Rudberg (1991) maintain that in traditional research about children's and adolescents' development, the development has been considered to be mainly the same for boys and girls. However, in several other studies it has been shown that there are great differences between the development of boys and girls during childhood and adolescence (Bjerrum Nielsen 1981, 1987, 1988; Ericsson and Rudberg 1983; Bjerrum Nielsen and Larsen 1985).

Girls and boys obtain different experiences from their social contexts, something which affects their development in different ways. Social background and family type have different importance for the way boys and girls evaluate their self-image. Also their school experiences seem to affect their self-image differentially. Finally, our results suggest that boys' and girls' TV consumption has different consequences, strengthening boys' self-image while inhibiting that of girls. An explanation of these gender differences is that through the socialization process girls become increasingly aware of men's greater power and higher prestige in society compared to women. Girls also meet appreciation for their very lack of independence and lack of self-assertion. This gender-specific socialization tends to encourage girls to a more self-critical attitude towards themselves. Thus, low self-esteem is a means for girls to be obedient to the cultural expectations of society, thus arriving at a measure of success.

The results of this study show that bivariate correlations and MCA are not always sufficient when trying to catch the entirety of all the complicated relations between agents of socialization. Bivariate correlations and MCA catch only a restricted part of the interaction, and that part is detached from its context. With LISREL however, it is possible to analyse and visualize complex structures in their entirety, as well as their interactions within a given context.

Mass media have here been studied as independent variables, and from only one aspect, namely, amount of consumption. Other aspects of media use and media relations may also be interesting to analyse, in order to gain a fuller knowledge of media's significance for self-evaluation. It would also be interesting to study media use as a dependent variable in an ecological perspective, much in the same way as self-esteem has been studied here. This will be a task for future research.

One of the most interesting results in this study is the importance of mass media for the longitudinal development of self-esteem. The results stress the need to study influence in a long-term perspective. The consequences of different experiences may be visible only after several years. The diametrically different role of mass media for the self-image of boys and girls is also rather striking. This points to the importance of studying boys and girls separately. Girls and boys are continuously being treated differently; they meet various demands, they have different experiences and, therefore, they also have different expectations about their future lives. It is no exaggeration to maintain that they live in separate worlds.

REFERENCES

Abrahamsson, U. (1985) *Kvinnor och män i teater och film*, Stockholm: SR/PUB.

Ahlgren, R.-M. (1991) *Skolelevers självvärdering*, Stockholm: Almqvist & Wiksell.

Alsaker, F.D. (1990) *Global Negative Self-Evaluations in Early Adolescence*, Bergen: Bergen University.

Andersson, B.-E. (1986) *Utvecklingsekologi*, Lund: Studentlitteratur.

Baron, R.A. and Byrne, D. (1987) *Social Psychology: Understanding Human Interaction*, (5th edn) Boston, Mass.: Allyn Bacon, Inc.

Beane, J.A. and Lipka, R.P. (1984) *Self-Concept, Self-Esteem and the Curriculum*, Mass.: Allyn and Bacon, Inc.

Becker, J.R. (1981) 'Differential treatment of females and males in mathematics classes', *Journal for Research in Mathematics Education* 12: 40–53.

Bjerrum Nielsen, H. (1981) 'Små piger, söde piger, stille piger', *Sosiologi idag* 3–4.

—— (1987) 'Kjönn og kontrol – om barns vennskap', in S. Berentzen and B. Berggren (eds) *Barns sociale verden*, Oslo: Gyldendal.

—— (1988) *Jenteliv og likestillingslaere*, Oslo: J.W. Cappelens Forlag.

Bjerrum Nielsen, H. and Larsen, K. (1985) 'Piger og drenge i klassoffentligheten', *Rapport* 2, Oslo: Universitetet i Oslo, Pedagogisk forskningsinstitutt.

Bjerrum Nielsen, H. and Rudberg, M. (1991) *Historien om flickor och pojkar. Könssocialisation i ett utvecklingspsykologiskt perspektiv*, Lund: Studentlitteratur.

Block, J.H. (1983) 'Differential premises arising from differential socialization of the sexes: Some conjectures', *Child Development* 54: 1335–1354.

Brock-Utne, B. (1983) 'Vårt utdanningssystem kvinneundertrykkende?', in M. Haavelsrud and H.H. Hartvigsen (eds) *Utdanning og likhetsidealer*, Oslo: Aschehoug.

Bronfenbrenner, U. (1979) *The Ecology of Human Development*, Cambridge, Mass., and London: Harvard University Press.

Chaffee, S.H., McLeod, J.M. and Atkin, C.K. (1971) 'Parental influences on adolescent media use', *American Behavioral Scientist* 14: 323–340.

Chaffee, S.H., McLeod, J.M. and Wackman, D.B. (1973) 'Family communication patterns and adolescent political participation', in J. Dennis, (ed.) *Socialization to Politics*, New York: Wiley.

Combs, A.W. (1969) *Florida Studies in the Helping Professions*, Tallahassee, Fla.: University of Florida Press.

Comstock, G. and Pail, H. (1987) *Television and Children: A Review of Recent Research*, Syracuse, NY: ERIC.

Comstock, G. and Paik, H. (1991) *Television and the American Child*, New York: Academic Press.

Coopersmith, S. (1967) *The Antecedents of Self-Esteem*, San Fransisco and London: W.H. Freeman and Company.

Crossman, M. (1987) 'Teachers' interactions with girls and boys in science lessons', in A. Kelly (ed.) *Science for Girls*, Milton Keynes: Open University Press.

Davies, R.H. and Davies, J.A. (1986) *TV's Image of the Elderly*, Lexington, Mass.: Lexington Books.

Donelson, F.R. (1986) 'An attributional analysis of students' reaction to success and failure', in R.S. Feldman (ed.) *The Social Psychology of Education*, New York: Cambridge University Press.

Einarsson, J. and Hultman, T. (1984) *Godmorgon pojkar och flickor. Om språk och kön i skolan*, Stockholm: Liber.

Ericsson, K. and Rudberg, M. (1983) 'Jentediskriminering i klasserommet. En eksplorerende studie av interaksjon mellom lærere og elever', *Tidskrift for Norsk Psykologforening* 5.

Erikson, E.H. (1963) *Childhood and Society*, New York: Norton.

Feshbach, N.D., Dillman, A.S. and Jordan, T.S. (1979) 'Portrait of a female on television: Some possible effects on children', in C.B. Kopp (ed.) *Becoming Female: Perspectives on Development*, New York: Plenum Press.

Gecas, V., Calonico, J.M. and Thomas, D.L. (1974) 'The development of self-concept in the child: Mirror theory versus model theory', *The Journal of Social Psychology* 92: 67–76.

Gerbner, G., Gross, L., Morgan, M. and Signorielli, N. (1986) 'Living with television: The dynamics of the cultivation process', in J. Bryant and D. Zillmann (eds) *Perspectives on Media Effects*, Hillsdale, NJ: Erlbaum.

Greenstein, F. (1969) *Personality and Politics*, Chicago: Markham.

Hansford, B.C. and Hattie, J.A. (1982) 'The relationship between self and academic/performance measures', *Review of Educational Research* 52: 123–142.

Houston, A., Donnerstein, R., Fairchild, H., Feshbach, N., Katz, P., Murray, J., Rubinstein, E., Wilcox, B. and Zuckerman, D. (1992) *Big World, Small Screen*, Lincoln and London: University of Nebraska Press.

Jarlbro, G. (1988) *Familj, massmedier och politik*, Stockholm: Almqvist & Wiksell.

Johanneson, I. (1966) 'Den allmänna utvecklingen under tonåren', in T. Husén and I. Carlsson (eds) *Tonåringarna och skolan*, Stockholm: Almqvist & Wiksell.

Johnsson-Smaragdi, U. (1983) *TV Use and Social Interaction in Adolescence. A Longitudinal Study*, Stockholm: Almqvist & Wiksell.

—— (1986) 'Familjen, kamraterna och TV-tittandet', in K.E. Rosengren (ed.) *På gott och ont: Barn och ungdom, TV och video*, Stockholm: Allmänna Barnhuset och Liber Utbildningsförlaget.

—— (1992) 'Learning to watch television: Longitudinal LISREL models replicated', *Lund Research Papers in Media and Communication Studies* 5, Lund: Department of Sociology, University of Lund.

Jönsson, A. (1985) *TV – ett hot eller en resurs? En longitudinell studie av relationen mellan skola och TV*, Lund: Gleerups.

—— (1986) 'TV: A threat or a complement to school?', *Journal of Educational Television* 12(1): 29–38.

—— (1989) 'Så här har vi det', *Pedagogisk psykologiska problem* 502, Malmö: Lärarhögskolan.

——— (1991) 'En bit på vägen och lite till ....', *Pedagogisk psykologiska problem* 554, Malmö: Lärarhögskolan.

Jöreskog, K.G. and Sörbom, D. (1988) *LISREL 7: A Guide to the Program and Applications*, (2nd edn) Chicago: SPSS Publications.

Kohlberg, L.A. (1966) 'A cognitive-developmental analysis of children's sex-role concepts and attitudes', in E. Maccoby (ed.) *The Development of Sex Differences*, Stanford: Stanford University Press.

Lagerroth, I. and Nilsson, R. (1992) *Grundsärskoleelvers självbild*, Malmö: Institutionen för pedagogik.

Lööv, T. and Jarlbro, G. (1989) 'Dröm och verklighet. En longitudinell studie av ungdomars yrkesförväntningar', *Lund Research Papers in the Sociology of Communication* 17, Lund: Department of Sociology, University of Lund.

Mead, G.H. (1934,1969) *Mind, Self and Society from the Standpoint of a Social Behaviorist*, Chicago and London: The University of Chicago Press.

Nash, R. (1974) *Teacher Expectations and Pupil Learning*, London: Routledge.

Openshaw, K.D., Thomas, D.L. and Rollins, B.C. (1983) 'Socialization and adolescent self-esteem: Symbolic interaction and social learning explanations', *ADOLESCENCE* XVIII (70): 317–329.

Pölkki, P. (1990) *Self-concept and social skills of school beginners*, Jyväskylä: University of Jyväskylä.

Prendergast, M. and Binder, D. (1975) 'Relationships of selected self-concept and academic achievement measures', *Measurement and Evaluation in Guidance* 8: 92–95.

Roe, K. (1989) 'School achievement, self-esteem and adolescents' video use', in M.R. Levy (ed.) *The VCR Age: Home Video and Mass Communication*, Newbury Park, Calif.: Sage.

Rollins, B.C. and Thomas, D.L. (1979) 'Parental support, power and control techniques in the socialization of children', in W.R. Burr, R. Hill, R.I. Nye and I.L. Reiss (eds) *Contemporary Theories About the Family*, (Vol 1), New York: Free Press.

Rosenberg, M. (1965) *Society and the Adolescent's Self-Image*, Princeton: Princeton University Press.

——— (1979) *Conceiving the Self*, New York: Basic Books Inc. Publishers.

Rosengren, K.E. and Windahl, S. (1989) *Media Matter. TV Use in Childhood and Adolescence*, Norwood, NJ: Ablex Publishing Corporation.

Samuels, S.C. (1977) *Enhancing Self-Concept in Early Childhood*, New York: Human Science Press.

Simon, W. and Simon, M. (1975) 'Self-esteem, intelligence and standardized academic achievement', *Psychology in the Schools* 12: 97–99.

Skaalvik, E.M. (1982) *Selvoppfatning og skoleerfaringer*, Universitetet i Trondheim: Pedagogisk Institutt.

Sonesson, I. (1989) *Vem fostrar våra barn – videon eller vi?*, Stockholm: Esselte Studium.

Spender, D. (1982) *Invisible Women. The Schooling Scandal*, London: Writers and Readers Cooperative Society Ltd.

Taube, K. (1987) *Läsinlärning och självförtroende*, Stockholm: Tema Nova.

Thomas, D.L. (1974) *Family Socialization and the Adolescent*, London: Lexington Books.

Wernersson, I. (1977) *Könsdifferentiering i grundskolan*, Göteborg: Acta Universitatis.

Zahran, H. (1966) *The Self-Concept in Relation to the Psychological Guidance of Adolescents: An Experimental Study*, London: University of London.

Ziehe, T. (1989) *Kulturanalyser: Ungdom, utbildning, modernitet*, Stockholm: Symposion.

Zuckerman, D.M., Singer, D.G. and Singer, J.L. (1980) 'Children's television viewing, racial and sex-role attitudes', *Journal of Applied Social Psychology* 10 (4): 281–294.

Chapter 9

Media use and social mobility

Keith Roe

INTRODUCTION

The use which individuals make of the media varies appreciably according to their position in the social structure (Roe 1983; Rosengren and Windahl 1989). It follows that any significant change in these positions, or in the configuration of the social structure as a whole, will influence individual and aggregate patterns of media use. In this chapter the relationship between social mobility and some aspects of media use will be examined theoretically and empirically.

THEORETICAL CONSIDERATIONS

Social mobility

In his seminal work on the subject, Sorokin (1964) defined social mobility as 'any transition of an individual or social object or value – anything that has been created or modified by human activity – from one social position to another'.

He then proceeded to identify two principle types of social mobility: 'horizontal', involving transition from one social group to another situated on the same level; and 'vertical', involving upward or downward movement, either by individuals or by whole social groups, from one social stratum to another. Vertical mobility was then further distinguished according to its 'velocity', i.e. the social distance or number of strata crossed by an individual in a definite period of time; and its 'generality', i.e. the number of individuals who have changed their social position in a definite period of time.

Despite the multidimensionality of this definition most analyses of social mobility have focused on just one of its aspects: the upward vertical mobility of individuals from one social class or status to another (for a recent exception, see Erikson and Goldthorpe 1992). This tendency has been signally apparent in Sweden, where the expansion of the opportunities for inter-generational upward mobility has been a central tenet of the Social

Democratic ideology which has dominated politics for most of this century. However, it is important that the other dimensions of social mobility also be taken into account; in particular, that vertical movement takes place in a downwards as well as an upwards direction, and that vertical movement in both directions may involve whole social groups as well as individuals.

As Sorokin noted, any change in any field of social life may lead to the decline of certain groups and the advancement of others. Such changes in group status may be rapid and spectacular, e.g. where new technology quickly renders skills obsolete, or they may be slow and intangible, as with changes in morals and beliefs. This continual realignment of groups in the status hierarchy means that the reference points for individual mobility are also continually changing. Moreover, this relativity is compounded when exceptional individuals move in the opposite direction to that of their original social group (up from a declining group or down from a rising group). If these contrapositional movements are commensurate, individual and group mobility will cancel each another out to give a misleading appearance of fixity.

Viewed from this perspective, social mobility is an objective, sociological concept associated with status inequality. As such it is usually analysed statically, at an aggregate level, with the resultant loss of its essentially dynamic character. In order to avoid this static context, it is necessary, as Merton (1968: 437) noted, to incorporate into the conceptual scheme, 'what everybody knows', namely, 'that not only his current status but also his past history of statuses affect the present and future behavior of the individual.'

The theory of status inequality also contains subjective elements which need to be taken into consideration. In order to have any efficacy, inequality must be perceived as such by the individual. 'What to do? How to act? Who to be?' According to Giddens (1991: 70) these questions of identity construction must be answered by everyone living in late modernity (for more detailed discussions see, for instance, Johansson and Miegel 1992 and Chapters 10–12 of this volume). However, the answers we give to these questions are not unconstrained. Since available social roles are unequally distributed, they are defined and reinforced by formal and informal sanctions and expectancies and by the differential predispositions set up by prior socialization. Although there is status inequality at all stages of development, at certain points – perhaps the most critical of which being the transition from adolescence to adulthood – there are marked changes in social expectancies and constraints, and the individual is confronted with the task of achieving a new status (De Vos 1990). It is at such times that status inequality is likely to be experienced most directly.

Status, self-esteem and identity

There is a substantial body of work linking the notion of status to the important social-psychological concepts of self-esteem and identity. On the basis of Veblen's (1934) observation, that those who fall short of some social standard, 'suffer in the esteem of their fellow-men', Lipset and Zetterberg (1966: 565) postulated two hypotheses as a basis for their theory of social mobility: that, 'the evaluation (rank, class) a person receives from his society determines in large measure his self-evaluation'; and that, 'a person's actions are guided, in part at least, by an insatiable desire to maximize a favourable self-evaluation'. This perspective is fruitful, they argued, because it places the motivations for mobility in the realm of the ego-needs of the individual, rather than merely as resulting from social norms.

The concept of identity, likewise, has been used as a bridge between ego-psychology and more general social and cultural approaches (Erikson 1959). Extending this model, De Vos (1990: 32) defined identity as, 'an internal experience of adherence to one's social status in age, gender, class, caste and ethnic behaviour'. In every culture, he argues, human interpersonal concerns are basically self-oriented and vertically differentiated in terms of status and power. However, since modern cultures are characterized by extreme occupational specialization, social dominance is linked to group identity, and status depends even more on group membership than on individual prowess. The psychological well-being of the individual thereby becomes inextricably linked to the status of the group to which he or she belongs.

The decreasing hegemony of inter-generational status ascription in contemporary culture conversely opens up an increasing area of choice. According to Giddens (1991: 81) one significant consequence of this development is that each of us is forced to choose a lifestyle; i.e. 'a more or less integrated set of practices..[that]..gives material form to a particular narrative of self-identity'; from a vastly increased number of available possibilities. Although lifestyle choice is usually seen as a leisure sphere task, increasingly mediated by the media, Giddens points out that choice of lifestyle is still strongly conditioned, especially by work. Where there is a complex division of labour, he argues, choice of work forms a basic element of lifestyle orientations, and 'strategic life planning' assumes a special importance. The heuristic value of such a lifestyle approach, and its implications for the media uses and gratifications of Swedish adolescents, has been demonstrated by Johansson and Miegel (1992 (cf. also chapters 10–12 below)).

Reference groups and subcultures

In theories of social mobility the main bridge between psychological and sociological perspectives, between the individual and the social structure, has generally been Reference Group Theory (see Lipset and Bendix 1962; Merton 1968; Merton and Rossi 1950). The primary reference group for infants is the family. However, children soon form their own 'us and them' group identifications, particularly after they start school and, at critical stages of development, there is significant movement between reference groups (De Vos

1990). Social institutions, particularly in the educational sphere, also begin to confer status on individuals and groups.

Reference group theory also provides a bridge between social mobility and important concepts that are frequently operationalized in analyses of adolescents' media use. With the onset of puberty, and for some years thereafter, peer group membership becomes an increasingly salient reference point for the vast majority of adolescents and is associated with a shift in media use patterns (Johnsson-Smaragdi 1983; Roe 1983; Rosengren and Windahl 1989; see also Chapter 4).

In some cases these groups form themselves into distinct subcultures. The subcultural model predicts that individuals sharing similar statuses will tend to interact more with each other than would be expected by chance and that from this interaction values, norms and collective identities develop which are to some extent unique, and which can be traced to the particular problems, facilities, and opportunities facing those individuals (Cohen 1970).

Subcultures generally become most visible during the final years of the educational career and can be seen as a collective defence against threats to self-esteem on the part of students who are experiencing failure or other status problems, or who feel that education is meaningless in terms of future prospects. By making alternative investments in the values and activities of subcultures, rather than in those of more socially legitimate agencies, an alternative identity may be constructed. Not infrequently, disapproved of media contents and flamboyant symbols of popular culture facilitate the spectacular expression of subcultural presence (Roe 1987a; 1987b; 1987c; 1989; 1992).

Anticipatory socialization

Implicit in status inequality and reference group theory is the existence of status aspiration. This postulation is based on the observation that individuals often orient their values and behaviour to groups other than those to which they currently belong. One of the most important mechanisms by which status aspiration is facilitated is by anticipatory socialization. This involves adopting the values and orientations of a group to which one aspires but does not belong, with the aim of aiding one's transition into membership of that group (Merton 1968). Anticipatory socialization occurs at all stages of the life cycle but is notably apparent during adolescence as a succession of social and biological changes must be traversed.

In sociological terms the function of anticipatory socialization is to prepare the individual for anticipated future statuses. It is composed of an explicit part, usually achieved by formal education, and an implicit, informal part achieved by responding to cues in behavioural situations. In this way,

The individual moves more or less continuously through a sequence of statuses and associated roles . . . although his 'official' (socially acknowledged) transfer into a new status may seem to be sudden, more often than not this is only because the informal antecedent preparation has gone unnoticed. There is less discontinuity in status sequences than might appear on the social surface, with its celebrative *rites de passage* and legally enacted changes of status. (Merton 1968: 439)

According to one perspective (Kelly 1963), anticipation also channelizes our psychological processes and forms the basis of our personal constructs, being carried on, 'so that future reality may be better represented'.

An important corollary to the theory of anticipatory socialization, which may go some way towards explaining, e.g., the weak correlations often obtained between adolescents' social backgrounds and their media uses and tastes, is that an individual's perceived future may be a significant factor influencing present behaviour and values (Bourdieu 1984; Roe 1992). In analyses of social mobility the existence of a future dimension necessitates the description of a double temporal trajectory composed of the individual's subjective experience of past, present, and anticipated future statuses, as well as objective indicators, such as his or her 'class of origin', 'class of context', and 'class of destination' (Rosengren and Windahl 1989).

At different stages in an individual's trajectory, however, status is attributed dissimilarly and signifies different social and psychological experiences. For adults, status is largely determined in the context of work (or the lack of it!). It is in this context that we are continually confronted with, 'the brute reality of differences in power, prestige and possession' (Rosenberg and Pearlin 1978: 61). The status of infants is ascribed by that of their parents, and status-related experiences occur largely in the context of home and neighbourhood. Older children and adolescents occupy an increasingly indeterminate zone where parental status ascription is diminishing but where work roles are, as yet, unavailable. However, the dominant institutional context here, the school, is not only a leading status dispenser in its own right, it also plays a central role in reproducing the occupational structure.

The school

According to one perspective (Bourdieu and Passeron 1977, 1979; Bowles and Gintis 1977; Collins 1979; Giroux 1981), a main purpose of schooling is precisely that of sorting students into hierarchically ordered classes by means of the allocation of grades and, with them, socially recognized status titles defining success or failure. These status allocations are given exchange value in the form of diplomas and certificates and, since occupations requiring lengthy schooling generally have a higher status than those requiring very little, the possession of scarce certificates has become essential for attaining most high status positions in the occupational structure. Consequently, 'trying to invent a status index that does not take education into account is like trying to invent a standard of living index that does not include income' (Jencks 1972: 180).

The strong correlation between academic qualifications and occupational status implies that schooling is one of the most important means by which individuals and social groups seek to retain or improve their social position. As a result, the competition for academic qualifications is aggravated and there is a vast increase in the demand for education. The expansion of educational provision, at a rate greater than that of the occupational structure, however, leads to the devaluation of diplomas and means that, in order to retain its position, each generation must attain an educational status at least one level higher than its predecessor. As a consequence, the struggle for educational qualifications becomes one of the key arenas of interclass competition (Bourdieu 1984; cf. Hurrelmann 1988).

Naturally, the starting stakes in this competition are unequal. Social background, as well as other family characteristics (Jarlbro 1988; see also Chapters 8 and 12) form the basis upon which school experiences are structured. However, while social and family origins define opportunities and the propensity to be able to exploit them, it is the school which mediates and legitimates actual outcomes by means of its status allocation activities. If education is then a major facilitator of vertical mobility, it follows that it is responsible not only for movement upwards but also for movement downwards.

While upward mobility may result in serious cultural dislocation and personal identity problems, anticipatory socialization tends to smooth the passage to some degree. For those being downclassed, especially from established middle-class professional and technical backgrounds, the problems of personal and cultural adjustment are likely to be felt more acutely. The collective disillusionment which results from a 'broken trajectory', that is,

> from the structural mismatch between aspirations and real possibilities, between the social identity the school system seems to promise ... and the social identity that the labour market in fact offers is the source of ... that refusal of social finitude which generates all the refusals and negations of the adolescent counter-culture. (Bourdieu 1984: 144)

Thus, the struggle against declassing is not only now one of the most important factors in the transformation of social structures; the strategies which groups employ in this struggle often revolve around cultural appropriation and innovation combined with entry into the most indeterminate, ill-defined and professionally unstructured occupations in the newest sectors of cultural production (Bourdieu 1984).

Bourdieu also argues that the tacit guarantee hidden behind the status allocation activities of the educational system is that the student possesses a general pattern of culture. In schools this process occurs continually by the manipulation of aspirations, self-esteem and identity which results from formally channelling students into prestigious or devalued positions. It is thereby partly via the school system that young people acquire the basis of their social world. Where legitimate achievement systems contribute to positive self-esteem and identity construction, students will be inclined to accept the culture legitimated by those systems; to the extent that they fail to do so, however – e.g. where the school holds out little promise of future rewards for some students – identification with and participation in less legitimate cultural activities may be substituted. In this way schools can be seen as creating particular status cultures (Bourdieu 1984; Dembo 1972; Roe 1992, 1993a; Stinchcombe 1964).

If, as Bourdieu argues, education is the means by which we acquire a practical command of the master patterns of culture and of the codes required to read and make sense of cultural products, then it follows that it is also the means by which the dispositions towards taste and cultural preferences are acquired, and by which the propensity to appropriate cultural products is reproduced. Seen from this perspective, taste (in media contents as well as all other cultural spheres) is nothing but a practical mastery of the sense of what is befitting to an individual occupying a given space (or status).

The theoretical link between status, mobility, and media use has received support from a number of empirical studies. For example, in Britain, Piepe *et al.* (1975) found that, associated with the changes in housing and consumption which accompany social mobility, there is a change in the patterns of television use towards those of the middle class. They also stressed the role of the school with respect to mobility, arguing that possibly the most intense form in which the re-socialization of the working-class child occurs is where the school operates as an avenue of social mobility. Increasingly distanced from their original class milieux, upwardly mobile individuals often use the media as sources of new values, attitudes and models of behaviour (cf. Piepe *et al.* 1978).

PREVIOUS EMPIRICAL FINDINGS

From a different perspective, Flodin (1986) found no direct relationship between television and the status dimensions of Swedish adolescents' occupational plans. Neither was there any significant tendency for students to choose those occupations frequently shown in TV programmes. Compared to family background and educational attainment, he concluded, TV consumption does not exercise any significant influence on such plans, despite the fact that young people often state that the media are an important source of information for occupational choice. Flodin also emphasized the strong repercussions which the school's grading activities have on students' educational and occupational plans.

In another Swedish study, Roe (1983; 1987a) found direct and indirect relationships between adolescents' social background, school achievement, anticipated future, and music preferences. He concluded that adolescents' music preferences are at least partly dependent upon earlier levels of school achievement. Subsequent studies (Roe 1990, 1992, 1993a; Roe and Löfgren 1988) have supported these findings with regard to music tastes, while others (Roe 1987b, 1993b) have reported similar relationships with regard to the use of socially disapproved of video contents such as violent video 'nasties'.

Some of these studies (Roe 1983, 1985, 1992) also indicated that, although the relationships between social background and most music preferences were very weak, some music tastes were related to anticipated future status. The structural models analysed supported the view that successful students, recognizing their current high status in the school and anticipating a trajectory into the higher levels of the status hierarchy, begin to cultivate a taste for cultural elements perceived as relevant to that future while acquiring a distaste for cultural elements perceived as inappropriate to it. Conversely, the unsuccessful, also conscious of their current position, and of the destination to which the school is consigning them, reject the academic world and the culture which it represents, and develop a taste for 'deviant' forms of culture; e.g. even after controlling for social background, 11-year-old female heavy users of popular music and 15-year-old males preferring socially disapproved of types of music anticipated getting lower status jobs after leaving school.

A number of researchers (e.g. Flodin 1986; Rosengren and Windahl 1989) have called for greater empirical attention to be paid to the media use patterns of socially mobile individuals who deviate markedly from their class trajectory, and the few studies which have touched upon this subject indicate the potential heuristic value of such an approach. In Sweden, recent studies of adolescents' occupational expectations and their actual social mobility have indicated significant relationships with media use (Jarlbro and Dalquist 1991; Lööv and Jarlbro 1989; cf. Chapter 7). On the basis of a typology based on socio-economic background and current educational status, Jarlbro and Dalquist classified respondents as status climbers, status fallers, or stationary. They found that individuals with media use patterns (and other leisure activities) which are atypical for their class of origin, also tend more often to change social position. However, on the bases of longitudinal analyses, they concluded that the atypical media use, far from being a cause of subsequent mobility, is actually part of a general pattern of anticipatory socialization.

Furthermore, they found that whereas 'climbers' retained media use patterns similar to those of their original status, 'fallers' moved closer to the media use pattern of their status destination. A similar observation was made by Piepe et al. (1978: 23) who gave the phenomenon a historical dimension by noting that, whereas the pre-war experience of upwards social mobility had typically involved the adoption of the cultural norms and style of life of the class of destination, from the 1960s onward the upwardly mobile often refused to relinquish many aspects of their working-class identity. This change, it was argued, was best explained by the changing meanings of social class.

According to Trondman (1990) this change is better understood in terms of shifts in the cultural legitimacy of popular culture in general, and of rock music in particular. He argues that, since tastes in rock music are now intimately related to the establishment of social hierarchies and mark social distance between classes and social settings, they can be used as a symbolic capital investment.

The importance of rock music for those adolescents experiencing status disjunction difficulties was also noted by Frith (1983: 223). He came to the conclusion that music was most important for adolescents (whether middle class or working class) who in some way rejected their class cultures (cf. Willmott 1969). Moreover, he argued, in the history of rock such 'deviants' have been of crucial importance as the link between the culturally adventurous of all classes, 'providing the continuity of bohemian concern that runs from the beats to the punks'. Bourdieu (1984: 18), too, emphasizes the pre-eminent role of music in the cultural legitimation of the differences and distinctions between the social classes. 'The flaunting of musical culture', he argues, 'is not a cultural display like others.' In fact, 'nothing more clearly affirms one's "class", nothing more infallibly classifies, than tastes in music.'

A THEORETICAL MODEL

On the basis of the theoretical and empirical review presented above a theoretical model of social mobility and media use has been constructed (see Figure 9.1). The model postulates that the passage from socio-economic status background and status destination is mediated by the educational system and the socially legitimated status it dispenses. The educational experience in turn structures individuals' perception of their likely futures in the occupational hierarchy which, via the process of anticipatory socialization, influences media use and taste patterns. The combined influence of these factors, which in effect amounts to a self-fulfilling prophecy, in turn has a direct bearing on the status destination of the individual (and social groups). As individuals move towards their status destination they increasingly synchronize their position in symbolic space with their position in social space to produce a structural homology. Where there is a serious discrepancy between origin and destination, as a result of successes or failures in the educational system, the model predicts that cultural strains will appear which will be associated with unique and 'deviant' media use and taste patterns.

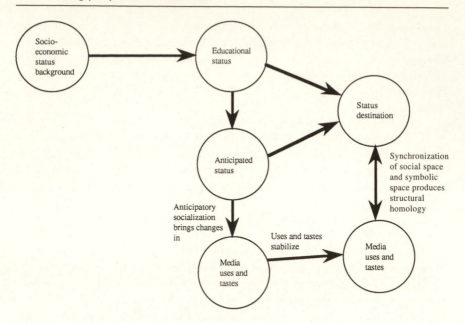

Figure 9.1 A theoretical model of the relationship between social mobility and media uses and tastes

Following the typology presented by Jarlbro and Dalquist (1991: 10) we can identify three major trajectories: climbers, moving upwards; the stationary, with no significant mobility; and fallers, moving downwards. Following Frith (1983: 223) we may then formulate two specific predictions:

1 That individuals or groups who have a 'broken trajectory' (i.e. become objectively or subjectively separated, in an upwards or a downwards direction, from their status origin) will tend to display music tastes 'deviant' from those typical of their status background.
2 That individuals and groups on a downward trajectory (i.e. those facing 'downclassing'), as a result of their negative experiences, *ceteris paribus*, face more severe problems of social and psychological adjustment than others and that consequently they will tend to display culturally 'illegitimate', or otherwise socially disapproved of music tastes.

Since the available data were not collected specifically to test these predictions, we shall here be able to undertake only a preliminary, exploratory analysis. Nevertheless, this will enable us to assess their heuristic potential.

THE DATA

The data analysed here come from the 1985 and 1990 waves of the Media Panel Program and are thus longitudinal in nature. Both Malmö and Växjö respondents are included. Further details of the data collection procedures employed can be found in Rosengren and Windahl (1989) and Johansson and Miegel (1992).

Occupational data were available in both collection waves for 201 individuals. Of these, 57 per cent originally lived in Malmö and 43 per cent in Växjö; by gender, 56 per cent were female and 44 per cent were male. By comparing parents' occupational status in the first wave with respondents' own occupational status in the second wave, 12 per cent were classified as 'climbers', 32 per cent as 'droppers', and 56 per cent as 'stationary'. Where the occupational status of parents differed, the higher status was used. Of the climbers, 80 per cent were female; 20 per cent, male. Of the droppers, 51 per cent were male, and 49 per cent female. In part the larger number of droppers can be explained by the fact that, in most cases, our respondents (aged only 20–21 at the second data collection) cannot be assumed to have reached their final status destination. Nevertheless, it should be recalled that we are here discussing trajectories towards, rather than actual status destinations.

There were educational data from both collection waves for 201 individuals. Of these, 52 per cent were from Växjö and 48 per cent from Malmö; 53 per cent were female and 47 per cent male. Parents' educational status in the first wave was compared with respondents' own educational status in the second wave to produce an educational mobility typology. Where there was a discrepancy of two or more places on the five-point scale used, respondents were classified either as 'educational climbers' (24 per cent), 'educational droppers' (9 per cent), or 'educationally stationary' (67 per cent). Where the educational status of parents differed, the higher status was employed. Of the educational climbers 59 per cent were female and 41 per cent male; of the droppers, 61 per cent were female and 39 per cent male; and of the stationary group, 49 per cent were female and 51 per cent male.

As an alternative indicator of educational mobility, respondents were classified into one of the following categories:

a) Having at least one parent with a higher (i.e. university or college) education but who had not themselves attained this level of education ('higher education droppers').
b) Having no parent with a higher education but who had themselves obtained entry to a university or college ('higher education climbers').
c) Having at least one parent with a university or college education and having themselves also attained this status ('higher education stationary').

According to these criteria 36 (19 males and 17 females) were classified as 'droppers', 24 (9 males and 15 females) as 'climbers', and 12 (5 males and 7 females) as 'stationary'.

The school achievement data consisted of the grades awarded to each respondent in 1985, during their ninth school year. According to the system then in operation, for each subject studied, pupils were awarded a grade on a scale from 1 (lowest) to 5 (highest). For the analyses presented here an overall mean grade was computed for each respondent.

During the first data collection respondents were asked to indicate which job they thought, realistically, that they would get after completing their education. The replies were then coded on the same basis as the other occupational status items. Henceforth, this variable will be referred to as 'anticipated occupational status'.

In both data collection waves respondents were asked to rate a wide range of musical genres according to their own likes and dislikes. On the basis of the results of previous research (e.g. Roe 1983; 1992; 1993a) three types of music, widely dispersed across the spectrum of cultural legitimacy, were selected for analysis: disco, heavy metal, and classical music. The variables from the 1985 data collection will be referred to as 'Disco 1', 'Heavy Metal 1', and 'Classical 1'; and those from the 1990 data collection as 'Disco 2', 'Heavy Metal 2', and 'Classical 2'.

Where appropriate the results from three types of analysis will be presented here: Pearson correlation, analysis of means, and analysis of variance. The significance level of any coefficient presented is at least <.01 unless marked with an asterisk, in which case the level is <.05.

RESULTS

Occupational mobility and music preferences

In the whole occupational mobility analysis group a large number of statistically significant bivariate correlations were found. Relationships between the occupational status of parents and the other variables in the model were weak or moderate (under r = .3). There were positive correlations with respondents' school achievement, anticipated occupational status, actual occupational status, and educational status. There was only one very weak correlation between parents' occupational status and the music preference variables ('Classical 2').

Relationships between respondents' school achievement and the other variables, however, were stronger. There was a strong (r = .52) positive relationship between school achievement and later educational status, and quite a strong one with anticipated educational status (.38). Moreover there were significant moderate correlations between school achievement and five of the six music variables: positive with 'Disco 1', 'Classical 1' and 'Classical 2'; and negative with 'Heavy Metal 1' and 'Heavy Metal 2'. Thus, higher school achievement is associated with liking classical music, while lower school achievement is associated with liking heavy metal. Moreover, the strength of these relationships appears to increase slightly over time. The correlation between school achievement and liking disco, on the other hand, disappears over time. These results indicate that school achievement may indeed play an important mediating role.

'Anticipated occupational status' also correlated, if less strongly, with five of the six music types: positively with 'Classical 1'; and negatively with 'Heavy Metal 1', 'Heavy Metal 2', and 'Disco 2'. The correlation between anticipated status and that actually attained five years later was very weak and non-significant, a result probably accounted for by the already noted fact that many respondents had not yet reached their final status destination. This interpretation is supported by the moderately strong positive association between anticipated occupational status and later educational status.

Among the second data collection wave variables, respondents' own occupational status was weakly associated with the music variables: positively with 'Disco 2' and 'Classical 2', and negatively with 'Heavy Metal 2'. Similarly, own educational status was associated positively with 'Classical 2' and negatively with 'Heavy Metal 2'.

Educational status at time two was also associated with music preferences at time one: positively with 'Disco 1' and 'Classical 1', and negatively with 'Heavy Metal 1'. However, relationships between music tastes at time one and own occupational status at time two were non-significant, presumably for the reason already noted.

As expected, there were also relationships between the music variables themselves. There were moderate negative correlations between 'Disco 1' and 'Heavy Metal 1', and between 'Disco 2' and 'Heavy Metal 2', and a weak positive correlation between 'Disco 1' and 'Classical 1'. Over time there was a moderate negative correlation between 'Disco 1' and 'Heavy Metal 2', and weak negative correlations between 'Heavy Metal 1' and 'Disco 2', 'Heavy Metal 1' and 'Classical 2', and between 'Classical 1' and 'Disco 2'.

The pattern of correlations provides appreciable support for the postulated model. The theoretically most important of these relationships are illustrated in Figure 9.2. Over time, music preferences are seen to be related to differential educational achievement and to anticipations of future status. Greater liking for heavy metal is related to lower educational achievement, as well as to the anticipation, and actual attainment, of a lower occupational status. Greater liking for classical music is associated with higher educational achievement, as well as with the anticipation, and actual attainment of, a higher occupational status. Thus, a taste for these types of music, which represent opposite ends of a continuum of legitimate culture, may be indicative of actual and anticipated social status. Disco appears to occupy an equivocal, intermediate position, being positively related to school achievement but, over time, negatively related to anticipated occupational status.

The pattern and strength of the correlations obtained from the status 'stationary' group were essentially similar to those for the group as a whole. For the 'droppers' group, however, there were interesting divergences (the small number of 'climbers' made this group too small for analysis at this

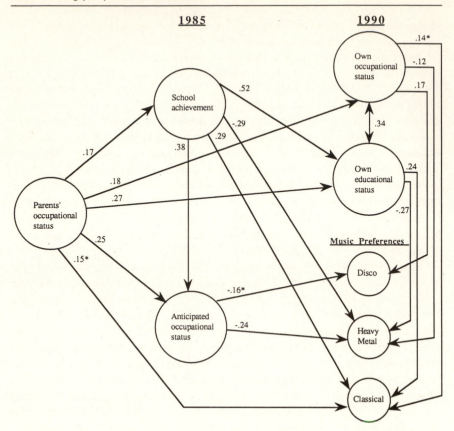

Figure 9.2 Occupational mobility and music preferences: an illustrative model containing bivariate correlation coefficients of major theoretical interest (n = 201)

level). Despite the substantially lower number of respondents, there was still a tight pattern of significant correlations. To begin with there were more, and stronger, relationships between parents' occupational status and the other variables in the model. In particular, in this group, not only was there a positive association between parents' status and liking for classical music, there was also a negative relationship with heavy metal. Conversely, there were fewer relationships between school achievement and the music preferences, although those that were found were stronger than previously: in a negative direction with the two heavy metal variables, and positive with 'Classical 1'. Over time, there were strong negative correlations between 'anticipated occupational status' and two music variables: 'Disco 2' and 'Heavy Metal 2'.

On the basis of an analysis of such a small group we should be wary of all but the most tentative conclusions. Nevertheless, there are indications here, first, that the downwardly mobile may have a tendency to fall back on their status origins, perhaps in an attempt to compensate for their own lack of attainment; and second, that those anticipating a drop in status develop a taste for disco and heavy metal. Analyses of the mean levels of liking for the music types, together with a one-way analysis of variance by parents' occupational status and respondents' own school achievement, provided more detailed information of the pattern of relationships between the variables.

At time one, disco was liked most by very high school-achievers from the lower working class. However, over time, the relationship changes. At time two, disco is liked most by very low achievers from the lower working class. Perhaps, over time, the high achievers move on to other tastes, more appropriate to their emerging educational status.

The data for liking heavy metal also reveal interesting changes over time. At time one, heavy metal was liked most by the low school achievers from the upper working class, while at time two, it was liked most by the low achievers from the upper middle class. A finding once more indicating a synchronization of status and taste.

By contrast, the pattern for liking classical music was more stable. At both time points the highest mean levels of liking are manifested by upper-middle-class high achievers.

The one-way analysis of variance in the liking for the music types by parents' occupational status failed to result in any significant 'eta' co-efficients. However, respondents' school achievement was a significant factor in relation to the variance in liking 'Disco 1', the two heavy metal variables, and the two classical music variables, providing further evidence of the mediating role of school achievement.

If we compare the mean preference levels for the music types across the occupational mobility groups, the results are once again in line with theoretical expectations: disco and classical music are liked most by the upwardly mobile, whereas heavy metal is liked most by the downwardly mobile.

Finally, an Analysis of Variance (Anova) of the music preferences at time two, by SES background, gender, school achievement, anticipated status, and actual occupational status was carried out on the data from all 201 respondents. The results indicated that, of the three music types, these five factors were best able to explain the variance in the ratings for heavy metal (26 per cent), compared to only 16 per cent for classical music and 13 per cent for disco. Of the three, only the explanation for heavy metal attained an acceptable level of significance. These levels of explanation were increased slightly by employing own educational status in the analysis instead of own occupational status (to 28 per cent, 19 per cent, and 15 per cent, respectively). Once again, however, only the explanation for heavy metal was significant.

Educational mobility and music preferences

The educational mobility group analysis manifested an overall pattern of bivariate correlations similar to that of the occupational mobility group described above. The educational status of parents was strongly correlated with their occupational status (r = .61). There were weak positive relationships between parents' educational status and respondents' own educational achievement, educational status, and anticipated occupational status, and there was a strong positive correlation between educational achievement and anticipated occupational status. With regard to the music tastes, there was a moderate positive correlation, at both time points, between parents' educational status and liking classical music, and a very weak negative one with 'Disco 2'. The theoretically most important of these relationships are illustrated in Figure 9.3.

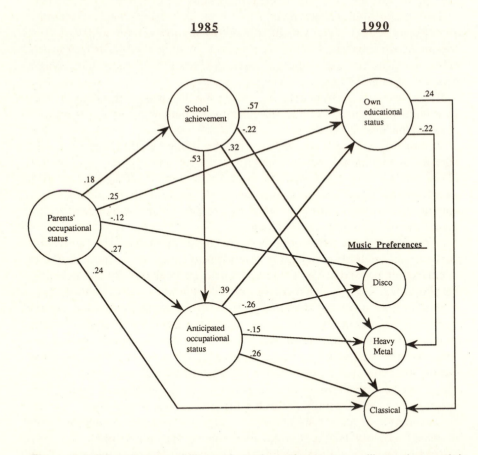

Figure 9.3 Educational mobility and music preferences: an illustrative model containing bivariate correlation coefficients of major theoretical interest (n = 201)

In the educationally 'stationary' group, the educational status of parents correlated moderately strongly with five of the six music variables: positively with the two classical music variables; negatively, with the two heavy metal variables. There was also a weak negative relation with 'Disco 2'. In addition, there were moderately strong relationships between own educational achievement and all six music variables: positive with the two classical music variables and 'Disco 1'; negative with the two heavy metal variables and 'Disco 2'. Similarly, own educational status was related negatively to both heavy metal variables and 'Disco 2', and positively to 'Classical 1' and 'Classical 2'.

Although the educational status 'climbers' and 'droppers' groups were small, some interesting strong correlations did reach acceptable levels of significance. As expected, for the 'climbers', these concerned classical music: 'Classical 1' correlated positively with anticipated occupational status, while 'Classical 2' was strongly related, also positively, to parents' educational status, own educational achievement, own educational status, and anticipated occupational status.

Once again, the results for liking disco were rather equivocal, with no significant correlations with any of the educational variables. However, there were three with the occupational variables: namely, moderate to strong negative correlations between parents' occupational status and 'Disco 1', and between anticipated occupational status and 'Disco 2'; but a positive correlation between own occupational status and 'Disco 2'.

Among these educational 'climbers' it is also worth noting that, with the exception of moderate negative correlations with the two classical music variables, no significant relationships were found between the two heavy metal variables and any other variables in the model. This can be interpreted as lending support to the view that, although the upwardly mobile may adopt legitimate cultural forms as they move up, they do not necessarily abandon less legitimate forms more typical of their status origins. Meanwhile, the negative correlation between 'Heavy Metal 2' and 'Classical 2' suggests that there are differences in this respect, i.e. it is possible that while some reject heavy rock as their status rises, others refuse to make this rejection.

Conversely, for the educational status 'droppers', the only correlations to reach or approach significance were those with liking for heavy metal. Most striking was the extremely strong negative correlation (−.82) between anticipated occupational status and 'Heavy Metal 2', which indicates that those anticipating lower status tend to have a very strong preference for heavy metal.

One extremely interesting result from the educational 'droppers' was the existence of moderately strong positive correlations between parents' occupational status and the heavy metal variables. This indicates that, among 'droppers', liking for heavy metal is greater the higher the occupational status of parents, a result running counter to the weight of existing evidence. This, coupled with the unusually strong negative correlation with anticipated status, supports the view that heavy metal is liked by the downwardly mobile from higher social status backgrounds.

As with the occupational mobility data, analyses of the mean levels of liking for the music types, together with one-way analyses of variance were carried out.

The results for disco largely paralleled those of the occupational mobility group: at both time points, it was liked the most by those whose parents had the lowest educational status. By own school achievement, at time one it was liked most by those with the highest level of school achievement; at time two, by the average achievers.

Heavy metal preferences also once again showed interesting temporal changes. At time one this type of music was liked most by very low achievers with the lowest educational status parents; at time two, low achievers with high (but not the highest) status parents recorded the highest mean.

By contrast, the pattern for classical music was once again more stable. At both points the highest mean levels of liking are reached by very high achievers whose parents had the highest level of educational status.

The one-way analysis of variance in liking for the music types by parents' educational status produced only one significant eta (for 'Classical 2'). However, school achievement was a significant factor in relation to the variance in liking 'Heavy Metal 1' and the two classical music variables.

If we compare the means of the preferences for the music types across the educational mobility groups, the results are once again in line with theoretical expectations: heavy metal is liked most by the educational 'droppers', whereas classical music is liked most by the educational 'climbers'. The pattern for disco once again appears to change over time. To begin with it is liked most by the educational 'climbers'; by time two, however, there are virtually no differences between the groups. Once again an Analysis of Variance (Anova) of the music preferences at time two, by parents' educational background, gender, school achievement, anticipated status, and own educational status was carried out. However, the results obtained were rather different from those of the occupational mobility group. Whereas occupational factors accounted best for the variance in liking heavy metal, educational status factors were best able to explain the variance in liking classical music. The results indicated that the five factors listed above were able to account for 25 per cent of the variance in classical music, 22 per cent of that in heavy metal, and 19 per cent of the liking for disco.

Inter-generational mobility in and out of higher education

Finally, the mean levels of liking for the music types were analysed for the higher education mobility analysis group. At time one, both disco and heavy metal were liked most by average achievers with low (but not the lowest) educational status parents. However, at time two, whereas disco was liked most by average achievers with the lowest educational status parents, heavy metal was liked most by low achievers with high educational status parents. Classical music, on the other hand, was liked most at time one by very high achievers with low educational status parents, and at time two by very high achievers whose parents had a high educational status. Across the mobility groups, disco and classical music were liked most by those climbing into higher education, while heavy metal was liked most by those dropping out of it.

Occupational and educational mobility collated

Which of the occupational and educational groups, then, had the highest mean preference levels for the various types of music at the two data collection times? To answer this question the group means of the music preference variables were collated across the mobility groups. The results revealed an interesting differential pattern.

To begin with, liking for disco was highest in two groups: the occupational status climbers, and those climbing into higher education from backgrounds where neither parent had been to university or college. By the second collection point, disco was most liked by the occupational status climbers. A very strong preference for disco, then, appears to be associated most with *upwards occupational mobility.*

At time one, the highest level of liking for heavy metal was also found in two groups, but this time among the occupational status droppers and the educational status droppers. By time two heavy metal was liked most by the latter group. Thus, a very strong preference for heavy metal seems to be related most to *downwards educational mobility.*

At both time points classical music was liked most by those who, inter-generationally, were climbing into higher education. Therefore, a very high level of liking for classical music appears to be most characteristic of inter-generational *upwards mobility into higher education.*

SUMMARY AND CONCLUSIONS

The starting point of this chapter was the premise that changes in social position will be associated with changes in media use. More specifically, inter-generational status mobility, occurring within a larger context of status inequality, is likely to be accompanied by distinctive shifts in the self-esteem, identity and lifestyle of individuals and groups which, in turn, leads to distinctive cultural taste and media use patterns. For adolescents and young adults the dominant institutional context for status allocation and repro-duction is seen to be education. Schools are identified as instrumental in creating particular status cultures, as well as specific dispositions towards taste and preferences.

Following this perspective, a model was specified which postulates that, as a result of its mediation of the passage from status origins to status destinations, the educational system is instrumental in structuring the perceptions which individuals and groups have of their probable futures in the status hierarchy, something which, in turn, via the process of anticipatory socialization, influences media use and taste patterns. Where there is a serious divergence between status origin and destination, the model predicts that unique and 'deviant' media use and taste patterns will emerge.

On the basis of this model two specific predictions were made. First, that those experiencing mobility will display music tastes deviant from those typical of their status background and, second, that the downwardly mobile will display an unusually high level of preference for culturally less legitimate types of music.

The heuristic efficacy of this theoretical model has received preliminary support from the results of this study. Different types of social mobility, upwards and downwards, occupational and educational, were found to be differentially related to preferences for music types differing in cultural legitimacy. Thus, the segmentation of the music audience can be seen, at least in part, as resulting from the trajectory of individuals and groups within various dimensions of the social status hierarchy (cf. Bourdieu 1984; Peterson 1992).

Whether or not these findings may be generalized to other forms of media use remains a task for future investigation. Nevertheless our results encourage us to predict that social mobility is a potentially important explanatory factor in connection with media use and should be given far greater attention than it currently receives.

REFERENCES

Bourdieu, P. (1984) *Distinction: A Social Critique of the Judgement of Taste*, London: Routledge.

Bourdieu, P. and Passeron, J.-C. (1977) *Reproduction in Education, Society and Culture*, London: Sage.

Bourdieu, P. and Passeron, J.-C. (1979) *The Inheritors: French Students and their Relation to Culture*, London: University of Chicago Press.

Bowles, S. and Gintis, H. (1977) *Schooling in Capitalist America*, London: Routledge.

Cohen, A. (1970) 'A general theory of subcultures', in D.O. Arnold (ed.) *The Sociology of Subcultures*, San Francisco: University of California Press.

Collins, R. (1979) *The Credential Society*, New York: Academic Press.

Dembo, R. (1972) 'Life-style and media use among English working class youths', *Gazette*, 18: 24–36.

De Vos, G.A. (1990) 'Self in society: A multi-level, psycho-cultural analysis', in G.A. De Vos and M. Suarez-Orozco (eds) *Status Inequality: The Self in Culture*, Newbury Park, Calif.: Sage.

Erikson, E.H. (1959) 'Identity and the life-cycle', *Psychological Issues* 1.

Erikson, R. and Goldthorpe, J.H. (1992) *The Constant Flux: A Study of Class Mobility in Industrial Societies*, Oxford: Clarendon.

Flodin, B. (1986) *TV och yrkesförväntan* (with an English summary), Lund: Studentlitteratur.

Frith, S. (1983) *Sound Effects: Youth, Leisure, and the Politics of Rock 'n' Roll*, London: Constable.

Giddens, A. (1991) *Modernity and Self-identity*, Cambridge: Polity.

Giroux, H.A. (1981) *Ideology, Culture and the Process of Schooling*, Philadelphia, Pa.: Temple University Press.

Hurrelmann, K. (1988) *Social Structure and Personality Development*, Cambridge: Cambridge University Press.

Jarlbro, G. (1988) *Familj, massmedier och politik* (with an English summary), Stockholm: Almqvist & Wiksell International.

Jarlbro, G. and Dalquist, U. (1991) 'Mot alla odds: En longitudinell studie av ungdomars sociala mobilitet', *Lund Research Papers in the Socilogy of Communication* 30, Lund: Department of Sociology, University of Lund.

Jencks, C. (1972) *Inequality: A Reassessment of the Effect of Family and Schooling in America*, New York: Harper & Row.

Johansson, T. and Miegel, F. (1992) *Do the Right Thing: Lifestyle and Identity in Contemporary Youth Culture*, Stockholm: Almqvist & Wiksell International.

Johnsson-Smaragdi, U. (1983) *TV Use and Social Interaction in Adolescence*, Stockholm: Almqvist & Wiksell International.

Kelly, G. (1963) *A Theory of Personality*, New York: Norton.

Lipset, S.M. and Bendix, R. (1962) *Social Mobility in Industrial Society*, San Francisco: University of California Press.

Lipset, S.M. and Zetterberg, H.L. (1966) 'A theory of social mobility', in R. Bendix and S.M. Lipset (eds) *Class, Status and Power*, New York: Free Press.

Lööv, T. and Jarlbro, G. (1989) 'Dröm och verklighet: En longitudinell studie av ungdomars yrkesförväntningar', *Lund Research Papers in the Sociology of Communication* 17, Lund: Department of Sociology, University of Lund.

Merton, R.K. (1968) *Social Theory and Social Structure*, New York: Free Press.

Merton, R. K. and Rossi, A.K. (1950) 'Reference group theory and social mobility', in R.K. Merton and P.F. Lazarsfeld (eds) *Continuities in Social Research*, New York: Free Press.

Peterson, R.A. (1992) 'Understanding audience segmentation: from elite and mass to omnivore and univore', *Poetics* 21: 243–258.

Piepe, A., Crouch, S. and Emerson, M. (1978) *Mass Media and Cultural Relationships*, Farnborough: Saxon House.

Piepe, A., Emerson, M. and Lannon, J. (1975) *Television and the Working Class*, Farnborough: Saxon House.

Roe, K. (1983) *Mass Media and Adolescent Schooling: Conflict or Co-existence?*, Stockholm: Almqvist & Wiksell International.

—— (1985) 'The school and music in adolescent socialization', in J. Lull (ed.) *Popular Music and Communication*, Newbury Park, Calif.: Sage.

—— (1987a) 'Swedish youth and music: listening patterns and motivations', *Communication Research* 12: 353–362.

—— (1987b) 'Adolescents' video use: a structural cultural approach', *American Behavioral Scientist* 30: 522–532.

—— (1987c) 'Schooling ourselves to heavy metal', in O. Stafseng and I. Frones (eds) *Ungdom mot år 2000*, Oslo: Gyldendal.

—— (1989) 'School achievement, self-esteem and adolescents' video use', in M.R. Levy (ed.) *The VCR Age: Home Video and Communication*, Newbury Park, Calif.: Sage.

—— (1990) 'Adolescents' music use: a structural-cultural approach', in K. Roe and U. Carlsson (eds) *Popular Music Research*, Gothenburg: NORDICOM-Sweden.

—— (1992) 'Different destinies – different melodies: school achievement, anticipated status, and adolescents' tastes in music', *European Journal of Communication* 7: 335–357.

—— (1993a) 'Academic capital and music tastes among Swedish adolescents: an empirical test of Bourdieu's model of cultural reproduction', *Young: The Nordic Journal of Youth Research* 1 (3): 40–55.

—— (1993b) 'Videovåldets första fans', in C. von Feilitzen, M. Forsman and K. Roe (eds) *Våld från alla håll: Forsknings-perspektiv på våld i rörliga bilder,* Stockholm: Symposion.

Roe, K. and Löfgren, M. (1988) 'Music video use and educational achievement', *Popular Music* 7: 303–314.

Rosenberg, M. and Pearlin, L.I. (1978) 'Social class and self-esteem among children and adolescents', *American Journal of Sociology* 84: 53–77.

Rosengren, K.E. and Windahl, S. (1989) *Media Matter: TV Use in Childhood and Adolescence*, Norwood, NJ: Ablex.

Sorokin, P.A. (1964) *Social and Cultural Mobility*, Glencoe: Free Press.

Stinchcombe, A.L. (1964) *Rebellion in a High School*, Chicago: Quadrangle.

Trondman, M. (1990) 'Rock taste – on rock as symbolic capital', in K. Roe and U. Carlsson (eds) *Popular Music Research*, Gothenburg: NORDICOM-Sweden.

Veblen, T. (1934) *The Theory of the Leisure Class*, New York: Random House.

Willmott, P. (1969) *Adolescent Boys in East London*, London: Routledge & Kegan Paul.

Part IV

Lifestyle and the use of media

Chapter 10

Values, lifestyles and family communication

Fredrik Miegel

LIFESTYLE, IDENTITY AND VALUE

The empirical study of youth culture and young people's lifestyles is by no means an easy task. Depending on the purpose of the study, it can be conducted from quite different theoretical and methodological points of view. In this chapter I shall apply what might be called a value perspective. This is not a very original perspective, since several theories in the field combine lifestyle theory with a more or less developed value theory (see, for instance, Mitchell 1983; Kamler 1984). The reason for this is that behind most of our actions and attitudes lie a number of values, and since lifestyles are almost always empirically conceptualized and identified in terms of (patterns of) attitudes and/or actions, the value concept is obviously of central importance in this respect.

The values embraced by an individual also form a fundamental component of that individual's identity, and the identity is crucial for which lifestyle the individual will develop. This confronts us with two obvious difficulties:

1 Theoretically, we must define what we mean by the terms 'value', 'identity', and 'lifestyle', and there is no single and commonly agreed upon definition of any of these terms.
2 Empirically, we must be able to construct relevant methods to make each of these three phenomena empirically accessible.

I cannot, of course, offer any final solutions to these problems here, but only give a brief summary of the discussions carried out in Johansson and Miegel's *Do The Right Thing* (1992), where each of these questions is dealt with rather thoroughly (see also Lööv and Miegel 1989, 1991; Miegel 1990; Miegel and Dalquist 1991).

LIFESTYLE

One can distinguish three different but interrelated levels at which it is possible to study aspects of living, in a way relevant to a discussion of lifestyle: a *structural*, a *positional*, and an *individual* level (Johansson and Miegel 1992: 22ff; Lööv and Miegel 1989; cf. Heller 1970/1984; Thunberg *et al*. 1981: 61). The distinction clearly resembles that made by Habermas in volume two of *The Theory of Communicative Action* (1987). Habermas distinguishes between three structural components of the lifeworld, namely *culture*, *society* and *personality*. To each of these components he connects a reproduction process: *cultural reproduction*, *social integration* and *socialization* respectively (Habermas 1987: 135–148).

On the structural level one can examine differences and similarities between various countries, societies and cultures, but also differences evolving over time within one and the same society. We may refer to configurations primarily reflecting differences in societal structure as *Forms of Life*. In short, these configurations can be said to represent different forms of society and its culture.

The positional level concerns differences and similarities in relevant aspects of living between large categories, classes, strata or groups situated at different positions within a social structure. Configurations of this kind, primarily determined by the position held in a given social structure, we term *Ways of Living*.

On the individual level, finally, one tries to understand differences and similarities between the ways in which individuals face reality and lead their lives, how they develop and express their personality and identity, their relations toward other individuals, etc. At this level we speak of *Lifestyles*. Lifestyles are thus expressions of individuals' ambitions to create their own specific personal, cultural and social identities within the historically determined structural and positional framework of their society. Thus, the term lifestyle is here defined as a structurally, posititionally *and* individually determined phenomenon.

The reason for making the above distinction is that the application of the concept of lifestyle has changed in accordance with societal and cultural change. In classical sociology, the concept was mainly used to distinguish between basically social classes or status groups on the basis of their cultural characteristics (see Weber 1922/1968; Simmel 1904/1971; Veblen 1899/1979). In contemporary society, on the other hand, lifestyle has become less tied to the social position of the individual; instead, individually determined conditions have become increasingly important for researchers within the area (see Toffler 1970; Zablocki and Kanter 1976; Schudson 1986; Turner 1988).

IDENTITY

We deal with the concept of identity by distinguishing three components inherent in the identity of an individual: *personal*, *social* and *cultural* identity (Johansson and Miegel 1992). These three components of identity are to be considered as aspects of one and the same phenomenon, namely, the total identity of the individual. The three aspects, then, are not to be mistaken for distinct types or categories of identity.

In brief one can explicate the differences between these aspects of identity in the following way. Through the *personal identity*, the individual develops the capacity to live and think in isolation from others as an autonomous being. This aspect of identity is formed and developed through the process of *individuation* which results in the *personality* of the individual (Blos 1962, 1967, 1979; Mahler 1963; Mahler *et al.* 1975). The personal identity consists of experiences, thoughts, dreams, desires as interpreted and comprehended by the individual in relation to other experiences and thoughts. Personal identity thus relates to the individual. It may be described as a unique system of relations between experiences, thoughts, dreams, hopes and desires.

Through his or her *social identity* the individual becomes a member of different groups, learning the roles he or she is expected to play. This aspect of identity serves the function of integrating the individual in different social contexts. Social identity is formed and developed through the process of *socialization* and is manifested in the processes of *role-enactment*, *role distance* and *role-transition* (Mead 1934/1962; Goffman 1969, 1982; Turner 1968, 1990; Burke and Franzoi 1988). It serves the function of making the individual capable of playing certain roles in social life. In a sense, social identity is non-individual. Its function is to define the individual's position within the society, relations toward other individuals sharing the same position, and the relations towards individuals holding other social positions.

Through the *cultural identity* the individual becomes able not only to express his or her unique characteristics within the group to which he or she belongs, but also to express towards other groups his or her own group membership or belongingness. The cultural identity is formed and developed through the process of *lifestyle development* (Johansson and Miegel 1992). The cultural identity can be said to have a double, or integrating, function. On the one hand, it is related to the personal identity, and on the other, to social identity. The individual uses his or her values, attitudes and actions to maintain and develop the personal identity, but also to distinguish him- or herself or relate to other individuals. Thus, one and the same value, attitude or action may on one hand serve the purpose of strengthening the self, and on the other function as a means of expressing a sense of belonging to, or holding distance toward, other individuals.

VALUE

Culture consists of the **values** the members of a given group hold, the **norms** they follow, and the *material goods* they create. Values are abstract ideals, while norms are definite principles or rules which people are expected to observe. (Giddens 1989/1991: 31).

The rather broad definition of the concept of value proposed by Giddens in the above quotation points to the theoretical as well as empirical difficulties inherent in the concept, one central characteristic being its abstract nature. However, in the same quotation Giddens also marks the importance of the concept within the social sciences by making it the most fundamental component of culture. Obviously, the lifestyles developed in a society constitute one aspect of that society's culture. Hence, the most important concept in relation to identity and lifestyle is value. Actually, value is the most fundamental component of lifestyle, and one can say that the lifestyle of an individual is an expression of his or her values, the norms related to these values, etc. But value is, indeed, a complicated concept to deal with, and in order to make it suitable for lifestyle analysis, I have to make a number of conceptual distinctions. On the one hand I distinguish between three conceptual levels on which lifestyle can be studied from a values perspective, and on the other, I distinguish between at least four different types of value (Miegel 1990; Johansson and Miegel 1992).

In brief, the lifestyle phenomenon can be studied on three conceptually different levels: a *value level*, an *attitude level*, and an *action level*. The value level consists of the individual's *general* and abstract ideas about material, aesthetic, ethical and metaphysical conditions and qualities. These rather abstract ideas are made concrete by the individual on the attitude level. The attitudes of an individual involves his or her outlook on *specific* objects, phenomena and conditions of reality. On the action level, finally, the individual manifests his or her attitudes in the form of different actions. The values and attitudes of the individual become visible and observable when they manifest themselves in action. To summarize: the individual embraces a number of values which he or she makes concrete in the form of attitudes. Such attitudes are expressed in the form of certain actions and behaviours.

As indicated above, I distinguish between four different types of value, namely, material, aesthetic, ethical, and metaphysical values. Each of these types of value corresponds to a type of attitude and a type of action (Figure 10.1).

Most empirical and a good deal of the theoretical lifestyle studies hitherto conducted are concerned basically with the left-hand side of the figure, that is, with material and aesthetic values, attitudes and actions. The most important reason for this is probably that material and aesthetic expressions of value are rather easy to make empirically accessible, since to a considerable extent they have to do with consumption. I will argue here that the right-hand side of the figure – that is, the ethical and metaphysical values – represents an important component of the lifestyle of an individual.

VALUES AND IDENTITY

To understand the relation between identity and value, we turn to the widely influential work of Milton Rokeach. According to Rokeach, a value is an

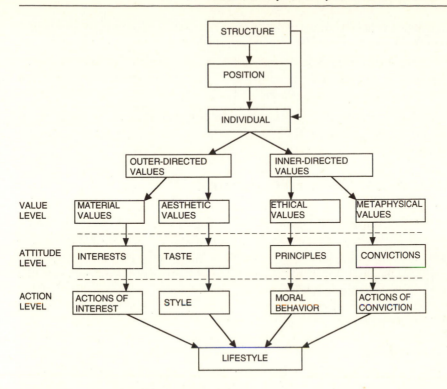

Figure 10.1 Values, attitudes and actions

enduring belief, either prescriptive or condemning, about a preferable or desirable mode of conduct or an end-state of existence. These values are organized into value systems along a continuum of relative importance (Rokeach 1973). Rokeach believes that values are taught to human beings, and once taught they are integrated into an organized value system in which each value is arranged in relation to other values. The values serve different functions for the individual. They constitute standards guiding our behaviour, helping us to make decisions, for example in our presentation of ourselves to others, in our comparisons of different actions or objects, in our attempts to influence others, in our formulations of our attitudes, in our evaluations and our condemning of others, and so forth.

Rokeach's theory of value is accompanied by a number of assumptions about human nature. He maintains that there is a group of conceptions more central to an individual than are his or her values. These are the conceptions individuals have about themselves. Rokeach argues that the total belief system of an individual is functionally and hierarchially structured, so that if some part of the system is changed, other parts of it will be affected, too, and consequently their corresponding behaviour as well. The more central the changing part of the belief system is, the more extensive the effects will be.

A change in the conception of one's self would thus affect and lead to changes also in the values. Rokeach's main thesis is that:

> . . . the ultimate purpose of one's total belief system, which includes one's values, is to maintain and enhance . . . the master of all sentiments, the sentiment of self regard. (Rokeach 1973: 216)

Before proceeding, it is useful to place Rokeach in a philosophic value theoretical context, since the assumptions inherent in his work are far from unquestioned.

SOME REMARKS ON VALUE THEORY

In Chapter 12, Thomas Johansson distinguishes between a cognitive and an affective dimension of lifestyle, maintaining that values constitute the former dimension, whereas the latter consists of affects, desires and pleasure. The dimension as such offers no great problem, but locating the values within the cognitive dimension calls for discussion. The reason for his doing this is that most social scientists involved in value studies have had what might be called a cognitivist definition of the value concept – including Rokeach, whose theory Johansson takes as his point of departure. In our joint dissertation, too, we somewhat unreflectedly applied a rather cognitivist value definition (Johansson and Miegel 1992: 62). Against this background it is hardly surprising that Johansson defines value in a cognitivist fashion and regards values as belonging to a cognitive dimension of lifestyle. The question, however, is whether values are to be defined in this way. It has long been disputed within the philosophy of value (cf. Bergström 1990; Frankena 1963/ 1973; Hare 1981; Moritz 1973).

In brief, one can identify two basic lines of argument in this debate, one represented by so called cognitivist theories of value, and the other by so called non-cognitivist theories.[1] In contrast to the cognitivist theories, the non-cognitivist theories state that value statements are not judgements, but expressions of emotions, or preferences, or imperatives, and thus neither true nor false.

Against this brief value theoretical background, it is clear that the theory suggested by Rokeach, and applied by us in our study, is not self-evident, but in fact rather questionable from a value theoretical point of view, especially since the non-cognitivist theories have been dominant in the post-war twentieth century philosophy of value. Aware of this theoretical limitation or naivety, we have, nevertheless, judged Rokeach's approach as the most suitable among the available social scientific empirical value studies.

VALUES, IDENTITY AND THE CONSTRUCTION OF LIFESTYLES

Lifestyles are routinised practices, the routines incorporated into habits of dress, eating, modes of acting and favoured milieux for encountering others; but the routines followed are reflexively open to change in the light of the mobile nature of self-identity. Each of the the small decisions a person makes every day – what to wear, what to eat, how to conduct himself at work, whom to meet with later in the evening – contributes to such routines. All social choices (as well as larger and more consequential ones) are decisions not only about how to act but how to be. (Giddens 1991: 81)

In studying the relation between values, identity and lifestyle, it is necessary always to keep in mind that the identity is a complex system of relations consisting of a multitude of conceptions about who one is, and how one is related to other individuals and to one's society and culture. Put in other words, identity has a number of different psychological functions for the individual.

First, it has the function of cultivating the personal self, that is, the qualities and characteristics we believe are tied to our own unique person. In this sense, identity functions as a means to help us to maintain and enhance the conceptions we have about ourselves, to identify ourselves, define ourselves for ourselves, to speak, as well as to express this unique self to others, to show others who we are.

Secondly, identity has a number of social functions for the individual. Apart from the desire to have a unique personal identity, people have a desire to be part of their society or culture, and of a variety of different groups existing within it. People often define themselves in relation to groups to which they feel they belong. People play different social roles. Consequently, they sometimes need to subordinate their personal identity in favour of various role expectations.

Thirdly, identity serves the function of integrating and making compatible with one another the desire to be unique with the desire to belong (Johansson and Miegel 1992; Ewen 1988).

The integration of these two desires is not always unproblematical. We are constantly occupied with the struggle to integrate these two poles of identity, and we do not always succeed; conflicts often occur (see Turner 1978).

First, the different expectations related to the roles one plays are not always entirely compatible with one's desire to develop and express one's personality. Thus, the expectations directed towards a certain role may be experienced as obstructing one's potential to achieve one's desire to maintain and develop the qualities and characteristics inherent in what one sees as one's own unique personality.

Secondly, the qualities and characteristics identified as one's own unique personality may lead to difficulties in adopting a certain role. Thus, although one would like to play a particular role, or to occupy a certain position in society, one is prevented from doing so by, say, low self-esteem, or political opinion, for example.

Thirdly, one's social identity consists of multiple roles, and it may be difficult to combine these different roles into a coherent picture of one's social self. One must constantly balance between these different roles, and at the same time take into consideration all the different role expectations. To find a satisfying balance between the different roles one has to play and these roles and one's own personal strivings and aspirations, is something which is difficult but which individuals must endeavour to achieve throughout their whole life.

The different psychological functions of the identity discussed above obviously correspond with different functions of values and lifestyles also. An important distinction is therefore that between *security* and *developmental* values (Johansson and Miegel 1992). This distinction resembles Rokeach's distinction between the *ego-defensive function* of values and the *knowledge* or *self-actualization function* of values (Rokeach 1973: 15). The security values (cf. ego-defensive values) serve the function of helping oneself to fit in and adapt in an unproblematic way to society, avoiding conflicts and ensuring that one's actions and attitudes are justified. In Rokeach's terms, such values represent 'ready made concepts provided by our culture that such justifications can proceed smoothly' (Rokeach 1973: 15f). The developmental values (cf. knowledge or self-actualization) serve the function of fulfilling the individual's needs and desires to search for meaning, understanding, knowledge and self-realization.

For some individuals, security is the most important function of values, and vice versa. Obviously, which function an individual emphasizes most has a considerable impact on the way his or her lifestyle is constructed (see Zablocki and Kanter 1976; Mitchell 1983).

In order to understand how individuals construct their identity, it is important to comprehend how they reason and act in order to solve the never-ending conflicts between their different roles; and between their roles and their self-images. Society's culture provides a large number of images and ideals for the ways in which particular roles may be successfully acted out, and an equally great number of ideals and images concerning individuality and personal identity. Finally, culture offers a number of ideals and images concerning solutions to the problem of bringing the two poles of identity together.

In the development of the lifestyle of an individual all the components of identity distinguished here are at work. Lifestyle consists of actions and attitudes based not only on material and aesthetic values, but also on metaphysical and ethical values, attitudes and actions. I have argued that any lifestyle involves a meaningful pattern of relations between values, attitudes and actions of all possible kinds. It is thus impossible to keep the different types of value apart in discussing identity and lifestyle. The same is true for the relation between the individual and society. In contemporary Western society the different types of value – material, aesthetic, ethical, and metaphysical – are mingled together in consumer goods and the mass media. As Stuart Ewen puts it:

. . . in the perpetual play of images that shaped the mass-produced suburbs, and in the ever-changing styles that kept the market in consumer goods moving, 'material values' and values of 'mind and spirit' were becoming increasingly interchangeable and confused. (Ewen 1988: 232)

Trust

So far I have argued that the values embraced by an individual are the most fundamental components of his or her identity and lifestyle. In order to function in society, a human being must share with his fellow human beings a set of commonly held values, norms, conceptions, etc. The individual must, therefore, internalize these values, norms and conceptions in order to become integrated in society. The process through which this internalization takes place is socialization. As a matter of fact, the most important function of socialization is to integrate the individual into society.

As modernization gradually made society increasingly complex, socialization became a complicated process indeed. While in pre-modern times socialization prepared the individual to function together with a relatively limited number of persons, socialization in late modern society must prepare the individual to function within highly complex systems and structures.

Against this background Niklas Luhmann and others have pointed to the importance of the concept of *trust* in socialization theory (Luhmann 1973/1979; cf. Giddens 1991). According to both Luhmann and Giddens, trust is necessary if the individual is ever to develop and to function in society. Without trust, everything in society will be experienced as threatening and uncontrollable, and the individual will experience a kind of isolation in reality, which may lead to existential anguish. Giddens and Luhmann believe that this important ability to experience trust is established during childhood in relation to the nearest environment, that is, parents, siblings, peers, etc. To establish this trust in the individual is thus a basic function in socialization.

Luhmann maintains that trust is a mechanism which helps the individual to deal with the complexity characterizing modern society. A complex society demands that an individual's trust be based on the insight that he or she is indeed dependent on a very complex system. According to Luhmann, individuals and social systems alike strive to create a kind of predictability in reality – that is, to establish reasonable expectations about how individuals and social systems work.

The establishment of trust during childhood and adolescence provides the individual with a sense of security. We learn what is expected of us, and what we can expect from others in different contexts. The establishment of trust, therefore, to a considerable extent is based on the learning of norms and rules of different kinds, the 'do's and don'ts' of social life. Once internalized, these norms and rules function as a kind of guarantee for individuals that they can expect some reasonable continuity and stability in the ways people act and react in different situations. In this sense, trust is related to that aspect of identity which I call social identity. Giddens (1991) uses the term *ontological trust* to describe the individual's need for a predictable environment over which he or she has at least some control, in order to be able to trust the existence of some continuity and stability in the numerous relations on different levels which constitute the individual's social network.

Thus, the ability to trust is an essential prerequisite for the individual to develop a stable identity and a socially acceptable lifestyle. The process through which the individual internalizes the necessary values, norms and conceptions is, therefore, one of the most important factors in the development of the individual's identity and lifestyle. A good deal of this process takes place during childhood and adolescence in relation to family experiences (cf. Chapter 1).

However, apart from learning social rules and norms, the individual is, of course, also developing his or her personal identity during childhood and adolescence. Here, too, the individual's family is of utmost importance in controlling the individual's degree of freedom, and in encouraging the development of his or her individual needs, desires, experiences, attitudes, etc. In short, on the one hand, the individual must learn a number of norms and rules in order to adopt and fit into a variety of social contexts, and, on the other, must develop an autonomous individual personality. The communication climate of the family in which the individual is brought up, therefore, sets the necessary conditions for the individual's identity and lifestyle development in adult life, one of the most important aspects of family related socialization being the relative importance assigned to social and personal identity development, respectively.

So far I have discussed theoretically the relation between the values embraced by the individual and the lifestyles the individual develops. I have furthermore discussed the fundamental role of the early socialization and the establishing of trust in the individual's value, identity, and lifestyle development. I have argued that a fundamental role in this process is played by the family in which the individual is brought up, and, thus, that the communication ideology within the family may have at least some impact on which values and lifestyles the individual will develop.

In the rest of this chapter I shall present some empirical findings in support of the previous arguments concerning the relation between values and lifestyle, and between socialization and the learning of values.

AN EMPIRICAL INTRODUCTION

In this section I will briefly report on the instruments used to measure values, lifestyle and family communication. Within the Media Panel Program a considerable amount of theoretical and empirical work has been conducted on these subjects. Family communication has been studied by Hedinsson (1981) and Jarlbro (1986, 1988). The relation between value and lifestyle has been analysed mainly by Lööv and Miegel (1989, 1991), Johansson and Miegel (1992), Miegel (1990) and Miegel and Dalquist (1991).

We have used three different sets of questions for studying the values of our respondents. Two are well-known empirical instruments developed by Ronald Inglehart (1977) and Milton Rokeach (1973), and one of them we have developed ourselves.

In brief, Rokeach identified eighteen values which he took to cover the entire and universal value sphere. His technique is usually termed List of Values (LOV). It may be used in at least two different ways. Rokeach himself used the ranking technique, which means that the respondents must arrange the eighteen values in order of preference. In our study, however, we have used a rating technique. We have also added six values to Rokeach's eighteen values. I cannot account for the theoretical and methodological reasons behind this choice of approach here, however. (For a thorough discussion of these matters, see Johansson and Miegel (1992). For a discussion of ranking vs. rating techniques, see, for instance, Munson (1984), Alwin and Krosnick (1985), De Casper and Tittle (1988).)

Contrary to Rokeach, Inglehart does not identify particular values. Instead, he uses what might be described as an indirect method of identifying the value orientations of the respondents: he measures the respondents' attitudes towards twelve concrete societal goals for the future. Like Rokeach he uses a ranking technique, whereas in our study we have employed a rating technique. In brief, Inglehart's method aims at identifying two different value orientations: a material one and a postmaterial one. Inglehart states that in contemporary society individuals have not only become more able to influence their own lives, but have also come to put higher value on self-development, personal growth, life satisfaction and the like. No longer having to put as much effort into the mere satisfaction of fundamental biological and material needs, the contemporary Western person has become increasingly preoccupied with self-development. Inglehart thus indicates that in Western societies a gradual shift in value orientation is taking place. The earlier emphasis on material welfare and physical security has decreased, greater attention being paid to such phenomena as self-fulfilment, self-realization and personal growth. This is the process he calls a shift from a material to a postmaterial value orientation in contemporary society (Inglehart 1977, 1990).

Part of our own constructed value measurements resembles Inglehart's, but we had our respondents rate their attitudes towards fourteen different goals for their own future, instead of using Inglehart's societal goals. Using this method we can identify four types of personal value orientation: individual security, individual development, social security and social development. In short, the value orientation of individual security encompasses such future goals as having a stable relationship and children; individual development goals such as travelling a lot, living abroad and having an exciting job. Social security stresses such personal goals for the future as earning money, having a safe job, a car of one's own, working full-time, and looking young. Social development, finally, includes goals such as investing in education and making a career.

Two types of lifestyle indicator were used in the study. We measured the individuals' attitudes towards music and film, and also the relative frequency with which they pursue different leisure time activities. We asked our respondents about their attitudes towards 53 different music genres, and 37 different film genres. To make the material more manageable we employed factor analysis to arrive at a number of *taste patterns*, as we like to call them. These taste patterns may be interpreted as a number of quite general patterns of taste in music and film, towards which the respondents relate in differing ways depending on their class, gender and education, and also depending on which values they hold. From these factors we created twelve additive indices of music taste and nine indices of film taste, each of which can be used in further statistical analysis (Johansson and Miegel 1992). The same procedure was used for the measurement of leisure time activities. From a list of 56 different activities we created eleven additive indices, or *activity patterns*.

In order to measure family communication we have applied two versions of Chaffee's measurement method (Chaffee *et al.* 1973; cf. Ritchie 1991). Chaffee distinguishes between *socio-oriented* family communication and *concept-oriented* communication patterns. Socio-oriented family communication tends to stress the importance of smooth social relations with other people, while the concept-oriented family emphasizes the importance of ideas and concepts (Chaffee *et al.* 1973; Jarlbro 1986; Rosengren and Windahl *et al.* 1989). In this study we use two different sets of questions to identify these dimensions. We applied the original set of questions when the respondents were 15 years old. At this time the respondents' parents reported on how the communication within the family took place. We used a revised version when the respondents were 21 years old. At this time they responded themselves on how they thought family communication ought to be.

There are, however, several difficulties involved in measuring family communication, some of which I will briefly mention here. One obvious problem is that we have measured one particular family member's (in most cases the mother's) perception of norms, rules and ideals governing family communication (Ritchie 1991). Different family members may have different views on these matters; daughters may be raised differently than sons; father and mother may have different attitudes concerning children's upbringing, and so on. Furthermore, the measurement does not account for gender or age related positions and distributions of power within the family. Nor does it account for the existence of different types and sizes of family. Communication within a family consisting of only a single parent and one child is probably radically different from that in a family with two parents and several children. There are also children with two families, two 'fathers', two 'mothers' and two sets of siblings, and communication in these families respectively may, indeed, vary.

Apart from the problems related to the family, there are also problems associated with the fact that from a rather early age, just like children in many other countries, most Swedish children spend a great deal of time in social institutions (first in child care centres, then at school). A considerable part of the early socialization, therefore, takes place outside the family, and in relation to adults and peers other than parents and siblings. The relative impact of the family and these institutions respectively on which values, norms and ideals the individual internalizes, are, therefore, of utmost importance when discussing how family communication may influence individually developed values.

The list of problems related to the measurement of family communication and its influence on the individual may be further extended (for instance, by the role of the mass media in the process of socialization), but I stop here by establishing the fact that the measurement of family communication and its impact on the individual entails several difficulties which I cannot solve here. I can only point them out and keep them in mind when interpreting the statistical analyses presented later in this chapter (cf. also Chapter 8).

ADAPTION AND PROGRESSION

Taking a close look at the different measurement scales used when measuring values, value orientation and family communication, we find that the dimensions supposedly tapped by these scales show interesting similarities. It may even be possible to locate them within two separate categories which we may call *Adaption* and *Progression* (Figure 10.2). The former category emphasizes the importance of fitting in and adapting in an unproblematic way to the environment, the avoidance of conflicts, smooth relations with other people, and the securing of social and material relations, whereas the latter stresses such aspects as personal growth, self-development, personal independence, self-actualization, supportiveness and open communication.

In the category of adaption we may place Rokeach's *ego-defensive values*, which serve the function of helping one to fit in and adapt in an unproblematic way to society. Inglehart's *material value orientation* can also be assigned to this category, emphasizing material needs, stable social relations, and societal order. Likewise, the personal value orientations of *individual* and *social security* belong to this category, since they stress stable social, material and economic relationships. Finally the *socio-oriented family communication pattern*, stressing the importance of smooth social relations with other people, the avoiding of conflict, and clear-cut power positions, also belongs to the category of adaption.

	ADAPTION	PROGRESSION
ROKEACH	EGO-DEFENSIVE	KNOWLEDGE OR SELF-ACTUALIZATION
PERSONAL VALUE ORIENTATIONS	SECURITY	DEVELOPMENT
INGLEHART	MATERIALISM	POSTMATERIALISM
CHAFFEE	SOCIO-ORIENTED	CONCEPT-ORIENTATION

Figure 10.2 The categories of adaption and progression

The category of progression includes Rokeach's *knowledge or self-actualization values*, serving the function of fulfilling the individual's needs and desires to search for meaning, understanding, knowledge, and self-realization. Also Inglehart's *postmaterial value orientation*, stressing self-development, personal growth, life satisfaction, etc., belongs to this category, as do the personal value orientations of *social* and *individual development* with their emphasis on social, material and personal development and growth. Finally, also, Chaffee's *concept-oriented family communication pattern* can be assigned to the category of progression, due to its emphasis on the importance of ideas, concept, personal independence, open communication, and the like.

From this we may argue that the four different measurement scales in different ways aim at capturing different aspects of one and the same phenomenon in modern society, namely, the process of individualization, which will be discussed in more detail in the concluding part of this chapter. This means that we should expect statistical correlations between the four adaption dimensions, and between the four progression dimensions. And, as a matter of fact, there are such correlations.

Table 10.1 presents the correlations between the four Rokeachean values most representative of his knowledge and self-actualization dimension (self-realization, inner harmony, self-esteem, wisdom), and the four values best describing his ego-defensive dimension (family security, national security, power, wealth); it also includes Inglehart's materialism and postmaterialism dimensions, and the four personal value orientations. The table speaks for itself. The variables belonging to the adaption category tend to correlate with each other, as do the variables belonging to the progression category. However, there are few correlations between the progression variables and the adaption variables.

These results further support the assumption that the different methods of measuring value may capture different aspects of one and the same phenomenon. As will be shown later in this chapter, the same seems to hold true for the relation between the values/value orientation and the socio-oriented family communication pattern. Furthermore, the statistical variation within the variables are generally considerably greater in the variables I have assigned to the adaption category. Whereas most people in our sample seem to agree more or less upon the statements used when measuring progression, they show generally much more variation in their attitudes toward the statements used to capture the dimensions included in the adaption category.

One may thus pose the question what kind of information we gain from the analysis of the relation between values and family communication. If the different scales measure basically the same phenomenon, albeit at different conceptual levels, the results obtained should be expected. And this is actually what I argued earlier in this chapter. According to the discussion, the value structure of a society has an impact on which values the individuals

Table 10.1 Knowledge or self-actualizing values, ego-defensive values, personal value orientations and Inglehart's value orientations (Pearson's correlations)

	Knowledge or self-actualization values				Ego-defensive values				Personal value orientations				Inglehart's value orientations	
	Accomplishment	Inner harmony	Self-respect	Wisdom	Family security	National security	Power	Wealth	Social security	Individual security	Social dev.	Individual dev.	Material	Post-materialism
Knowledge or self-actualization values														
Accomplishment	–													
Inner harmony	.39**	–												
Self-respect	.44**	.37**	–											
Wisdom	.28**	.24**	.40**	–										
Ego-defensive values														
Family security	.25**	.47**	.18*	.00	–									
National security	.13	.18*	.28**	.08	.27**	–								
Power	.13	.02	.11	.18*	.02	.30**	–							
Wealth	.05	-.08	.10	.12	-.01	.26**	.66**	–						
Personal value orientations														
Social security	.01	.06	.02	-.02	.19*	.38**	.38**	.44**	–					
Individual security	.15*	.26**	.00	-.06	.44**	.25**	.12	.09	.37**	–				
Social development	.23**	.13	.18*	.23**	.11	.17	.29**	.27**	.17*	.12	–			
Individual development	.31**	.22**	.16*	.16*	.05	-.01	.12	.19*	.03	-.14	.34**	–		
Inglehart's value orientations														
Material	.13	.13	.09	.03	.33**	.41**	.26**	.36**	.36**	.27**	.17*	-.01	–	
Postmaterialism	.32**	.45**	.21**	.19	.27**	.01	-.17**	-.20*	-.19*	.05	.07	.24**	.15	–

of that society internalize, which in turn influences their attitudes towards, in this case, how family communication ought to take place. Put in another way, if the value structure of a society (Inglehart) has impact on which values the individuals within this structure embrace (Rokeach), and if the values the individual embraces constitute the basis for that individual's attitudes in various areas (Chaffee), we should expect correlations between the variables used to measure each of these levels. That is precisely the results obtained. I will return to a discussion of these matters later in the chapter.

YOUTH CULTURE AND LIFESTYLE: THE IMPORTANCE OF VALUES

The empirical results presented in Tables 10.2, 10.3 and 10.4 may be regarded as providing a rough and preliminary indication of how young people's lifestyles are structured.

There are a large number of different relations present in the tables, and these can be interpreted on the basis of several different theoretical perspectives. I shall briefly discuss three such theoretical perspectives: a class- and status-oriented perspective, a gender perspective and a human values perspective.

The class and status perspective may be regarded as the dominant perspective within the sociological literature on popular culture and lifestyles (see Weber 1922/1968; Gans 1974; Bourdieu 1984). According to this perspective, the most important structural principle here is the distribution of wealth and status in society. The most thoroughgoing theoretical and empirical work within this tradition is probably Bourdieu's *Distinction*. Our empirical results give some support to the assumption that class and education are important factors in the development and maintenance of lifestyles.

We note that several taste and activity patterns correlate with either class or education or both. Thus, the levels of education and class background seem to be related to the development of certain tastes and leisure time interests. Even though class and education constitute important and necessary explanations of the way young people develop particular lifestyles, these variables do not suffice for providing an adequate explanation. Also age, which, however, is kept constant in the analyses, and gender are important factors to consider.

On the basis of our empirical data we conclude that differences between men and women in their tastes and leisure time activities, and in their lifestyles, are considerable. These differences are, of course, related to gender roles. On a more general level it is also possible to discuss these differences in terms of two differing cultural spheres, namely, a male and a female sphere. However, just as with class and education, gender is a necessary but not sufficient explanation of the differentiation of lifestyles within a society.

Apart from gender, class and education, there are also other structurally,

Table 10.2 Musical taste related to positional variables, values and value orientations (Pearson's correlations)

	Jazz	Post-Punk	Heavy Metal	Folk & Rock	Main-stream	Country	Modern Dance	Opera/ Musical	Ethnic	Symph/ Southern	Socially Conscious	50s & 60s Rock
Gender	-.09	-.19***	-.20***	-.07	.13	.05	-.10	.19***	-.09	-.24***	.26***	-.08
City	-.05	-.08	.05	-.10	.13	-.09	-.01	-.01	-.05	-.09	-.15**	-.13
Class	.06	.08	-.03	.11	-.05	-.18**	-.04	.15**	.01	.02	-.09	-.01
Education	-.01	-.08	-.27***	.03	-.08	-.15**	-.01	.28***	-.03	-.04	-.12	-.10
Material security	-.08	-.16**	.09	-.23***	.29***	-.05	.03	-.18**	-.12	.00	-.09	-.19***
Personal security	.01	-.14	-.08	-.13	.31***	.07	-.07	-.07	-.13	-.03	.00	-.08
Social security	.06	-.06	.00	.01	.20***	-.02	.12	.12	.01	-.03	.11	.01
Personal development	.19***	.09	-.08	.14	-.01	.01	.25***	.23***	.20***	.02	.10	.04
Material development	.13	.05	-.11	.08	.04	-.04	.13	.19***	.07	.12	-.02	-.03
Material	.01	-.16**	.02	-.09	.31***	-.09	.07	-.01	-.01	.02	-.03	-.10
Postmaterial	.19***	.04	-.09	.20***	-.02	.01	.05	.24***	.13	-.01	.18**	.12
A clean world	.08	-.04	-.09	.18**	.09	-.01	-.05	.17**	.10	.04	.14	.14
Technical development	.17**	.06	.06	-.03	.10	-.08	.14	.04	.06	.12	-.18**	-.04
A comfortable life	.03	-.04	-.03	-.00	.13	-.04	.02	.05	-.08	.07	.04	-.04
An exciting life	.14	.01	.01	.07	.02	-.09	.09	.08	.10	.09	.01	-.00
Accomplishment	.16**	.02	-.11	.11	.09	-.14	.08	.19***	.11	.07	.02	.04
Peace	.02	-.15	-.07	.07	.26***	.04	.03	.08	-.02	-.09	.23***	.07
A world of beauty	.13	.02	-.00	.04	.13	.07	.05	.07	.16**	-.00	.23***	.07
Equality	.03	-.10	-.10	.02	.06	.00	-.01	.09	.02	-.12	.17**	.06
Family security	.01	-.16**	-.07	-.00	.28***	.11	-.01	.10	-.10	-.04	.12	.00
Freedom	.00	-.15	-.13	-.01	.21***	.03	.08	.01	-.01	-.12	.06	.02
Happiness	-.00	-.05	-.07	-.02	.14	.07	-.06	.01	-.05	.00	.10	-.03
Inner harmony	.10	.02	-.03	.09	.12	-.04	.08	.18	.03	.06	.15**	.07
Love	.05	-.05	-.07	.09	.20***	.08	-.08	.10	-.03	.03	.21***	.06
National security	.01	-.12	.01	-.09	.28***	-.02	.10	-.04	.04	-.00	-.09	-.15**
Pleasure	.08	-.06	.03	-.05	.20***	.01	.02	.01	.01	.04	.09	-.04
Salvation	.07	-.01	.02	-.11	.12	.05	-.02	.03	-.03	-.09	.01	-.05
Self-respect	.13	.09	-.01	.14	.11	-.10	.08	.24***	.18**	.14	.05	.14
Social recognition	.03	.02	.01	-.7	.18**	.06	.01	-.10	.08	.05	-.02	-.04
Wisdom	.18**	.14	-.04	.10	-.07	-.09	.02	.22***	.15**	.05	-.03	.09
Justice	-.01	-.09	-.15**	-.05	.16**	.06	.02	.04	.03	-.08	.11	.07
Power	.09	.10	.00	-.11	.08	.03	.09	-.07	.11	.07	-.15**	-.10
Health	-.06	-.11	-.03	-.01	.25***	-.05	-.02	.02	-.09	.02	.07	-.00
Wealth	.02	.04	.07	-.11	.11	-.07	.16**	-.11	.05	.12	-.16**	-.09

Table 10.3 Film taste related to positional variables, values and value orientations (Pearson's correlations)

	Romantic	Poetic/ Psycho	Socially Conscious	SF/ Fantasy	Horror	Porno & Violence	Agent	Comedy	War & Gangster
Gender	.55***	-.01	-.02	-.30***	-.30***	-.40***	-.33***	-.15**	-.31***
City	.04	-.10	-.07	-.07	-.04	-.01	.15**	-.06	-.03
Class	-.15**	.01	.09	-.04	-.05	-.19**	.09	-.12	.00
Education	-.15	-.01	.01	-.19**	-.29***	-.34***	.00	-.26***	-.10
Material security	.20***	-.26***	-.20***	.25***	.24***	.37***	.26***	.46***	.19***
Personal security	.33***	-.14	-.08	.04	-.02	.05	.06	.20***	-.04
Social security	.24***	.01	.03	-.04	.01	-.09	.05	.14	-.04
Personal development	.06	.23***	.23***	-.01	.02	-.14	-.03	-.09	-.04
Material development	-.02	.05	.12	-.05	-.01	-.03	.15**	-.01	.11
Material	.24***	-.22***	-.12	.06	.18**	.18**	.16**	.37***	.15**
Postmaterial	.18**	.20***	.22***	-.11	-.17**	-.24***	-.10	-.11	-.14
A clean world	.14	-.03	.08	-.06	-.13	-.16**	-.06	-.01	-.07
Technical development	-.13	-.04	.02	.19***	.21***	.22***	.30***	.15**	.23***
Comfortable life	.22***	-.06	.05	-.01	.01	.07	.09	.25***	.01
Exciting life	.01	-.17**	.17**	.00	.10	-.01	.08	.00	-.01
Accomplishment	.10	.08	.21***	-.04	-.02	-.03	.15	-.01	.03
Peace	.29***	-.03	.05	-.07	-.02	-.06	-.10	.16**	-.07
World of beauty	.22***	.10	.15**	.04	.09	.03	.00	.11	.01
Equality	.25***	.15	.16**	-.04	-.10	-.18**	-.23***	.00	-.10
Family security	.33***	-.07	.01	-.04	.02	.01	-.02	.20***	.00
Freedom	.16**	.06	.09	-.06	.02	-.04	-.01	.09	.00
Happiness	.29***	.01	.02	-.04	.00	.03	-.02	.22***	-.08
Inner harmony	.18**	.07	.14	-.03	-.03	-.06	.03	.01	-.04
Love	.30***	.02	.07	-.08	-.06	-.07	-.02	.16**	-.04
National security	.19***	-.12	-.04	.11	.12	.22***	.22***	.23***	.24***
Pleasure	.25***	.00	.05	.04	.08	.19***	.16**	.26***	.13
Salvation	.07	-.05	-.04	.07	-.05	.06	.03	.07	-.05
Self-respect	.08	.10	.23***	.10	-.02	-.04	.21***	-.01	.13
Social recognition	.08	.00	-.02	.14	.11	.24***	.25***	.17**	.19***
Wisdom	-.15**	.15**	.21***	.06	-.07	-.13	-.04	.15**	-.05
Justice	.17**	.04	.13	-.06	-.05	-.08	-.08	-.02	.05
Power	-.09	.01	.01	.14	.20***	.31***	.27***	.14	.20***
Health	.17**	-.05	.00	.05	.05	.03	.02	.25***	-.02
Wealth	-.01	-.01	-.05	.20***	.27***	.28***	.24***	.27***	.21***

Table 10.4 Leisure time activities related to positional variables, values and value orientations (Pearson's correlations)

	Culture	Party	Music	Sports	Domestic	Fashion	Religious	Hunting/Fishing	Exercise	Media	Travel
Gender	.24***	-.10	-.04	-.34***	.40***	.38***	.11	-.22***	.18**	-.20***	.09
City	.17**	.01	.18**	.21***	-.15	-.13	-.02	.07	.05	-.11	.14
Class	-.06	.09	-.01	.17**	-.13	-.07	-.07	.18**	.06	-.05	-.08
Education	.29***	-.02	.16**	.12	-.11	-.04	.03	.01	.10	-.25***	.17**
Postmaterial	.26***	-.12	.17**	-.21***	.20***	.09	.07	-.17**	.03	-.11	.19***
Material	-.24***	.10	-.12	.10	.07	.19***	-.05	-.01	.07	.05	-.10
Material security	-.43***	-.12	.17**	-.21***	.20***	.09	.07	-.17**	.03	-.11	.19***
Material	-.24***	.10	-.12	.10	.07	.19***	-.05	-.01	.07	.05	-.10
Material security	-.43***	.06	-.18**	.10	.10	.19***	-.08	.08	.05	.26***	-.12
Personal security	-.10	-.05	-.13	.00	.29***	.26***	.09	.08	-.01	.09	-.05
Social security	.08	.14	.07	.09	.15**	.28***	.07	-.04	.19***	.10	.14
Personal development	.29***	.19***	.14	.07	-.03	.03	.03	.10	.26***	-.04	.41***
Material development	.20**	.18**	.10	.17**	-.02	.06	.01	.13	.25***	-.10	.18**
A clean world	.12	-.14	.07	-.09	.12	.05	.08	-.06	.03	.06	.02
Technical development	-.17	.02	.06	.18**	-.11	-.02	.01	.08	-.06	.12	.01
A comfortable life	.03	.10	.00	.05	.26***	.21***	.10	.02	.13	.06	.01
An exciting life	.14	.20***	.10	.03	.05	.07	.07	.13	.16**	.07	.20***
Accomplishment	.19***	.13	.02	.04	.11	.05	.05	.05	.10	-.10	.16**
Peace	.05	.02	-.01	-.02	.22***	.21***	.12	-.05	.12	-.01	.12
A world of beauty	.02	.08	-.01	-.12	.26***	.20***	.15**	-.03	.08	.16**	.17**
Equality	.14	-.02	-.01	-.15**	.28***	.19***	.15**	-.11	.09	-.02	.15**
Family security	.03	.01	-.10	-.14	.34***	.30***	.18**	-.02	.10	.04	.07
Freedom	.03	.00	-.04	-.09	.06	.14	.04	-.02	.09	-.01	.03
Happiness	.03	.02	.01	-.07	.32***	.18**	.07	.06	.18**	.05	.11
Inner harmony	.14	.02	.08	-.10	.23***	.12	.13	-.02	.11	-.06	.10
Love	.09	.00	.00	-.07	.30***	.20***	.08	.05	.11	.08	.05
National security	-.21***	.12	-.12	-.01	.05	.22***	.08	.06	.09	.10	.02
Pleasure	-.12	.11	-.07	.01	.24***	.12	.07	.12	.13	.11	.07
Salvation	.05	.02	.10	.03	.15	.14	.64***	.02	.08	.19***	.02
Self-respect	.15	.14	.07	-.03	.07	.09	.12	-.01	.06	.01	.12
Social recognition	-.20***	.05	-.12	.00	.05	.10	.01	.00	.05	.16**	.02
Wisdom	.24***	-.08	.19***	-.06	-.03	-.08	.16**	-.01	.07	.02	.09
Justice	.10	-.04	-.06	-.04	.20***	.17***	.11	.01	.13	-.01	.04
Power	-.17**	.12	-.16**	.09	-.04	.03	-.14	.11	.01	.16**	.03
Health	-.04	.03	-.11	.02	.16**	.13	-.01	-.03	.04	.10	.08
Wealth	-.21***	.15**	-.13	.13	.02	.08	-.16**	.14	.07	.24***	.05

positionally or individually determined phenomena which influence an individual's lifestyle. Among these are identity and the values embraced by the individual him- or herself.

In one way or another, all the different taste and activity patterns distinguished in this study are related to at least some values and/or value orientations. The relations between values and value orientations on the one hand, and taste and activity patterns on the other, are rather complex. These relations are partly explained by the ways in which values among youth in Western society are structured along the gender, class and status dimensions. From the simple correlation matrices presented in Tables 10.2, 10.3 and 10.4 we cannot gain insight into the complex relations between values, societal position, and tastes or activities. Thus we have conducted a number of combined Anova–MCA analyses in order to arrive at a more thorough knowledge of the empirical relations between these different variables.

In order to carry out a complete analysis of the relations between these variables, we would have to conduct an Anova–MCA analysis for all the thirty values and value orientations concerning their relation to each of the twelve musical taste patterns, the nine film patterns and the eleven activity patterns, making for a total of 30x32=960 Anova–MCA analyses. I cannot, of course, present such a number of analyses here. Instead I have chosen three such analyses to exemplify the complex relations to be found between structure, position, values and lifestyle which I have discussed in the theoretical part of this chapter (see Figures 10.3, 10.4 and 10.5).

It should be noted that the Anova–MCA analyses presented here are chosen among the fifteen showing the strongest correlation between a value and a taste or activity pattern.

Obviously, not every Rokeachean value is correlated with every taste or activity pattern. I could, therefore, just as well have presented a handful of examples of Anova–MCA analyses showing no correlation between a particular value and a taste or activity pattern. By presenting the Anova–MCA analyses in Figures 10.3, 10.4 and 10.5, I am thus not aiming at proving that each given taste or activity pattern is determined by a particular value. All I want to do is to show that at least some taste and activity patterns are clearly correlated with a value, and that some of the variation within a given such pattern seems to be explained by the degree to which that value is held. That is, the very existence of such correlations is what is interesting in this context; not the particular correlation. Put differently, the existence of correlations between some values and some taste and activity patterns, even when controlling for other variables, can be taken as an indication that the values which an individual embraces constitute one explanation, among others, for that individual's tastes in music and film, and her leisure time pursuits.

I am, of course, aware that in order to let the unique influence from each particular value on each particular taste or activity pattern stand out, we should have to keep not only gender, education, city and socio-economic

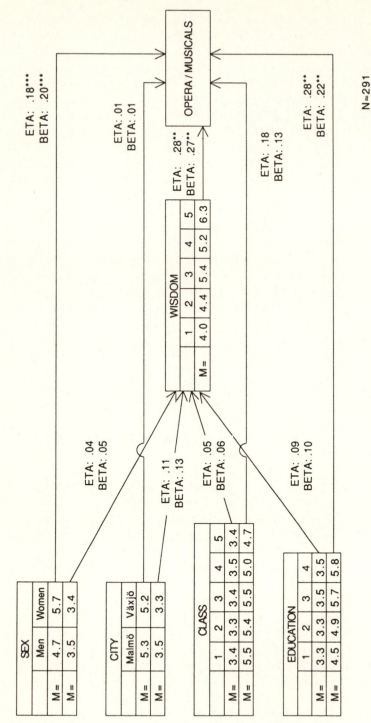

Figure 10.3 Anova–MCA analysis of the relations between structural and positional variables, the value of wisdom and the musical taste pattern of opera musicals

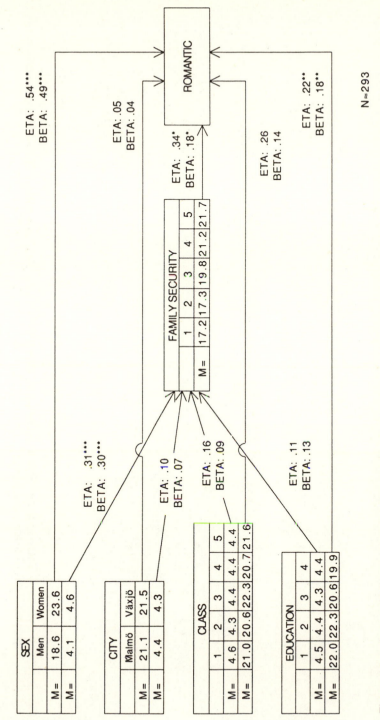

SEX

	Men	Women
M =	18.6	23.6
M =	4.1	4.6

CITY

	Malmö	Växjö
M =	21.1	21.5
M =	4.4	4.3

CLASS

	1	2	3	4	5
M =	4.6	4.3	4.4	4.4	4.4
M =	21.0	20.6	22.3	20.7	21.6

EDUCATION

	1	2	3	4
M =	4.5	4.4	4.3	4.4
M =	22.0	22.3	20.6	19.9

FAMILY SECURITY

	1	2	3	4	5
M =	17.2	17.3	19.8	21.2	21.7

ROMANTIC

ETA: .54*** BETA: .49***

ETA: .05 BETA: .04

ETA: .34* BETA: .18*

ETA: .26 BETA: .14

ETA: .22** BETA: .18**

ETA: .31*** BETA: .30***

ETA: .10 BETA: .07

ETA: .16 BETA: .09

ETA: .11 BETA: .13

N=293

Figure 10.4 Anova–MCA analysis of the relations between structural and positional variables, the value of family security and the romantic film taste pattern

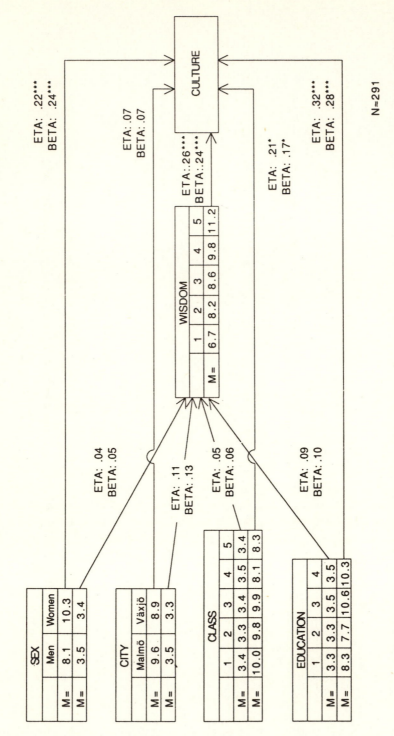

SEX		
	Men	Women
M =	8.1	10.3
M =	3.5	3.4

ETA: .04
BETA: .05

ETA: .22***
BETA: .24***

CITY		
	Malmö	Växjö
M =	9.6	8.9
M =	3.5	3.3

ETA: .11
BETA: .13

ETA: .07
BETA: .07

WISDOM					
	1	2	3	4	5
M =	6.7	8.2	8.6	9.8	11.2

ETA:.26***
BETA:.24***

CLASS					
	1	2	3	4	5
M =	3.4	3.3	3.4	3.5	3.4
M =	10.0	9.8	9.9	8.1	8.3

ETA: .05
BETA: .06

ETA: .21*
BETA: .17*

EDUCATION			
	1	2	3	4
M =	3.3	3.3	3.5	3.5
M =	8.3	7.7	10.6	10.3

ETA: .09
BETA: .10

ETA: .32***
BETA: .28***

CULTURE

N=291

Figure 10.5 Anova–MCA analysis of the relations between structural and positional variables, the value of wisdom and the culturally oriented activity pattern

status constant, but also all the other values and probably some other variables. Given the capacity of the Anova-MCA, where only five variables can be kept constant during an analysis, this is, unfortunately, impossible to accomplish.

In the figures we account for each positional variable's unique influence on a value, and on a taste or activity pattern. In the same figure we account for the unique influence of a specific value on a specific taste or activity pattern. Each figure is based on nine single analyses in which the relation between two variables was investigated while the influence of other relevant variables was kept constant.

The figures show that even when positional variables are held constant the relations between values and taste or activity patterns are strong. Thus, the values and value orientations of the individual tell a great deal about the way the individual's own personal lifestyle develops within the structurally and positionally determined framework characterizing the person's society and culture.

The values embraced by the individual are inculcated into him or her by parents and peers at school or at work, as well as through other societal institutions, during the processes of individuation and socialization. Eventually all persons learn to function as individuals who incorporate the general material, aesthetical, ethical and metaphysical codes of society and culture, as well as those of the particular groups and social networks in which they become involved during their lifetime. This adjustment to more or less commonly held values, norms, mores, etc. is necessary in order to function as a social being. However, there are considerable variations, both between different groups in society and between different individuals, with respect to the relative importance put on these values, norms, mores, and the like.

One might say that although most individuals share a common set of values, norms and mores with their fellow people, they nevertheless deviate from one another in their unique ways of relating to these values, mores and norms. Thus, the values and value orientations distinguished by Rokeach and Inglehart are all embraced more or less by all individuals, but the relative importance ascribed to each single value varies from person to person. These variations are important; obviously, they exert a strong influence on the more specific attitudes and actions of the individual. These individual variations, in their turn, are translated into the many highly differentiated lifestyles found in society.

The social and cultural structure of modern Swedish society is characterized by rather small variations in values between different classes and status groups among youth, but by rather strong variations between young men and women (see Table 10.5). It should be noted in this context that this state of affairs concerns young people in Sweden. The results may look different for other age-groups or for the Swedish population as a whole.

In our sample it is thus difficult to distinguish between the values and value

Table 10.5 Values and value orientations related to gender, class and education (Pearson's correlation)

	Gender	Class	City	Education
Material security	−.14	−.07	−.03	−.14
Personal security	.15**	−.07	.04	−.10
Social security	.19***	.04	.03	.02
Personal development	.11	.15**	−.04	.08
Material development	−.08	.20***	.06	.20***
Material	.02	.04	−.01	−.08
Postmaterial	.35***	−.04	−.12	−.02
A clean world	.18**	−.05	.00	−.07
Technological development	−.39***	.15	.04	.08
A comfortable life	.11	.04	−.09	−.15
An exciting life	.05	−.04	−.04	−.11
Sense of accomplishment	.14	.03	.06	.00
Peace	.30***	−.07	−.11	−.14
A world of beauty	.22***	−.08	−.10	−.23***
Equality	.39***	−.14	−.17**	.11
Family security	.30***	−.07	−.10	−.08
Freedom	.16**	.06	−.03	−.07
Happiness	.30***	−.02	−.16**	−.10
Inner harmony	.24***	.06	−.08	−.01
Love	.27***	.00	−.10	−.12
National security	.02	.00	.10	−.03
Pleasure	.09	−.09	−.09	−.16
Salvation	−.02	−.03	−.08	.00
Self-respect	.09	.15	−.02	.18**
Social recognition	−.08	−.04	.03	−.10
Wisdom	−.04	−.01	−.12	.07
Justice	.26***	.03	−.09	−.06
Power	−.23***	.03	.02	−.07
Health	.10	.03	−.07	−.07
Wealth	−.22***	.06	−.01	−.08

orientations embraced by different classes or status groups. Young people possessing higher education and coming from higher-class backgrounds do tend to emphasize the importance of development as opposed to security more than do individuals of lower education and of lower-class background. But the major differences are to be found along the gender dimension. Actually, we can identify a large number of values and value orientations tied to gender differences.

These gender differences are also expressed in variations in taste and activity patterns. Although there are class- and status-related taste and activity patterns, there are even greater gender-related patterns. Tables 10.2, 10.3, 10.4 and 10.5 show that there are strong relations between the gender-related values and value orientations, and the gender-related taste and activity patterns. This seems to imply that values and value orientations, as well as taste and activity patterns, are strongly influenced by gender. The interesting fact, though, is that even when gender is kept constant, the often rather strong influence of a particular value or value orientation on a taste or activity pattern remains intact (see Figures 10.3, 10.4 and 10.5). Thus, the tendency to embrace certain values and value orientations and to develop certain taste and activity patterns is closely related to gender. At the same time, irrespective of gender, class and education, individuals embracing particular values are more or less likely to develop certain taste and activity patterns.

FAMILY COMMUNICATION AND THE ESTABLISHMENT OF VALUES AND TRUST

So far I have argued that behind lifestyles in contemporary society lie a number of individually embraced values. At the structural level, these values are part of a long-term cultural heritage. At a positional level they are tied to the various positions which individuals occupy within these structures. At an individual level they are part of the individual's own identity. I have furthermore presented support for these assumptions in some empirical findings regarding the relations between positional variables, lifestyle variables and value variables. Investigating how these values are transmitted to the individual from various agents of socialization (be it parents, siblings, peers, the mass media, church, school or any other societal institution), I now turn to the notion of socialization.

As individuals, we must all be able to trust our environment to a certain degree, in order to adopt the basic values and become able to act upon them and thus to function socially and to establish a lifestyle and identity of our own. The basic aspect of this necessary trust is founded during childhood and early adolescence in relation to one's family. Therefore, the family is an agent of socialization of extreme importance. The communication pattern of a family may be regarded as one plausible indicator of how socialization is taking place within a family.

In this section I will supply some empirical findings with a bearing on the relation between the family communication pattern and the values developed by individual family members. Taking as our point of departure Chaffee's socio-oriented dimension of family communication (see above), I shall investigate differences in values between the individuals in our sample. (I will not use his concept-oriented dimension since the variables used to measure this dimension show only little variation in our sample. That is, most respondents seem to agree upon the desirability of a concept-oriented family communication.)

Socio-oriented communication may be described as rather authoritarian, involving clear power relations between the family members (i.e., parents and children), stressing such factors as avoiding conflict, obeying, not getting angry, not arguing, showing respect for the elderly, etc.

234 Lifestyle and the use of media

We can first establish that there is a certain degree of stability between how the respondents' parents scored on the socio-oriented communication dimension when the respondents were 15 years old, and how they themselves scored at the age of 21 (Pearson's correlation .24***). The really important question, however, is whether the degree of socio-oriented communication pattern in the family has any impact on how the respondents score on the value variables.

I divided the population into three groups. One-third scored low on the socio-oriented dimension, one-third scored medium, and the remaining third scored high. When comparing the low-scoring third with the high-scoring third, I found some interesting differences in the scores also on the value and value orientation variables (Tables 10.6 and 10.7). In the tables the fifteen Rokeachean values which show the largest variations between the groups are included, together with the four personal value orientations, and Inglehart's postmaterial and material value dimensions. The values not included in the table show only small or no variation between the groups.

Turning first to Table 10.6, which includes the parental reports on the family communication when the individuals were 15 years old, and the values they held at the age of 21, we find that the individuals whose parents scored high on the socio-oriented dimension, tend to score higher on values and

Table 10.6 Scores on value and value orientation variables at age 21, for low, medium, or high scores on the socio-oriented dimension of family communication at age 15 (parental reports; means)

Value	Low	Medium	High
Power	0.75	0.49	1.24
Pleasure	2.78	2.86	3.22
Social recognition	1.61	1.43	1.98
Exciting life	2.46	2.62	2.76
A beautiful world	2.82	3.22	3.12
National security	2.79	2.70	3.08
Salvation	0.24	0.47	0.51
A comfortable life	3.17	3.27	3.43
Wealth	1.41	1.08	1.66
Happiness	3.38	3.41	3.60
Family security	3.18	3.41	3.39
Love	3.58	3.59	3.74
Health	3.58	3.78	3.73
Equality	3.01	2.89	2.93
Social security	13.16	12.95	14.36
Individual security	5.71	5.84	6.15
Social development	5.55	4.86	5.38
Individual development	7.86	2.30	7.35
Material	16.53	16.64	17.09
Postmaterial	20.14	19.16	19.51

Table 10.7 Scores on value and value orientation variables at age 21, for self-reported low, medium, or high scores on the socio-oriented dimension of family communication at age 21 (means)

Value	Low	Medium	High
National security	2.79	2.80	2.13
Technological development	2.19	2.02	2.50
Wealth	1.44	1.27	1.74
Salvation	0.35	0.45	0.64
Pleasure	2.95	2.93	3.20
Self-respect	2.91	2.72	2.66
Power	0.92	0.76	1.17
Social recognition	1.68	1.71	1.92
A beautiful world	2.95	3.11	3.19
A comfortable life	3.23	3.38	3.43
Equality	3.07	2.95	2.89
Family security	3.31	3.38	3.47
Wisdom	2.55	2.30	2.39
Freedom	3.76	3.75	3.61
Happiness	3.47	3.51	3.60
Social security	12.61	13.69	14.81
Individual security	5.55	5.89	6.41
Social development	5.57	5.28	5.31
Individual development	7.77	7.50	7.23

value orientation which have to do with security, materialism and status. As to the Rokeachean values, we find that those individuals whose parents scored high on the socio-oriented dimension tend to score higher also on the kind of values which Rokeach interprets as ego-defensive, and values which emphasize security, that is, values such as *social recognition, family security, salvation, wealth, a comfortable life, national security, happiness, love* and *health.* We also note that they tend to score higher on values stressing power and status, for instance, *power, social recognition,* and *wealth.* This indicates that individuals raised in families oriented towards socio-oriented communication – stressing the importance of avoiding conflict, fitting in unproblematically with society, enjoying security, appreciating a fixed and rather authoritarian distribution of power between the family members – themselves tend to adopt values expressing such features. This tendency gains further support from the fact that these individuals also tend to score higher on the personal value orientations which emphasize the security dimension, i.e. *social security* and *individual security,* but lower on the development dimensions, i.e. *social development* and *individual development.* They also tend to score higher on Inglehart's dimension of *material value orientation,* and lower on his *postmaterial value* dimension.

We may thus conclude from these results that the scores on those values and value orientations which I assigned to the category of adaption tend to be higher if the score is high also on the socio-oriented family communication pattern.

The results presented in Table 10.7 show basically the same pattern. On the one hand, individuals scoring high on the socio-oriented communication pattern tend to score higher also on the values and value orientations belonging to the adaption category, and lower on these belonging to the progression category. On the other hand, the individuals scoring low on the socio-oriented communication pattern tend to score higher on the values and value orientations belonging to the progression category and lower on these belonging to the adaption category.

It is indeed tempting to take these results as supporting our assumption that there is a relation between the family communication and the values internalized by the individual, and to some extent that is so. The relations accounted for in Table 10.6 describe the relations between the scores of the respondent's parents on the socio-oriented communication pattern when the individuals were 15 years old, and the respondents' own reports on the values and value orientations at the age of 21. These results thus indicate that the family communication pattern during upbringing influences the strength with which the individual embraces certain values at adult age. Although the patterns found in Tables 10.6 and 10.7 are clear enough, the tendencies are rather weak and statistically not significant. This has probably several explanations. In the first place, the variations within each of the variables used are rather small, and so is the sample analysed. Another explanation may be that the measurement scales used are not sufficient to capture successfully the variations in the phenomena they are supposed to measure. Yet another, perhaps more plausible and definitely more tempting and interesting explanation is that the absence of statistically significant correlations reflects a gradual long-term change of the overall societal structure. It is to this explanation I shall now direct my attention.

CONCLUSIONS

In this chapter I have argued that the values embraced by an individual constitute a fundamental part of that individual's identity and lifestyle, and that these values are internalized by the individual through the process of socialization. Assuming that an important part of the socialization takes place within the family, I hypothesized that the communication climate in the family is related to the values internalized by the individual. These assumptions are not very controversial – as a matter of fact they are rather commonly held among those involved in socialization theory. Empirically to study and measure values, family communication and the process of socialization is, however, difficult. Hence the statistical analyses which I have presented as supporting our assumptions must be interpreted with some caution.

The first question to consider is whether the different instruments used

when measuring values, value orientations and family communication basically aim at capturing one and the same phenomenon. During the last few
decades there has been a discussion within sociology and social psychology
regarding the development of a new personality type during the twentieth
century. In brief, this discussion emphasizes the view that during the last
century or so, most people in Western societies have experienced a rise in
the satisfaction of material needs. They do not have to put as much effort into
satisfying these basic needs; consequently they have become more concerned
with phenomena such as life-satisfaction, self-expression, personal growth
and fulfilment, etc. This is the process Inglehart (1977) tries to capture in his
The Silent Revolution. Although Inglehart does not use the term personality
type himself, we can, nevertheless, use his terminology and describe the new
personality type as post-materialistic. Inglehart is far from alone in having
noticed this process, however. It has been studied and analysed by several
social scientists during the latest fifty years or so.

> A number of commentators have suggested that a new personality type has
> emerged in the course of the twentieth century. David Riesman (1950), for
> example, refers to the replacement of the 'inner-directed' by the other-
> directed type and Daniel Bell (1976) mentions the eclipse of the puritan
> by a more hedonistic type. Interest in this new personality type has been
> sharpened recently by discussions of narcissism. (Featherstone 1991: 187)

Also Rokeach's discussion of the 'master of all sentiments, the sentiment of
self regard' (1973: 216) follows this line of argument. Featherstone (1991)
speaks about the new personality type in terms of a 'performing self', and
Goffman has noted the increasing importance of the 'presentation of self in
everyday life' (Goffman 1982).

Following these theoreticians there is no doubt that the twentieth century
has witnessed an increased interest in identity, lifestyle and personality. It
is this process which Inglehart and Rokeach study, and it may be argued that
Chaffee's studies of family communication basically concern the same
process, the concept-oriented individual representing the new personality
type. Given this state of affairs, we may interpret our empirical findings
about the relations between family communication and values as providing
further support for the hypothesis about the increasing importance of the
individual's personality development. This is reflected, for example, in the
fact that all our respondents scored high on the concept-oriented communication dimension.

It is indeed probable that there exists a relation between family communication and the individual's values. All the same, the results presented in this
chapter are best interpreted as suggesting a long-term process taking place in
modern Western societies, a gradual change of the societal structure affecting
also the positional and individual levels of society and culture.

It is mandatory, then, that media and communication research concerned with youth and youth culture look closer at how this process is also reflected in the mass media. There is no doubt that popular culture and the mass media constitute leading sources from which young people receive the images and ideas they use in their identity and lifestyle work. The mass media, therefore, have an important role as agents of socialization and as transmitters of values, norms and attitudes, something which obviously has considerable impact on the importance of the role of the family in the process of socialization. The relation between the two agents of socialization, the family and the mass media, therefore remains an important issue to study if we are ever fully to understand the role of family communication in the shaping of young people's lifestyles and identities.

NOTE

1 Although it is impossible to account for the entire scope of this extensive philosophical debate here, it is nevertheless important to pay at least some attention to it. The notion of value has been, and is, an extremely ambiguous and ever-disputed concept within philosophy. Thus the location of value within a cognitive dimension of lifestyle is not at all self-evident, but, as we shall see, actually a rather questionable standpoint.

To begin with the cognitivist theories, we can identify at least two leading types of theory, namely, naturalistic and objectivistic value theories. The former seem to be the most common ones within the social sciences. Mitchell's (1983) and Inglehart's (1977; 1990) theories both rest on naturalistic assumptions about the nature of values. Also Rokeach's (1973) theory is founded on a special branch of value naturalism, namely, subjectivism (see Johansson and Miegel 1992). In brief, naturalist theories of value state that norms and valuations are natural, scientific or empirical statements. That is, an ethical or aesthetic term can be defined in terms of non-ethical or non-aesthetic terms. Such theories have been subject to severe and devastating criticism within the philosophy of value, and within modern philosophy they are almost totally abandoned. The best-known argument held against naturalistic theories is different formulations of *Hume's Law*, stating in its most commonly known form that it is impossible to derive 'ought' from 'is' (Hume 1740/1982; Mackie 1980; Hare 1981).

The other basic form of value cognitivism is the so-called objectivistic value theories. These theories are also called non-naturalist theories; they deny that value statements express empirical value judgements, but agree that value judgements can be objectively true or false. This is the kind of theory held by, for instance, Plato, Kant, Sidgwick, and Moore (Bergström 1990; Frankena 1963/1973). Although objectivistic theories of value have not been totally abandoned, they have nevertheless been somewhat out of fashion in the twentieth-century value philosophy.

During the twentieth century different forms of non-cognitivist theories of value have emerged and become dominant. Several different forms of such theories have developed throughout the century, the best-known being the so-called emotivism – which according to Bergström (1990) gained almost total acceptance in Sweden – and later also the so-called prescriptivism (Bergström 1990; Mackie 1980) and universal prescriptivism (Hare 1981). Mackie (1980) describes the differences between the theories as follows:

Emotivism: a moral statement expresses, rather than reports, a sentiment which the speaker purports to have, and, by expressing it, tends to communicate it to a suitable hearer. . . .

Prescriptivism: in judging morally about a proposed action, a speaker is commanding or forbidding it. This is developed into Universal Prescriptivism: a moral statement endorses a universalizable prescription which the speaker is implicitly applying, or is prepared to apply, to all relevantly similar actions, irrespective of their relation to himself. (Mackie 1980:73)

REFERENCES

Alwin, D.F. and Krosnick, J.A. (1985) 'The measurement of values in surveys: A comparison of ratings and rankings', *Public Opinion Quarterly* 49: 535–552.

Bell, D. (1976) *The Cultural Contradictions of Capitalism*, London: Heinemann.

Bergström, L. (1990) *Grundbok i värdeteori*, Stockholm: Bokförlaget Thales.

Blos, P. (1962) *On Adolescence*, New York: The Free Press.

—— (1967) 'The second individuation process of adolescence', *The Psycho-analytic Study of the Child* 22: 162–186.

—— (1979) *The Adolescent Passage: Developmental Issues*, International Universities Press.

Bourdieu, P. (1984) *Distinction. A Social Critique of the Judgement of Taste*, Cambridge, Mass.: Harvard University Press.

Burke, P.J. and Franzoi, S.L. (1988) 'Studying situations and identities using the experiental sampling method', *American Sociological Review* 4: 559–568.

Chaffee, S. H., McLeod, J.M. and Wackman, D.B. (1973) 'Family communication patterns and adolescent political participation', in I.J. Dennis (ed.) *Socialization to Politics*, New York: Wiley.

Dalqvist, U. (1991) *Insamlingsrapport 1988 och 1990*, Lund: Sociologiska Institutionen.

De Casper, H.S. and Tittle, C.K. (1988) 'Rankings and ratings of values: counseling uses suggested by factoring two types of scales for female and male eleventh grade students', *Educational and Psychological Measurement* 48: 375–384.

Ewen, S. (1988) *All Consuming Images. The Politics of Style in Contemporary Culture*, New York: Basic Books.

Featherstone, M. (1991) 'The body in consumer culture', in M. Featherstone, M. Hepworth and B.S. Turner (eds) (1991) *The Body. Social Process and Cultural Theory*, London: Sage.

Frankena, W.K. (1963/1973) *Ethics*, London: Prentice Hall Inc.

Gans, H.J. (1974) *Popular Culture and High Culture. An Analysis and Evaluation of Taste*, New York: Basic Books.

Giddens, A. (1989/1991) *Sociology*, Cambridge: Polity Press.

—— (1991) *Modernity and Self-identity. Self and Society in a Late Modern Age*, Oxford: Polity Press.

Goffman, E. (1969) *Where the Action Is: Three Essays*, London: Penguin Books.

—— (1982) *The Presentation of Self in Everyday Life*, Harmondsworth: Penguin Books.

Habermas, J. (1987) *The Theory of Communicative Action. Volume 2. Lifeworld and System: A Critique of Functionalist Reason*, Boston, Mass.: Beacon Press.

Hare, R. M. (1981) *Moral Thinking. Its Levels, Method and Point*, Oxford: Clarendon Press.

Hedinsson, E. (1981) *TV, Family and Society: The Social Origins and Effects of Adolescents' TV Use*, Stockholm: Almqvist & Wiksell International.

Heller, A. (1970/1984) *Everyday Life*, London: Routledge & Kegan Paul.
Hume, D. (1740/1982) *A Treatise of Human Nature. Books Two and Three*, London: Fontana/Collins.
Inglehart, R. (1977) *The Silent Revolution: Changing Values and Political Styles Among Western Publics*, Princeton, NJ: Princeton University Press.
—— (1990) *Culture Shift in Advanced Industrial Society*, Princeton, NJ: Princeton University Press.
Jarlbro, G. (1986) 'Family communication patterns revisited: reliability and validity', *Lund Research Papers in the Sociology of Communication* 4, Lund: Department of Sociology, University of Lund.
Jarlbro, G. (1988) *Familj, Massmedier och Politik*, Stockholm: Almquist & Wiksell International.
Jarlbro, G., Lööv, T. and Miegel, F. (1989) 'Livsstilar och massmedieanvändning. En deskriptiv rapport', *Lund Research Papers in the Sociology of Communication* 14, Lund: Department of Sociology, University of Lund.
Johansson, T. and Miegel, F. (1992) *Do The Right Thing. Lifestyle and Identity in Contemporary Youth Culture*, Stockholm: Almqvist & Wiksell International.
Kamler, H. (1984) 'Life Philosophy and Lifestyle', *Social Indicators Research*, 14 (1): 69–81.
Lööv, T. and Miegel, F. (1989) 'The Notion of Lifestyle: Some Theoretical Contributions', *The Nordicom Review* 1: 21–31.
Lööv, T. and Miegel, F. (1991) 'Sju livsstilar. Om några malmöungdomars drömmar och längtan', *Lund Research Papers in the Sociology of Communication* 29, Lund: Department of Sociology, University of Lund.
Luhmann, N. (1973/1979) *Trust and Power*, Chichester: John Wiley & Sons.
Mackie, J.L. (1980) *Hume's Moral Theory*, London: Routledge & Kegan Paul.
Mahler, M.S. (1963) 'Thoughts about development and individuation'. *The Psychoanalytic Study of the Child* 18: 307–324.
Mahler, M.S., Pine, F. and Bergman, A. (1975) *The Psychological Birth of the Human Infant*, New York: Basic Books.
Mead, G.H. (1934/1962) *Mind, Self and Society: From the Standpoint of a Social Behaviorist*, Chicago: University of Chicago Press.
Miegel, F. (1990) 'Om värden och livsstilar. En teoretisk, metodologisk och empirisk översikt', *Lund Research Papers in the Sociology of Communication* 25, Lund: Department of Sociology, University of Lund.
Miegel, F. and Dalquist, U. (1991) 'Värden, livsstilar och massmedier. En analytisk deskription', *Lund Research Papers in the Sociology of Communication* 31, Lund: Department of Sociology, University of Lund.
Mitchell, A. (1983) *The Nine American Lifestyles. Who We Are and Where We Are Going*, New York: Warner Books.
Moritz, M. (1973) *Inledning i värdeteori*, Lund: Studentlitteratur.
Munson, M. (1984) 'Personal values: considerations on their measurement and application to five areas of research inquiry', in R.E. Pitts and A.G. Woodside (eds) *Personal Values and Consumer Psychology*, Toronto: Lexington Books.
Riesman, D., Glaser, N. and Denny, R. (1950) *The Lonely Crowd*, New Haven, Conn.: Yale University Press.
Ritchie, L.D. (1991) 'Family communication patterns. An epistemic analysis and conceptual reinterpretation', *Communication Research* 18 (4): 548–565.
Rokeach, M. (1973) *The Nature of Human Values*, New York: The Free Press.
Rosengren, K.E. (1991) 'Media use in childhood and adolescence: invariant change? Some results from a Swedish research program', in J.A. Anderson (ed.) *Communication Yearbook* 14: 48–90, Newbury Park, Calif.: Sage.

Rosengren, K.E. and Windahl, S. (1989) *Media Matter. TV Use in Childhood and Adolescence*, Norwood, NJ: Ablex Publishing Corporation.

Schudson, M. (1986) *Advertising, the Uneasy Persuasion: Its Dubious Impact on American Society*, New York: Basic Books.

Simmel, G. (1904/1971) 'Fashion', in D.N. Levine (ed.) *On Individuality and Social Forms*, Chicago: University of Chicago Press.

Thunberg, A.M., Nowak, K., Rosengren, K.E. and Sigurd, B. (1981) *Communication and Equality. A Swedish Perspective*, Stockholm: Almqvist & Wiksell.

Toffler, A. (1970) *The Future Shock*, New York: Random House.

Turner, B.S. (1988) *Status*, Milton Keynes: Open University Press.

Turner, R.H. (1968) 'Role', in D.L. Sills (ed.) *International Encyclopedia of the Social Sciences*, New York: Macmillan and the Free Press.

Turner, R.H. (1978) 'The role and the person', *American Journal of Sociology*, 1: 1–23.

Turner, R.H. (1990) 'Role Change', *Annual Review of Sociology* 16: 87–110.

Veblen, T. (1899/1979) *The Theory of the Leisure Class. An Economic Study of Institutions*, Harmondsworth: Penguin Books.

Weber, M. (1922/1968) 'Class, status, party', in H.H. Gerth and C.W. Mills (eds) *From Max Weber. Essays in Sociology*, London: Routledge & Kegan Paul.

Zablocki, B.D. and Kanter, R. (1976) 'The differentiation of life-styles', *Annual Review of Sociology* 2: 269–298.

Chapter 11

Seven lifestyles[1]

Fredrik Miegel

INTRODUCTION

The lifestyles developed among the young of a given society contain significant information about the youth culture of that society. When studying young people's lifestyles, therefore, we study aspects of young people's culture. That is, we study youth culture. The concepts of lifestyle and culture are thus conceptually interwoven and can hardly be kept separate. Lifestyles are expressions of culture.

It is argued in Chapter 10 in this volume that lifestyle may be studied at different levels, and the same holds true for culture. The three different but interrelated levels at which lifestyle are determined – structural, positional, and individual (see Johansson and Miegel 1992; Lööv and Miegel 1989a) – are relevant also to the concept of culture. Besides the three *levels of determination*, there is, however, another important distinction to be made when it comes to the study of lifestyle and culture. This is the methodological distinction between two *levels of analysis*: the two levels we call the macro and the micro level. As pointed out by, for instance, Alexander and Giesen (1987), this is a purely analytical distinction:

> We will argue that the macro–micro dichotomy should be viewed as an analytic distinction and that all attempts to link it to concrete dichotomies – such as 'individual versus society' or 'action versus order' – are fundamentally misplaced. Only if it is viewed analytically, moreover, can the linkage between micro and macro be achieved. (Alexander and Giesen 1987: 1)

Alexander (1987) thus holds that there can be no empirical referents for micro or macro as such. Instead they are analytical contrasts within empirical units.

> There can be no empirical referents for micro or macro as such. They are analytical contrasts, suggesting emergent levels within empirical units, not antagonistic empirical units themselves. (Alexander 1987: 290)

Although there is some confusion about what micro and macro actually are, most theoreticans seem to agree that a micro perspective is usually applied when studying interaction among individuals or small groups, whereas the macro perspective is used when studying those social structures within which the individuals operate. A good overview and discussion of the different meanings which the micro–macro distinction can have for different authors is supplied by Münch and Smelser (1987; cf. Giddens 1984/1989). The authors themselves prefer the following definition:

> We see the micro level as involving encounters and patterned interaction among individuals (which would include communication, exchange, co-operation, and conflict) and the macro level as referring to those structures in society (groups, organizations, institutions, and culture productions) that are sustained (however imperfectly) by mechanisms of social control and that constitute both opportunities and constraints on individual behavior and interactions. (Münch and Smelser 1987: 357)

The definition suggested by Münch and Smelser clearly resembles that advocated by, for instance, Anthony Giddens, who describes the difference between the two levels like this:

> The study of everyday behaviour in situations or face-to-face interaction is usually called **microsociology**. **Macrosociology** is the analysis of large scale social systems, such as a business firm, the political system or the economic order. . . .
>
> Macro analysis is essential if we are to understand the institutional background of day-to-day life. The ways in which people live their everyday lives are greatly affected by the broader institutional framework within which they exist . . . .
>
> Micro studies are in their turn necessary for illuminating broad institutional patterns. Face-to-face interaction is clearly the main basis of all forms of social organization, no matter how large in scale. (Giddens 1989/1991: 113f)

On the one hand, culture, as well as lifestyle, can be studied as a macro phenomenon, that is, as an important component of the societal structure. On the other, it can be studied as a micro phenomenon, that is, as an important aspect of people's everyday life. Culture is thus present both in the abstract structures of the system world, and in the more concrete structures of the lifeworld. On the macro level of analysis we are concerned with social and cultural structures, and with those positionally distinguished formations within the structures which set the framework for individual action and interaction. At this level of analysis we use observational data such as historical documents and aggregated individual data. The unit of study at the micro level is the single and unique individual possessing distinctive features and having established more or less unique relationships to the various social and cultural conditions to be found on the structural and positional levels of determination.

In this chapter I am basically interested in young people's everyday culture. It consists, on the one hand, of routines and practices aimed at securing the basic necessities of life and living, and, on the other, of dreams, thoughts, desires, longings and strivings. Everyday culture is homogeneous: it is constructed in relation to certain fundamental or basic values, norms, ideals, rules and beliefs common to most people within a given culture. It is, however, at the same time, heterogeneous: a vast number of different and partly contradictory cultural expressions coexist within the framework of a common overarching culture (Lööv and Miegel 1991).

The point of departure in this chapter is the assumption that the individual's choice of lifestyle and everyday life is not only determined by which society or culture that individual belongs to, or by which different positions the individual occupies within it. On the contrary. Within certain given cultural, social and material frames, people develop individual lifestyles. In this context, we thus use the notion of lifestyle to designate the individual's active choice of cultural expressions. People's dreams, desires, hopes, fears, ideals and goals in life are not completely governed by their social or cultural affiliations (although these, of course, are of utmost importance). Lifestyles are developed and maintained in the intersection between a) social and cultural structures, and b) the individual's own initiatives and actions.

In the remaining part of this chapter I shall briefly discuss different possible methods to employ when studying young people's lifestyles empirically. I shall argue for the importance of studying lifestyle from both a macro and a micro perspective, by means of different methods. Depending on which perspective we choose, we obtain very different information. But rather than looking upon the two perspectives as conflicting alternatives, I shall see them as complementary. I shall also discuss and account for some results obtained within the Media Panel Program, where a combination of quantitative and qualitative methods was used (Johansson and Miegel 1992).

GENERAL PATTERNS AND INDIVIDUAL VARIATIONS

Lifestyle is a rather complex and difficult concept with which to deal. There is, however, no need to discuss the concept of lifestyle and its relations to a number of related concepts such as value, identity, taste and style, in any detail here. (For discussions of these matters, see Chapters 1, 10 and 12 in this volume; see also Johansson and Miegel 1992). We note, however, that the empirical study of young people's lifestyles can be conducted from a large number of different perspectives; also, a variety of methods can be employed in order to capture different aspects of the phenomenon. We must, therefore, decide what kind of study we want to conduct, and what kind of information we want to obtain in order to choose adequate research methods and ways of collecting data.

Broadly speaking, there are at least two types of perspective to choose between. On the one hand, we may aim to identify what we shall here call *general patterns of lifestyle*, and, on the other, we may aim to capture what we shall refer to as *individual variations of lifestyle*. There is a third possibility, however. We may aim to capture both general patterns and individual variations. That was the strategy used in the particular study accounted for in this chapter.

DIFFERENT STRATEGIES, DIFFERENT INFORMATION

In the particular study on which this chapter builds, two different methods of investigating young people's lifestyles were employed. A quantitative analysis was carried out, and also a qualitative analysis in the form of seven case studies was conducted. This combination of quantitative and qualitative data is a strategy well suited for studying various aspects of lifestyle. The advantages of using multiple methods – often referred to as triangulation – have been observed and discussed by numerous researchers (see Denzin 1970/ 1978; Jensen and Jankowski 1991; Taylor and Bogdan 1984).

> Triangulation is often thought of as a way of guarding against researcher bias and checking out accounts from different informants. By drawing on other types and sources of data, observers also gain a deeper and clearer understanding of the setting and people being studied. (Taylor and Bogdan 1984: 68)

In Johansson and Miegel (1992) we quantitatively identified a number of rather abstract and general patterns of taste in film and popular music and leisure time activities among the 21 year olds included in our sample. The patterns which we distinguished in this way are to a considerable extent the products of the measuring instruments used. The latter represent operationalizations or indicators of lifestyles; the taste and activity patterns used in our study can all be seen as possible and very likely components of young people's lifestyles. On the basis of the operationalizations selected for the examination of taste and leisure time activities, we thus arrived at a number of music taste patterns, film taste patterns and leisure time activity patterns, which provide at least a rough picture of how tastes and activities are related and distributed in this particular age-group in Swedish society (see Chapter 10).

The reasons for distinguishing such patterns are manifold. Most important is that they may serve as lifestyle indicators. We can apply the taste and activity patterns in analyses of the way the different patterns are structured along dimensions such as gender, class, education, age, etc. We can also get a rough estimation of how large a part of the population belongs to each of these patterns. Finally we can analyse the relations between these patterns and a number of other variables of interest, for example, values and attitudes in various areas.

Although we could have called these patterns lifestyles, we refrained from so doing, since when statistically identifying patterns of taste or activities in one area or another, we consider only a limited segment of lifestyle patterns in society. It is more accurate, therefore, to call these patterns taste and activity patterns rather than lifestyles. In order to reach a more thorough understanding of the individual's lifestyle, one must consider a wide range of attitudes and actions based on all the different types of value embraced by the individual. When sorting young people into different categories on the basis of, for instance, their musical taste only, lifestyle becomes, of course, defined in terms of taste in music, which means that neither attitudes based on other aesthetic values, nor attitudes based on other types of value – material, political, ethical, metaphysical, etc. – are included in the definition.

Making use of the notion of *ideal types*, one can quantitatively discern a number of more or less clearly articulated lifestyle patterns within a society by operationalizing and measuring phenomena considered to be relevant as lifestyle indicators of that society. Further theoretical refinement of the various patterns thus distinguished can allow them to be conceived in a gradually purer form, so that they finally represent what we may call *ideal types of lifestyle*.

Whereas such general patterns of tastes and activities may be very useful for understanding major trends in the lifestyles of youth culture, they do not tell us very much about how particular individuals build their own individual lifestyle. To arrive at such an understanding, intensive studies of a number of single individuals are required.

Individuals within a society take on elements from several of these lifestyle patterns, and depending on which pattern is predominant for a given individual, one can locate him or her within one or more ideal types of lifestyle. Most individuals have characteristics which make them candidates for more than one – sometimes even seemingly contradictory – lifestyles. The ideal types of lifestyle are aggregates consisting of individually determined characteristics, and are thus analysed from a macro perspective. In fact, however, every individual has her or his own personal and unique lifestyle, that is, something which we may call an *individual lifestyle*. In order to cope with this dilemma we must move to the micro level. Individual lives are, of course, partly determined by structural and positional characteristics. However, within existing societal structures individuals also adopt their own, specific, individual lifestyles. These should be studied at the micro level of analysis.

One of the main theses in *Do the Right Thing* (Johansson and Miegel 1992) was that, although in order to arrive at a basic picture of young Swedes' lifestyles it is both possible and meaningful to identify and distinguish empirically a number of general patterns of lifestyle in the areas of leisure time activities and tastes in popular music and film, and whereas we could assign each of the some 300 individuals included in our sample to one or more of the taste and activity patterns we distinguished, this is nevertheless not enough if we are to understand the role and importance of the lifestyle phenomenon for the individuals themselves. To accomplish this, we must also carry out intensive studies of single individuals and their specific lifestyles.

Therefore, during a three-year period, we conducted a number of intensive case studies in an attempt to comprehend the core of the individual lifestyle, which are the individual's own and unique way of structuring a multitude of cultural artefacts and phenomena. The general patterns which we constructed by means of different statistical methods are important, for they visualize *the unity within the diversity* of Swedish youth culture. The case studies, in their turn, illustrate *the diversity within the unity* portrayed by our theoretical and empirical lifestyle constructions. One of the main reasons for carrying out such very time-consuming case studies is that they provide us with information about both the regularities and the peculiarities in young people's lifestyles. They give information about how individuals use culture to express their adherence to different social and cultural groupings, and they indicate how they use culture to express their own individuality and uniqueness. The case studies may thus shed some light on conflicts resulting from the individual's cleavage between a private and a public self, between individuality and sociability, etc.

> As a research endeavor, the case study contributes uniquely to our knowledge of individual, organizational, social and political phenomena. . . . the distinctive need for case studies arises out of the desire to understand complex phenomena. In brief, the case study allows an investigation to retain the holistic and meaningful characteristics of real-life events – such as individual life cycles, organizational and managerial processes, neighborhood change, international relations, and the maturation of industries. (Yin 1984: 14)

The case study method has several advantages, especially when combined with other quantitative and qualitative methods. Randy Stoecker (1991) discusses the application and the advantages of the case study, arguing that case studies may be used as a means of showing specific processes involved both in general trends and in exceptions to such trends. In this manner the case study method can be used to make measurement instruments and predictions more specific (see Yin 1984).

The importance of having an elaborated theoretical framework when using case studies has often been stressed by social sciences (see Jensen and Jankowski 1991; Mitchell 1983; Stoecker 1991; Yin 1984).

> In case studies statistical inference is not involved at all. Instead the inferential process turns exclusively on the theoretically necessary linkages among the features of the case study. The validity of the extrapolation depends not on the typicality or representativeness of the case study but upon the cogency of the theoretical reasoning. (Mitchell 1983: 207)

Although Stoecker (1991) argues that theory plays an important role in case studies, he also emphasizes the difficulties involved.

Theorizing 'idiosyncrasy' then, refers to bringing all possible theoretical perspectives to bear, and discarding and weighing each until we have built a valid and useful explanation. The difficulty involves determining the extent to which we rely on theory to guide us in choosing what to look for and how to explain what we find. Just how much to rely on theory, and thus risk missing important idiosyncrasies of particular cases, or restrain theory and thus risk overemphasizing the idiosyncratic, is a tricky question. (Stoecker 1991: 102)

In *Do the Right Thing* (Johansson and Miegel 1992) we tried to solve this problem in different ways. First, we used a fairly open theory which took account of the main contributions thus far to an emerging, overall theory of lifestyle. Second, we introduced the distinction between ideal types of lifestyle and individual lifestyles briefly discussed above. Third, in discussing the case studies we also drew on the results of the more general quantitative study. In all, this enabled us to capture both general tendencies in young people's lifestyles and idiosyncracies inherent in the individual lifestyles.

Validity is a problem when using the case study method. According to Stoecker (1991) the best validity check comes from the participants themselves. Even if participants do not agree with the theoretical explanations provided by the researchers, they must agree that the behaviours, tastes and attitudes we attribute to them are indeed *their* behaviours, tastes and attitudes. Such a validity test was also made during the case studies included in our study. Our respondents read and commented on our descriptions of them during the three years we followed them. Our descriptions coincided almost perfectly with the respondents' own views. The validity of our descriptions may, therefore, be considered as high.

TWO LIFESTYLES ...

The seven individuals chosen for case studies belonged to the statistically most typical representatives of two statistically identified ideal types of lifestyle. They were thus strategically chosen. As previously mentioned, the questionnaires used within the later Media Panel Program data collection waves contain a large number of lifestyle-related questions (about, for instance, tastes in music, film, clothes, actors and leisure time activities, etc.). On the basis of such items we constructed a scale for measuring gender specific cultural patterns or lifestyles. The outcome was one male and one female pattern, or two ideal types of lifestyle.

The male lifestyle was characterized, among other things, by preferences for heavy metal and heavy rock music, thriller and horror books, science fiction and action films, and the like.

The female lifestyle included preferences for romantic media content, in books, films and music, an interest for fashion and domestically oriented leisure time activities, and so on.

The two ideal types of lifestyle were rather distinct and clear-cut. Therefore, they serve well to describe some of the gender-related lifestyle variations among young Swedish adults. The two patterns thus provide us with some substantial information about how tastes and leisure time interests differ along the gender dimension. As a matter of fact, the two patterns give a good general picture of the differences in these areas between young men's and women's cultural spheres in contemporary Sweden. Despite its significance and usefulness in the study of the relation between gender roles and lifestyles, the picture obtained is nevertheless rather abstract, as we shall see. (This abstractness, of course, is its very point. There are also other points to be made, however.)

... OR SEVEN?

Altogether we met the seven young people included in the case study on three different occasions. The method used is probably best described as in-depth qualitative interviewing, a method described by Taylor and Bogdan in the following way:

> By in-depth qualitative interviewing we mean repeated face-to-face encounters between the researcher and informants directed toward understanding informants' perspectives on their lives, experiences, or situations as expressed in their own words. (Taylor and Bogdan 1984: 77)

The length of the interviews varied from two to three hours; they were recorded on tape and later transcribed in order to facilitate our analysis of the material. We managed to establish a very good relationship generally with these young people. The interviews were thus characterized by a great deal of openness and trust. The interviews were based upon questions concerning the individuals' values, tastes and leisure time interests. The informants were asked to try to recapitulate their lives, that is, telling us about persons and events in the past which had influenced their lives in one way or another, so as to supply us with what is best described as their life histories.

> In the life history, the researcher attempts to capture the salient experiences in a person's life and that person's definitions of those experiences. The life history presents people's views on their lives in their own words, much the same as in a common autobiography. (Taylor and Bogdan 1984: 78)

Each case study also contained a so-called *life plan*. The informants were asked to describe their future in two ways: as they thought it would be, and how they wanted it to be. In the following, I shall briefly account for the seven cases separately. The presentation contains a number of quotations from the interviews, and in order to make these quotations accessible for the reader I have combined quotations from different parts of the interviews. Where this is done, it is marked in the text. In order to protect their integrity and to ensure their anonymity, we have changed the names of our interviewees, as well as other pieces of information which might otherwise reveal their identity. I cannot, unfortunately, give but a rather summary account of the case studies here. For a full description of the seven cases and our analyses of them, see Johansson and Miegel (1992) (see also Lööv and Miegel (1989b; 1991)). In this chapter only brief descriptions of the individual's lifestyles may be offered; most of their reported life histories and life plans have had to be left out. What remains, nevertheless, illustrates well how different the seven individual lifestyles were, and how different the meanings the seven young people ascribed to their behaviour, tastes, interests and so on in spite of the fact that all of them belonged to one of two main ideal types of lifestyle.

Case one: Magical mystery Tor

Tor grew up in a lower middle-class family; he had completed two different schools oriented towards graphic design. Tor devoted most of his time to two main interests: he constructed and took part in so-called role games within the fantasy genre; he also sketched and painted. His plans for the future were concrete and well-defined, and his occupational plans and extra-curricular activities almost totally overlapped. He wanted to become a draughtsman or an illustrator, preferably within the genres of fantasy or science fiction.

> Hopefully I'll become a commercial artist, or a cover designer for books, book jackets or games and such things. I like to draw fantasy characters like dragons and monsters. . . . I'd like to develop this form of art in making book jackets or book covers, but I'll probably not get the chance to do this for a long time. However, this is what I'm aiming at.

Tor was indeed very purposeful in his ambitions. He was deeply committed to his interests in drawing and in fantasy culture, and these interests formed the dominant elements in his cultural identity. During his leisure time, Tor designed and constructed fantasy games; he also painted mythical motifs, themes from fairy tales and fantasy stories. He was also a member of a fantasy club where he could attend lectures and play role games and the like. His devotion to the fantasy culture was expressed also in his cultural tastes.

> Most of the films I care for are fantasy and science fiction, or other types of adventure films, like, for instance, *Indiana Jones*. George Lucas and Steven Spielberg are my favourite directors. I also like Harrison Ford. I seldom watch any really 'deep' or 'serious' films. In my opinion, people should go to the movies to be entertained and excited, not to become depressed. . . . On the rock scene, my favourites right now are 'The Mission', 'Magnum' and 'Gandalf'. I bought 'Gandalf' because of their

name. It's one of Tolkien's characters, but I discovered that the music was really good, too. . . . From what I say about books I guess you understand that it's mainly fantasy books I'm reading. I also read quite a bit of horror fiction, and some occult stuff.

During the three years we followed Tor, he continually developed his interests in painting and fantasy culture, and they became increasingly integrated into his personality and lifestyle. He was an imaginative and artistically talented person, skilfully balancing between the realms of fantasy and reality. Although he dreamed about becoming a recognized artist, he knew this was basically a dream. His actual plans for the future were much more realistic. Among the seven young people we followed, he was probably the one with the most stable identity. He was sure about, and satisfied with, who he was and what he wanted to do and become.

I'm determined to become an illustrator. You have to have a goal, and I know that I'll become an illustrator, one way or another. At first I might have to work at an office doing something simple, but as you learn the trade you can do more and more, and finally you'll have enough knowledge and skill to do what you want. Maybe I'll have to get more education. There's an interesting school in Copenhagen, and there's a private school in Stockholm that I've been thinking about. . . . I wouldn't mind being an artist, but to be one you have to be damned lucky. You need to become recognized and known. What you do is basically the same as when you're an illustrator. The difference is that as an artist you have no regular customers, no secure income. Art is something you create in your leisure time.

Like many young people's lifestyles, Tor's lifestyle was closely related to popular culture. Popular culture serves a double function for young people. They use it to explore, develop and express what they consider to be their unique personal identity, and they use it to show their adherence to various groups and persons.

This double function was obvious in Tor's case. For him it was the engagement in a variety of activities associated with the fantasy genre. He spent his leisure time playing role games with his friends, and he was a member of an international fantasy organization. A fundamental feature of Tor's involvement with popular culture was that he created it rather than merely consumed it. He constructed role games, wrote adventure stories, painted fantasy motifs, etc.

It would seem that the overriding element in Tor's identity and in his personality was his need and desire to make use of his imagination and artistic talent. His interest in the popular cultural sphere of fantasy can thus be regarded as a result of his more fundamental personal characteristics. That fantasy was his main popular cultural interest may be explained by the fact that the fantasy genre better than any other form of popular culture provided him with opportunities to utilize his imagination and artistic creativity. It helped him to develop his cultural competence, and through his engagement in role games, fantasy clubs, and the like, he strengthened and developed his social competences.

Case two: The dancing queen

Anna-Karin grew up in a working-class family, and she was working as a nursery school teacher. She had no plans to change her occupation in the future, and was fully satisfied with working with children.

Her tastes in music and film were rather mainstream. She was not very interested in either music or film, but listened to what was played on the radio and occasionally went to see some of the popular American films going the rounds. The same held true for her literary taste. She did not read very much, but when she did, she read bestsellers by, say, Judith Krantz or Jackie Collins.

Anna-Karin's most dominant interest was dance. For a long period of time she had been a member of a team of folk-dancers, and she was active as a leader and instructor. She was also a member of the team's committee. Her interest in folk-dancing was expressed not only through dancing, but she also read a lot of books on the subject.

> I dance folk-dance and I'm an instructor for the youth team. This takes quite a bit of time. We practise once a week, but we also have lots of courses and performances. Last weekend, for example, we were off performing down in Germany. We also have performances quite often in Malmö and in the vicinity. . . . I'm really fond of Schottische, Hambo, and other types of big festival dances, since they have so many rotations and you're doing different things all the time. Everything has to match if it's going to work out all right. *Weave Rough Homespun* is a really nice dance symbolizing weaving. There are eight couples standing in a line, and there are lots of fusions which are supposed to be the weaving. You bend down again and again, and you're active all the time. Then we have the *Frykdals-dance*. It's quite a difficult dance, and it takes a long time to learn, but when you know it, it's really great to dance. *English For Three Couples* is another dance that's difficult – that is, before you know how to do it, since everyone is doing things at the same time. . . . I've become ever more interested in folk-dance and everything surrounding it. I read a lot of different books and I have lots of notebooks I use to research, which keeps me busy all the time. The costumes are really interesting. They have so many symbols, and ornaments symbolizing different things. These symbols are so abundant. Many are about marriage and such things. . . . We've had courses that deal with costumes, with dance, and with handicraft. All these things are part of our history. I have

a costume with a white blouse and a big loose top, with a waist and waistcoat. It has lots of silver jewellery, and buckles on it, and a chain. All this had meaning, showing how rich you were. The costumes we use nowadays were once used only by the rich.

Apart from folk-dancing, Anna-Karin was very interested in fashion and sewing, and when she did not work or dance, she sewed. On the whole Anna-Karin, much like Tor, had a genuine need to create and to express herself aesthetically, not with the aim of gaining recognition from others, but rather to develop her own competence and skills in different areas.

> I find it rather enjoyable to look for sewing patterns and to see if they turn out the way I thought. I feel I create something. I haven't got enough imagination to design clothes myself, except for simple things. Sometimes my friends ask me if I can make them a dress or whatever, then I make it and hope it will fit. . . . The more you sew, the more experienced you become, so you can make more complicated things. It's stimulating with such small challenges. . . . Being creative is important. Besides my sewing, dancing also contains creative elements. I try to use rhythm and motion in my work. Many children who have difficulties with reading and writing also have problems with their movement.

Anna-Karin showed a social consciousness in the sense of being highly concerned about the welfare of physically and mentally disabled children, of children with problematic home situations, and the like. She tried in many ways to help such children develop their capacities in her nursery school work. She also did a lot of reading about physically and mentally disabled children and about different methods used to help them. This concern for others suggests that ethical values constituted an important part of her value system. However, her interest in expressing herself aesthetically also characterized her. This suggests strong aesthetic values as well. Anna-Karin's lifestyle was strongly influenced by both her aesthetic and her ethical values, attitudes and actions. She was not much concerned about what other people might think of her lifestyle. What was important to her was to be satisfied with, and to make use of, her creativity, by developing and enhancing her skills and competence within the areas of folk-dancing, sewing and child care. This was important for her, not because it increased her social or cultural status; basically, it increased her own satisfaction and helped her to develop her cultural identity and lifestyle.

Case three: The mother

Sonja grew up in a lower middle-class family. She worked on and off as a nurse's aid. Her thoughts regarding her future were rather diffuse, but she wanted a job with much freedom and travelling. During our first two interviews with Sonja she expressed dreams about being a photographer or a film director, though she knew that these dreams were hard to realize. She also expressed a strong desire to travel. Travelling was, no doubt, her major leisure time interest. She wanted to see the world. Therefore, she had spent a year in Israel working in a kibbutz, and half a year in Iceland working as a fisherwoman.

> Since we last met I've been to Mallorca for two weeks and I was also working in Iceland last autumn as a fisherwoman. I'd really like to travel more, preferably to Asia or South America. I certainly don't have any plans at the moment to go there, but it would be nice to spend a year or so there. I could also imagine living abroad for a couple of years, or having a job where you travel a lot. . . . I thought about becoming a photographer, so I applied for a kind of media education, but there was only room for sixteen persons so they didn't let me start. I'll probably have to attend a lot of evening classes instead, but right now it's hard to find the time. . . . In one way or another, I think it would be great to work with pictures. You can always dream, of course, about having the opportunity to make a film and to stand behind the camera.

Sonja's cultural tastes were clearly influenced by her interest in travelling. Her favourite author was Leon Uris, and she listened much to so-called world music, especially music influenced by Spanish rhythms. Considering her dreams about becoming a film director or a photographer, it was only natural that she was very interested in film. She watched almost everything, from Fassbinder films to the *Texas Chainsaw Massacre*.

When we met Sonja the third time, she had given up almost all her dreams of becoming a film director or a photographer. Also her interest in travelling had decreased. The reason was that she was expecting a child. She had not totally abandoned her dreams, but she had come to realize that she probably was never to achieve them. Instead she thought much of her future role as a mother. She wanted a safe, comfortable and secure life for herself and her child. She was also preparing for marriage and family life. She was looking forward to having a child, a house, and a husband. Security was very important to Sonja.

> Probably I'll be moving into a terraced house. But I'm still working at the hospital. And in January I'm going to become a mother. I like that. I keep growing and growing. . . . I still have the same dreams, but they've become weaker. First I have to think about my child. In a few years I'll start working again. It'll probably be the same kind of job as I had before. It's nothing I'm looking forward to, I don't think it's so great. I know I'll probably never achieve the dreams I have. To do that you've got to be lucky, and usually I don't have that much luck. Well I'm not pessimistic. I'm pretty realistic. It depends on your ambitions. You can always aim at

the stars, but I'll probably only reach the grass-roots. But I don't care. The important thing is to have a stable income.

During our first two interviews, Sonja wanted to experience different cultures and express herself aesthetically in the areas of film and photography. This had changed dramatically by the third interview. Whereas previously she was continually searching for new influences and experiences, she had now found her place in reality. Sonja's change of lifestyle was clearly related to the fact that she had become pregnant (which, of course, is one of the most crucial changes in a woman's life). Her desire to find and create meaning in life through travelling, experiencing different cultures and meeting people from other cultures, as well as her desire to create and express herself aesthetically, diminished when she found another way to create meaning in her life. This new meaning was anchored in giving birth to and raising a child, and in living a good family life. Sonja's lifestyle had become almost entirely related to living a family life.

Case four: Wounded knee

Agneta grew up in a lower middle-class family. She graduated from high school with special training as an assistant nurse and was working at an orthopaedic clinic. Her plans for the future were very uncertain, most of them having the character of fleeting dreams and immediate impulses. A common theme in them was, however, the hope of being able to travel. She was not very satisfied with the job she had, but did not know what to do instead.

> I don't feel so good at my job. I'm looking for another one, any kind of job where they don't require anything more than a high school education. I've applied for a job at a travel agency. I'm so tired of the the medical area, nothing but work, not rewarding at all. I've thought about applying for nurses' training but I'm not at all sure I want to continue working in medical care. It's hard not knowing what you want to do. I'll soon be 22. Everybody seems to have their dreams, but I don't have any real dreams at all. . . . I'd like to become an air hostess. It must really be great to travel so much. I would probably rather become an air hostess than a tourist guide. Yes, it would probably suit me well to be an air hostess. I really ought to apply for the air hostess course, but I'm too lazy. . . . It bothers me that I never get going on things, and that I have a job I don't feel satisfied with.

As long as she could remember, Agneta's major leisure time interest had been playing and watching soccer, live and on TV. But because of a wounded knee she was forced to give up her soccer career. This was quite a blow for her, because before that her life had been totally dominated by soccer.

> Actually I don't have any leisure time interests left since I quit playing soccer. I was active for eight years. My knee-cap was broken. It was a girl

who kicked me on the knee. It was really hard to be forced to stop playing soccer. I grew up in a soccer family. My brother, father, sister – they all play soccer. Soccer meant so much to me. You had so many friends, the team spirit and all the fun to go with it. It feels really bad to have to be without it.

During our first two interviews with Agneta she was rather pessimistic about life and her future. It was really hard for her to cope with the fact that she was never going to be able to play soccer again. It made her depressed and coloured her attitudes towards other aspects of life as well.

When we met Agneta the last time she had become a little bit more optimistic, but nevertheless returned, during the interview, over and over again to the burden of not being able to play soccer. She still did not know what she wanted to do in the future, and had developed a *laissez-faire* kind of lifestyle and a rather hedonistic attitude towards living. 'Why care about tomorrow, it is now that you live' seemed to have become her motto.

I think it's important to enjoy yourself while you're young. Not that I'm afraid of getting old, but I'm afraid of how fast time flies. Why not have fun while you're young?

Agneta's desire to make the most of life while she was young, and not to worry too much about the future, could be interpreted as an indication that she was the one among the seven informants who went through the most dynamic lifestyle and identity changes. She did not know what she wanted or what would become of her. She thought of herself as not mature enough to plan for the future. She first had to find out who she was and what she really wanted to do. She had no fixed lifestyle, but one that was constantly changing. This state of affairs can be explained at least partly by the difficulties she experienced when she had to give up soccer, her major interest. During the earlier part of her youth, almost everything circled around soccer. Soccer thus constituted the fundamental component of her identity and lifestyle. In a sense, when she suddenly lost soccer, she lost her lifestyle and part of her identity as well, finding herself forced to develop a new one. For many years, however, she was incapable of replacing soccer. This created problems for her in finding meaning in other areas of life. One might say that Agneta went through a minor identity crisis, which she finally managed to solve, at least partly. She still missed soccer, but she had come to realize that even though she would never be able completely to replace it, there were other ways in which she might develop herself and her lifestyle.

Case five: The twentieth-century girl

Annika grew up in an upper middle-class family. After completing three years of the social studies curriculum at high school she began studying at the university. Characteristic of Annika was that she had rather clear-cut thoughts about her future profession. She was a girl of high ambitions, and she wanted a job that could promote her personal growth. She had taken some courses at the university in the area of marketing, which was the area in which she wanted to work in the future.

> I know what I want to do. I want to work with marketing. I've been interested in it for a long time. I just can't change my mind about it. I've started to learn how things work within the marketing area. It's got the creative aspect that appeals to me. Thinking about getting a job is a problem. You know, I don't just want any job, it's got to suit me. It has to allow me to develop as a person.

Annika's leisure time interests and tastes were clearly associated with her studies and plans for her future occupation. She was aesthetically minded. Interior decorating, art, literature and music composed important aspects of her lifestyle. Annika's taste was rather distinct and can be characterized as conventional 'high culture'.

> Both my boyfriend and I have become interested in art. In this way we've come to visit different art exhibitions. Art has made me realize that something can be really strange but still very good. However, if you want to reach most people with it, it also has to be realistic. . . . At home I like to listen to Vivaldi, and it can be nice listening to good opera music and modern jazz. . . . I'm quite fond of somewhat odd films, but now and then I also like to see an American film. The former kind of films have a more lasting value. Still, Tom Cruise is the all-American guy and I can't deny the fact that I like him. . . . I read quite a lot. I don't like detective stories. I read Jan Guillou [a Swedish popular author of agent novels], but I didn't like him at all. What I'm most fond of is stories about everyday life. I like authors who can describe life as it is.

Most of Annika's mass media use was oriented towards gathering information and knowledge, but now and then she escaped into a romantic love story. She was very ambivalent towards reading romantic novels. Although she liked to read them, she expressed her distaste for them. She had the same attitude towards the films she saw, and she felt that some activities – like reading weekly gossip magazines, engaging in fashion, idolizing handsome film stars and reading romance stories – were natural parts of a young girl's development.

> I also read those sickly-sweet novels, of course. They don't give you anything in return, but it can be an amusing pastime. It's dreaming and forgetting reality. It's a kind of escape, you know, not because I dislike reality the way it is, but still it's a nice feeling to read a romantic novel. . . . This Friday *Cocktail* was released, with Tom Cruise, an actor who's

that kind of handsome guy who all girls like. . . . I buy a lot of clothes I guess, even if it's become less now. I'm not as fixed on it as I was earlier. But anyhow it's probably a pretty common thing for most girls my age.

During the three years we followed Annika, she gradually became more certain of herself. She matured and developed a more stable identity and lifestyle. At the first interview her taste was rather mainstream, common to girls of her age. By the time of our second meeting she had become aware of the distinction between high culture and popular culture. She referred primarily to high culture in describing her tastes, but also admitted that she still consumed what she described as cheap and vulgar cultural goods. The third time we met her, she did not make such clear distinctions. She had become more self-confident and more certain of her tastes. It was not as important to her what others thought of her tastes. She had become self-confident enough to have her own opinion of what she liked, and to accept those things in her taste of which she had felt a bit ashamed earlier. She described herself thus:

> Young, curious, has partly decided what she wants to do in life, but still pretty mouldable. Rather influenced by advertising, likes quality, has some cultural interests. A twentieth-century girl. I suppose I aim at this thing of becoming something. Not merely for the money, but to get the money to buy that particular table. To be able to live somewhat outside everyday life, that's important.

Case six: The medicine man

Lasse grew up in a middle-class family. After graduating from high school he started to work within the building trade. He also took law courses at the university. He regarded himself as a theoretician and, consequently, he felt that the right path for him was to carry on with his academic studies. He aimed to become a doctor, and was rather determined to actually become one.

> I've always wanted to become a doctor and that's what I'm going to be. It's the only thing that feels right. I've read quite a bit about medicine, so it would be nice to get started in medical school. There are new ways of applying now which may increase my chances of getting in. . . . I've pretty definite plans, but it's still possible to change. You've got to always have some sort of escape route. I could imagine myself as a builder, but if everything works out as I want to, I'll become a doctor.

During the first interview with Lasse, his main leisure time interests were karate and music. He played in several rock bands, and devoted many hours a week to karate training to keep himself fit. He then had some dreams about becoming a professional musician, a rock star, but by the second interview he had given up those dreams. He had also ceased karate training. Instead he had developed a new interest in scuba-diving and amateur archaeology. The music, however, was still important to him.

My dreams of becoming a professional musician were shattered. I had some ideas about applying to a music school, but it didn't turn out that way because of my parents, and maybe that was good. But I think I would have been happy as a poor musician. Somewhere deep inside me I still have that dream, but it's far away now. I suppose it was those boyish dreams; they've changed a bit. You become aware of what it's really all about. For example, playing the piano professionally takes a lot of time, so you have to accept it as a hobby. I suppose there's a certain bitterness over the fact that it never came into being. . . . I played in a pretty well-known group before, and if I had quit school I could still have been playing with them. But I've no regrets. I've gone through all that and realized that it doesn't feel so bad if you are forced to accept something. What I'm doing today is my own free choice and it feels all right. But it took some careful consideration. If you've spent two and a half years in high school you don't quit like that. There are kind of norms from those around you, friends and parents. I could be furious about such norms when I was younger. I was a member of a country band once, and we really were top level. It was a full-time job and they have a record contract now. I've become calmer about it now, I'm not that angry anymore. . . . I've almost entirely abandoned karate. Music. . . well, I listen a lot but I play less. I've got rid of all my electric equipment and bought myself an acoustic piano, which was a good move. Now I play when I want to, not because I have to. The electronics were so pretentious. But karate I'll probably never pick up again. I'm doing a lot of scuba-diving in the Sound. I help some environmental researchers take samples. It's fun but it's also scary. You know, in ten or twelve years there won't be any oxygen left, no vegetation, no animal life. It will be completely dead. Also, I help some marine archaeologists diving for wrecked viking ships. It's really interesting when you find a piece of wood or something and the archaeologists make sense of it and tell you what it is. It's really fantastic. I read a lot about it. It's a great feeling being down in the deep, looking for Swedish history.

Lasse's tastes were, just as Annika's, rather high culture but also included, as he expressed it himself, 'a lot of shit'. In Lasse's tastes popular culture and high culture coexisted naturally. He did not make as hard distinctions as Annika. He was not ashamed of listening to heavy metal or punk music and watching cheap action films and thrillers, but he clearly knew the difference in status between the different cultural products he consumed.

Maybe it's easier to get heavily carried away by modern music, but listening to classical music, like Mozart, for example, makes you quite poetical. When it comes to modern music, I listen to a lot of trash and

American West Coast rock, and to 'Docenterna', 'Ebba Grön' and that kind of stuff. You become a little bit nostalgic. When it comes to modern music I'm not changing my tastes. I'll probably be an old man when the rock bands I listen to stop playing. 'Tubes', 'Scritti Politti', 'Van Halen' have been there all along, and they've been releasing records all the time. . . . I like both commercial films and other types of film. I spend more time now watching films than before. I watch a lot of documentaries, like portrayals of different countries, descriptions of nature, films with an educational purpose. . . . I watch quite a few trash films. For instance, I saw a Dolph Lundgren film, it was real rubbish, just like *My Stepmother Is an Alien* was. Those are real junk films. . . . Shit films are good, because for a couple of hours you can rest your brain. The bad thing is that everything is so stereotyped and show-offish, but sometimes there are some really good parts in those films. . . . Portrayals of family relations, problem films, and films about ordinary families, I think, tend to be good.

Lasse's lifestyle developed considerably during the three years we studied him. In the beginning he was rather self-centred and occupied with his own development. By the end of our study he had become much more concerned about his relationships with others. He almost entirely gave up the individual leisure activities in which he used to be involved and had replaced them with activities of a group character. His interest in scuba-diving was closely connected with his concern for the environment and ecological problems. He had also become interested in psychology and people's psychological well-being.

Case seven: The spirit in the sky

Tobias grew up in a lower middle-class family. He graduated from a high school programme specializing in metal industry work. Tobias was the only one of the seven informants who had been a member of a genuine youth subculture.

I constantly questioned everything the teachers said, so they wanted to get rid of me. For that reason, I was thrown out, in ninth grade and had to start again in a new school. I've probably been some kind of a problem child. I really felt good when I was accepted by this gang. I became a kind of psychiatrist for these guys. I got involved with a heavy gang of punks or whatever they were. Long shabby hair, rivets on their jackets, leather jackets with fifteen zippers, tight black trousers, ragged jeans, constant boozing, and lots of cursing. Not exactly the dream of a mother-in-law. I spent most of my time with them and I enjoyed it, but I was dressed the same as now. It was trash metal, hardcore, well it's the same shit. They were problem children. . . . We weren't criminal in any way, but if they were harassed or drank too much beer, they often beat somebody up.

Several of them have been nailed for assault and battery. One of the guys works as a bouncer in a porno-club in the USA, but he's trying to get something going with his music.

At the same time as Tobias was spending most of his time with this gang, he also met Christian people, and he was a member of the youth organization of the Swedish State Church. In this organization he developed a faith of his own in his strong belief in Jesus and God. He also developed plans to become a parish assistant and a recreation leader, and even considered being a clergyman in the future.

> It all started after confirmation. I then began taking part in youth activities in church. It was not exactly a religious thing. Instead, you treated the place just like any kind of youth recreation centre. . . . And then, well, I just discovered that this was the way it was. It came sneaking upon me, so to say. It took probably two or three years. And then when you started believing in things, you were eager to know more about them. . . . I felt I wanted to become a parish assistant. I wanted to work with people on the basis of my faith. I felt it would be really terrific. I applied to this school but was rejected. Later I heard that you could work and get practical experience, so I moved to Stockholm and stayed there for a year with a really lousy standard of living. Then I was accepted at the school, and I've been here for a year now this summer. I can't see anything negative about it. Theology, education, psychology, almost everything is nice and I benefit privately from it too. . . . I've got some thoughts about becoming a clergyman, but then I'd have to study quite a lot. These are only small, very small, thoughts. You don't simply become a clergyman, it's a vocation, a pretty heavy one, and in fact more than a profession, it's a way of living. When you're hungry you know it; when you feel called, you know what to do. It's simply a feeling you get.

Tobias's lifestyle was very complex; from a conventional point of view, it contained incoherent and inconsistent elements. His Christian faith was combined with his taste in such seemingly contradictory music genres as speed metal, trash metal, punk and Christian music. He watched violent films, but also Christian films. Also his leisure time interests were quite varied. He took part in different kinds of sport activity, spent a great deal of time photographing and processing photos, he made his own video films, participated in church services, and read books. He was also interested in guitar playing and in old cars. He owned an Austin A-35 from 1957, which he liked to work with now and then. He was eager to play down his being a Christian, and felt that his daily lifestyle was not particularly influenced by his Christian faith. For example, he had always been rather fond of hanging around in bars, and he did not change this habit when he became a Christian. Drinking beer had taken on a new meaning for him, however. Through drinking beer, smoking and swearing, Tobias wanted to counteract the prejudices he felt many young poeple had against Christians.

> If I go to a pub, and I do that a lot, I often end up talking with somebody about what I'm doing. When I tell them I'm at a Christian school, their mouths often drop. They seem rather puzzled and surprised at my using bad language, drinking a few beers, laughing, and even occasionally going for a pee.

Tobias's studies, future plans, leisure time activities, and tastes in popular culture were all coloured by his metaphysical convictions. At the same time, he was rather concerned about what other people thought of him. Consequently he deliberately used different symbols and artefacts to express and visualize his taste and style. He did this in order not to be identified, as he expressed it, as a boring Christian. Tobias's style, therefore, can be seen as a symbolic expression of his need to express what he considered as his unique and individual way of relating both to Christianity and to profane culture.

CONCLUDING DISCUSSION

In this chapter I have been preoccupied with the study of lifestyle using qualitative interviews and case studies. I have, however, also argued for the advantages of combining quantitative and qualitative data when studying a phenomenon as complex as lifestyle. The Media Panel Program, of course also contains a substantial amount of aggregated individual quantitative data. Within the project both sources have been used to illuminate different aspects of lifestyle. The rather abstract patterns of culture, identified in the quantitative part of the study, may serve as a map against which the dynamic character of an individual's lifestyle stands out. In studying individual lifestyles, one is studying subtle variations which are impossible to capture by means of the instruments used to identify more general patterns of culture. Looking at the brief portraits of the seven individuals, we can conclude that each of them can be described in terms of such general patterns, and that they also deviate from them in various and important respects.

Although this statement may seem obvious and self-evident, it is nevertheless important, since herein lies the key to the distinction between ideal aggregated lifestyles and individual lifestyles. Whereas the former term designates general, theoretically, methodologically and empirically constructed patterns of culture common to several individuals, the latter term designates the individual's relations to such patterns. Whereas the former concept is used to distinguish characteristics common to a large number of people so as to characterize them in terms of a limited number of lifestyles, the latter is used to distinguish the single individual as a unique person with his or her own individual way of relating to the social and cultural phenomena inherent in lifestyle. General patterns of lifestyle allow us to find unity within diversity, whereas individual lifestyles allow us to find diversity within unity.

The lifestyle studies conducted within the Media Panel Program may perhaps best be described in terms of a continuous oscillation between *categorizations* and *particularizations*. On the one hand, we have categorized empirically a multitude of leisure time activities or genres of film and music in terms of a limited number of aggregates, and on the other hand, we have shown how seven particular individuals can be described in terms of these categories, at the same time as they deviate considerably from them. One advantage of such an oscillation between different levels of analysis is that one can identify, and thereby take into consideration, the various limitations and problems related to lifestyle studies on both the aggregated and the individual, the micro and the macro, level of analysis.

NOTE

1 The major part of this chapter builds on what is presented in the doctoral dissertation *Do the Right Thing. Lifestyle and Identity In Contemporary Youth Culture* (1992), which I wrote with Thomas Johansson. All the interviews accounted for in the text were conducted jointly by Johansson and me, and much of the theoretical discussions are the product of our joint efforts.

REFERENCES

Alexander, J.C. (1987) 'Action and its environments', in J.C. Alexander, B. Giesen, R. Münch and N.J. Smelser (eds) (1987) *The Micro–Macro Link*, Berkeley, Calif.: University of California Press.
Alexander, J.C. and Giesen, B. (1987) 'From reduction to linkage: The long view of the micro–macro debate', in J.C. Alexander, B. Giesen, R. Münch and N.J. Smelser (eds) (1987) *The Micro–Macro Link*, Berkeley, Calif.: University of California Press.
Denzin, N.K. (ed.) (1970/1978) *Sociological Methods. A Sourcebook*, New York: McGraw-Hill Book Company.
Giddens, A. (1984/1989) *The Constitution of Society*, Oxford: Polity Press.
—— (1989/1991) *Sociology*, Cambridge: Polity Press.
Jensen, K.B. and Jankowski, N.W. (eds) (1991) *A Handbook of Qualitative Methodologies for Mass Communication Research*, London: Routledge.
Johansson, T. and Miegel, F. (1992) *Do the Right Thing. Lifestyle and Identity in Contemporary Youth Culture*, Stockholm: Almqvist & Wiksell International.
Lööv, T. and Miegel, F. (1989a) 'The Notion of Lifestyle. Some Theoretical Contributions', *The Nordicom Review*, No 1, 21–31.
Lööv, T. and Miegel, F. (1989b) 'Vardagsliv, livsstilar och massmedieanvändning. En studie av 12 malmöungdomar', *Lund Research Papers in the Sociology of Communication* 16, Lund: Department of Sociology, University of Lund.
Lööv, T. and Miegel, F. (1991) 'Sju livsstilar. Om några malmöungdomars drömmar och längtan', *Lund Research Papers in the Sociology of Communication* 29, Lund: Department of Sociology, University of Lund.
Mitchell, A. (1983) *The Nine American Lifestyles. Who We Are and Where We Are Going*, New York: Warner Books.

Münch, R. and Smelser, N.J. (1987) 'Relating the micro and macro', in J. C. Alexander, B. Giesen, R. Münch and N.J. Smelser (eds) (1987) *The Micro–Macro Link*, Berkeley, Calif.: University of California Press.

Stoecker, R. (1991) 'Evaluating and rethinking the case study', *The Sociological Review* 1:88–112.

Taylor, S.J. and Bogdan, R. (1984) *Introduction to Qualitative Research Methods. The Search for Meanings*, New York: Wiley.

Yin, R.K. (1984) *Case Study Research. Design and Methods*, London: Sage.

Chapter 12

Late modernity, consumer culture and lifestyles: toward a cognitive-affective theory

Thomas Johansson

INTRODUCTION

> Lifestyle is not a term which has much applicability to traditional cultures, because it implies choice within a plurality of possible options, and is 'adopted' rather than 'handed down'. Lifestyles are routinised practices, the routines incorporated into habits of dress, eating, modes acting and favoured milieux for encountering others; but the routines followed are reflexively open to change in the light of the mobile nature of self-identity. Each of the small decisions a person makes every day – what to wear, what to eat, how to conduct himself at work, whom to meet with later in the evening – contributes to such routines. All social choices (as well as larger and more consequential ones) are decisions not only about how to act but what to be. The more post-traditional the settings in which an individual moves, the more lifestyle concerns the very core of self-identity, its making and remaking. (Giddens 1991: 81)

Theoretical and empirical discussions of consumer culture, lifestyles, the mass media, popular culture and youth culture are intimately connected to more fundamental philosophical and ontological questions concerning subjectivity, societal and cultural change and the meaning of life. The terms 'lifestyle' and 'identity' are currently in vogue (Featherstone 1987). They are used as conceptual tools for trying to grasp how societies and individuals are changing. In post-traditional societies lifestyle has become an issue for most people and, as Giddens points out, the more post-traditional the settings in which an individual moves, the more lifestyle concerns the very core of self-identity.

The concept of lifestyle is often associated with market research, consumer attitudes and consumer styles (Holman and Wiener 1985; Mitchell 1983; Pitts and Woodside 1984; Schwartz *et al.* 1979). One of the most influential books in lifestyle research during the 1980s was Arnold Mitchell's work *The Nine American Lifestyles* (1983). In brief, Mitchell conceptualizes and describes *The Nine American Lifestyles* on the basis of Maslow's well-known hierarchy of needs. Maslow's theory states that certain elementary physical needs have to be fulfilled before people will become concerned about activities and interests aiming at self-realization (Maslow 1968). Accordingly, Mitchell distinguishes between three different categories of lifestyle: *need-driven* lifestyles, *outer-oriented* lifestyles and *inner-oriented* lifestyles.

Mitchell's work has had a considerable impact on lifestyle research in Western countries (see, for example, Zetterberg 1983). One of the advantages of Mitchell's work is that he has developed a theoretical framework of lifestyle and empirical methods for measuring lifestyles. There are also several problems inherent in Mitchell's theoretical and methodological approach, however. (For a critique of Mitchell, see Johansson and Miegel 1992a: 19, 58.)

Although the notion of lifestyle has strong connotations to market research and consumer styles, it also has strong roots in sociological theory. In classical sociology, the notion of lifestyle was connected with the Weberian distinction between classes and status groups (Turner 1988; Weber 1922/1968). According to Weber, it is appropriate to use the term 'class' to designate a large number of persons with similar, economically determined living conditions and life experiences. In contrast to classes, status groups are determined by assessments of social honour or esteem. Status distinctions are often linked with class distinctions, but income and property as such are not always acknowledged as qualifications for status. Social status is normally expressed in the form of a specific style of life. As Weber puts it in an oft-quoted passage:

> With some over-simplification, one might thus say that 'classes' are stratified according to the reproduction and acquisition of goods; whereas 'status groups' are stratified according to the principles of their *consumption* of goods and represented by special 'styles of life'. (Weber 1922/1968: 193)

Through the consumption of goods and the creation of specific and distinguished lifestyles, status groups and societal hierarchies are made visible. Possessing wealth is not enough; it has to be put in evidence – for example, through the conspicuous consumption of clothes and jewellery or other accessories. However, as soon as the lower classes succeed in imitating the lifestyle of the higher classes by means of mass produced, cheap copies of former aristocratic status symbols, new symbols are appropriated and made into status symbols (Simmel 1904/1971; Veblen 1899/1979). This perpetual play between different classes and status groups creates a constant need for change, and for those new sensations and experiences which, according to Simmel, are so typical of modern city life in particular and modernity in general. This symbolic play and creation of different lifestyles is also gradually extended to large parts of the labouring population. Thus, according to modern lifestyle theoreticians, the creation of lifestyles becomes intimately interwoven with the twin processes of modernization and individualization (Blumer 1969; Johansson and Miegel 1992a; Zablocki and Kanter 1976).

The notion of lifestyle and the theoretical discussion of this concept is thus closely related to some of the most central sociological questions of the twentieth century, such as the differentiation of classes and status groups, the rise of a consumer society, the process of individualization and the increasing importance of self-identity. During the 1980s we have also witnessed a renewed interest in questions concerning lifestyle and self-identity (Featherstone 1987; Giddens 1991; Johansson and Miegel 1992a, b; Reimer 1989). There are several reasons for this renewed interest in the lifestyle discourse.

Firstly, the cultural dimension has increasingly come to occupy a more central position in theorizing about different social phenomena. In order to understand central sociological questions such as the relation between different social groups, struggles for power, the relation between self and society, the process of socialization, etc., it is necessary to grasp the complex relationship between social processes and individuals' utilization of different symbols, artefacts, styles and tastes. Culture does not only have an ideological impact upon different types of social action, it also has a material impact. Cultural symbols are not only reflections of class relations, gender relations, etc., they also have an impact of their own on the formation and maintenance of these relations. In this sense, the notion of lifestyle is a powerful tool that can be used to study the relation beween social and cultural processes.

Secondly, mass produced culture has come to play an increasingly greater part in the creation of identities and lifestyles of short or long durability. This particular function has become widely recognized in modern mass media research. In the intersection of everyday life, culture and the mass media, symbols are constantly being interpreted and transformed. The 'whole way of life' created and maintained in everyday culture no longer merely embraces the 'original' or 'authentic' culture, but also a wide array of mass media produced symbols and notions. It is also in this meeting between culture in the sociological or anthropological sense of the word, and culture as mass produced symbols and artefacts, that lifestyles are created and maintained. The concept of lifestyle may thus be used to analyse this intricate interplay between mass produced culture and the culture of everyday life.

Thirdly, the concept of lifestyle cuts across such important distinctions as those between public and private, social and personal, high culture and popular culture, global and local culture, and so on. Such dualistic conceptions of society, culture and human life have increasingly become criticized and questioned. A general theme in postmodern theories of culture and society is an emphasis upon the effacement of the boundary between art and everyday culture and the collapse of the distinction between high culture and mass/popular culture (Baudrillard 1987; Featherstone 1991). Also the dual conceptions of man and society are criticized, and replaced by other theoretical constructions within social theory (see, for example, Alexander

1988; Giddens 1991; Habermas 1987). Consequently, the lifestyle concept can be used to find new paths to the solution of old questions and new ways of theorizing sociological questions.

In this chapter, I will further elaborate and develop some of the theoretical issues and thoughts briefly touched upon in this introduction. I will begin by discussing the fundamental issue of the formation of self-identity and lifestyle in late modern Western societies. The relation between values and lifestyle plays a central role in the lifestyle discourse. I will therefore discuss the formations of personal as well as societal value systems. Finally, I will try to tie all the notions and ideas together in the fourth section, 'Towards a Theory of Late Modern Identity and Lifestyle'.

SELF-IDENTITY AND LIFESTYLE

Introduction

Modernity confronts the individual with a complex diversity of possibilities and choices. The existential terrain of late modern life is thus characterized by an increased awareness of the opportunity to construct and reconstruct one's life history. Whereas tradition or established habit orders life into a relatively fixed numbers of channels, the late modern terrain offers a wide range of different lifestyle alternatives to individuals. However, even though lifestyle choices in late modern societies are multiplied and the individual's choices often seem arbitrary, it is always necessary to study the structuration of lifestyles within a specific social and cultural context. Lifestyles are constituted and maintained within a more or less structured field of different positions and movements (Bourdieu 1984). As Grossberg (1992: 99) puts it: 'People are never only Black or female or working-class; people's identities are defined precisely by the complex articulations between different positions in a variety of systems of social difference.'

The development of lifestyle repertoires is also intimately related to fundamental existential issues, such as the reflexively organized construction and reconstruction of self-identity and life history, the creation of meaning in life and the development of a sense of ontological security. The conspicuous and imaginative character of lifestyle offers individuals a wide variety of means to strengthen and develop their self-identity and body awareness. However, it also offers them opportunities to hide their 'real' personality and socio-cultural origin and to create a kind of dream-world. Through the development of different lifestyles, individuals are articulating various kinds of needs, desires and *life-plan calendars*, but at the same time they are gradually integrated and drawn into a system of structurally and positionally determined social and cultural processes and formations (Berger *et al.* 1974; Giddens 1991).

The development of lifestyles is therefore to be considered as the parallel and continuous processes of individualization and social and cultural integration. These two different aspects of lifestyle thus engender an accelerating lifestyle differentiation in late modern society. This characteristic *duality of lifestyle* was also observed by Georg Simmel (1904/1971) in his classic essays on the fashion mechanism and city life. According to Simmel, this double and sometimes contradictory urge for both individuality and cultural belonging is a typical characteristic of modernity (Frisby 1985; Nedelmann 1991).

Lifestyle and symbolic democratization: hiding in the light

Individual identity is formed and structured in relation to others. Contemporary child psychology, as well as research about infants' early interactions with their parents, show that infants take active part in this developmental process, and thus also continuously populate the world with samples of their own inner lives (Stern 1985; Winnicott 1965/1987). The infant's growth takes the form of a continuous interchange between inner and outer reality. Or as Winnicott (1965/1987: 86) expresses it: 'All the processes of a live infant constitute a *going-on-being*, a kind of blue-print for existentialism.' It is through this constant interaction with, and reflection by, significant others that the self and the body-ego is formed and developed.

Adolescence and youth may be regarded as periods during which the individual has to work through his or her earlier life experiences in order to develop a sense of identity (Blos 1962; Erikson 1968; Kroeger 1989). A positive, more self-evident awareness of personal identity emerges. During late adolescence the capability to form one's own view of the past, present and future emerges (Blos 1962). It is also during adolescence and youth that people experiment with different roles and more or less consistent lifestyles. The growth and maturation of the body are central components during these developmental stages. The body is decorated and used in different ways to express identity and lifestyle choice.

A central aspect of lifestyle is its visibility. Through the development and choice of different lifestyles, individuals express parts of their self and identity. The conspicuous and visible character of lifestyle is also a key to the understanding of the differentiation of lifestyles in late modern society. By means of relating to others, young people gradually develop a self-identity. The visualization of different lifestyle characteristics plays an important role in this development. The experimentation with different lifestyles is primarily an experimentation with different group memberships and socio-cultural identities. Individuals thus enact their 'private' drama on the societal stage, and through the participation in various groups they transform it into a social and cultural experience. 'All the world's a stage, And all the men and women merely players: They have their exits and their entrances; And one man in his time plays many parts, His acts being seven ages' (Shakespeare, *As You Like It*: II, vii).

Central characteristics of late modernity are the rise of a consumer society and the growing importance of the mass media as agents of socialization (Featherstone 1991; Giddens 1991; cf. Chapter 1). A wide range of commodities and commercial leisure facilities are provided, and new images are constantly superimposed on the old ones. Images and symbols are used as means to mark boundaries and articulate identity and difference, but they are also used to create an ambiguous surface which is often disengaged from what Raymond Williams calls a 'whole way of life', that is, everyday culture, class conditions, gender relations, and so on (Williams 1975). In a sense, this is a 'postmodern' vision of society and culture. In my view, however, lifestyles mediate between material and social conditions, on the one hand, and popular cultural products produced within consumer culture, on the other. Lifestyles are created in order to enhance the development of self-identity through their visibility, but they may also function as generators of an illusory transcendence of class (Ewen 1988; Johansson and Miegel 1992a). It is thus a 'hiding in the light' (Hebdige 1988).

During the nineteenth century, lifestyles were intimately connected to class and status. According to Weber, different status groups at the time could be distinguished on the basis of their material monopolies. Such honorific preferences consisted, for example, of the privilege of wearing special clothes, of eating special food and of playing certain musical instruments. This meant that in public life it was not very difficult to distinguish between different status groups (and their lifestyles), since they were rather conspicuous and easily identified through such symbolic signs (Heller 1970/ 1984; Sennett 1976).

At this time, lifestyles were well-integrated parts of the individual's self-identity. Status characteristics formed coherent and visible parts of bodily presentation, lifestyle and of the habitus (Bourdieu 1984). Marcel Proust describes how subtle variations in gestures and speech could be used to distinguish one status group from another.

> . . . but I nevertheless had no hesitation in placing the stranger in the same class of society, from the way not only in which he was dressed but in which he spoke to the man who took the tickets and to the box-openers who were keeping him waiting. For, apart from individual characteristics, there was still at this period a very marked difference between any rich and well-dressed man of that section of the aristocracy and any rich and well-dressed man of the world of finance or 'big business'. Where one of the latter would have thought he was giving proof of his exclusiveness by adopting a sharp and haughty tone in speaking to an inferior, the nobleman, affable and mild, gave the impression of considering, of practising an affectation of humility and patience, a pretence of being just an ordinary member of audience, as a prerogative of good breeding. (Proust 1920/1983: 32f)

During the nineteenth century, it was more or less easy to distinguish between people from different walks of life by their clothes, the way they used the language, and the style they embraced. Fashion was used in order to make status distinctions and to express membership in well-defined classes and status groups. Also in the early industrial societies which confronted Weber, Simmel and Veblen, class and status conditions were the obvious points of departure in lifestyle analysis. If different persons belonged to a particular class or status group, they were regarded as having approximately the same lifestyle. In contemporary society, where individual variations in terms of lifestyle are supposedly much greater, this obviously provides an insufficient notion of lifestyle.

To identify the social position of a person by means of what clothes he or she wears is not as easy today as it once was. Although still very unevenly distributed, in pace with the growing prosperity in Western industrialized societies, individuals' incomes have become more equal. There are still great differences, of course, in access to economic capital, both between and within different classes and status groups. However, the welfare state has given most people enough money not only to satisfy their basic needs, but also to consume for pleasure. Discretionary income has grown. Therefore, one way of labelling late modern society is to describe it as a *consumer society* (Bell 1976; Featherstone 1991).

Style and fashion have become important matters for late modern humanity, not least among youth, and the style market supplies an infinite number of images and symbols by means of which one can try to construct what and whom one wants to be or become. This is not always synonymous with what one actually is or can become, however.

In late modern society, style is a very complicated phenomenon, and it functions in differing ways. One way it functions is as a generator of illusory transcendence of class. Stuart Ewen calls this process *symbolic democratization*. Thus, by developing a certain style in clothes or other material objects the individual can create a sense of partaking in what is seen as a desirable style of life, as it is presented by mass media (Ewen 1988; Schudson 1986).

By possessing the goods identified with the powerful, the free and the beautiful, the individual develops a feeling of having power, beauty and freedom. Prior to the consumer society, the symbols of power, beauty and freedom were possessed only by those who had actual power. In the modern consumer society, however, the very symbols, due to their mass production, have been made available to common humanity on a massive scale (Benjamin 1968; Ewen 1988). Real power, of course, is still in the hands of an élite. The increasingly equal distribution of power symbols, then, does not correspond with a more equal distribution of actual power. In this sense, symbolic democratization is a form of false consciousness.

If the style market constitutes a presentation of a way of life, it is a way of life that is unattainable for most, nearly all, people. It is very relevant. It is the most common realm of our society in which the need for a better, or different way of life is acknowledged, and expressed on a material level, if not met. It constitutes a politics of change, albeit a 'change' that resides wholly on the surface of things. The surfaces themselves are lifted from an infinite number of sources. (Ewen 1988: 16)

In late modern society lifestyle characteristics such as clothes and other artefacts constitute what Fredric Jameson has called a *depthless culture*; that is, the overproduction of signs and reproductions of images and simulations leads to a loss of stable meaning, and an aestheticization of reality. The consumer public becomes fascinated by the endless stream of bizarre symbols and images which takes the viewer beyond a stable perception of reality (Baudrillard 1987; Jameson 1991; Johansson 1992).

When analysing late modern culture, it is important that one does not fall into the 'postmodern trap', losing sight of everyday culture and material conditions. The increasing effacement of the boundary between everyday culture and mass produced culture, so well described by Stuart Ewen, creates an open symbolic space which is filled with dreams, desires, hopes, wishes, Utopias and so on. In analyses of late modern culture, identity and lifestyles, it is thus necessary to grapple with the dynamic relation between popular/mass culture and everyday culture. Basically, lifestyles are produced and maintained in the intersection of popular/mass culture and the culture of everyday life.

The process of symbolic democratization has two aspects. It may create an illusion, an inhibiting factor on the individual's capability to analyse and influence his or her social and cultural position; the person may become an obedient, submissive, uncritical and conformable citizen. Alternatively, symbolic democratization may help one to develop one's self-confidence, personality and identity, which in turn may generate an awareness of one's capability to influence one's own situation, thus assuming at least some degree of real power. Popular or mass culture may be used to oppose the validated cultural capital of the bourgeoisie. 'Bad taste' may be turned into a weapon directed toward the legitimate culture (Fiske 1987; Johansson and Miegel 1992a, b).

The process of symbolic democratization is intimately interwoven with the process of individualization and youth culture (Johansson 1992). In late modern society, people often refuse to be labelled in terms of traditional categories such as class, status, gender and race. It is important for them constantly to reflect upon their possibilities in life, and their future destiny. The self consequently becomes an object of deliberate attention and thorough examination. It is important for individuals to feel engaged in what they do, and they therefore constantly ask themselves questions such as: 'Is this right for me?', 'Do I feel emotionally engaged in what I am doing?', 'Is this the kind of life I want to live?'. This search for self-identity is to a large extent canalized into consumption of popular culture. The late modern world is thus characterized by the cultivation of consumer lifestyles based on conspicuous consumption (Denzin 1991; Ewen 1988; Featherstone 1991).

Self-identity and lifestyles are increasingly defined by a media-oriented popular/mass culture in which youth, health, sexuality and body appearance have taken on premium values. As earlier mentioned, the effacement of the boundary between everyday culture and mass produced culture creates an open space which may be filled with dreams and desires. But it may also lead to frustrations over unrealized dreams, hopes and desires. Symbolic demo-cratization thus contributes to the creation of a 'postmodern vision' of transcendence, individuality and lifestyle experimentation. This 'vision' may result in a more reflexive and active way of relating to social and cultural conflicts and problems, but it may also result in a passive and conservative reaction (Denzin 1991). Thus, symbolic democratization may be a hiding in the light as well as a way of confronting the repressive features of late modern culture.

Ontological security, self-identity and lifestyle

In a post-traditional order the self becomes a *reflexive project*, that is, individuality, worth and dignity are not automatically given to us by nature, but assigned to us as tasks we have to solve (Giddens 1991; May 1958/1986). Individuals often feel bereft and alone in a world where they lack emotional and psychological support and the sense of security provided by a more traditional milieu. According to some social scientists, late modern indi-viduals are therefore afflicted with a permanent identity crisis (Berger *et al.* 1974; Featherstone 1991). Identity and lifestyle become a life-long project (Featherstone 1991). However, when touching upon the subject of identity and identity crisis, it is important to point out that there are great variations between different individuals, different classes and status groups, men and women, etc.

In human life basic trust plays an essential role. Basic trust links self-identity to the appraisals and loving attention of significant others (Erikson 1968; Giddens 1991; Winnicott 1965/1987). Basic trust is thus developed through constant and reliable everyday interaction with significant others. From early childhood, habit and routine play a fundamental role in the shaping of the individual's self-identity. In a society characterized by increasing complexity, there is a corresponding growth in the need for assurances about the present and the future. According to Luhmann, trust accumulates as a kind of capital which opens up more opportunities for extensive action (Luhmann 1979). In his book *Modernity and Self-Identity*, Anthony Giddens has de-veloped similar thoughts regarding trust and daily life.

The trust which the child, in normal circumstances, vests in its care-takers,

I want to argue, can be seen as a sort of emotional inoculation against existential anxieties – a protection against future threats and dangers which allows the individual to sustain hope and courage in the face of whatever debilitating circumstances she or he might later confront. Basic trust is a screening-off device in relation to risks and dangers in the surrounding settings of action and interaction. It is the main emotional support of a defensive carapace or *protective cocoon* which all normal individuals carry around with them as a means whereby they are able to get on with the affairs of day-to-day life. (Giddens 1991: 40)

The maintaining of certain habits and routines are thus a way of developing a crucial bulwark against threatening anxieties and insecurity. All individuals develop a framework of ontological security based on routines, habits and cognitive and emotional ways of interpreting the world and life itself. This process is closely related to the development and maintenance of an individual biography (Luckmann 1983; Schutz and Luckmann 1974). The biography of the individual is a designed project consisting of long-range life-plans regarding what the individual will do with his or her life and what he or she wants to become. When the individual, as Berger and his co-authors express it, 'plots the trajectory of his life on the societal "map", each point in his projected biography relates him to the overall web of meanings in the society' (Berger *et al.* 1974: 76). Self-identity is thus not a psychological entity, but instead a psychosocial entity which relates individuals' aspirations, desires, goals and needs to societal and cultural structures of meaning. In this way self-identity is also intimately related to the development of lifestyles.

A lifestyle may be defined as a more or less integrated set of values, attitudes and actions which an individual embraces, not only because it constitutes a foundation for meaningful practices, but because it gives material form to a particular narrative of self-identity (Giddens 1991; Johansson and Miegel 1992a). A lifestyle has a certain unity important to a continuing sense of ontological security. Although the notion of lifestyle is often associated with the area of consumption, it is also related to the work context. Work conditions and material conditions strongly condition life chances in Weber's sense.

Life chances may also be understood in terms of the availability of potential lifestyles. A plurality of lifestyle choices do exist, but only within a socially, economically and culturally structured space of lifestyle (Bourdieu 1984). Lifestyles are structurally, positionally and individually determined phenomena (Johansson and Miegel 1992a). The range of feasible lifestyle alternatives in a society constitute a *cultural pool* of symbols, artefacts, habits and orientations. In this way we could talk about a *potential space* of lifestyles. In his book *Playing and Reality* (1971), Winnicott speaks of a potential space, which exists between inner psychic reality and the outer social world. Through playing and through use of cultural symbols, the child (and the adult!) try to bridge the incongruity between inner and outer reality. Culture is thus created in this continuous interplay between personal experiences and the outer social and cultural reality. Such a potential space opens up for longings, dreams and desires, but also for more objective goals and aspirations. Lifestyle choices may thus form an important part of an individual's life planning and development of a self-identity.

Self-identity and lifestyle: concluding remarks

Contemporary culture and society has been described in many different ways: as a post-industrial society, a narcissistic culture, a postmodern culture, a risk society and so on (Beck 1986; Bell 1976; Lasch 1985; Lyotard 1986). Although social scientists disagree concerning the description of contemporary culture and society, they agree that the formation of self-identity and lifestyle has turned into a complicated issue for modern humanity. In pre-industrial Western societies there was no problem of order, everybody being so clearly labelled (Sennett 1976). There was also a greater coherence between social, cultural and personal identity – they formed an integrated whole. In late modern culture individuals often deliberately scramble all the codes and symbols, by quickly shifting from one to another. They combine different styles and tastes and construct what could be called *postmodern collages* (Johansson 1992; Ziehe 1989). Through such combinations of different and often contradictory styles, people explore the symbolic possibilities in their culture. People's use of different popular cultural elements may lead to the creation of a kind of dream-world, i.e. a condition in which one has the possibility, in a symbolic way, to realize all kinds of dreams and desires. However, the consumption of popular cultural goods may also increase individuals' possibilities to reflect upon their own situation and consequently also to change their lives.

A central characteristic of late modern culture is thus the refusal to be labelled in terms of traditional categories such as class, status, gender, religion, race, and so on. This does not mean, however, that self-identity is fluid and ever-changing. Lifestyle and identity experimentation is always taking place within a cultural and social context. The effacement of the boundary between everyday culture and mass/popular culture has led to the creation of a potential space of lifestyles. Dreams and desires are mixed with more realistic goals for the future. These dreams, desires and goals are organized into lifestyles and different narratives of self-identity. Accordingly, a lifestyle constitutes a foundation for meaningful practices and gives material form to a particular narrative of self-identity. Lifestyle and self-identity are thus constructed through complex articulations between different positions in a variety of different systems of social difference.

Basic trust plays a central role in human life. Human existence is ordered through the maintenance of certain habits, routines, values, attitudes, and so on. People develop a framework of ontological security through the development of everyday routines and modes of social interaction. These routines may, of course, be reflexively changed. In fact, late modern culture is characterized by more or less constant changes of everyday routines and rituals. 'The notion of risk becomes central in a society which is taking leave of the past, of traditional ways of doing things, and which is opening itself up to a problematic future' (Giddens 1991: 111).

Late modern man is thus constantly engaged in the construction of reliable and coherent narratives of self-identity. The process of symbolic democratization has opened up an imaginative space of possible narratives of self-identity, but it also puts great stress on people. This may lead to an identity crisis, but may also be enriching and strengthening. The historical appearence of the *performing self*, which places great emphasis upon appearance, display and the management of impressions, has led to an ever-increasing popularity of autobiographies, soap operas, self-therapy, psychoanalysis, and so on (Denzin 1991; Featherstone 1991; Giddens 1991; Wouters 1992).

> Although feelings of ambivalence, insecurity and disorientation will to some extent accompany each new round in the process of self-distantiation, articulating and emphasizing one's distinctive features still seems to have become a sport and an art, and increasing numbers of people seem to have become more and more aware both that they have to put their minds and hearts into it, and of how it is to be done. (Wouters 1992: 243)

THE SPACE OF LIFESTYLES: TOWARD A COGNITIVE–AFFECTIVE THEORY

Lifestyles are formed and maintained through the constant interaction between different individuals and different groups of individuals. Late modern individuals put strong emphasis on appearance, the body look and the management of impressions (Featherstone 1990; Goffman 1969). Self-identity and lifestyles are constituted and developed through the presentation of self in everyday life. The potential space of lifestyles in a specific society may be conceptualized in many different ways. I will here discuss three different models of constructing the social and symbolic space of lifestyles. Firstly, I will present and discuss a *power and status perspective* on lifestyle, considering some crucial parts of Bourdieu's theory of lifestyles as it is presented in *Distinction* (1984). I will also account for Mike Featherstone's discussion of the new cultural intermediaries and symbolic production. Secondly, I will present and discuss an *affective perspective* on lifestyle, accounting for Lawrence Grossberg's theoretical discussion on popular culture, consumption and everyday life. *Finally*, I will discuss a *cognitive value perspective* on lifestyle and say something about an alternative way to conceptualize the social and symbolic space of lifestyles.

Pierre Bourdieu and the will to power

Pierre Bourdieu maintains that there is an ever-ongoing struggle for power and status, not only between, but also within different classes in society. This struggle concerns not only position in relation to matters of production (income, occupation, education), but rather, Bourdieu also defines a class or a class fraction in terms of such features as sex-ratio, geographical distribution, ethnic origin and so on. Struggles of this sort take place within what he calls a social space, where relations between the classes are structured in accordance with the amount of, and access to, the different forms of capital (economic, cultural and social capital).

It is the dominant classes and class fractions that primarily interest Bourdieu; that is where he finds the most accentuated struggle for power, the struggle for not only economic, but also cultural dominance. According to Bourdieu, the dominant class in a society has a monopoly on legitimate culture, defining it and determining what tastes are the best and what lifestyles are to prevail.

Other classes and class fractions constantly try to promote their cultural preferences and lifestyles so as to become legitimate and predominating. The struggle for dominance between classes and class fractions leads to continual changes in lifestyle. The symbolic battle is fought in different fields of cultural preference. The fields consist of different cultural goods within the areas of, say, music, art, theatre and literature. Bourdieu claims that the heart of these symbolic struggles is taste, and that the aim is to achieve acceptance of a specific taste as the legitimate one within a particular field of preference. The 'right' taste and lifestyle thus stand as symbols of power and status.

Thus, the social space of lifestyles is structured according to the rules of power. Consequently, the most powerful classes and class fractions are setting the lifestyle agenda. Even though Bourdieu is trying to avoid being a determinist, he presents a perspective of society and lifestyles where the Nietzschean *will to power* is determining all relations and lifestyle discourses. In Bourdieu's theory, the development of habitus and the individual lifestyle is only comprehensible when conceptualized within a specific social field of power relations. Thus, the cultural game of identity and the urge for individuality and authenticity is an illusion. It is the will to power that brings things and people together or separates them.

> Distinction and pretension, high culture and middle-brow culture – like, elsewhere, high fashion and fashion, haute coiffure and coiffure, and so on – only exist through each other, and it is the relation, or rather, the objective collaboration of their respective production apparatuses and clients which produces the value of culture and the need to possess it. (Bourdieu 1984: 250)

When describing the dynamics of the symbolic field, Bourdieu touches upon the important relation between *being and seeming* (cf. May 1958/1986;

Winnicott 1965/1987). This discussion has great similarities with what has been described as the process of symbolic democratization. The symbolic struggles over being and seeming deal with the distinction between 'natural' grace and style, on the one hand, and usurped airs and graces, on the other. People who exhibit external signs of wealth and status associated with a condition higher than their own often have a self-image too far out of line with the image others have of them. However, strategies of pretension and the creation of symbolic illusions are not merely imaginary phenomena. As Bourdieu (1984: 253) expresses it: 'The reality of the social world is in fact partly determined by the struggles between agents over the presentation of their position in the social world and, consequently, of that world.' A class and status fraction highly involved in this construction of reality is the so-called *petite bourgeoisie*.

The *petite bourgeoisie* is torn by contradictions between objectively dominated conditions and would-be participation in dominant values and lifestyles. They are committed to symbolic consumption and to taste. The presentation of a specific and distinguished social character is central to these groups. They are constantly occupied trying to modify the positions in the objective classifications by modifying the representation and principles of the ranks and status distinctions.

Following Bourdieu, Mike Featherstone argues that beside the new middle class in modern consumer society (for instance, managers, scientists and technicians), there has also developed an expanding group which he calls the new cultural intermediaries. Thus he describes this group:

> These are engaged in providing symbolic goods and services that were referred to earlier – the marketing, advertising, public relations, radio and television producers, presenters, magazine journalists, fashion writers, and the helping professions (social workers, marriage counselors, sex therapists, dieticians, play leaders, etc.). (Featherstone 1991: 44)

Still following Bourdieu, Featherstone also calls this group the new intellectuals. They are important in the lifestyle discussion, because they may be regarded as a kind of professional lifestyle creator, constantly engaged in seeking new experiences. Therefore, the group is also called 'the new heroes of consumer culture', depending on their making lifestyle into a life project. Life is conceived as essentially open-ended, and they are fascinated by identity and the endless quest for new experiences.

The function served by these new intellectuals is to legitimize for intellectual analysis such traditional non-intellectual areas as sport, fashion and popular music, in this way supplying new symbolic goods and experiences to the adherents of lifestyles of the new middle-class audience which they themselves have partly helped to create (Featherstone 1987, 1990, 1991).

In the social and symbolic space constructed by Bourdieu, lifestyle and self-identity are closely associated with the will to power. As Nietzsche

(1883/1977: 229) expressed it: 'The world seen from within, the word described and defined according to its "intelligible character" – it would be "will to power" and nothing else.' Lifestyle and self-identity are constructed within a fairly closed space, and identity games are turned into status games. Bourdieu is constantly occupied with demystifying and unveiling power structures and power relations. Lifestyles are embraced either in order to signify people's status and as a means of recognition, or as means of the creation of self-images and identities that are merely symbolic illusions. Bourdieu has been criticized on several different issues: lack of empirical relevance, theoretical obscurity, determinism, etc. (DiMaggio 1979; Fenster 1991; Fiske 1987; Rosengren 1991). In my opinion, however, the most constructive critique of Bourdieu's use of the concept of capital and his conceptualization of the social and symbolic space of lifestyles is to be found within the tradition of *cultural studies* (Fiske 1987; Grossberg 1992). We will therefore turn our attention to one of the authors within this theoretical tradition – Lawrence Grossberg.

Postmodern structures of feeling

In his book *We Gotta Get Out Of This Place*, Grossberg (1992) presents an analysis of popular culture, everyday life and postmodern sensibilites. Although there are many similarities between Pierre Bourdieu's and Lawrence Grossberg's lifestyle analyses, there are also some crucial differences. To a greater extent than Bourdieu, Grossberg emphasizes the importance of desire and affects in the creation of a symbolic space of identities and lifestyles. According to Grossberg, cultural formations – that is, structures that distribute, place and connect cultural practices and social groups – may be understood only if one grasps the 'structure of feeling' affecting people's practices and identities, or, as Grossberg prefers to call it, a particular sensibility.

> A sensibility can be understood in a number of different ways. For the individuals living within it, it defines a historically determined and socially distributed mode of engagement with (or consumption of) particular practices. It determines the 'proper' and appropriate way of selecting cultural practices, of relating to them, and of inserting them into daily life. In other words, the notion of sensibility replaces and refines the concept of taste, for the sensibility of a particular formation determines the very meaning of 'taste' within it. Taste means entirely different things in different formations. (Grossberg 1992: 72)

Cultural practices may have different types of effect on the structuration of everyday life and the space of lifestyles: economic effects, libidinal effects, political effects, aesthetic effects, and so on. They may also bypass meaning altogether and act directly on the body of the consumer (Grossberg

1992). Practices and effects are connected to each other through the process of articulation. Articulation is a continuous struggle to locate practices within a shifting and dynamic field of forces. The effects of any practice are always the product of its position within a social and cultural context. It is only within specific contexts that identities and relations exist. Thus, a context is a structured field, a configuration of practices and relations between different practices.

When analysing lifestyles and identities, there are always different levels of structures that have to be taken into account. Cultural analysis involves an attempt to construct the specificity of an articulated context, according to Grossberg. However, in order to analyse a certain field of forces, it is necessary to describe the dominant sensibility structuring the field in question. Or as Grossberg (1992: 73) expresses it: 'How the specific sounds, styles and behaviors of a specific alliance (e.g., surf music and surf culture, or trash music and skateboards, or the particular configuration of "mod" culture) make sense together depends upon the sensibility at work.'

Grossberg emphasizes that sensibilities may operate within the field of ideology or morality, but the dominant sensibilities often involve desire, fantasy and especially pleasure. Pleasure is indeed a complex phenomenon, and the term covers a great number of different relations: the fun of breaking the rules, the enjoyment of doing what you want, the temporary fulfillment of desires, etc.

Popular culture and consumption occupy a central position in Grossberg's analysis of late modern society. Popular culture is an important site of people's passions and desires. People spend a lot of time with popular culture, and it matters to them (Fiske 1987, 1989; Fornäs 1990; Frith 1988). Popular culture is always more than ideological or a mark of class and status relations. It provides sites of relaxation, privacy, pleasure, fun, passion, desire and emotion. Popular culture often has a direct impact upon the body. It generates laughter, screams, tears, and other kinds of emotional reaction. Popular culture therefore seems to work at the intersection of the body and emotions (see Csikszentmihalyi and Larson 1984; Larson and Kubey 1985).

Affect is a central concept in Grossberg's analysis of popular culture and everyday culture. Affect operates across all our senses and experiences. 'Affect is what gives "color", "tone" or "texture" to the lived' (Grossberg 1992: 81).

Affect actually points to a complex set of effects which circulate around notions of investment and anchoring; it circumscribes the entire set of relations that are referred to with such terms as 'volition,' 'will,' 'investment,' 'commitment,' and 'passion.' Affective relations always involve a quantitatively variable level of energy (activation, enervation) that binds an articulation or that binds an individual to a particular practice. Affect identifies the strength of the investment which anchors people in particular experiences, practices, identities, meanings and pleasures, but it also determines how invigorated people feel at any moment of their lives, their level of energy or passion. In this quantitative dimension, affect privileges passion and volition over meaning, as if simply willing something to happen were sufficient to bring it about (e.g., as one ad campaign continuously declares, 'Where there's a will, there's an A'). (Grossberg 1992: 82)

So, popular culture is a crucial ground where people are influenced by others (individuals and/or social groups) and mass media. Through such affective investments people are also drawn into, and located within, various circuits of power and power relations. Thus, affect concerns both belonging and identification (see Simmel 1904/1971). People tend to feel at home when they care about something. As Grossberg (1992: 84) expresses it: 'The very notion of "the popular" assumes the articulation of identification and care; it assumes that what one identifies with (including moments of identity) matters and what matters – what has authority – is the appropriate ground for identification.' Consequently, self-identity and lifestyle are organized and structured on the basis of what Grossberg calls 'mattering maps', that is, emotional and affective structures that 'tell' people how to navigate their way through various moods, pleasures and passions (see Williams 1975; cf. also Bourdieu's concept of habitus).

People are always located within a social and cultural sphere, but the relationship between different individuals and various groups is never static. People and groups of people are continuously moving through the social sphere. However, daily life is always structured and constrained. Therefore, it is appropriate to conceptualize people's self-identity and lifestyle development in terms of *structured mobility*. Such a structured mobility defines the places and spaces, the stabilites and mobilities within which people work and live.

> A structured mobility describes the ways fractions of the population travel across the surfaces of culture and the ways they anchor themselves into their imaginary depths. It is a historical organization, both spatial and temporal, which enables and constrains the ways space and place, mobility and stability, are lived. Consequently, it is neither a rigid system of places nor a predefined itinerary of imagined mobility. It is precisely the condition which makes both stability and mobility possible. . . . It describes the sites people can occupy, the ways they can take up practices constituting these sites, and the paths along which they can connect and transform them so as to construct a consistent livable space for themselves. (Grossberg 1992: 109)

The individuals that Grossberg portrays are ruled by passions, affects and desires. The *affective individual* is always a multiple and multidimensional person, taking on the shape and colour of the affective structure through which he or she moves. However, coherence and stability is always possible, even though identity is also fleeting and changing. It is thus possible to talk about preliminary structurations of self-identity. The affective individual must always struggle to develop his or her self-identity and lifestyle. In so doing, he or she is constantly involved in the construction of new maps and in the movement between different sites of daily life. The affective individual is also always drawn into a complex network of power relations and political projects. Practices and cultural consumption produce pleasure and even empowerment, but also displeasure, boredom, insecurity and disempowerment. Power describes a constantly changing state of play in this shifting and multidimensional field of forces, relations and sensibilities.

In contrast with Bourdieu's relatively closed and more or less stable social space of lifestyles, Grossberg's symbolic space is fairly open and transitional. The sensibility of postmodernity is characterized by an ironic nihilism where it has become increasingly difficult to differentiate between reality and its images. Most traditional values and pleasures (love, family, sex, work, etc.) have turned into treacherous traps which never seem to deliver on their promise (Berman 1983; Grossberg 1992). It is no longer possible to speak of a singular group identity or a coherent self-identity, but instead of multiple identities and fluid communities. Consequently, lifestyles and identities are articulated and constructed within a multidimensional symbolic space.

A cognitive perspective on lifestyle

A common analytical approach in lifestyle research is the value perspective (see, for example, Johansson and Miegel 1992a; Reimer 1988, 1989; Reimer and Rosengren 1990). Social scientists often use and define the value concept in terms of cognitions. This view is radically questioned within philosophy. (see Chapter 10) However, in this section I will discuss a cognitive value perspective.

According to Rokeach, a value is an enduring belief (i.e. cognition), either prescriptive or condemning, about a preferable or desirable mode of conduct or an end-state of existence (Rokeach 1973). The values of an individual are organized into value systems. A value system is described as 'an enduring organization of beliefs concerning preferable modes of conduct or end-state of existence along a continuum of relative importance' (Rokeach 1973: 5).

Rokeach maintains that there is a group of conceptions more central to an individual than are his or her values. These are the conceptions individuals have about themselves. This self-identity proves itself in its ability to lend continuity to an individual's life history (cf. Giddens 1991). Rokeach's main thesis is that 'the ultimate purpose of one's total belief system, which includes one's values, is to maintain and enhance . . . the master of all sentiments, the sentiment of self-regard' (Rokeach 1973: 216).

Values constitute the most fundamental component of lifestyle. From this perspective, the lifestyle of an individual is basically an expression of his or her values. The lifestyle phenomenon can, therefore, be studied on three conceptually different levels: *the value level*, *the attitude level* and *the action level* (Miegel 1990; Johansson and Miegel 1992a: 71). The value level consists of the individual's general and abstract conceptions about material, aesthetic, ethical and metaphysical conditions and qualities. These conceptions are made concrete by the individual on the attitude level. The attitudes of an individual involve his or her outlook on specific objects, phenomena and conditions of reality. On the action level the individual, finally, manifests his or her attitudes in the form of different actions. The values and attitudes of an individual become visible and observable when they manifest themselves in action.

In order to construct a social and symbolic space of lifestyles, it is necessary to develop an understanding of the values and value orientations lying behind the development of such a space. Ronald Inglehart provides us with a theoretical understanding of how structural changes taking place in Western societies during late modernity contribute to changes in human values and competences, and how in their turn these changes affect the social and symbolic structure in society (Inglehart 1977, 1990). In accordance with this assumption, Inglehart maintains that the values of the Western public have undergone a change from an emphasis on material welfare and physical security, to an increased emphasis on quality of life values. The former type of value he calls *material*; the latter, *postmaterial*. His main thesis is thus that post-war Western societies have witnessed a gradual shift in their value structure, a shift from materialist to postmaterialist values.

The value changes result in an increasing emphasis on needs for belonging, self-esteem and self-realization, whereas changes in skills have led to more people having the skills needed to cope with politics on a national scale (cf. Giddens 1991; Habermas 1975).

Yet another important distinction with respect to the social and symbolic space of lifestyle, is between security and developmental values (Johansson and Miegel 1992a: 69; Rokeach 1973: 15f.). The security values serve the function of helping us to fit in and to adapt in an unproblematic way to society, avoiding conflicts and ensuring that one's actions and attitudes are justified. In Rokeach's terms such values represent 'ready made concepts provided by our culture that such justifications can proceed smoothly' (Rokeach 1973: 15f.). The development of security values are probably related to what Giddens (1991) discusses in terms of basic trust and ontological security. The developmental values, on the other hand, serve the function of fulfilling needs and desires to search for meaning, understanding, knowledge and self-realization. The individual's identity is not to be found in behaviour, values, attitudes, beliefs, etc., but in the capacity to 'keep a particular narrative going' (Giddens 1991). The biography that the individual reflexively develops is only one story among a number of potential stories about his or her development as a self.

In studying young people's popular culture consumption, one is likely to find indications of individuals' need and desire for security as well as their desire for development (Johansson and Miegel 1992a, b). In order to be recognized as being part of one's society and culture, one must have a basic knowledge and awareness of its fundamental values, norms, mores, language, and so on, whereas being recognized as a distinct individual requires that one develop and transcend common taste, competence and knowledge in at least some cultural area, and possibly in several. In most popular cultural phenomena there also exists a mainstream, expressing the values of security and belonging, and a number of more specific and distinct tastes expressing the values of transcendence and development. Thus, security and development are two basic aspects of human life. It is important to emphasize the fact that security and development always exist at the same time, and that they are intimately related to each other, expressing two fundamental aspects of human existence, like a Janus face.

The dimensions of postmaterialism/materialism and security/development, seem to capture some important aspects of late modern culture. However, there is an ongoing discussion concerning the validity of Inglehart's value conceptualization, and several attempts have been made to reconstruct Inglehart's materialist/postmaterialist dimension (Flanagan 1987; Reimer 1988, 1989). The dimension of security/development is also quite problematic and in need of a more penetrating theoretical elaboration (Johansson and Miegel 1992a: 227f.). The important achievement in these theoretical and empirical works, however, is the connection made between values and value orientations on the one hand, and lifestyles on the other. The often superficial actions and artefacts constituting a lifestyle have their origins in an individual and societal value structure. In order fully to understand the anatomy of the lifestyle concept, one must realize that behind all visible expressions and signs which we designate as a lifestyle, there exists a number of fundamental values (Johansson and Miegel 1992a; Miegel 1990).

The social space of lifestyle: concluding remarks

Bourdieu and Grossberg represent two different ways of constructing a social and symbolic space of lifestyles and identities. Whereas Bourdieu emphasizes power relations, constructing a rather stable and rigid social and symbolic system, Grossberg opens up a space for a more imaginative theoretical analysis of lifestyle and self-identity. Comparing Bourdieu and Grossberg, it is possible to use Mitchell's distinction between outer-directed and inner-directed lifestyles (Mitchell 1983).

People belonging to outer-directed lifestyles create ways of structuring everyday life that are geared to the visible, tangible and materialistic. Outer-directed lifestyles are arranged in a hierarchy placing the successful status-seeking American at the top, emphasizing the will to power. Inner-directed lifestyles are so named because their driving forces are internal, not external.

People embracing inner-directed lifestyles often seek the new, resenting old values and lifestyles. They are oriented towards inner exploration, a quest for the mystical and new experiences, that is, towards new sensibilities and new structures of feeling. Both these perspectives and constructions of a social and symbolic space of lifestyles capture central aspects of the lifestyle discourse, but they are merely dealing with what could be called *affective aspects* of lifestyle such as the will to power and pleasure.

The construction of values and value orientations occupies a central position within the lifestyle discourse. I have touched upon two such constructions of value dimensions: materialism/postmaterialism and security/development. However, it is probably quite difficult to construct a social and symbolic space of lifestyle, capturing the complexity of late modern culture, on the basis of such dualisms. Late modern culture is not an either/or culture, but a both/and culture (Reimer 1988, 1989, 1992). In order to construct a space of late modern lifestyles, it is thus necessary to reconstruct the different dimensions in question and find concepts that are less rigid and more relevant for a late modern context.

In several articles, Bo Reimer claimed that Inglehart's materialist/postmaterialist dichotomy may be too rigid to capture the complexity of people's value orientations in late modern Western society (Reimer 1988, 1989; Reimer and Rosengren 1990). Using a combination of Inglehart's and Rokeach's measurements of values and value orientations, Reimer found that Rokeach's value set captures young people's values better than the Inglehart value battery (Reimer 1988). Following this, Reimer suggests that instead of treading the postmaterialist path, young people seem to move in a multitude of more individual and personal directions. 'This movement may be regarded as a characteristic of what I prefer to call "postmodern structures of feelings"; feelings too diverse to be contained inside a materialist/postmaterialist value construction' (Reimer 1988: 357).

Reimer describes certain tendencies influencing young people in our time. The two characteristics of individuality and immediacy comprise major components in young people's lifestyles. Youth culture is characterized by an orientation toward new social formations and a reflexively grounded distrust toward earlier political solutions on the one hand, and an orientation toward life itself, pleasure and the fulfilment of desire on the other. Thus, there are both cognitive and affective reasons influencing the constellation of new formations and collectivities (see Ziehe 1989). The affective dimension has also gradually gained more attention from social scientists (Maffesoli 1991; Wouters 1992). According to Michel Maffesoli, it would be appropriate to speak about a collective narcissism emphasizing the aesthetic and involving a particular mode of life, of dress, of sexual manners, etc. In short, it is everything that could be described as collective passion.

. . . for while the official institutions and the professional sociologists may continue to use their eternal socio-professional categories, other signs of social affiliation are emerging to cut right across them: cultural practices, age groupings, participation in affective collectivities. In a word, we have now to deal with the practice of networks. (Maffesoli 1991: 12)

In order to construct a social and symbolic space of lifestyle in late modern Western socities, it is necessary to include both cognitive and affective dimensions (Giddens 1991; Grossberg 1992; Maffesoli 1991; Reimer 1988, 1989; Wouters 1992). Values and value orientations – that is, the *cognitive dimension of lifestyle* – are intimately interwoven with affects, desires and pleasure – the *affective dimension of lifestyle*. The development and maintenance of different lifestyle sectors – 'time-space slices of individuals' overall activities, within which a reasonably consistent and ordered set of practices is adopted and enacted' (Giddens 1991: 83) – is closely related to the development of different structures of feelings as well as to changes in the individual and societal value structure (Reimer 1988, 1989; Williams 1975). Pierre Bourdieu, Lawrence Grossberg and the value theoreticians mentioned in this chapter all discuss different aspects of the complex social and symbolic space of lifestyle. They identify different actors on the societal stage and different driving forces. An important question is this: Are these different approaches incompatible, or is it possible to integrate and synthesize them, formulating a more comprehensible theory of lifestyle in late modern society?

In the concluding section of this chapter I will try to draw the different threads together, and say something about the future of lifestyle research.

TOWARDS A THEORY OF LATE MODERN IDENTITY AND LIFESTYLE

It would be mistaken to speak here of individuation alone. Individuation is only the indispensable personal stamp of all human existence. The self as such is not ultimately the essential, but the meaning of human existence given in creation again and again fulfills itself as self. (Buber 1965: 84)

The individual is always realizing his or her possibilities and choices within a more or less structured social and cultural environment. From the early days of life, habit and routine play a fundamental role in the shaping of self-identity. Routines are incorporated into habits of dress, modes of consumption, leisure time activities, working conditions, and so on. The maintenance of such habits and routines is a way of coping with threatening anxiety and insecurity (Giddens 1991). Basic trust and security are thus central aspects of human existence obtained through the constant interaction and loving attentions of early caretakers. Basic trust, routines and habits link self-identity to the appraisals of others. The routines followed are, however, reflexively open to change – thus, it is possible to abandon old routines and develop new ones. Trust functions as a protective cocoon, making it possible for individuals to cope with the expectations and demands of everyday life, providing them with a certain amount of *trust capital*. Trust capital makes it possible for individuals to take certain risks and to change certain parts of their self-identity and lifestyle.

The process of individualization – the historical process in which the individual gradually becomes separated from society – and the notion of individuation – a maturational process in which the individual has to work through his or her earlier experiences in order to develop a relatively stable identity – have come to occupy a central position in the lifestyle discussion (Johansson and Miegel 1992a: 29ff.). It is even appropriate to speak about an *individualistic turn* within lifestyle research. Researchers within this area have frequently showed a tendency to put too much emphasis on the sole individual (see, for example, Mitchell 1983). Individuality is never developed in a vacuum; it is always developed in a cultural and social context. 'The tension of our lives would be even greater if we did not, in fact, engage in practices that constantly limit the effect of our isolating individualism, even though we cannot articulate those practices nearly as well as we can the quest for autonomy' (Bellah *et al.* 1985: 151). The value of individualism is not equally embraced within the whole population. Men tend to place great importance on expressing and claiming their material and social status and their individuality, whereas women seem to put more importance on developing their individuality without abandoning their values of security and concern for others, for example (Chodorow 1978; Miller 1976, 1984). Basically, however, the continuity of self-identity – that is, the persistence of feelings of personhood in a continuous self and body – is only maintained through constant interaction with others. An elegant description of this process may be found in Gidden's book *Modernity and Self-Identity*:

> The existential question of self-identity is bound up with the fragile nature of the biography which the individual 'supplies' about herself. A person's identity is not to be found in behaviour, nor – important though it is – in the reactions of others, but in the capacity *to keep a particular narrative going*. The individual's biography, if she is to maintain regular interaction with others in the day-to-day world, cannot be wholly fictive. It must continually integrate events which occur in the external world, and sort them into the ongoing 'story' about the self. (Giddens 1991: 54)

In late modern Western society, the construction of this ongoing story of the self is closely related to lifestyle development and consumerism. Through the process of symbolic democratization a wide variety of symbols and signs have been made available to common people. As Willis expresses it: 'Commercial cultural forms have helped to produce an historical present from which we cannot now escape and in which there are many more materials – no matter what we think of them – available for necessary symbolic work than ever there were in the past' (Willis 1990: 19). These symbols and signs are constantly being reinterpreted and used to create more or less durable identities and lifestyles.

Using Winnicott's somewhat metaphorical language we could speak about a potential space of lifestyles (Ogden 1986; Winnicott 1971). A potential space is an intermediate area of experiencing that lies between fantasy and reality. The cultural experience is obtained through the interplay between fantasy – inner psychic reality – and actual or external reality. The potential space is filled with illusions, with playing and with symbols (Ogden 1986). Distinct forms of failure to create or adequately maintain the psychological interplay of reality and fantasy may occur: the dialectic of reality and fantasy may collapse in the direction of fantasy or collapse in the direction of reality, for example (Ogden 1986).

Winnicott's and Ogden's discussion of the potential space has important implications for the theoretical discussion of symbolic democratization and lifestyles. Through the process of symbolic democratization the symbols of power, beauty, freedom, etc., have been disengaged from their earlier rather restricted meanings and become available to common people. As mentioned above, this may lead to an illusory transcendence of everyday culture – that is, a collapse into fantasy – but it may also lead to *symbolic work* and creativity – that is, a dialectic process involving both fantasy and reality (Kinkade and Katowich 1992; Ogden 1986; Willis 1990; Winnicott 1971).

Lifestyle development and cultural consumption may thus lead to a more integrated and flexible self-identity, but it may also lead to a more fictive, disintegrated and illusory 'story' about the self. Popular/mass culture is, no doubt, something to be looked upon as a positive factor of pleasure and meaning in people's lives, but it may also conceal and disguise the real power relations in society. In order to understand people's use of popular culture and the function of lifestyles it is necessary to study these processes in a cultural and social context. One way of doing this is to construct a social and symbolic space of lifestyles (Bourdieu 1984; Grossberg 1992; Johansson and Miegel 1992a, b ; Reimer 1992).

The theoretical construction of a social and symbolic space of lifestyle is, no doubt, the most central question within lifestyle research today. Such a theoretical model may be used as a heuristic tool when empirically studying lifestyles in late modern Western society. In constructing such a space it is necessary to define *driving forces* (will to power, affects, cognitive development, and so on), *actors* (classes and status groups, affective collectivities, value collectivities, individuals, and so on) and the *relations* between these actors.

The most elaborate attempt to construct a social and symbolic space of lifestyle is to be found in Pierre Bourdieu's *Distinction*. There are, however, several limitations inherent in Bourdieu's theoretical construction: lifestyles and tastes are exclusively defined in terms of interaction between different classes and status groups; the social space constructed by Bourdieu is relatively closed and static; the struggle for power is the dominant driving force in people's lives and thus the ultimate value in life. These aspects of the social and symbolic space of lifestyle are, of course, of great significance, but it is also important to take into consideration other aspects of symbolic production and lifestyle development, for instance, the development of values, sensibilities, affects, and so on, not necessarily related to power and status relations (Johansson and Miegel 1992a).

A central thesis in this chapter is that in order to construct a symbolic space of lifestyle which adequately captures the essence of the differentiation of lifestyles in late modern Western societies, it is necessary to construct a *cognitive-affective theory of lifestyle*. A basic assumption in the theories of Pierre Bourdieu and Lawrence Grossberg is that human behaviour and the formation of lifestyle collectivities are ruled by the will to power and/or passion, desire and affects. (Or, as Freud would have it, by Eros and Thanatos.) However, human behaviour and lifestyle development is also intimately related to people's striving for meaning, identity and ontological security. Individuals are continuously shaping and constructing a 'story' about the self – a biography. In doing so, they are guided by passions, desires and affects, but this exploration of identity implies a reflexive and cognitive monitoring of the self.

The complex process of lifestyle development thus involves a great variety of different mechanisms and driving forces. These processes sometimes lead to an increased fragmentation of self-identity, but the most fundamental power in human life is the striving for a sense of continuity and meaning (Antonovsky 1987; Giddens 1991; May 1958/1986). The development of one's lifestyle plays an important part in the formation of a more or less stable self-identity. Self-identity and lifestyle are always developed and maintained in relation to others. The construction of a social and symbolic space of lifestyle, therefore, serves the purpose of analysing and describing the various relations between individuals and between social and cultural formations in a society. Important concepts in a future theory of lifestyle are, therefore, space, values, desires, affects, power, capital and identity (see Giddens 1991; Grossberg 1992; Johansson and Miegel 1992a, b; Reimer 1988, 1989).

In his book *Love's Executioner and Other Tales*, the American psychiatrist and author Irvin Yalom has captured the essence of contemporary culture and identity (Yalom 1989). The needs and desires which people try to fulfil through consumption and lifestyle experimentation will never cease to influence their expectations in life. These desires are always going to be present, and they will never be fulfilled. Consequently, the search for a more adequate and general theory of lifestyle will always lead us toward the more fundamental and existential questions in life concerning life and death, love and hate, security and development, and so on.

So much wanting. So much longing. And so much pain, so close to the surface, only minutes deep. Destiny pain. Existence pain. Pain that is always there, whirring continuously just beneath the membrane of life. Pain that is all too easily accessible. Many things – a simple group exercise, a few minutes of deep reflection, a work of art, a sermon, a personal crisis, a loss – remind us that our deepest wants can never be fulfilled: our wants for youth, for a halt to aging, for the return of vanished ones, for eternal love, protection, significance, for immortality itself. (Yalom 1989: 4)

SOME EMPIRICAL AND METHODOLOGICAL CONSIDERATIONS

This chapter represents an attempt to elaborate some of the theoretical concepts and views presented in *Do The Right Thing. Lifestyle and Identity in Contemporary Youth Culture* (Johansson and Miegel 1992a). Concepts such as identity, values and lifestyle have come to occupy a central position within contemporary cultural studies. In this final section, I will briefly touch upon three different problems in lifestyle and cultural research, and point towards some solutions to these problems.

The most important theoretical and empirical problem in a theory of lifestyle and identity is the construction of a social and cultural space. The most successful attempt made hitherto is to be found in Pierre Bourdieu's works (Bourdieu 1984, 1990). In my view, however, it is necessary to criticize and elaborate Bourdieu's conceptualization of the social space of lifestyles. In a future theory of lifestyles, concepts such as value, affect, desire and identity will have to occupy a central position. In order to construct such a theory it is necessary to operationalize the different concepts and to discuss the relation between them. Concepts such as desire and affects will, of course, present some difficulties in this respect. (For a discussion of the conceptualization and measurement of mood, affects, etc., see, for instance, Csikszentmihalyi and Larson 1984; Larson and Kubey 1985.) During the last two decades the concept of value has once again proved central in discussions of social and cultural development (Inglehart 1977, 1990; Johansson and Miegel 1992a; Miegel 1990; Reimer 1988, 1989, 1994; Rokeach 1973; Rosengren 1984, 1992).

Johansson and Miegel (1992a: 53ff), for instance, have discussed four different dimensions for conceptualizing values and value orientations: the material/postmaterial, the security/development, the material/aesthetic and the ethical/metaphysical dimension. Another important theoretical and methodological task will be the conceptualization and operationalization of the relation between desire and values. However, the work on formulating a social and cultural space of lifestyle and on developing adequate instruments of measurement has only just begun.

Another important issue in lifestyle and cultural research is the choice of methods. In order to study such complex phenomena as lifestyle and identity formation in contemporary society, it is important to combine different types of method (Johansson and Miegel 1992a). Quantitative methods must be used when studying social and cultural patterns and the formation of different groups and collectivities (Bourdieu 1984, 1990; Johansson and Miegel 1992a; Reimer 1988, 1989). However, when studying the construction of self-identity, biography and the individual lifestyle, it is necessary to use qualitative methods such as interviews, ethnographic methods, observations, etc. (Johansson and Miegel 1992a; Willis 1977, 1990). Lifestyle research may perhaps best be described in terms of a continuous oscillation between *categorizations* and *particularizations* (Johansson and Miegel 1992a: 301).

Finally, I will say something about the complex relation between everyday life and the production of dream-worlds within the media. The study of this relation brings to the fore the relation between the new cultural inter-mediaries and different audiences (Featherstone 1987, 1990, 1991). The new cultural intermediaries actively promote and transmit the intellectuals' lifestyles to a greater audience. In order to study the relation between the mass media and different audiences, it is necessary, therefore, to study the reception of the products, transmitted by the cultural intermediaries, in specific social and cultural contexts. The 'postmodern' cultural products created and transmitted by these fractions will be received in different ways dependent on people's values, attitudes, habitus, cultural and economic capital, desires and sensibilities.

REFERENCES

Alexander, J.C. (1988) *Action and Its Environment. Toward a New Synthesis*, New York: Columbia University Press.

Antonovsky, A. (1987) *Unraveling the Mystery of Health*, New York: Jossey-Bass Inc. Publishers.

Baudrillard, J. (1987) *The Ecstasy of Communication*, New York: Semiotexts.

Beck, U. (1986) *Risikogesellschaft. Auf dem Weg in eine andere Moderne*, Frankfurt a.M: Suhrkamp.

Bell, D. (1976) *The Cultural Contradictions of Capitalism*, London: Heinemann.

Bellah, R.N., Madsen, R., Sullivan, W.M., Swidle, A. and Tipton, S.M. (1985) *Habits of the Heart. Individualism and Commitment in American Life*, Berkeley: University of California Press.

Benjamin, W. (1968) *Illuminations*, London: Fontana.

Berger, P., Berger, B. and Kellner, H. (1974) *The Homeless Mind. Modernization and Consciousness*, New York: Vintage Books.

Berman, M. (1983) *All That Is Solid Melts into Air. The Experience of Modernity*, London: Verso Editors.

Blos, P. (1962) *On Adolescence*, New York: The Free Press.

Blumer, H. (1969) 'Fashion: From class differentiation to collective selection', *The Sociological Quarterly* 3: 275–291.

Bourdieu, P. (1984) *Distinction. A Social Critique of the Judgement of Taste*, Cambridge, Mass.: Harvard University Press.

—— (1990) *Homo Academicus*, Oxford: Polity Press.

Buber, M. (1965) *The Knowledge of Man. A Philosophy of the Inter-Human*, New York: Harper Touchbooks.

Chodorow, N. (1978) *The Reproduction of Mothering: Psychoanalysis and the Sociology of Gender*, Berkeley: University of California Press.

Csikszentmihalyi, M. and Larson, R. (1984) *Being Adolescent. Conflict and Growth in the Teenage Years*, New York: Basic Books.

Denzin, N.K. (1991) *Images of Postmodern Society. Social Theory and Contemporary Cinema*, London: Sage.

DiMaggio, P. (1979) 'Review essay: On Pierre Bourdieu', *American Journal of Sociology* 6: 1460–1474.

Erikson, E.H. (1968) *Identity, Youth and Crisis*, New York: W.W. Norton & Company.

Ewen, S. (1988) *All Consuming Images. The Politics of Style in Contemporary Culture*, New York: Basic Books.

Featherstone, M. (1987) 'Lifestyle and Consumer Culture', *Theory, Culture & Society* 1: 55–70.

—— (1990) 'The body in consumer culture', in M. Featherstone, M. Hepworth and B.S. Turner (eds) *The Body. Social Process and Cultural Theory*, London: Sage.

—— (1991) *Consumer Culture & Postmodernism*, London: Sage.

Fenster, M. (1991) 'The problem of taste within the problematic of culture', *Communication Theory* 1–2: 87–105.

Fiske, J. (1987) *Television Culture*, London: Routledge.

—— (1989) *Understanding Popular Culture*, Boston, Mass.: Unwin Hyman.

Flanagan, S.C. (1987) 'Controversy: Value change in industrial society', *American Political Science Review* 81: 1303–1319.

Fornäs, J. (1990) 'Popular music and youth culture in late modernity', in K. Roe, and U. Carlsson (eds) *Popular Music Research*, Göteborg: NORDICOM.

Frisby, D. (1985) 'Georg Simmel: First sociologist of modernity', *Theory, Culture & Society* 3: 46–67.

Frith, S. (1988) *Music For Pleasure. Essays in the Sociology of Pop*, Oxford: Basil Blackwell.

Giddens, A. (1991) *Modernity and Self-Identity. Self and Society in a Late Modern Age*, Oxford: Polity Press.

Goffman, E. (1969) *The Presentation of Self in Everyday Life*, London: Allen Lane.

Grossberg, L. (1992) *We Gotta Get Out Of This Place. Popular Conservatism and Postmodern Culture*, New York: Routledge.

Habermas, J. (1975) *Legitimation Crisis*, Boston, Mass.: Beacon Press.

—— (1987) *The Theory of Communicative Action. Volume Two: Life-World and System: A Critique of Functionalist Reason*, Boston, Mass.: Beacon Press.

Hebdige, D. (1979) *Subculture. The Meaning of Style*, London: Methuen.

—— (1988) *Hiding in the Light. On Images and Things*, London: Routledge.

Heller, A. (1970/1984) *Everyday Life*, London: Routledge & Kegan Paul.

Holman, R.H. and Wiener, S.E. (1985) 'Fashionability in clothing: A values and lifestyle perspective', in M.R. Solomon (ed.) *The Psychology of Fashion,* Toronto: Lexington Books.

Inglehart, R. (1977) *The Silent Revolution: Changing Values and Political Styles Among Western Publics*, Princeton, NJ: Princeton University Press.

—— (1990) *Culture Shift in Advanced Industrial Society*, Princeton, NJ: Princeton University Press.

Jameson, F. (1991) *Postmodernism. Or, The Cultural Logic of Late Capitalism*, New York: Verso.

Johansson, T. (1992) 'Music video, youth culture and postmodernism', *Popular Music and Society* 16 (3): 9–22.

Johansson, T. and Miegel, F. (1992a) *Do the Right Thing. Lifestyle and Identity in Contemporary Youth Culture*, Stockholm: Almqvist & Wiksell International.

Johansson, T. and Miegel, F. (1992b) 'Trygghet och protest. En kultur-sociologisk studie av splatter och gore', *Research Reports*, Lund: Department of Sociology, Lund University.

Kinkade, P.T and Katowich, M.A. (1992) 'Toward a sociology of cult films: Reading rocky horror', *The Sociological Quarterly* 2: 191–209.

Kroeger, J. (1989) *Identity in Adolescence. The Balance Between Self and Other*, New York: Routledge.

Larson, R. and Kubey, R. (1985) 'Television and music – contrasting media in adolescent life', *Mass Communication Review Yearbook*, 5: 395–413.

Lasch, C. (1985) *The Culture of Narcissism. American Life in an Age of Diminishing Expectations*, London: Abacus.

Luckmann, T. (1983) *Life-World and Social Realities*, London: Heineman Educational Books.

Luhmann, N. (1979) *Trust and Power*, Chichester: John Wiley & Sons.

Lyotard, J.F. (1986) *The Postmodern Condition: A Report on Knowledge*, Manchester: Manchester University Press.

Maffesoli, M. (1991) 'The ethic of aesthetics', *Theory, Culture & Society* 1: 7–20.

Maslow, A. (1968) *Toward a Psychology of Being*, New York: Van Nostrand Company.

May, R. (1958/1986) *The Discovery of Being. Writings in Existential Psychology*, New York: W.W Norton & Company.

Miegel, F. (1990) 'Om värden och livsstilar. En teoretisk, metodologisk och empirisk översikt', *Lund Research Papers in the Sociology of Communication* 25, Lund: Department of Sociology, University of Lund.

Miller, J.B. (1976) *Towards a New Psychology of Women*, Boston, Mass.: Beacon Press.

—— (1984) 'The development of women's sense of self', *Work In Progress: 84: 01*, Wellesley: Stone Center Working Papers Series.

Mitchell, A. (1983) *The Nine American Lifestyles. Who We Are & Where We Are Going*, New York: Warner Books.

Nedelmann, B. (1991) 'Individualization, exaggeration and paralysation: Simmel's three problems of culture', *Theory, Culture & Society* 3: 169–193.

Nietzsche, F. (1883/1977) *A Nietzsche Reader*, Harmondsworth: Penguin Books.

Ogden, T. (1986) *The Matrix of the Mind: Object Relations and the Psychoanalytic Dialogue*, Northvale, NJ: Aronson.

Pitts, R.E. and Woodside, A.G. (1984) *Personal Values and Consumer Psychology*, Toronto: Lexington Books.

Proust, M. (1920/1983) *Remembrance of Things Past. Volume Two: The Guermantes Way. Cities of The Plain*, Harmondsworth: Penguin Books.

Reimer, B. (1988) 'No values – new values? Youth and postmaterialism', *Scandinavian Political Studies* 11.

—— (1989) 'Postmodern structures of feeling. Values and lifestyles in a postmodern age', in J.R. Gibbins (ed.) *Contemporary Political Culture in a Postmodern Age*, London: Sage.

—— (1992) 'Inte som alla andra. Ungdom och livsstil i det moderna', in J. Fornäs, U. Boethius, H. Ganetz, B. Reimer (eds) *Unga stilar och uttrycksformer*, Stockholm: Symposion.

—— (1994) *The Most Common of Practices*, Stockholm: Almqvist & Wiksell International.

Reimer, B. and Rosengren, K.E. (1990) 'Cultivated viewers and readers: A lifestyle perspective', in N. Signorelli and M. Morgan (eds) *Cultivation Analysis. New Directions in Media Effects Research*, Newbury Park, Calif.: Sage.

Rokeach, M. (1973) *The Nature of Human Values*, New York: The Free Press.

Rosengren, K.E. (1984) 'Cultural indicators for the study of culture', in G. Melischek, K.E. Rosengren and J. Stappers (eds) *Cultural Indicators: An International Symposium*, Vienna: Austrian Academy of Sciences.

—— (1991) 'Combinations, comparisons and confrontations: Towards a comprehensive theory of audience research', *Lund Research Papers in Media and Communication* 1, Lund: Unit of Media and Communication Studies, University of Lund.

—— (1992) 'Cultural indicators research: a thumbnail sketch, a Swedish perspective, *Newsletter of the Sociology of Culture*, 6(4): 17–20.

Schudson, M. (1986) *Advertising, The Uneasy Persuasion: Its Dubious Impact on American Society*, New York: Basic Books.

Schutz, A. and Luckmann, T. (1974) *The Structures of the Life-World*, London: Heinemann.

Schwartz, S.H., Moore, R.L. and Krekel, T.H. (1979) 'Lifestyle and the Daily Paper: A Psychographic Profile of Midwestern Readers', *Newspaper Research Journal* 1: 9–18.

Sennet, R. (1976) *The Fall of Public Man*, Cambridge: Cambridge University Press.

Simmel, G. (1904/1971) 'Fashion', in D.N. Levine (ed.) *On Individuality and Social Forms*, Chicago: The University of Chicago Press.

Stern, D. (1985) *The Interpersonal World of the Infant: A View From Psychoanalysis and Developmental Psychology*, New York: Basic Books.

Turner, B.S. (1988) *Status*, Milton Keynes: Open University Press.

Veblen, T. (1899/1979) *The Theory of the Leisure Class. An Economic Study of Institutions*, Harmondsworth: Penguin Books.

Weber, M. (1922/1968) 'Class, status, party', in H.H. Gerth and C.W. Mills (eds) *From Max Weber. Essays in Sociology*, London: Routledge & Kegan Paul.

Williams, R. (1975) *The Long Revolution*, Harmondsworth: Penguin Books.

Willis, P (1977) *Learning to Labour. How Working Class Kids Get Working Class Jobs*, Aldershot: Gower.

—— (1990) *Common Culture. Symbolic Work at Play in the Everyday Cultures of the Young*, Milton Keynes: Open University Press.

Winnicott, D.W. (1965/1987) *The Maturational Process and the Facilitating Environment*, London: The Hogarth Press.

—— (1971) *Playing and Reality*, London: Tavistock Publications.

Wouters, C. (1992) 'On status competition and emotion management: The study of emotions as a new field', *Theory, Culture & Society* 9 (1): 229–252.

Yalom, I.D. (1989) *Love's Executioner and Other Tales of Psychotherapy*, London: Bloomsbury.

Zablocki, B.D. and Kanter, R. (1976) 'The differentiation of lifestyles', *Annual Review of Sociology* 2: 269–298.

Zetterberg, H. (1983) *Det osynliga kontraktet*, Stockholm: SIFO.

Ziehe, T. (1989) *Kulturanalyser: ungdom, utbildning, modernitet*, Stockholm: Symposion.

Part V

Conclusion

Chapter 13

Starting up

Karl Erik Rosengren

In this chapter an attempt will be made, not to summarize the contents of the preceding chapters – the various chapters and their authors are perfectly able to speak for themselves – but to highlight some themes representing potential starting points for future research in the wide fields covered by the Media Panel Program (MPP).

THEORETICAL AND METHODOLOGICAL POINTS OF DEPARTURE

A casual reading of the preceding chapters may give an impression of heterogeneity. A wide array of seemingly disparate phenomena have indeed been presented, but the heterogeneity is more apparent than real. Actually, the meta-theoretical, theoretical and methodological homogeneity within the Media Panel Program is quite considerable, and much the same is true for the various chapters of this book.

A *meta-theoretical* starting point of the MPP is the conviction that in order to be even moderately successful, all scientific and scholarly activities have to be characterized by a systematic interplay between substantive theory, formal models, and empirical data. By means of logical, mathematical, and/or statistical models the intricacies of young people's media use, its causes, consequences and effects as they develop over time may be disentangled in a way which would otherwise be impossible. In addition, when visualized as graphic models, even fairly complex statistical models – say, the systems of equations constituting a LISREL analysis of individual media use, its causes, effects and consequences – become intuitively comprehensible.

Deliberately refraining from the use of formal models may be a quite fruitful approach in an introductory phase of scientific and scholarly activities. In the long run, however, it will have devastating consequences for cumulativity and growth. Any tradition of research refusing to include also the use of formal models in its routine activities is doomed to remain a fad. Like all fads it will have its time, and then it will disappear and be forgotten (Rosengren 1992, 1993). Only the combined use of substantive theory, formal models and empirical data will ensure cumulative growth in certified knowledge, and the MPP is characterized by just such a combination.

Theoretically, our main perspective has been outlined in Chapter 1. It is a perspective which calls for detailed micro analysis to be carried out within an overarching macro framework. More specifically, we are – and will continue to be – interested in the two basic processes of development and socialization, taking place within a framework constituted by the *societal* system of institutions and by the *social* system of action as fundamentally structured by the basic variables of age and gender, class and status. Within this overarching theoretical perspective, we focus on the mass media as increasingly important agents of socialization, today standing out as very serious rivals to more traditional agents of socialization such as priests and teachers and law agents, and perhaps even to those primordial agents of socialization, the family, the peer group and the working group. Within this perspective of socialization, again, we try to combine the two mass communication research traditions of effects studies and uses and gratification studies into what has sometimes been called a uses and effects approach. We also try to transcend this approach by means of theoretical, methodological and empirical developments of lifestyle research (see below).

Methodologically, we have tried systematically to combine so-called qualitative and quantitative methods. In the early phases of the programme, we drew heavily on essays on television and television use written by a number of children in the age-groups under study. Later, we turned to large survey studies based on classroom and mail questionnaires. Later again – in the latest phase of the programme – intensive informal interviews were carried out with a number of type-representative young adults (see Chapter 12).

Apart from this, the methodological backbone of the programme, of course, is the combined cross-sectional design presented in Chapter 3 and used in Chapter 4 and other chapters of the book. This design, applied in two geographical locations, has allowed us to disentangle in the best possible way the intricacies of young people's media use, its character, causes and consequences, as developed during the period under study, a period first characterized by relatively high structural stability of the media scene, then by a thorough-going structural change of that same scene.

Although new specific problems of research will always turn up, of course, we are convinced that much the same meta-theoretical, theoretical and methodological considerations will remain the overall guidelines of the continued work within the MPP. We also believe that in future MPP research, the substantive focus will remain basically the same: the use made of mass media by young people under shifting societal conditions and within a media structure which for years to come will still be in a state of more or less continuous change. More specifically, this means that in our continued research we shall have to consider three broad areas of theoretical and empirical problems:

1 The relationship between overall societal culture and other societal systems.
2 The process of socialization as developing in a complex interplay between a number of socialization agents.
3 The truly basic theoretical problems usually subsumed under the heading 'agency and structure'.

In the rest of this concluding chapter, some main themes which have emerged in the previous chapters of the book will be discussed in terms of these three problematics.

CULTURE, MEDIA AND SOCIETY

Culture is the ideational system of society. As developed in Chapter 1, values are at the heart of culture, so that the main societal institutions – religion and science, art and technology, etc. – may be conceptualized as having developed around two pairs of value orientations: instrumental/expressive, and cognitive/normative value orientation (see Figure 1.1). There are innumerable *horizontal* relations betweens these institutions and their actors. There are also innumerable *vertical* relations between the macro, meso and micro levels of society, by means of which society's culture flows from the macro to the micro level and back again – never-ending processes in which societal culture and individually internalized culture incessantly interact, constitute and shape each other. In these processes, eight main types of socialization agent are always at work: family, peer group and working group; priests, teachers and law agents; social movements and the mass media. With particular regard to the mass media, the role of these processes in the lives of young people is what this book is about. The task of disentangling them is not easy. It takes a number of theoretical perspectives, implemented by means of various methodological approaches, realized within a combined cross-sectional/longitudinal design applied for a decade or two.

No societies are closed systems, and certainly not Sweden in the late twentieth century. A strong flow of ideational, social and material impulses is incessantly crossing the borders from the outside, affecting the internal processes of change always at work in any society. Sometimes the external inflow brings about changes not only *in*, but *of* the system. Such a change was brought about, for instance, by the introduction of TV into Sweden in the 1950s. Another such change was brought about by the introduction of cable and satellite television and the video cassette recorder in the 1980s. The latter change brought about an immense increase of media output produced under a radically different reward system than that dominating the public service system which had previously enjoyed monopoly status (see Figure 1.8; see also Chapters 2 and 4 above). As it happened, the latter change fell into the mid-period of the Media Panel Program, and this both complicated and enriched our work. Since this process of change has by no means come to an end, the task of charting its future effects will remain an important one for the MPP – perhaps the most important one.

As our panels grow older, and as new panels are added to the previous ones, there will be opportunity to compare both levels and structures of media use during radically different structural conditions. One problem to monitor carefully will be the differential influence on individual media use exerted by the two positional variables of gender and social class. Two rather different MPP studies, it will be remembered, have found that the influence of gender seems to be increasing; the influence of social class, decreasing (see Chapters 4 and 11). Do these results just represent temporary flucuations, or do they forebode some more permanent change in social structure? Future MPP studies of the structural and positional determinants of individual media use will be able to provide some answers to that question.

We shall be in a position, however, to take a long look not only at the determinants of individual media use among young people, but also at the consequences and effects of that use – in both a short-term perspective and a long-term. Hopefully, we shall also have the opportunity to do so with respect to various sectors of the 'great wheel of culture in society' (some of which have already been given considerable attention within the MPP but will certainly call for more).

Within the normative sectors, for instance, the political life of young adults as affected by their media use in childhood and adolescence promises to become a fruitful field of research (which, incidentally, has already been opened up by Jarlbro (1988)). Similarly, in the instrumental sectors, a promising area of research will concern the relationships between the use made of mass media by MPP children and adolescents and the character of their future working lives (including, alas, also the alternative of no work at all). Future studies in this area will be in a position to build on previous MPP studies by, for instance, Hedinsson (1981) and Flodin (1986); (see also the results summarized and presented in Chapters 7 and 9). In the cognitive sectors, of course, continued education and training as affected by previous mass media use also should be looked into, as should the expressive aspects of life, such as tastes and preferences in art and literature, high culture and popular culture.

All these studies will also offer a chance to cast new light on the classic problems of temporal effects related to age, generation and situation, dealt with in Chapters 1 and 4. It has already been mentioned that they will also provide opportunities to follow in some detail the changing relations of power between various agents of socialization which the changing media structure will no doubt bring about, presumably diminishing the role of school and family, at the same time increasing the importance of mass media and the peer group as agents of socialization.

CHANGING PROCESSES OF SOCIALIZATION

During the last century or so, there has been a secular trend changing the relative importance of society's agents of socialization. The role of the primordial agents of socialization – the family, the peer group and the working group – has probably been reduced, while historically more recent agents of socialization – particularly school, the mass media and some social movements – have grown more important.

Especially during the last few decades, this secular trend has taken on a new development, in that the role of the mass media as agents of socialization has been both strengthened and changed. More time is given to mass media use, and greater proportions of that time is dedicated to entertainment. During the last few years, this tendency has been further strengthened by the advent on the media scene of cable and satellite television and the video cassette recorder. Technically, all this means that more choice has been given to the media audience. Substantively, though, diversity in media fare may actually have been reduced (see Rosengren *et al.* 1992; Jshikawa 1994). All this will no doubt affect the many socialization processes continuously at work in modern society. More specifically, two types of effect may be expected; in some cases, they have already been observed.

In the first place, the relative importance of different agents of socialization has changed and very probably will continue to do so. For instance, the relative importance of school as an agent of socialization will be reduced, in that substantial parts of formal and informal socialization will be taken over by the mass media – a process which has probably already started. Also, more socialization will take place at home, in the family circle. At the same time, however, the role of the family may well be reduced – in relative terms, at least – since the agent of socialization will often be television distributed by the various TV sets of the family, more or less independently used by different members and/or generations of the family.

In the final analysis, again, all this may well appear in a different light, given the simple fact that what you prefer to receive from the TV set is to a considerable extent controlled – directly and indirectly – by your family background (as manifesting itself, for instance, in the family communication climate; see Chapters 1, 8 and 10). *Mutatis mutandis*, much the same goes for those other two agents of socialization so important to young people: school and the peer group.

Depending upon what happens in the family, at school and in the peer group, then, the same amount of mass media use may have very different meanings and have very different effects. This has been forcefully demonstrated in several previous chapters dedicated to this or that chain of mutual influence between the individual and various agents of socialization (see Chapters 7–10). For better or for worse, you often seem to want to choose the media content which agents of socialization around you tell you to choose. We thus all of us start long chains of mutually reinforcing influences, during which we ourselves and our surroundings build a lifestyle within which we may feel more or less at home. The continued study of such chains will be an important task for future studies within the Media Panel Program.

What may well happen in a not too distant future, however, is that a historical process having been on its way for quite some time may introduce or strengthen yet another complication in the already quite complicated process of socialization. That is the second effect on patterns of socialization brought about by basic changes in societal structure, an effect which may be expected to come about some time in a not too distant future.

AGENCY AND STRUCTURE: FORMS OF LIFE, WAYS OF LIFE AND LIFESTYLES

Socialization is a process of individuation: during the process of socialization, the human being becomes an individual. Historically, the process of individuation has grown ever more important and thorough-going, so that increasingly, the individual has come to stand out as a unique actor, very much in his or her own right. Superimposed upon the billions of primordial processes of *individuation*, that is, there has been a secular process of *individualization* (see Chapters 10–12). This process has been much discussed in social science during the last decade or so; witness, for instance, the agency/structure debate (see Chapter 1).

While these discussions have been rich and subtle, they have often been characterized by a strange absence of two important components necessary for cumulative growth in science. There has been no lack of sophisticated substantive theory expressed in eloquent, if sometimes rather fuzzy, verbal formulations. Formal models and hard empirical data, however, have been less common. Among the few who have actually combined substantive theory, formal models and empirical data relevant to the agency/structure debate, Pierre Bourdieu is outstanding in the richness of his theory, the sophistication of his formal models, and the wealth of empirical data used in his studies as presented, for instance, in his *Distinction* (1984).

Bourdieu gives short shrift to the notion of agency. When societal structure and individual position in that structure have had their say, nothing much, if, indeed, anything at all, is left for the individual to decide. Even personal taste in a number of aesthetical and other areas of life – that individual characteristic often felt to be the very essence of the individual – is characterized by Bourdieu as nothing but 'a virtue made of necessity which continuously transforms necessity into virtue' (Bourdieu 1984: 175). He thus neglects the basic distinction between form of life, ways of life and lifestyles explicated, for instance, in Chapter 1.[1] That is his privilege, of course, but empirical data may show whether he is wise in so doing. If Bourdieu is right, individually held values should have no influence on attitudes, tastes and related patterns of action, once the influence from societal structure and individual position in that structure have been controlled for.

That individually held attitudes, tastes, etc. have an influence on individual use of mass media, is a tenet within the uses and gratifications tradition, of course. It has been shown again and again that this is actually so – most efficently, perhaps, within the branch of uses and gratifications research informed by so-called expectancy-value theory as launched by Fishbein and Aijzen (Fishbein 1963; Fishbein and Aijzen 1981) and exemplified, say, by Palmgreen and Rayburn (1985) and Swanson and Babrow (1989). Presumably, Bourdieu would have no quarrel with these results *per se* (had he condescended to pay any attention to them at all). He would have taken for granted only that those expectancies and values were predetermined by societal structures and individuals' positions within those structures, so that there could be no true 'actors', only 'agents' of blind structural and positional forces:

> Dominated agents, who assess the value of their position and their characteristics by applying a system of schemes of perception and appreciation which is the embodiment of the objective laws whereby their value is objectively constituted, tend to attribute to themselves what the distribution attributes to them, refusing what they are refused ("That's not for the likes of us"), adjusting their expectations to their chances, defining themselves as the established order defines them, reproducing in their verdict on themselves the verdict the economy pronounces on them, in a word, condemning themselves to what is in any case their lot, *ta heautou*, as Plato put it, consenting to be what they have to be, "modest", "humble" and "obscure". (Bourdieu 1979/84: 471)

According to Bourdieu, then, beliefs, values, attitudes, tastes, etc. are just epiphenomena. Once societal structure and individuals' position within that structure have had their say, the rest is silence. That, of course, is an empirical statement which may be tested by means of empirical research. No doubt, individually held beliefs, values and attitudes are to no small extent determined by structure and position – nobody denies that. What is at stake is two other, closely related but different questions:

1 Are individually held beliefs, values, attitudes, tastes, etc. completely determined by structure and position?
2 Are individual patterns of action completely determined by structure and position, so that individually held beliefs, values, attitudes, tastes, etc. have no influence of their own on such patterns?

These are hardly new questions, and when tested (be it by concrete experiences of life or by systematic research), more often than not, the answer to both of them has been 'No'. Recent lifestyle research, however, sometimes forgetting the basic distinction between structurally, positionally and individually determined patterns of action, has not always given the same answer. To Bourdieu, as we have just seen, the answer to both questions is 'Yes'.

Johansson and Miegel (1992: 200 ff.) have produced a wealth of data relevant to this discussion, some of which are briefly presented in Chapter 10. The reader may see that, in a number of cases, at least, individually held values do exert an influence of their own on individual patterns of activity, even after careful controls for societal structure (place of living) and positional variables (gender, class of origin, and own education). Individually encompassed basic values, as well as individually entertained tastes, are certainly influenced by structural and positional conditions. But that is not – as Bourdieu would have it – the whole story. The whole story tells us that when those basic influences are removed by means of statistical controls or in other ways, there still remains some choice. Within a given form of life, within a given way of life, you may still – sometimes to no small extent – make a choice of your own. All of us (especially young people, perhaps) grasp those opportunities for choice. Bourdieu may not think so, but most people, indeed, most social scientists, are convinced that structure is not everything. Individual lifestyles do exist. Agency does exist.

Once we have agreed on this, two important tasks immediately announce themselves. The first concerns the relative role of the three determinant forces: structure, position, and agency. The second concerns the more specific question about the consequences of agency for traditional effects studies in communication research.

The former question calls for comparative research on a grand scale: the effects of structure and position are certainly very different in different societies, and the strength of these effects determine the space left for agency. Such comparative studies should preferably include comparisons over both time and space (see Rosengren *et al.* 1992). [2] After all, a petit-bourgeois in Bourdieu's Lille of northern France in the 1960s may not be quite the same as a computer operator in, say, Copenhagen or Boston in the mid-1990s. Very probably, the differences are quite considerable, and these differences vary from time to time and from place to place. The basic model for understanding them, however, is quite clear, and the techniques of research necessary to produce the needed data are well understood. [3] Most of the work remains to be done, though.

The second question calls for theoretical reconsiderations which may well affect our basic understanding of the whole tradition of effects studies. If as an individual you have some space for personal choice, and if your choice will affect your future life, then your future life – and your present life as well – may be regarded, not as a product of blind forces, the effects of behaviour mechanically following this or that position within this or that societal structure, but as a result of your own choice, an expression of your own basic values and attitudes.

This is where the difference between substantive theory and formal model enters the argument. The formal models do not recognize the difference between statistical relations arrived at through more or less well-considered personal preferences and statistical relations arrived at through brute social and societal forces. But substantive theory does. The effects of your media use may be regarded as part and parcel of your individual *lifestyle*, shaped by yourself within options offered by the *way of life* determined by your social position and also by the *form of life* prescribed by societal structure. Consequently, the causal perspective of effects research will have to be supplemented by the finalistic perspective of uses and gratifications research within a uses and effects design. This line of argumentation will also call for continued efforts within lifestyle-oriented research in communication studies, along the lines exemplified by Chapters 10–12 and foreboded in Chapters 7–9. In the long run, then, efforts such as these will also have to transcend the uses and effects perspective.

Such research will be able to find a platform in the wealth of data already collected within the Media Panel Program. In addition, new waves of data collection within the programme, undertaken by means of formal and informal interviews, mail and classroom questionnaires, and archival data, will hopefully be able to offer follow-ups of previous panels, and comparative data from new panels and cohorts.

The research councils willing, and other circumstances permitting, then, the needs of both a long-term uses and effects perspective and a long-term structural comparisons perspective will thus be served in future lifestyle-oriented MPP research – in the interest of that vital and basic debate about agency and structure.

NOTES

1 In addition, when explicating his theories in terms of a formal model, he chooses a very impractical and clumsy model (see Rosengren 1992).
2 For a recent temporally comparative study of media use and other habits under different societal conditions, see Werner (1993).
3 No doubt, however, considerable advances will be made in the necessarily somewhat provisional techniques of analysis sometimes used today. For instance, the series of repeated MCA analyses undertaken by Johansson and Miegel (1992) will gradually be replaced by structural modelling techniques such as LISREL.

REFERENCES

Bourdieu, P. (1984) *Distinction. A Social Critique of the Judgement of Taste*, Cambridge, Mass. and London: Harvard University Press and Routledge.
Fishbein, M. (1963) 'An investigation of the relationships between beliefs about an object and the attitude toward that object', *Human Relations* 16: 223–240.
Fishbein, M. and Aijzen, I. (1981) 'Acceptance, yielding, and impact', in R.E. Petty,

T.M. Ostrom and T.C. Brock (eds) *Cognitive Responses in Persuasion*, Hillsdale, NJ: Lawrence Erlbaum.

Flodin, B. (1986) *TV och yrkesförväntan: En longitudinell studie av ungdomars yrkessocialisation*, (TV and Adolescents' Occupational Socialisation. A longitudinal study, with a summary in English) Lund: Studentlitteratur.

Hedinsson, E. (1981) *TV, Family and Society: The Social Origins and Effects of Adolescents' TV Use*, Stockholm: Almqvist & Wiksell International.

Jarlbro, G. (1988) *Familj, massmedier och politik*, (Family, Mass Media and Politics; with a summary in English) Stockholm: Almqvist & Wiksell International.

Johansson, T. and Miegel, F. (1992) *Do the Right Thing. Lifestyle and Identity in Contemporary Youth Culture*, Stockholm: Almqvist & Wiksell International.

Jshikawa, S. (1994) 'Retrospect and prospect of the five countries joint research project on quality assessment of broadcasting', *Studies of Broadcasting*, 30.

Palmgreen, P. and Rayburn, J.D. (1985) 'An expectancy-value approach to media gratifications', in K.E. Rosengren, L.A. Wenner and P. Palmgreen (eds) *Media Gratifications Research: Current perspectives*, Beverly Hills, Calif.: Sage.

Rosengren, K.E. (1992) 'Substantive theories and formal models: Their role in research on individual media use', *Lund Research Papers in Media and Communication Studies* 4.

—— (1993) 'From field to frog ponds', *Journal of Communication* 43 (3): 6–17.

Rosengren, K.E., Carlsson, M. and Tågerud, Y. (1991) 'Quality in programming: Views from the North', *Studies of Broadcasting* 27: 21–80.

Rosengren, K.E., McLeod, J.M. and Blumler, J.G. (1992) 'Comparative communication research: From exploration to consolidation', in J.G. Blumler, J.M. McLeod and K.E. Rosengren (eds) *Comparatively Speaking: Communication and Culture Across Space and Time*, Newbury Park, Calif.: Sage.

Swanson, D.L. and Babrow, A.S. (1989) 'Uses and gratifications: The influence of gratification-seeking and expectancy-value judgments on the viewing of television news', in B. Dervin, L. Grossberg, B.J. O'Keefe and E. Wartella (eds) *Rethinking Communication, Vol 2: Paradigm Exemplars*, Newbury Park, Calif.: Sage.

Werner, A. (1993) 'The impact of new media on children: The case of Finnmark, 1967–1990', in H. Arntsen (ed.) *Media, Culture and Development*, Oslo: Department of Media and Communication, University of Oslo.

Indices

Connie Tyler

Subject index

Note: Those page numbers which are italicized are figures; those emboldened are plates.

heavy, and school achievement 145; increase in 36; more stable in childhood and young adulthood 115; parental viewing, indirect influence of 127; pre-school, effects of *142*, 143; related to age 60–2; relationship with aggressiveness and violent behaviour 141, 143–4; and self-esteem 176–7; and social class **68**, 69; stability of 100; under structural change 54–9
TV viewing pattern 66
TV/reading comics 119
TV/VCR use: effects/consequences of 141–5
TV/VCR viewing, related 119

Universal Prescriptivism 238, 239
upward mobility 183–4, 189, 201; problems of 188
uses and effects approach 134
uses and gratifications research 134, 303, 305

value changes 283
value orientations 3–4, 286, 290; material and postmaterial 217, 221, **222**, 235; personal 217–18, 219
value systems 14, 211, 282
value theory 211–12; cognitivist and non-cognitivist 212, 238; naturalistic and objectivistic 238
values 207, 209–10, 274, 286, 290; and identity 210–12; identity and lifestyle 212–16; importance of in youth culture and lifestyle 223–33; individual 227, 303, 304; and

lifestyle 282–3; types of 210, *211*
values/family communication relationship 217–23, 231, 236
values/value orientations 227; individual 231; related to gender, class and education 231–2, **232**
VCR viewing 60, 63, 122; development of *65*; stability and change in 103, *104*, 105
VCR/TV viewing 119
VCRs 35, 54, 64, 73, 97, 117, 299–300; induced rise in TV viewing 60, *61*, 61; and social class 71
vertical comparisons 52
vertical linkages: between levels of society 7, 20–1, 30, 49, 299
vertical mobility 183–4; and education 188; individual or group 184, *see also* upward mobility
violence, violent 133, 134, 141–3
visibility: of lifestyle 269, 270
voice 11–12

ways of life 9, 78, 135, 147, 302, 305; *see also* lifestyle
will to power 277–9, 289
working group 7, 16, 153, 299

young adults 36, 106, 120; political life of 300
young people: early experience and later self-image 169–77
youth 269; acceptance of new media appliances 54, 59–60; subcultures 260–2
youth culture 285–6; and lifestyle, importance of values 223–33

Name index

Abrahamsson, U. 177
Aijzen, I. *see* Fishbein, M. and Aijzen, I.
Alexander, J.C. 242, 267–8; *et al.* 7; and Giesen, B. 242
Andersson, B.-E. 150
Archer, M. 8

Babrow, A.S. *see* Swanson, D.L. and Babrow, A.S.
Ball-Rokeach, S. 138
Bandura, A. 123
Becker, H.S. 17

Becker, J.R. 173
Bell, D. 237
Bellah, R.N. *et al.* 287
Berger, P. *et al.* 274
Bibbee, R.C. *see* Namenwirth, J.S. and Bibbee, R.C.
Bjerrum Nielsen, H. and Rudberg, M. 178
Block, J.H. 154
Blos, P. 209
Blumer, H. 133
Bogdan, R. *see* Taylor, S.J. and Bogdan, R.